FRANKLIN RICHARDS
SON OF A GENIUS

ULTIMATE COLLECTION

FRANKLIN RICHARDS
SON OF A GENIUS
ULTIMATE COLLECTION

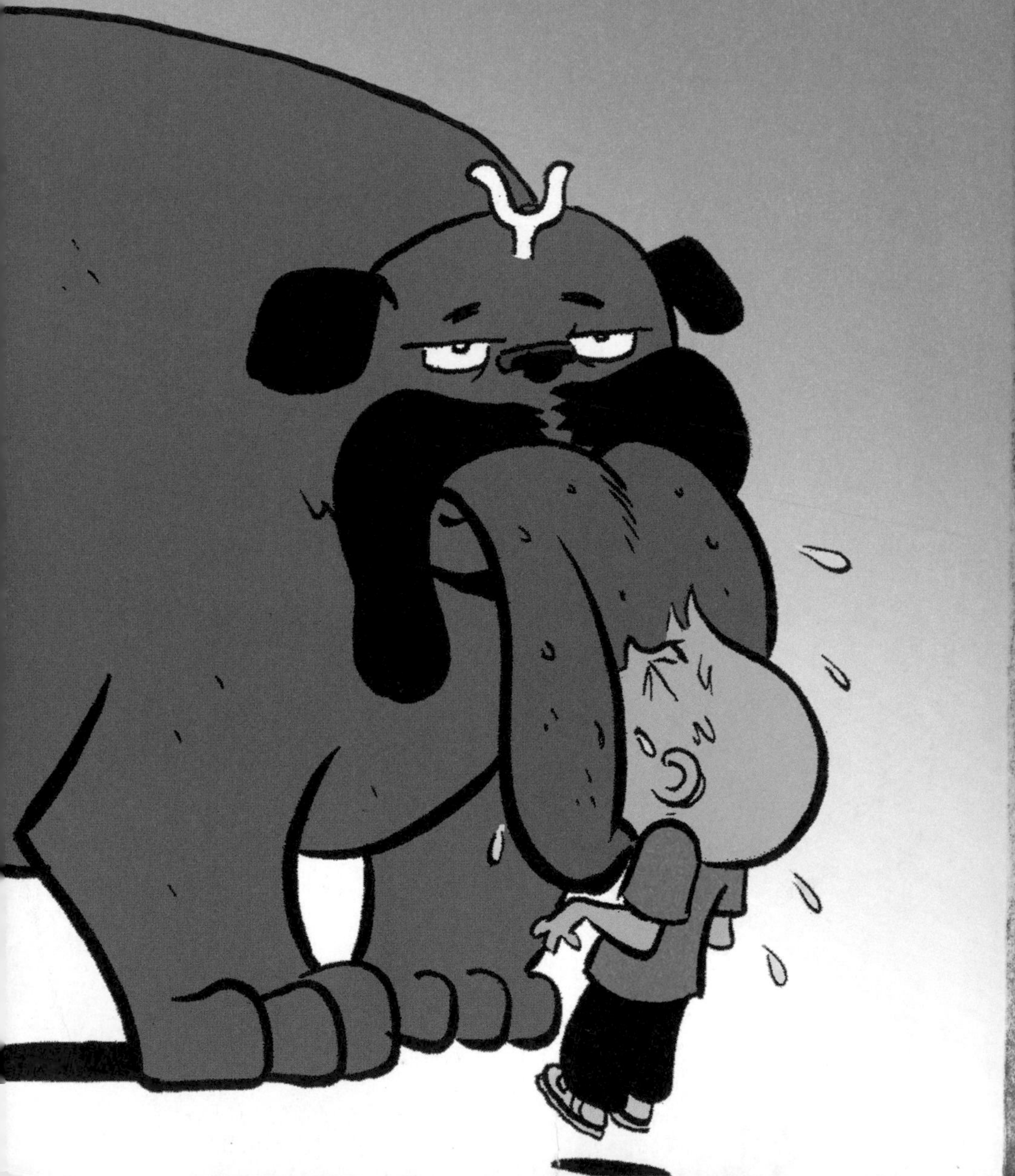

Story & Script:
Chris Eliopoulos & Marc Sumerak
Art & Letters:
Chris Eliopoulos
Color:
**Chris Eliopoulos, GuriHiru,
Lovern Kindzierski & Brad Anderson**
Editors:
Nathan Cosby, Mackenzie Cadenhead & Mark Paniccia

Collection Editor:
Cory Levine
Editorial Assistants:
James Emmett & Joe Hochstein
Assistant Editors:
Alex Starbuck & Nelson Ribeiro
Editors, Special Projects:
Jennifer Grünwald & Mark D. Beazley
Senior Editor, Special Projects:
Jeff Youngquist
Senior Vice President of Sales:
David Gabriel

Editor in Chief:
Joe Quesada
Publisher:
Dan Buckley
Executive Producer:
Alan Fine

• Son of an Introduction •

I was sitting in a meeting with the then-President of Marvel. He asked me if I had any comic book ideas that I could write and draw that would appeal to an all-ages market.

I told him I had an idea for Franklin Richards, the son of Reed and Sue Richards, two members of the Fantastic Four, and how his parents were always running off to save the world and leaving him home alone.

"I don't know who Franklin Richards is. Any other ideas?"

That was the end of Franklin, I thought. That is until two years later. I was sitting in the office of C.B. Cebulski, who was an editor at the time, and we were talking about the same old things. The former president had left the company by this time and Marvel was now starting on an all-ages line of kids books, so C.B. was telling me. I offhandedly said that they should use my Franklin Richards idea. He didn't know what I was talking about.

I mentioned to him that as a fairly new parent, I noticed that any chance my kids had, they would find my things and want to play with them. My tools, my office equipment, anything was fair game. I could only imagine what it would be like for a ten-year-old to be left at home with all the amazing things that the smartest man in the world had invented. He would go crazy. I told him it was like *Home Alone* meets the Marvel universe.

C.B.'s reaction? He started making a phone call mid-sentence.

I figured I had bored him and he moved on. But, he was actually calling David Gabriel, Marvel's Senior VP of Sales and all-around great guy. He was telling David that they had a new book for the kids line.

It happened just like that. But then the kids line went on without Franklin for a bit.

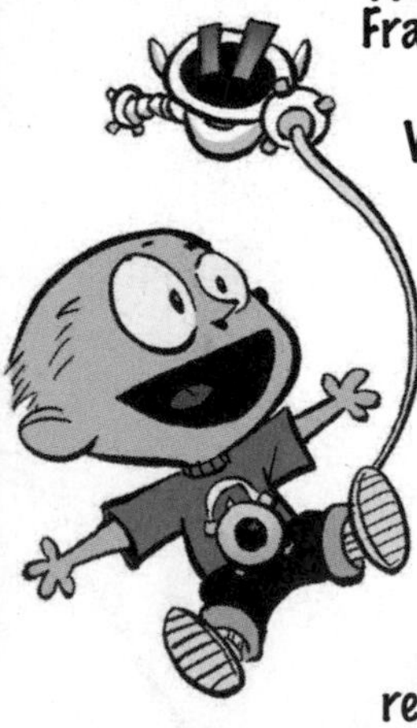

We originally had planned to do a 5-issue miniseries on Franklin, but some people got worried. They weren't sure what it was that we were doing exactly. It was a comic strip, but a comic book. It was for kids or for adults? It was decided that maybe we should try a couple of short backup stories just to see what we got.

Enter MacKenzie Cadenhead.

It was then that my new editor, MacKenzie Cadenhead, the real force behind Franklin, got things rolling. When we discussed it and I mentioned I wanted to write, draw, letter and color it by myself, some folks got nervous. I was untested and they were worried I wouldn't be able to handle all that work. MacKenzie was also my bodyguard. On the cover to this very book, MacKenzie watched traffic for me in Midtown Manhattan as I lay down in the middle of a street to take the background picture. I'd be roadkill if it weren't for her.

Enter Marc Sumerak.

Marc, a former editor at Marvel, was someone I had worked with before and MacKenzie had recommended him to provide scripting duties. He loves the Muppets, I love the Muppets, it was cool with me.

So, off we went, thinking we would do 4 5-page stories and be done with it. Funny thing was, though, people really liked it. It was a breath of fresh air in a marketplace filled with grim and gritty super heroes. It was funny and it had jokes for the adults as well as the kids.

We were asked to do more. And more, we did. Franklin went on for 4 years coming out quarterly with a series of short stories. It was a blast. We were having fun, the audience was having fun and then MacKenzie left Marvel for greener pastures about 2 years into the run.

Enter Nathan Cosby.

Nate is another Muppet-lover, so he clicked right into place as the new editor on Franklin. He had an energy and excitement that really pumped me up. He continued to guide Franklin along in all the trouble he and we got into. People continued to love what we were doing and so did we.

Exit Marc.

As we moved along, I was getting stronger and stronger as a writer and folks felt Marc needed to move up to more mainstream super-hero work and they felt I was able to carry on on my own. So Marc left and I picked up all the writing duties. But it didn't last too long.

We eventually felt we told all the Franklin stories we could and figured it was time to take a break. But then, it was decided that Franklin needed to have all his stories collected in giant volumes and I couldn't be happier.

Re-reading these stories makes me want to do more. Hope I do some day. There are always more adventures, but in the meantime, enjoy these.

Chris Eliopoulos
September 2010

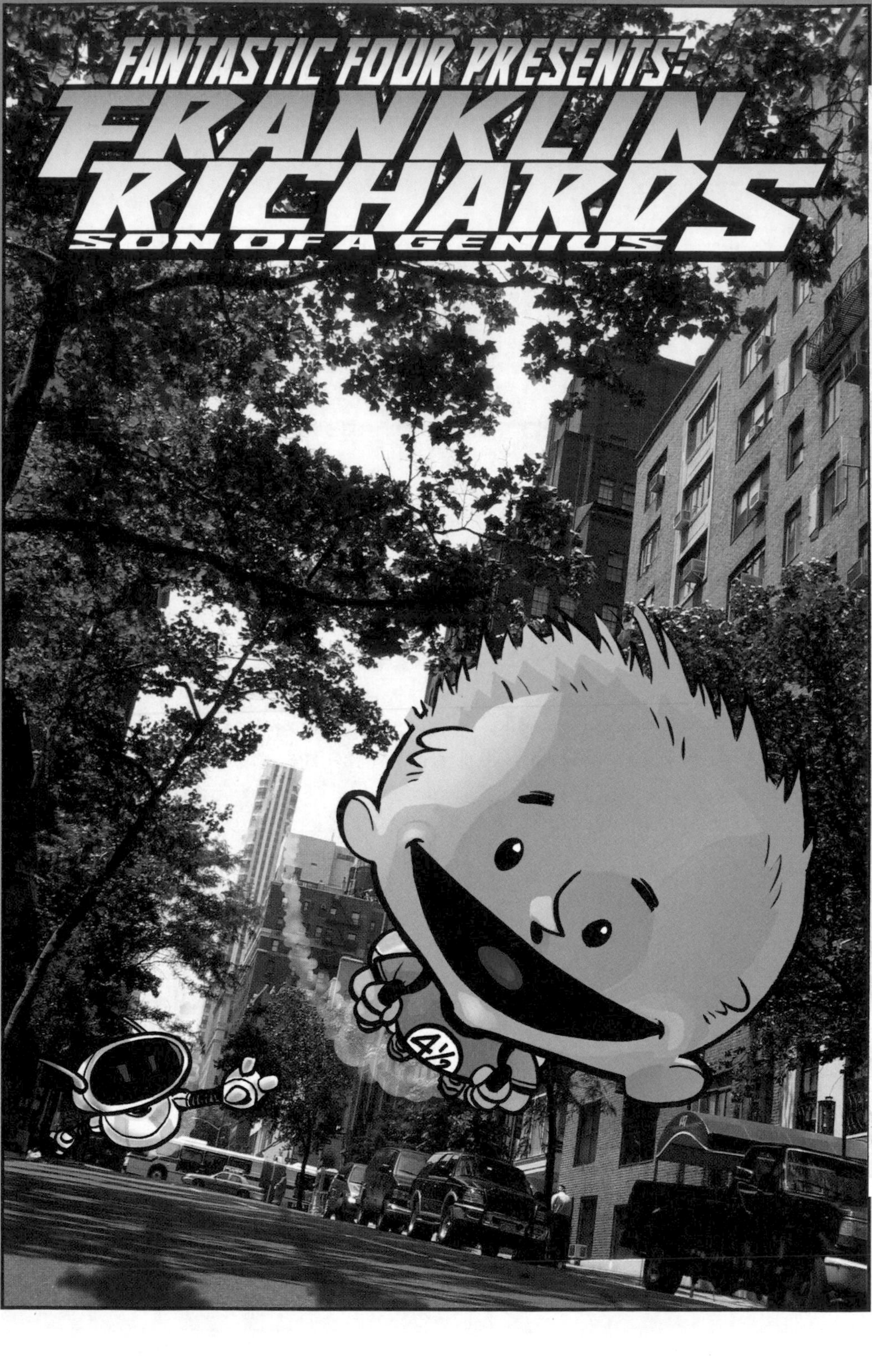
FANTASTIC FOUR PRESENTS:
FRANKLIN RICHARDS
SON OF A GENIUS
4½

FANTASTIC FOUR PRESENTS:
FRANKLIN RICHARDS
SON OF A GENIUS

STORY ONE **MICROSCOPIC** ④ STORY TWO **TONS OF FUN**

STORY THREE **VEGGIN' OUT** ④ STORY FOUR **WEATHER OR NOT**

STORY FIVE **SEND IN THE CLONES**

CHRIS ELIOPOULOS AND MARC SUMERAK
STORY

MARC SUMERAK
S C R I P T

CHRIS ELIOPOULOS
ART & LETTERS

JACOB CHABOT
PRODUCTION

NATHAN COSBY
ASSISTANT EDITOR

MARK PANICCIA
CONSULTING EDITOR

MACKENZIE CADENHEAD
EDITOR

JOE QUESADA
EDITOR IN CHIEF

DAN BUCKLEY
PUBLISHER

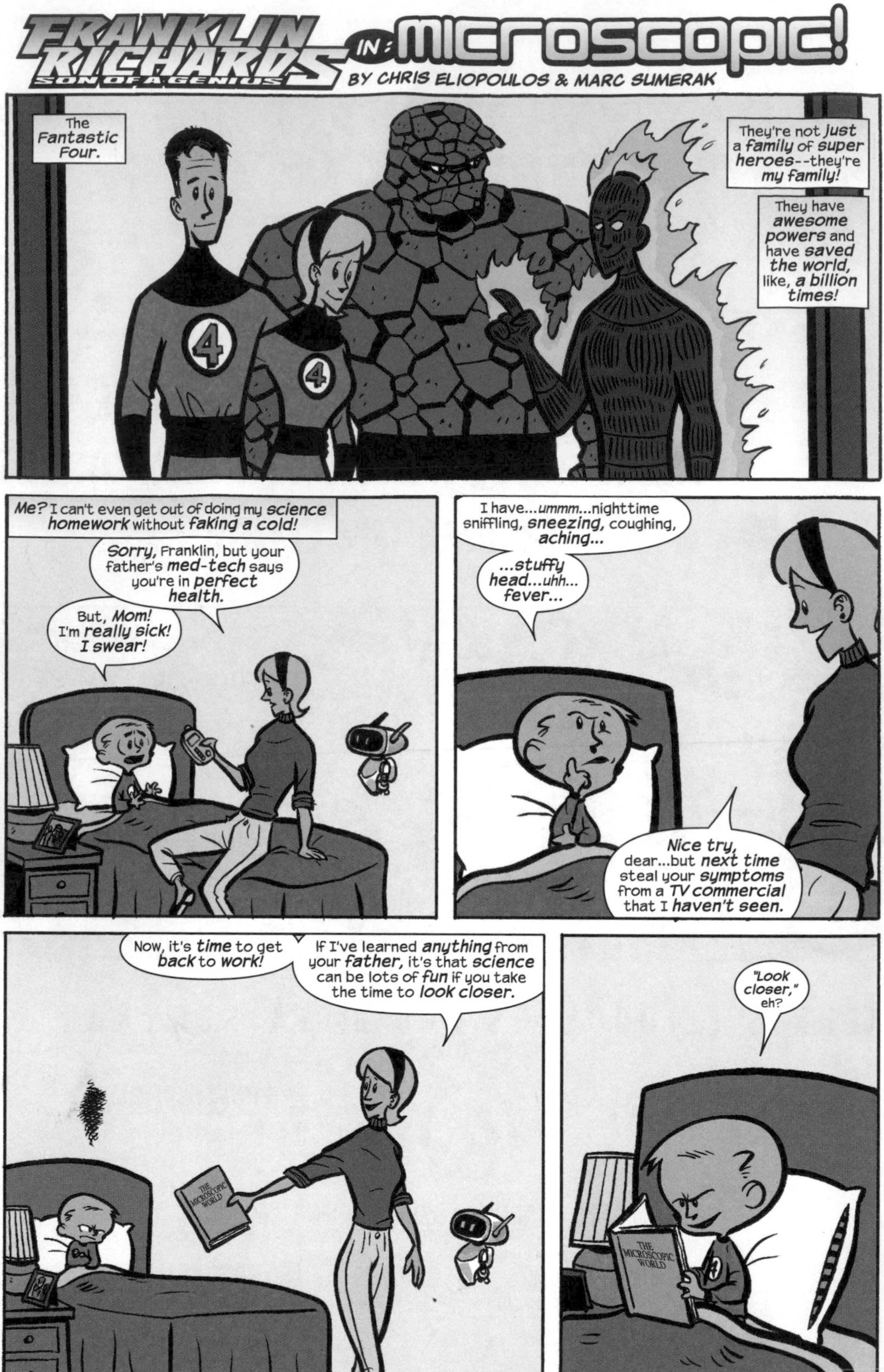
FRANKLIN RICHARDS
SON OF A GENIUS
IN: MICROSCOPIC!
BY CHRIS ELIOPOULOS & MARC SUMERAK
The Fantastic Four.
They're not just a family of super heroes--they're my family!
They have awesome powers and have saved the world, like, a billion times!
Me? I can't even get out of doing my science homework without faking a cold!
Sorry, Franklin, but your father's med-tech says you're in perfect health.
But, Mom! I'm really sick! I swear!
I have...ummm...nighttime sniffling, sneezing, coughing, aching...
...stuffy head...uhh... fever...
Nice try, dear...but next time steal your symptoms from a TV commercial that I haven't seen.
Now, it's time to get back to work!
If I've learned anything from your father, it's that science can be lots of fun if you take the time to look closer.
THE MICROSCOPIC WORLD
"Look closer," eh?
THE MICROSCOPIC WORLD

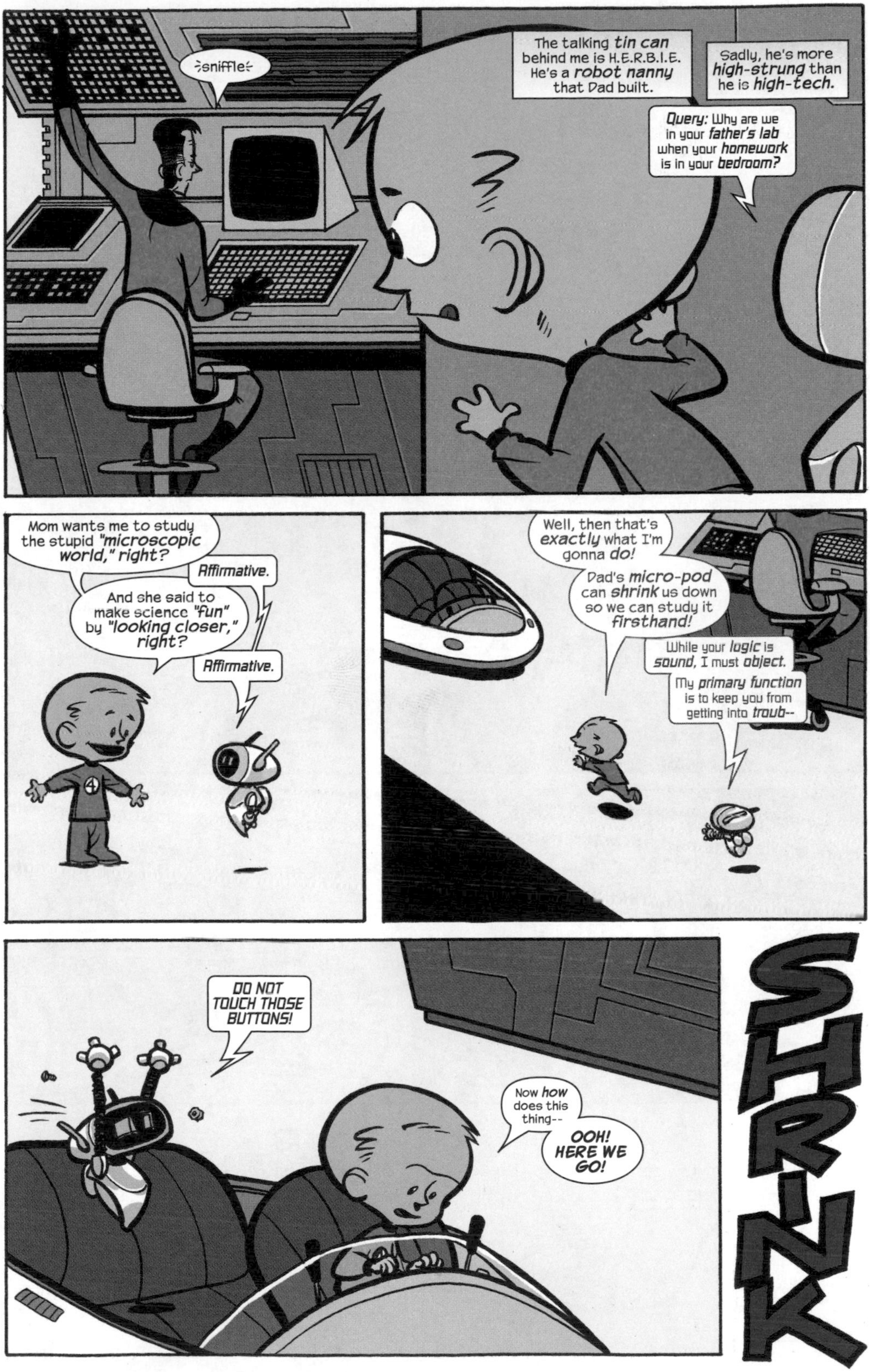

The talking *tin can* behind me is H.E.R.B.I.E. He's a *robot nanny* that Dad built.
Sadly, he's more *high-strung* than he is *high-tech.*
sniffle
Query: Why are we in your *father's lab* when your *homework* is in your *bedroom?*
Mom wants me to study the stupid *"microscopic world,"* right?
Affirmative.
And she said to make science *"fun"* by *"looking closer,"* right?
Affirmative.
Well, then that's *exactly* what I'm gonna *do!*
Dad's *micro-pod* can *shrink* us down so we can study it *firsthand!*
While your *logic* is *sound,* I must *object.*
My *primary function* is to keep you from getting into *troub--*
DO NOT TOUCH THOSE BUTTONS!
Now *how* does this thing--
OOH! HERE WE GO!
SHRINK

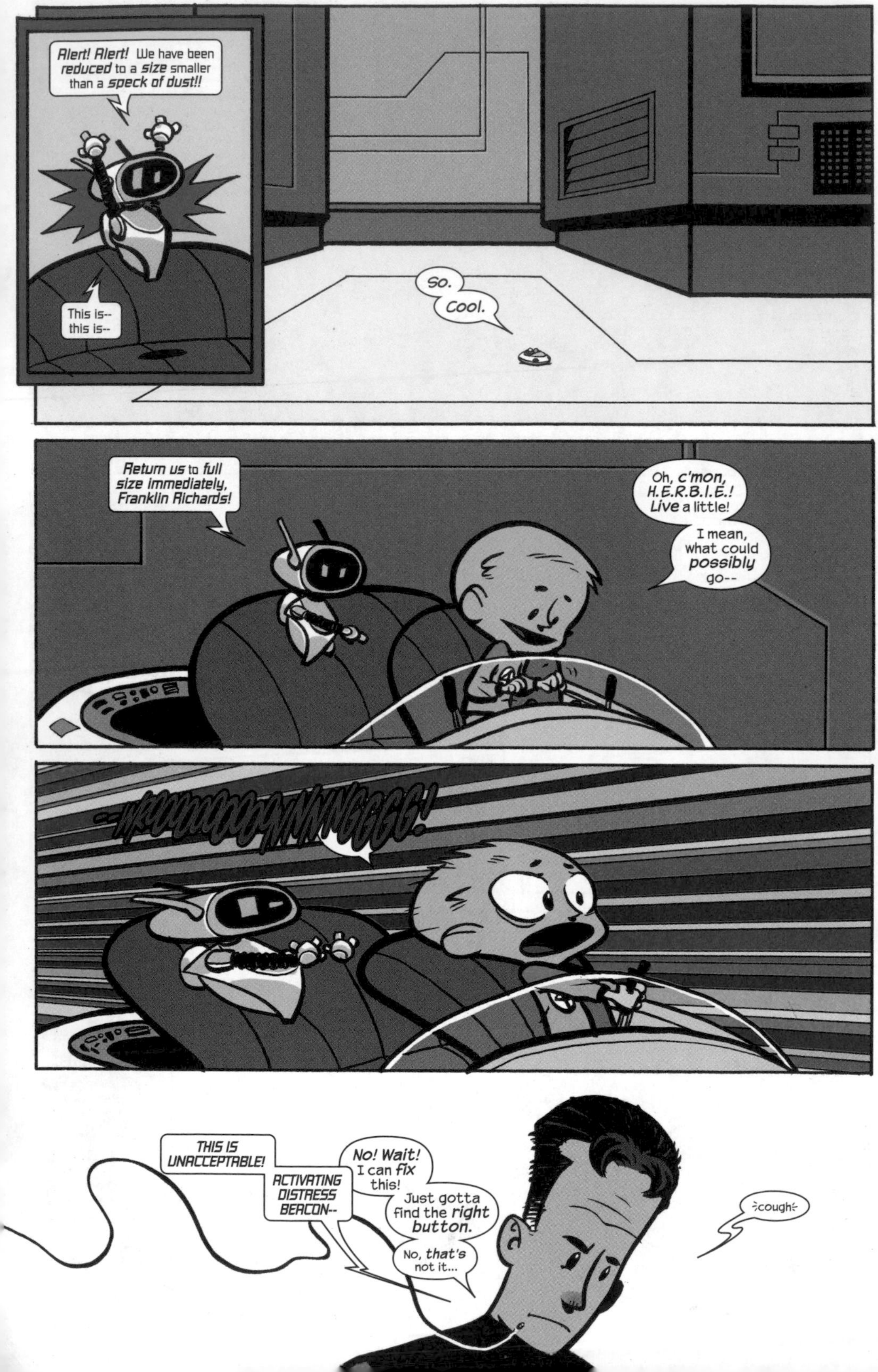
Alert! Alert! We have been reduced to a size smaller than a speck of dust!!
This is-- this is--
So.
Cool.
Return us to full size immediately, Franklin Richards!
Oh, c'mon, H.E.R.B.I.E.! Live a little!
I mean, what could possibly go--
--WRRRRRRRRROOOOONNNNNGGGG!
THIS IS UNACCEPTABLE!
ACTIVATING DISTRESS BEACON--
No! Wait! I can fix this!
Just gotta find the right button.
No, that's not it...
cough

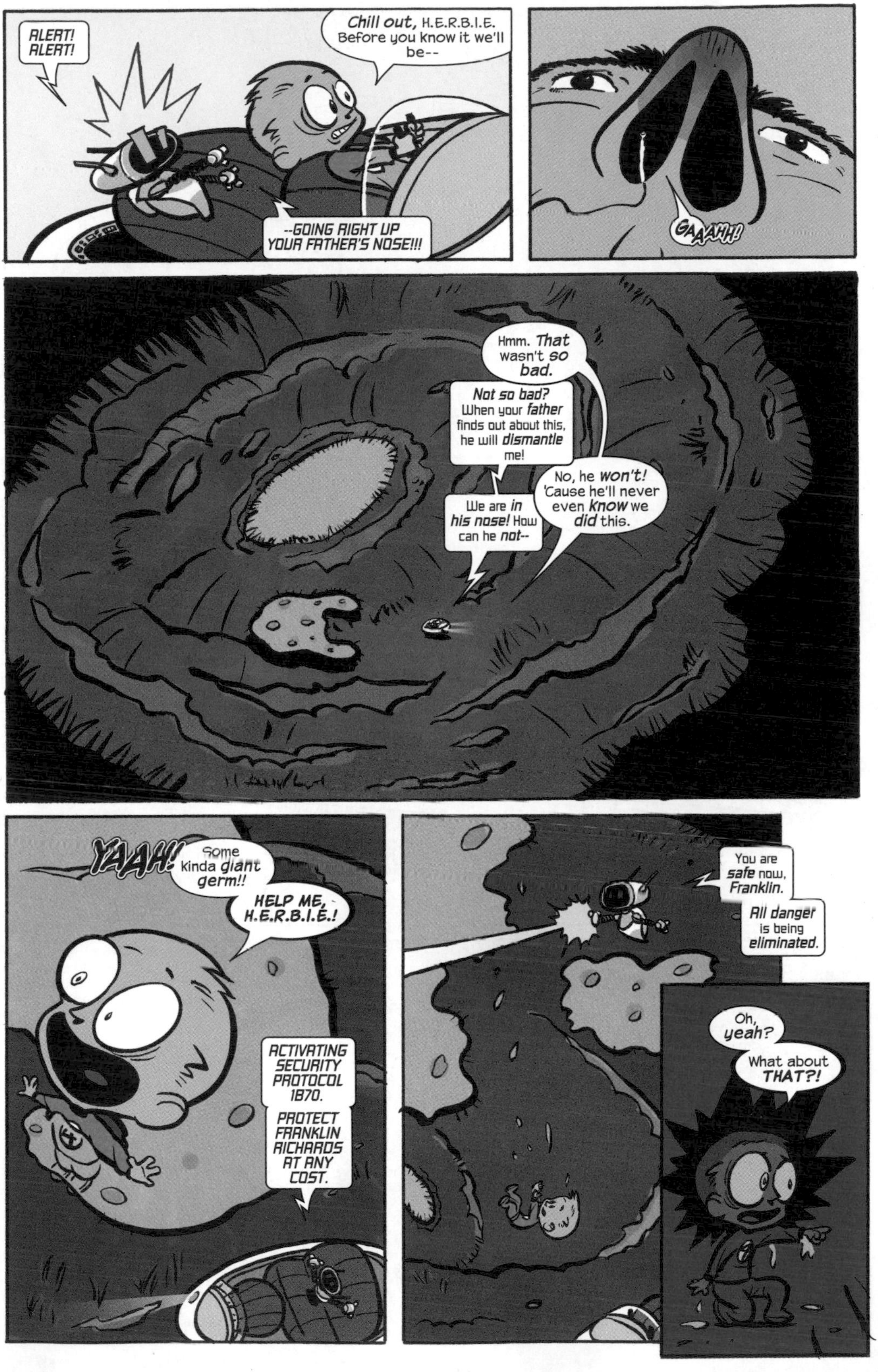
ALERT! ALERT!
Chill out, H.E.R.B.I.E. Before you know it we'll be--
--GOING RIGHT UP YOUR FATHER'S NOSE!!!
GAAAHH!
Hmm. That wasn't so bad.
Not so bad? When your father finds out about this, he will dismantle me!
No, he won't! 'Cause he'll never even know we did this.
We are in his nose! How can he not--
YAAH!
Some kinda giant germ!!
HELP ME, H.E.R.B.I.E.!
ACTIVATING SECURITY PROTOCOL 1870.
PROTECT FRANKLIN RICHARDS AT ANY COST.
You are safe now, Franklin.
All danger is being eliminated.
Oh, yeah?
What about THAT?!

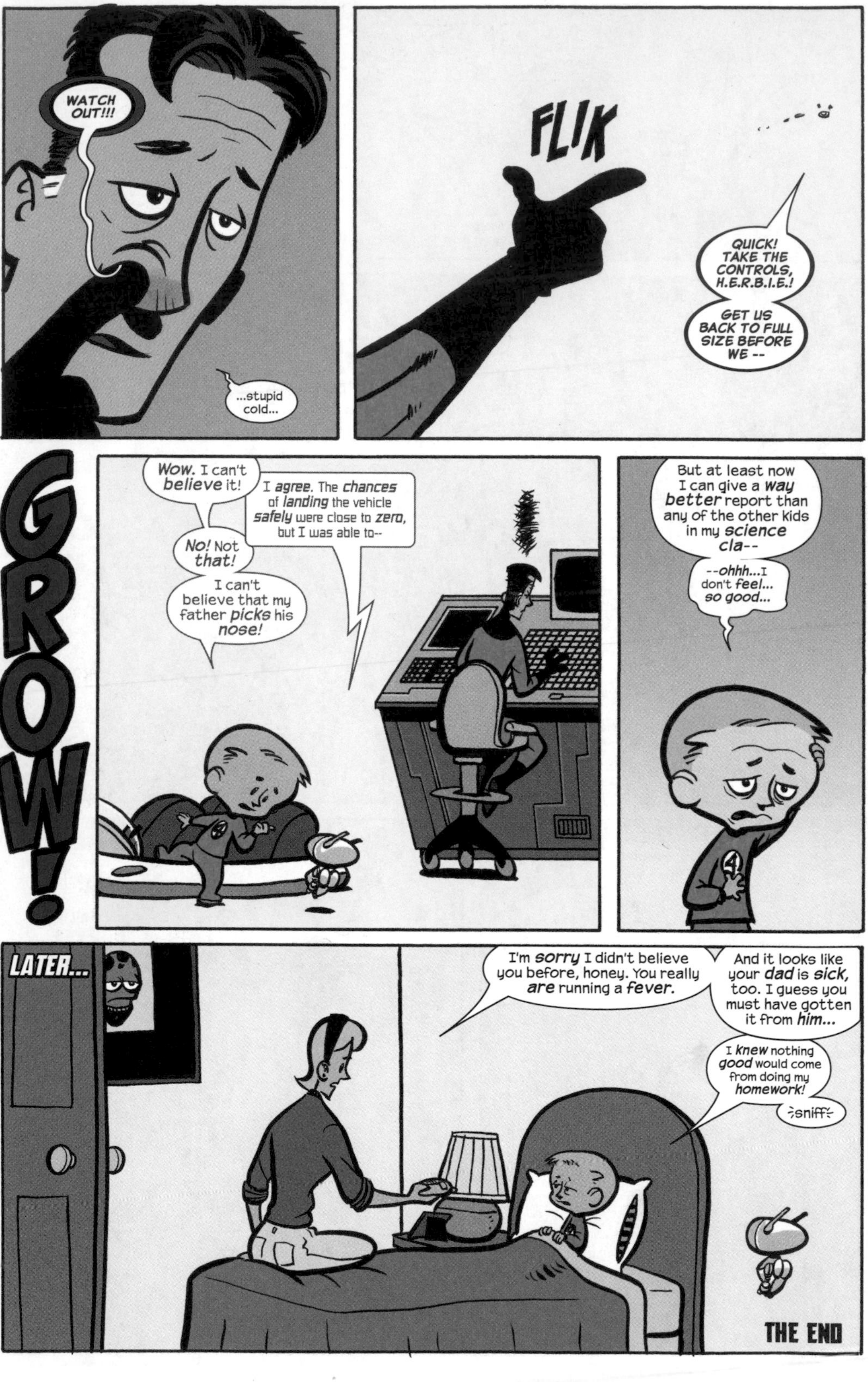

WATCH OUT!!!
...stupid cold...
FLIK
QUICK! TAKE THE CONTROLS, H.E.R.B.I.E.!
GET US BACK TO FULL SIZE BEFORE WE --
GROW!
Wow. I can't believe it!
I agree. The chances of landing the vehicle safely were close to zero, but I was able to--
No! Not that!
I can't believe that my father picks his nose!
But at least now I can give a way better report than any of the other kids in my science cla--
--ohhh...I don't feel... so good...
LATER...
I'm sorry I didn't believe you before, honey. You really are running a fever.
And it looks like your dad is sick, too. I guess you must have gotten it from him...
I knew nothing good would come from doing my homework!
sniff
THE END

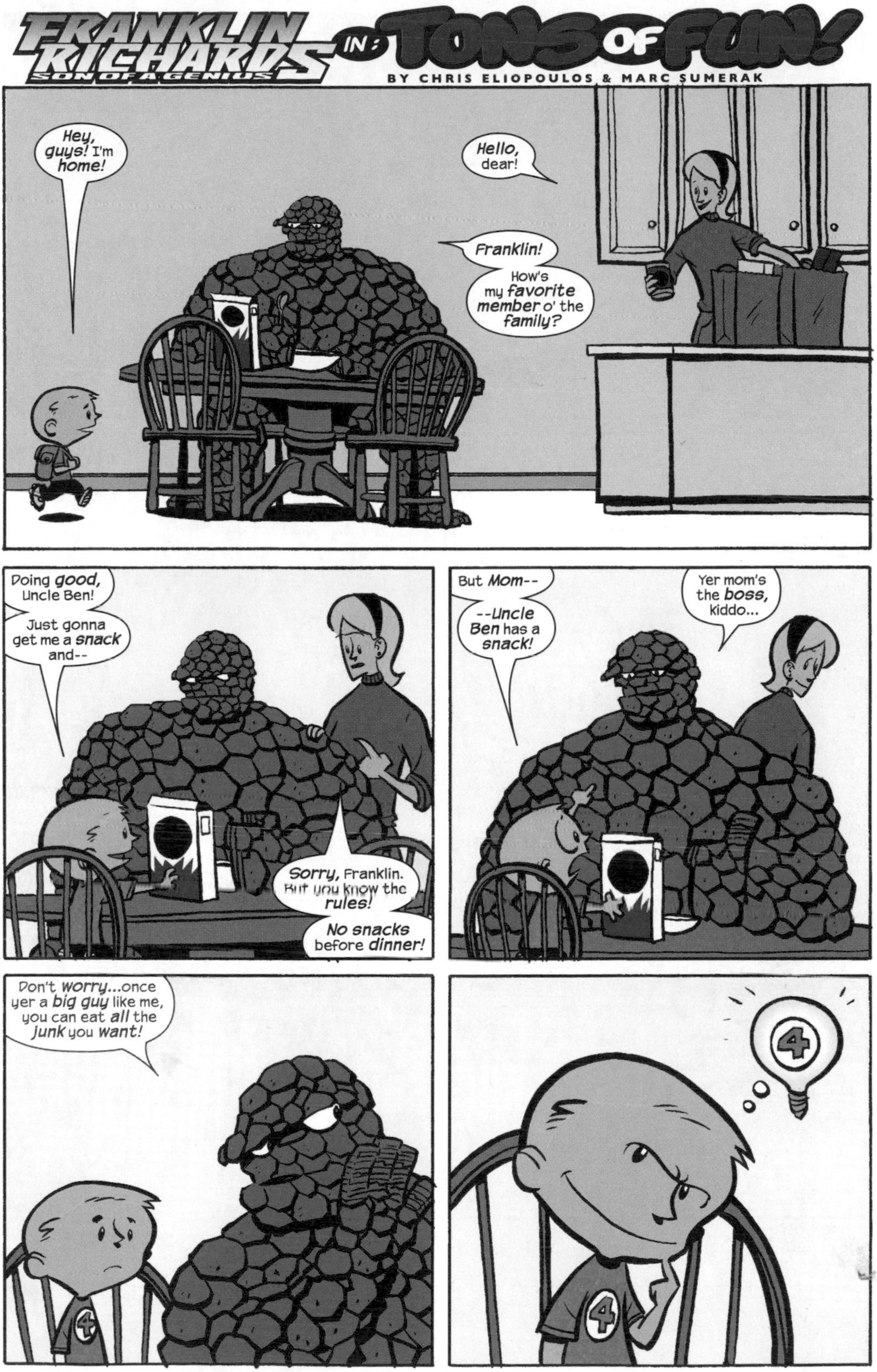
FRANKLIN RICHARDS SON OF A GENIUS
IN: TONS OF FUN!
BY CHRIS ELIOPOULOS & MARC SUMERAK
Hey, guys! I'm home!
Hello, dear!
Franklin!
How's my favorite member o' the family?
Doing good, Uncle Ben!
Just gonna get me a snack and--
Sorry, Franklin. But you know the rules!
No snacks before dinner!
But Mom--
--Uncle Ben has a snack!
Yer mom's the boss, kiddo...
Don't worry...once yer a big guy like me, you can eat all the junk you want!
4

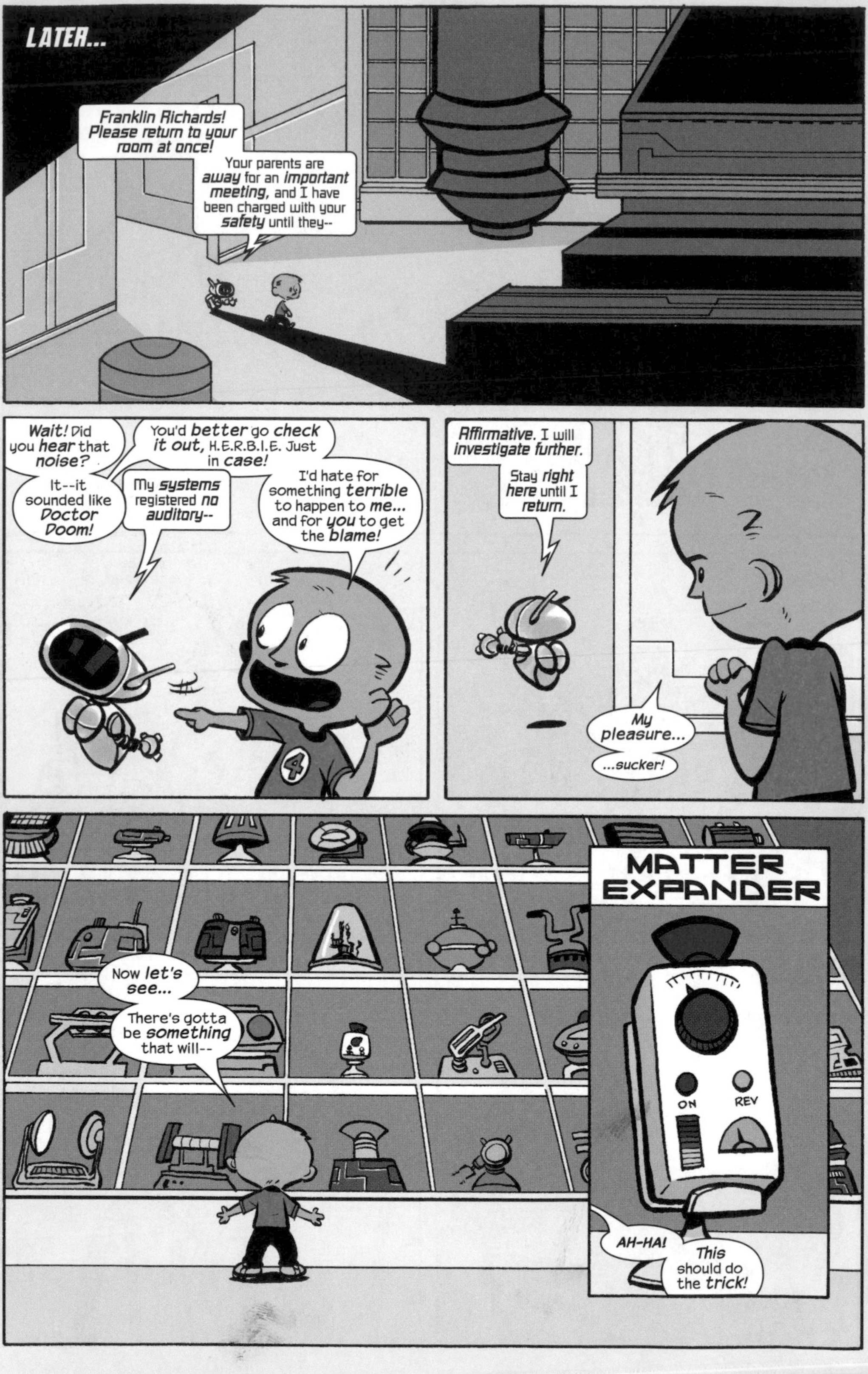
LATER...
Franklin Richards! Please return to your room at once!
Your parents are away for an important meeting, and I have been charged with your safety until they--
Wait! Did you hear that noise?
It--it sounded like Doctor Doom!
You'd better go check it out, H.E.R.B.I.E. Just in case!
My systems registered no auditory--
I'd hate for something terrible to happen to me... and for you to get the blame!
Affirmative. I will investigate further.
Stay right here until I return.
My pleasure...
...sucker!
Now let's see...
There's gotta be something that will--
MATTER EXPANDER
ON
REV
AH-HA!
This should do the trick!

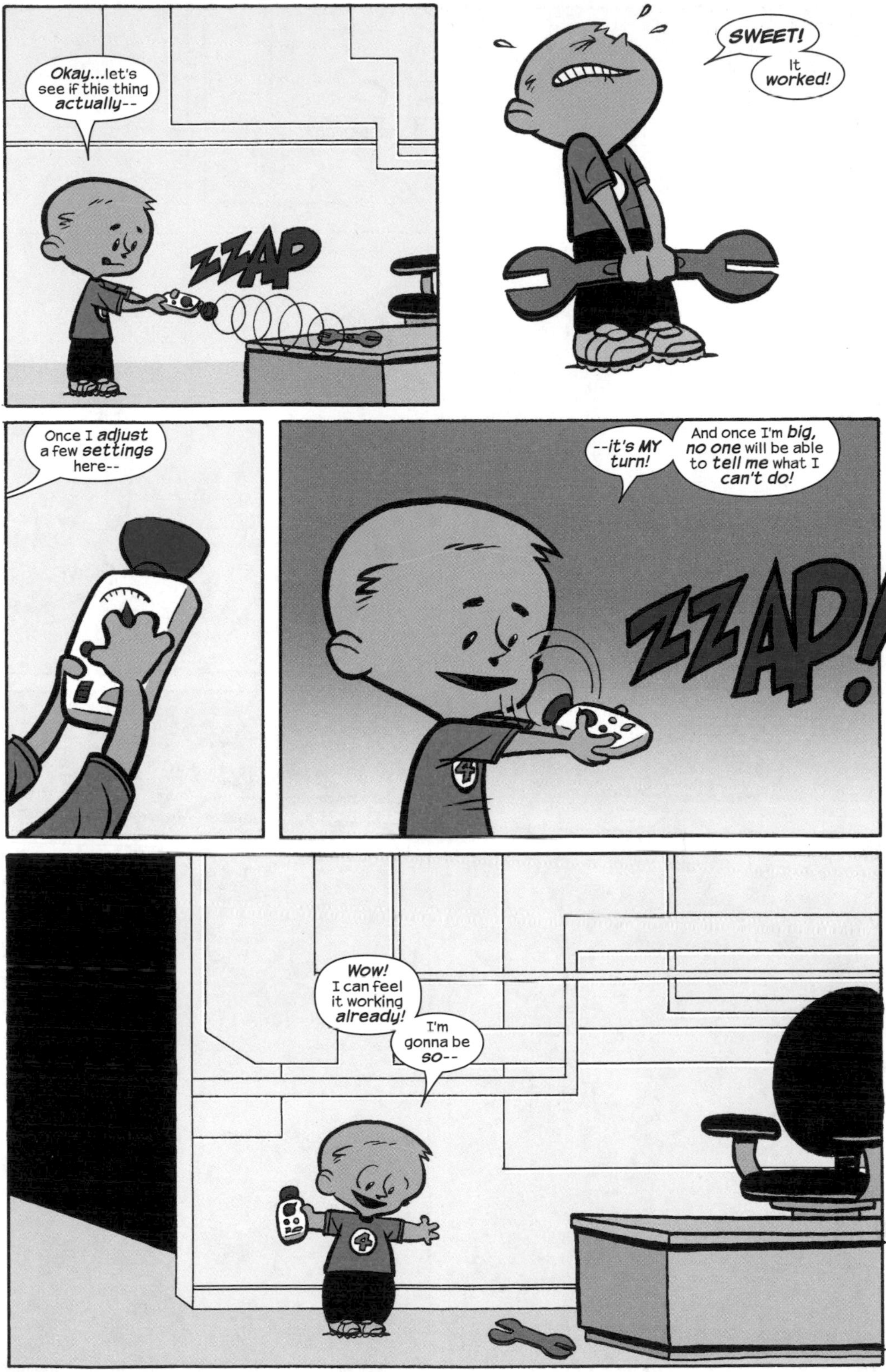

Okay...let's see if this thing actually--
ZZAP
SWEET!
It worked!
Once I adjust a few settings here--
--it's MY turn!
And once I'm big, no one will be able to tell me what I can't do!
ZZAP!
Wow! I can feel it working already!
I'm gonna be so--

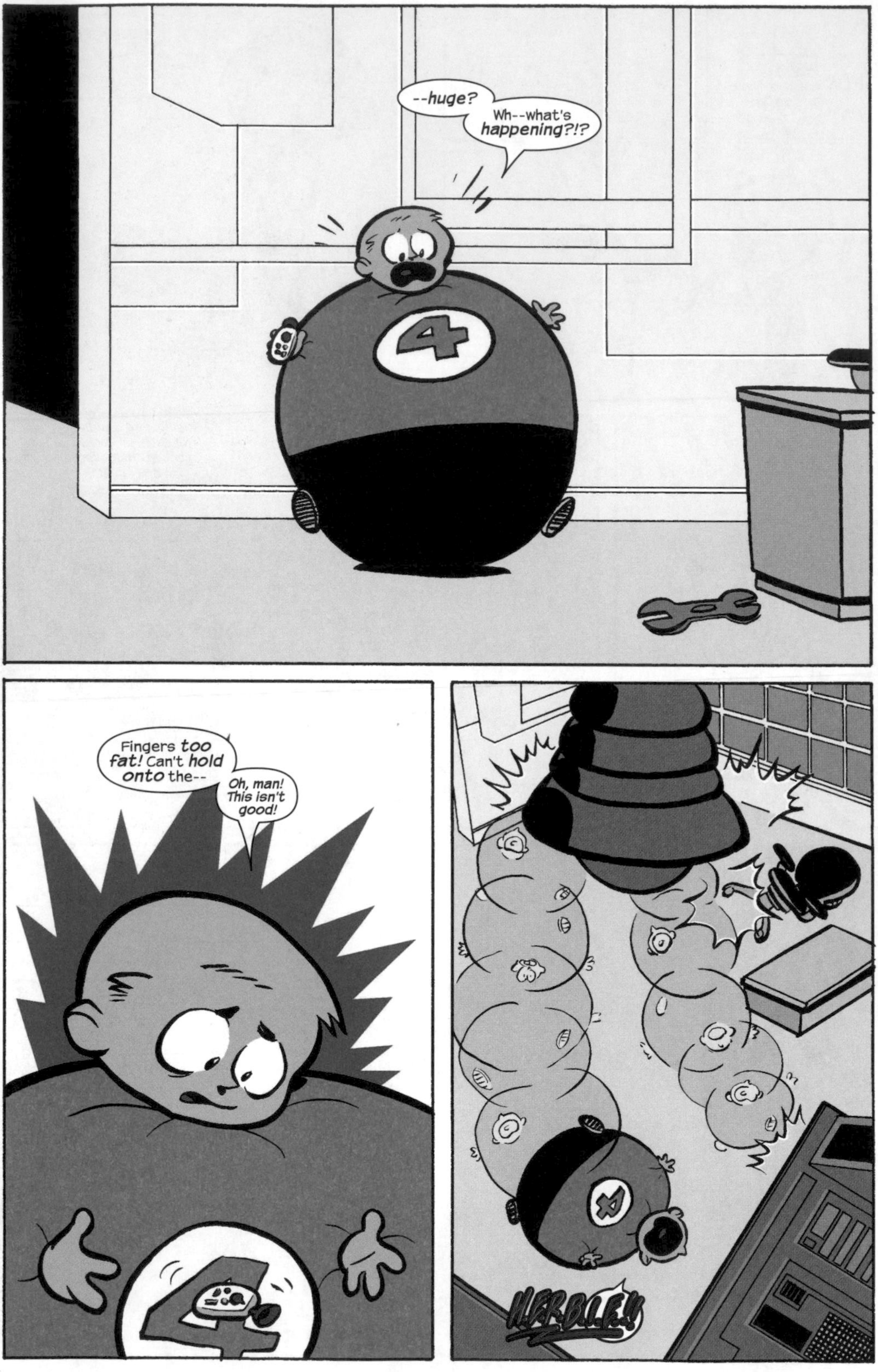
--huge?
Wh--what's happening?!?
Fingers too fat! Can't hold onto the--
Oh, man! This isn't good!
H.E.R.B.I.E.!!

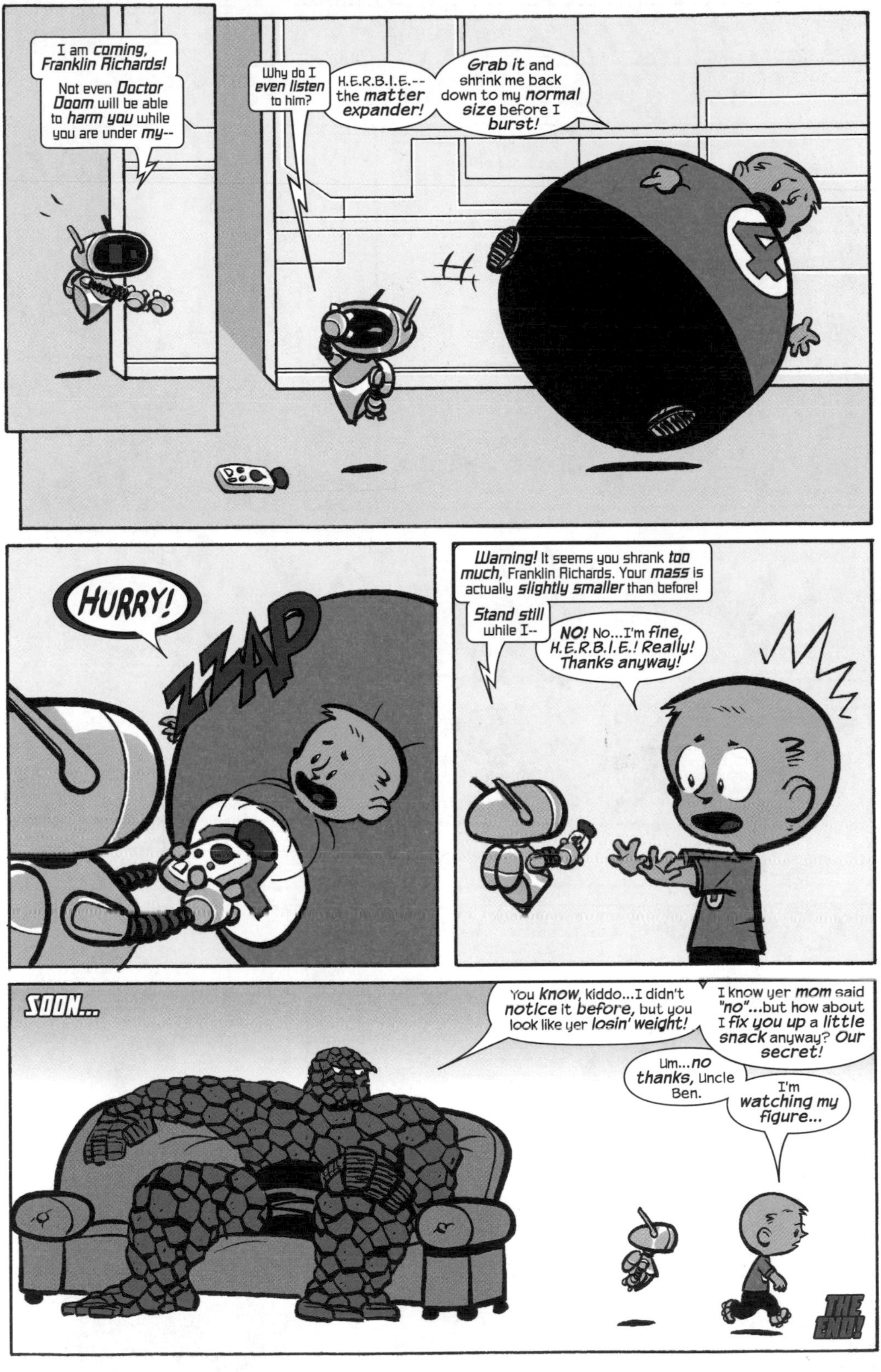
I am coming, Franklin Richards!
Not even Doctor Doom will be able to harm you while you are under my--
Why do I even listen to him?
H.E.R.B.I.E.-- the matter expander!
Grab it and shrink me back down to my normal size before I burst!
HURRY!
ZZAP
Warning! It seems you shrank too much, Franklin Richards. Your mass is actually slightly smaller than before!
Stand still while I--
NO! No...I'm fine, H.E.R.B.I.E.! Really! Thanks anyway!
SOON...
You know, kiddo...I didn't notice it before, but you look like yer losin' weight!
I know yer mom said "no"...but how about I fix you up a little snack anyway? Our secret!
Um...no thanks, Uncle Ben.
I'm watching my figure...
THE END!

FRANKLIN RICHARDS SON OF A GENIUS IN: "VEGGIN' OUT!"

STORY BY **CHRIS ELIOPOULOS & MARC SUMERAK**
MARC SUMERAK SCRIPT **CHRIS ELIOPOULOS** ART

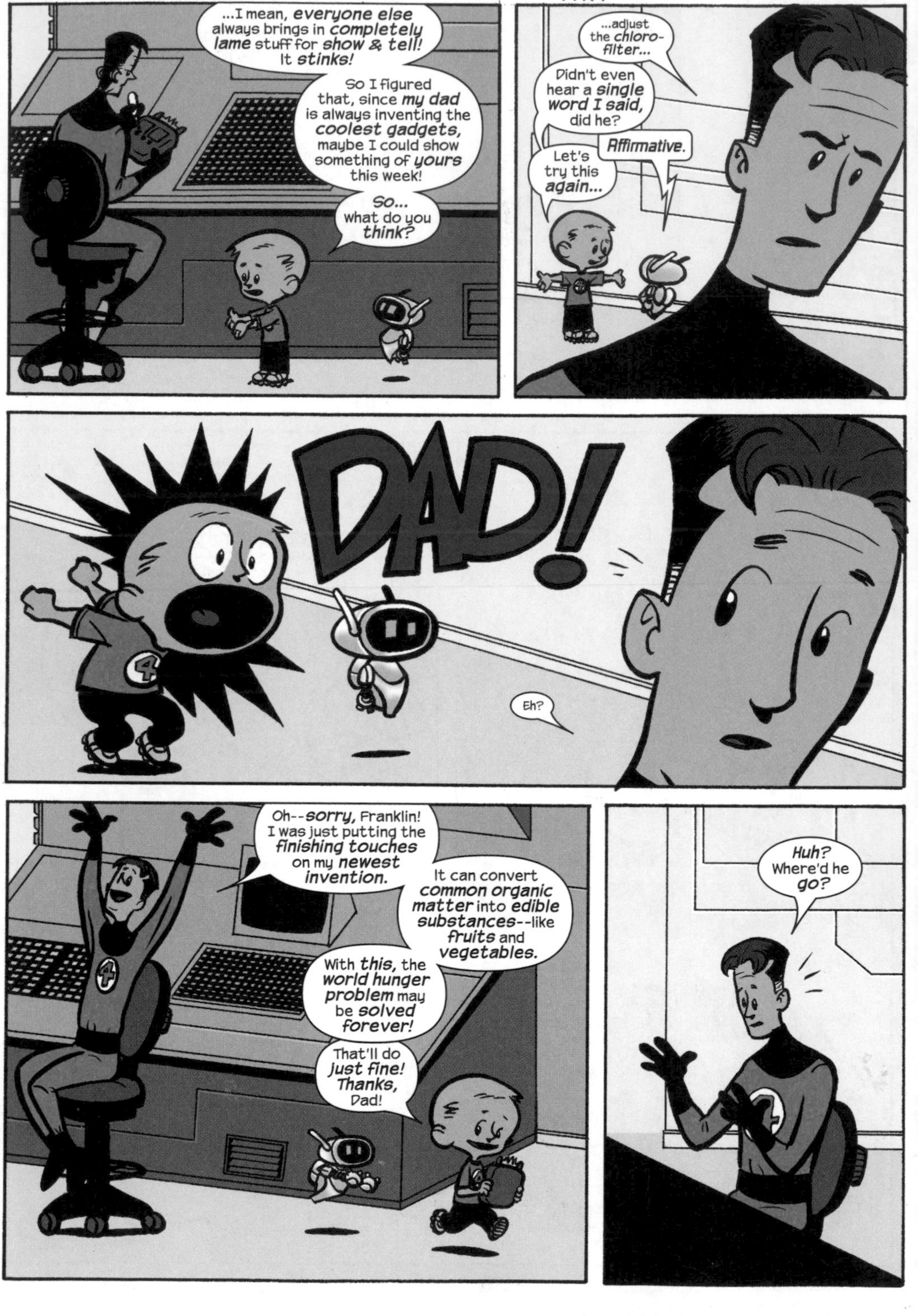
...I mean, everyone else always brings in completely lame stuff for show & tell! It stinks!
So I figured that, since my dad is always inventing the coolest gadgets, maybe I could show something of yours this week!
So... what do you think?
...adjust the chloro-filter...
Didn't even hear a single word I said, did he?
Affirmative.
Let's try this again...
DAD!
Eh?
Oh--sorry, Franklin! I was just putting the finishing touches on my newest invention.
It can convert common organic matter into edible substances--like fruits and vegetables.
With this, the world hunger problem may be solved forever!
That'll do just fine! Thanks, Dad!
Huh? Where'd he go?

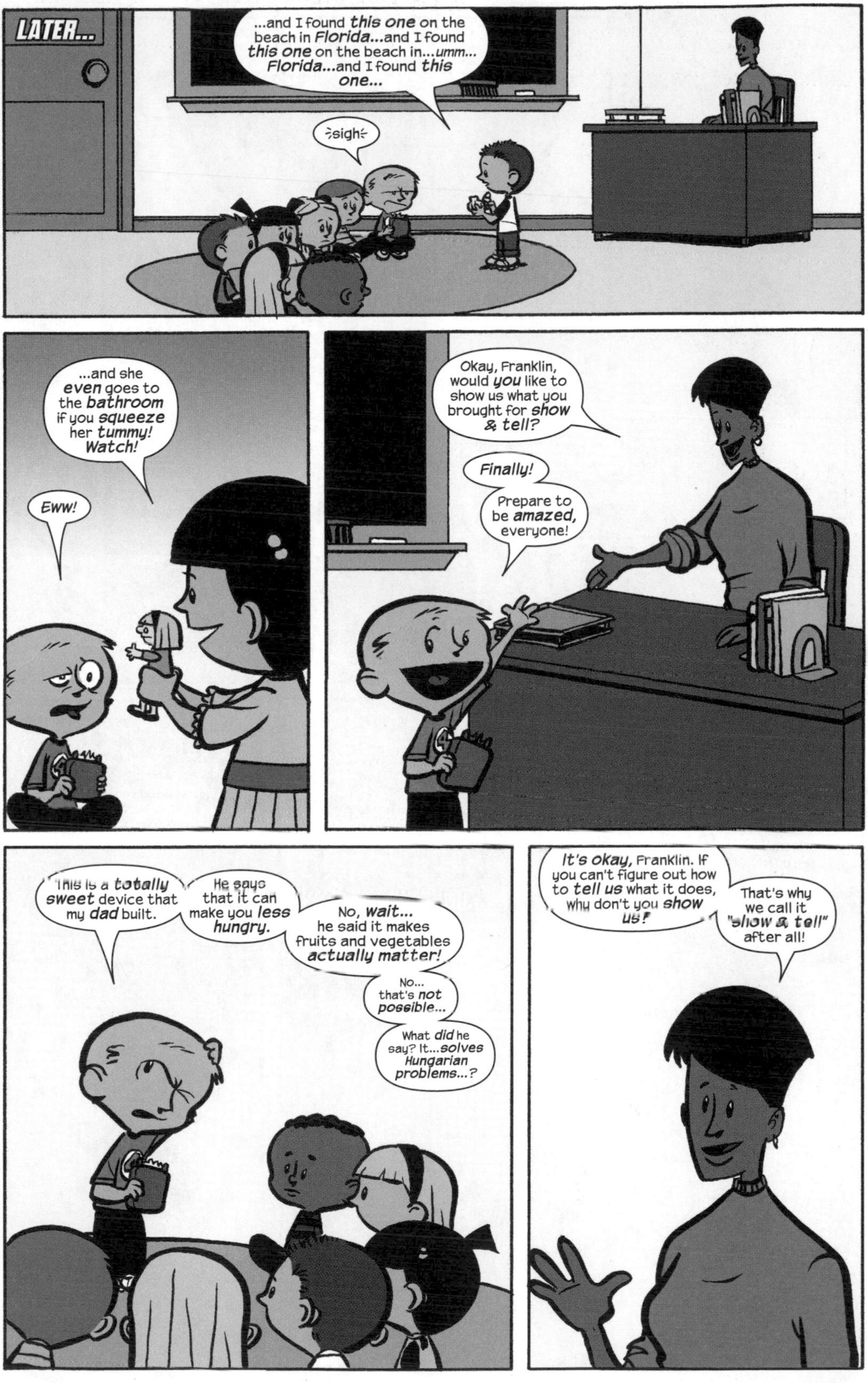

LATER...
...and I found this one on the beach in Florida...and I found this one on the beach in...umm... Florida...and I found this one...
sigh
...and she even goes to the bathroom if you squeeze her tummy! Watch!
Eww!
Okay, Franklin, would you like to show us what you brought for show & tell?
Finally!
Prepare to be amazed, everyone!
This is a totally sweet device that my dad built.
He says that it can make you less hungry.
No, wait... he said it makes fruits and vegetables actually matter!
No... that's not possible...
What did he say? It...solves Hungarian problems...?
It's okay, Franklin. If you can't figure out how to tell us what it does, why don't you show us!
That's why we call it "show & tell" after all!

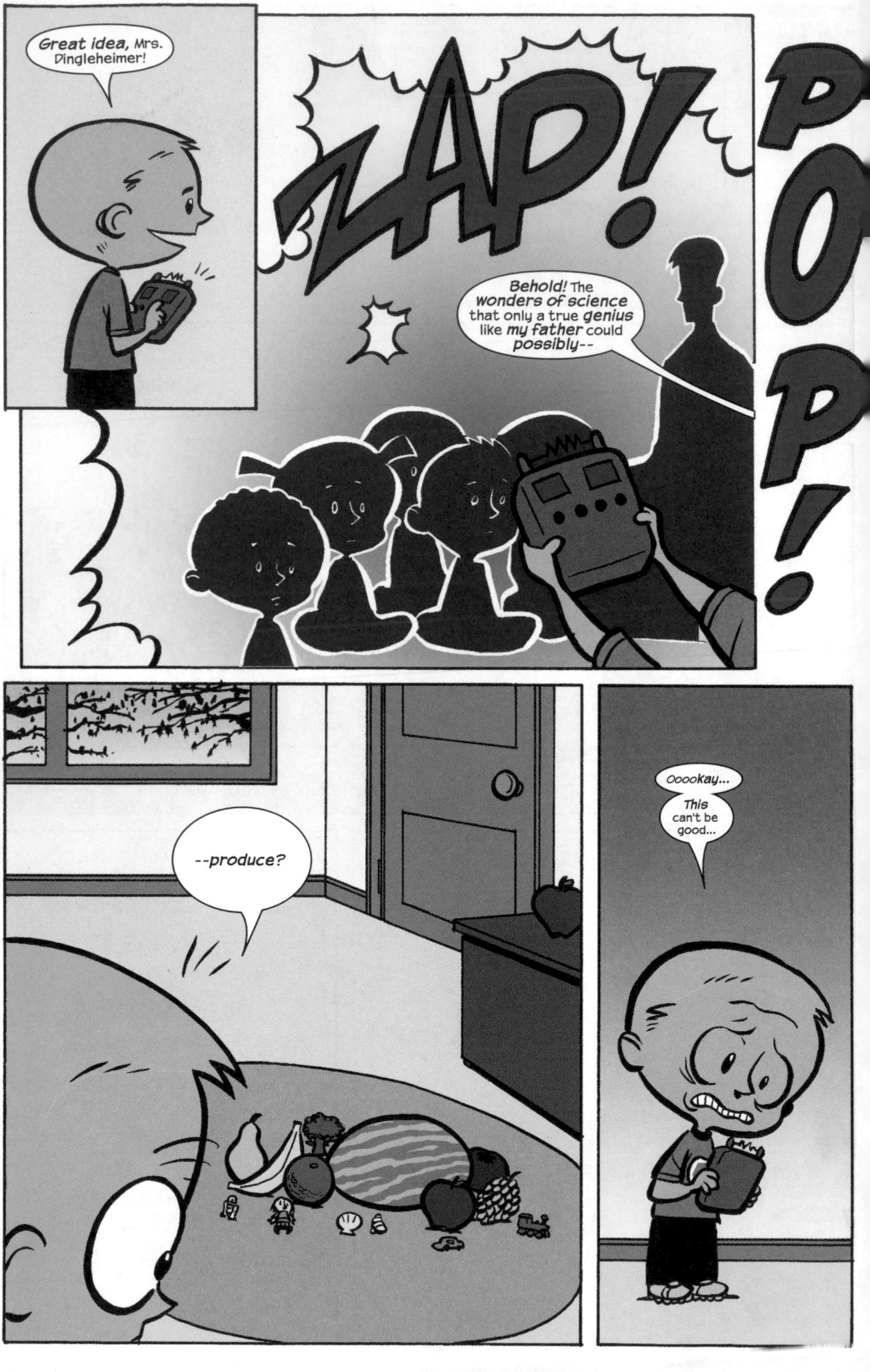
Great idea, Mrs. Dingleheimer!
ZAP!
POP!
Behold! The wonders of science that only a true genius like my father could possibly--
--produce?
Ooookay...
This can't be good...

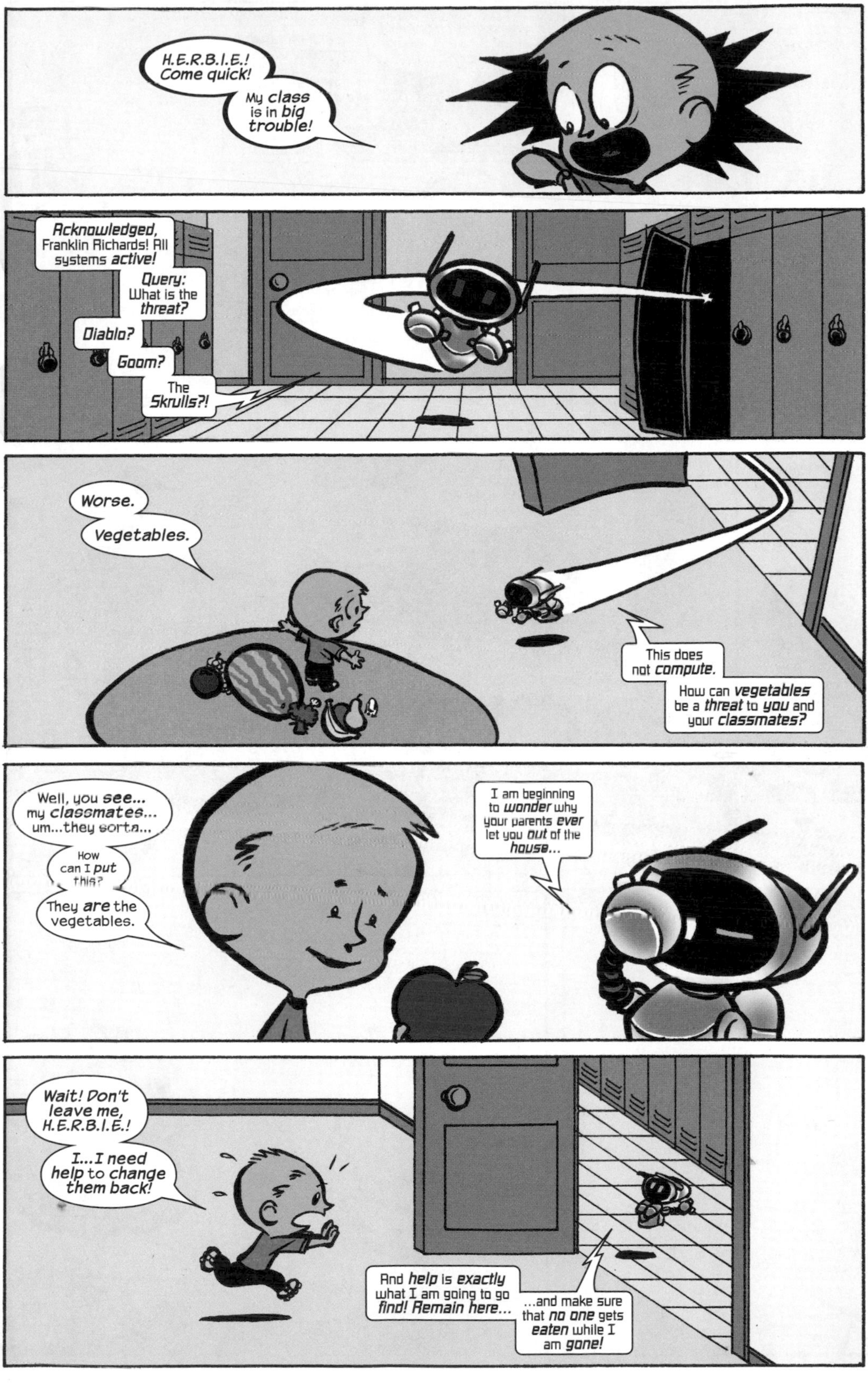
H.E.R.B.I.E.! Come quick!
My class is in big trouble!
Acknowledged, Franklin Richards! All systems active!
Query: What is the threat?
Diablo?
Goom?
The Skrulls?!
Worse.
Vegetables.
This does not compute.
How can vegetables be a threat to you and your classmates?
Well, you see... my classmates... um...they sorta...
How can I put this?
They are the vegetables.
I am beginning to wonder why your parents ever let you out of the house...
Wait! Don't leave me, H.E.R.B.I.E.!
I...I need help to change them back!
And help is exactly what I am going to go find! Remain here...
...and make sure that no one gets eaten while I am gone!

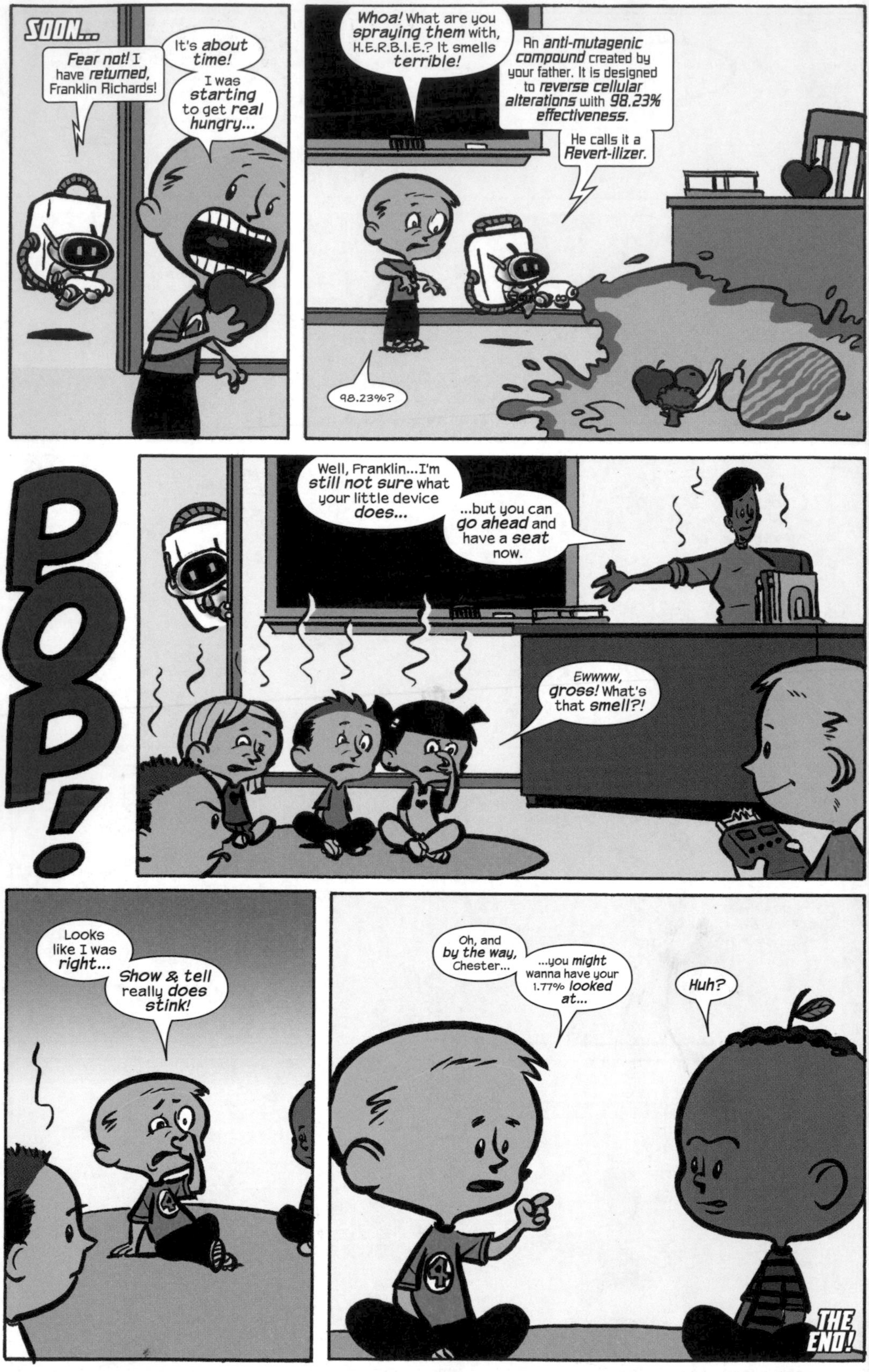
SOON...
Fear not! I have returned, Franklin Richards!
It's about time!
I was starting to get real hungry...
Whoa! What are you spraying them with, H.E.R.B.I.E.? It smells terrible!
An anti-mutagenic compound created by your father. It is designed to reverse cellular alterations with 98.23% effectiveness.
He calls it a Revert-ilizer.
98.23%?
POP!
Well, Franklin...I'm still not sure what your little device does...
...but you can go ahead and have a seat now.
Ewwww, gross! What's that smell?!
Looks like I was right...
Show & tell really does stink!
Oh, and by the way, Chester...
...you might wanna have your 1.77% looked at...
Huh?
THE END!

Franklin Richards: Son of a Genius in: Weather or Not

STORY BY **CHRIS ELIOPOULOS & MARC SUMERAK**
MARC SUMERAK SCRIPT
CHRIS ELIOPOULOS ART

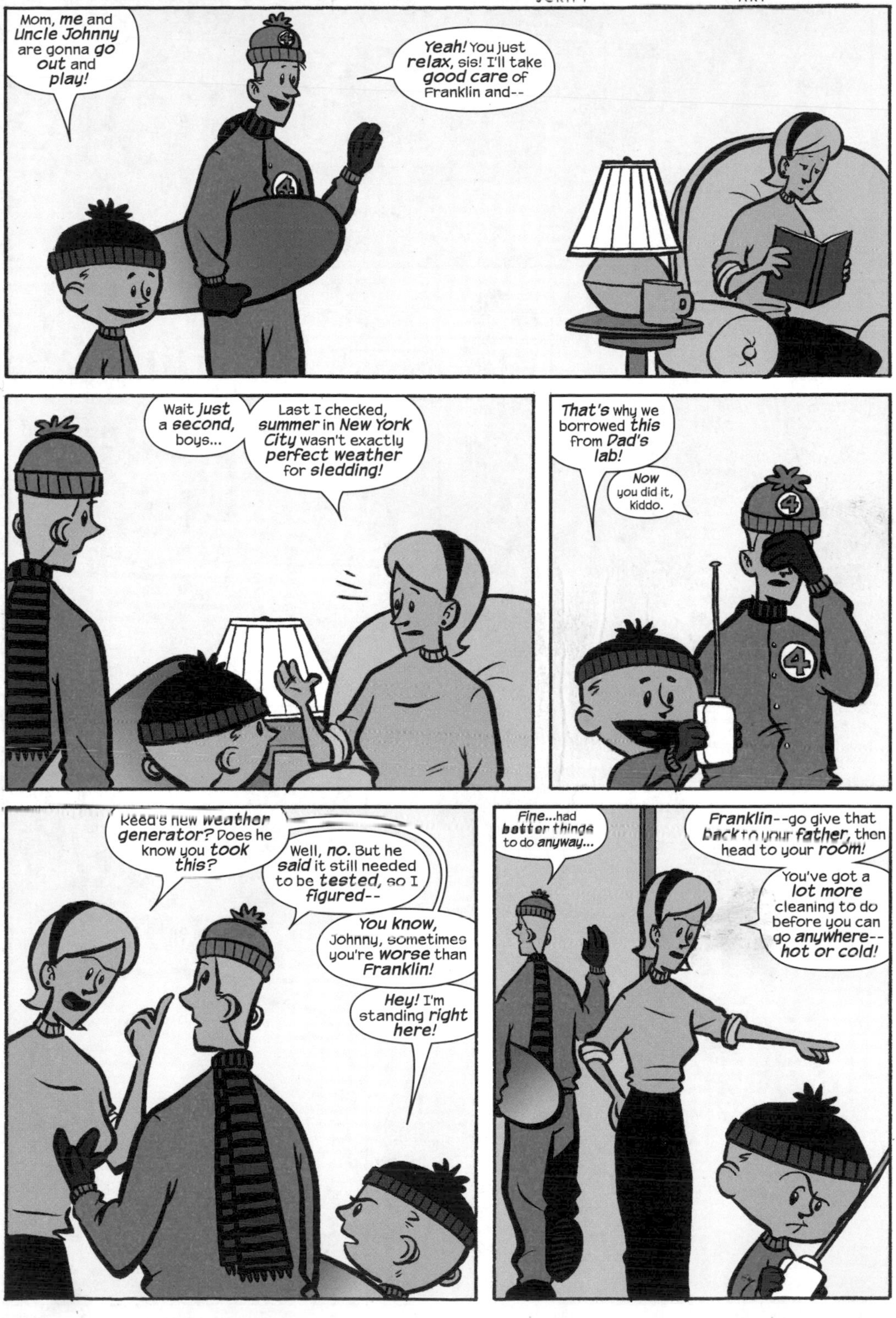
Mom, me and Uncle Johnny are gonna go out and play!
Yeah! You just relax, sis! I'll take good care of Franklin and--
Wait just a second, boys...
Last I checked, summer in New York City wasn't exactly perfect weather for sledding!
That's why we borrowed this from Dad's lab!
Now you did it, kiddo.
Reed's new weather generator? Does he know you took this?
Well, no. But he said it still needed to be tested, so I figured--
You know, Johnny, sometimes you're worse than Franklin!
Hey! I'm standing right here!
Fine...had better things to do anyway...
Franklin--go give that back to your father, then head to your room!
You've got a lot more cleaning to do before you can go anywhere--hot or cold!

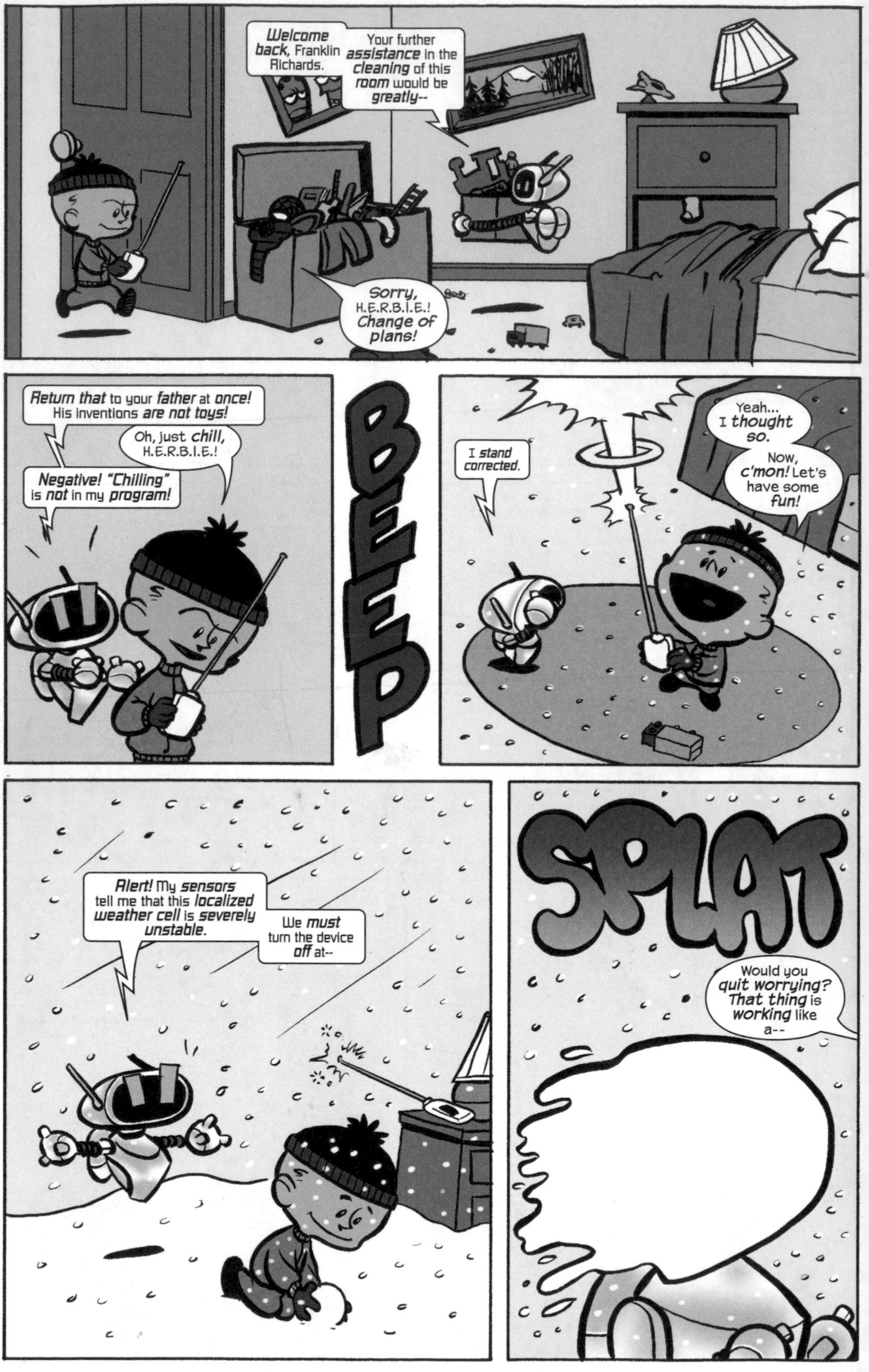

Welcome back, Franklin Richards.
Your further assistance in the cleaning of this room would be greatly--
Sorry, H.E.R.B.I.E.! Change of plans!
Return that to your father at once! His inventions are not toys!
Oh, just chill, H.E.R.B.I.E.!
Negative! "Chilling" is not in my program!
BEEEP
I stand corrected.
Yeah... I thought so.
Now, c'mon! Let's have some fun!
Alert! My sensors tell me that this localized weather cell is severely unstable.
We must turn the device off at--
SPLAT
Would you quit worrying? That thing is working like a--

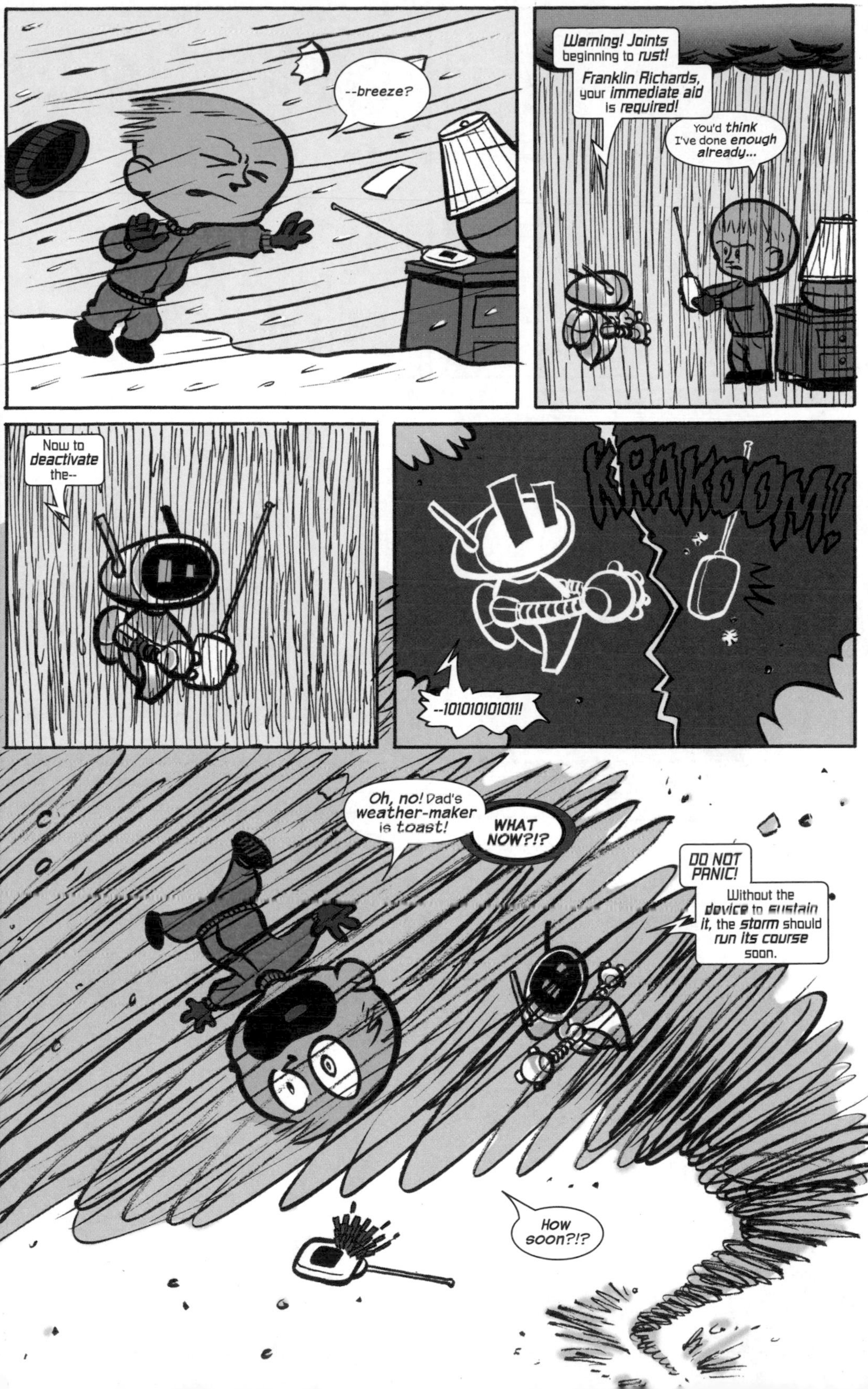
--breeze?
Warning! Joints beginning to rust!
Franklin Richards, your immediate aid is required!
You'd think I've done enough already...
Now to deactivate the--
KRAKOOM!
--101010101011!
Oh, no! Dad's weather-maker is toast!
WHAT NOW?!?
DO NOT PANIC!
Without the device to sustain it, the storm should run its course soon.
How soon?!?

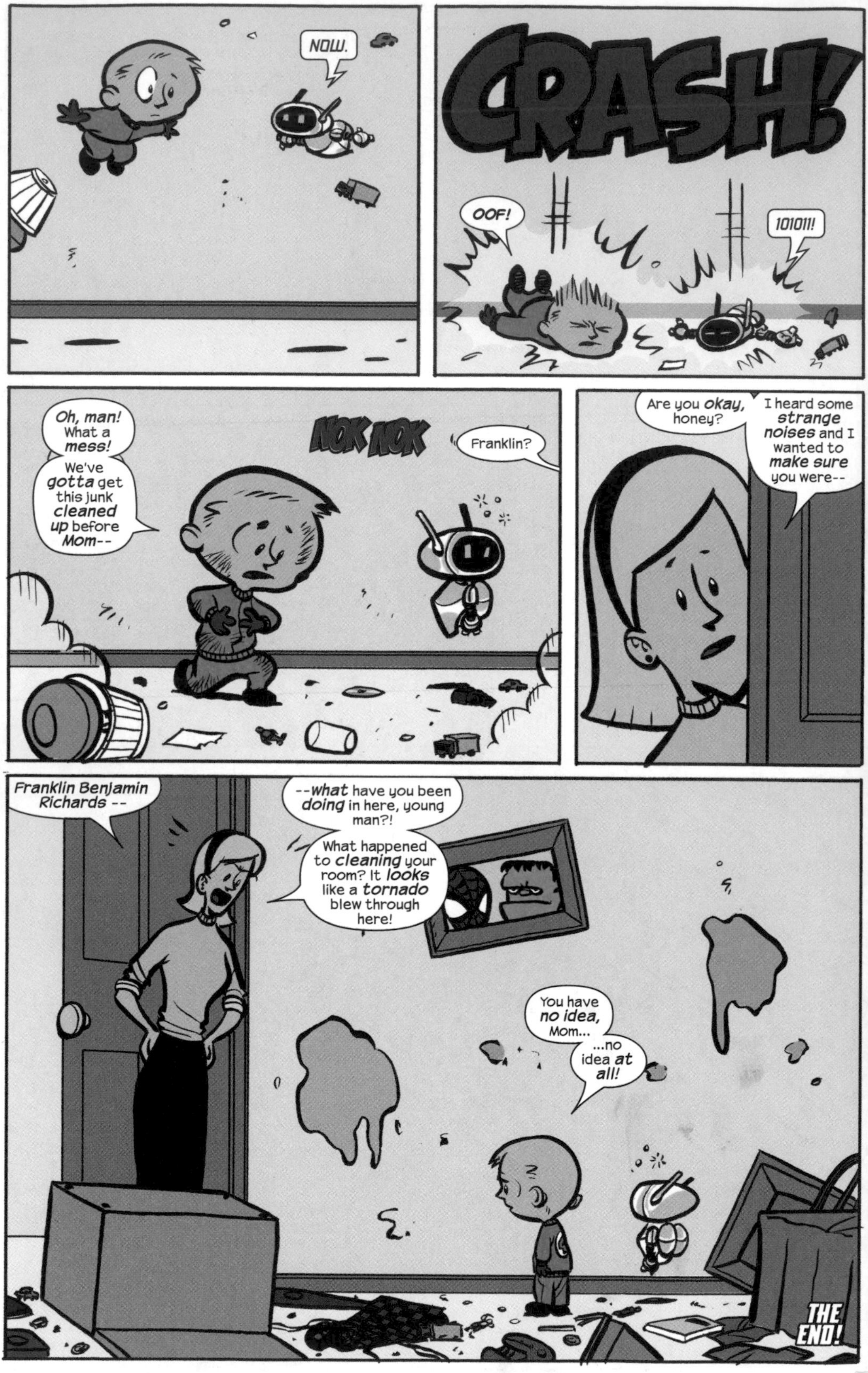
NOW.
CRASH!
OOF!
101011!
Oh, man! What a mess!
We've gotta get this junk cleaned up before Mom--
NOK NOK
Franklin?
Are you okay, honey?
I heard some strange noises and I wanted to make sure you were--
Franklin Benjamin Richards --
--what have you been doing in here, young man?!
What happened to cleaning your room? It looks like a tornado blew through here!
You have no idea, Mom...
...no idea at all!
THE END!

FRANKLIN RICHARDS SON OF A GENIUS IN: "SEND IN THE CLONES"

STORY BY CHRIS ELIOPOULOS & MARC SUMERAK

MARC SUMERAK SCRIPT — CHRIS ELIOPOULOS ART

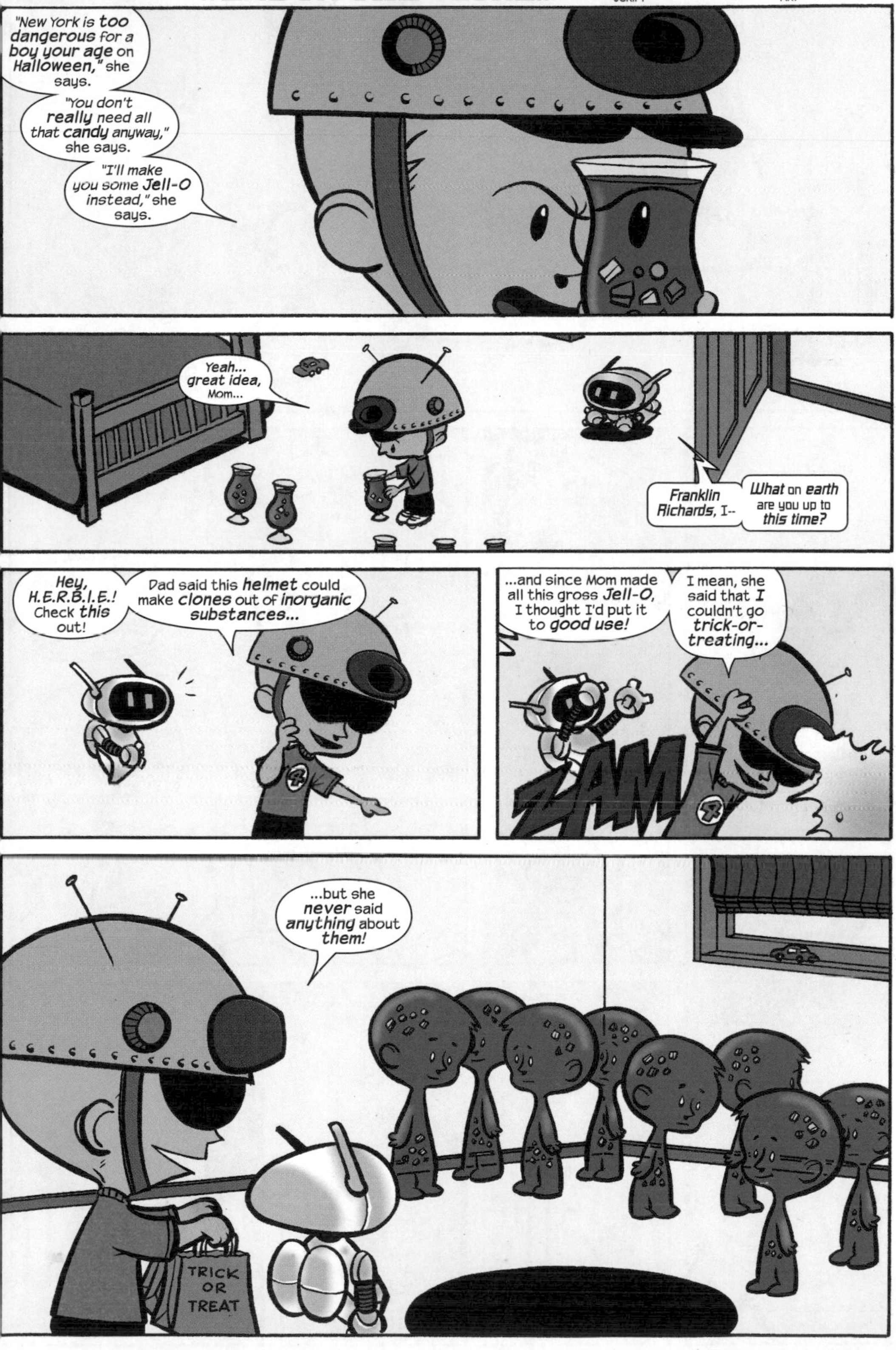
"New York is too dangerous for a boy your age on Halloween," she says.
"You don't really need all that candy anyway," she says.
"I'll make you some Jell-O instead," she says.
Yeah... great idea, Mom...
Franklin Richards, I--
What on earth are you up to this time?
Hey, H.E.R.B.I.E.! Check this out!
Dad said this helmet could make clones out of inorganic substances...
...and since Mom made all this gross Jell-O, I thought I'd put it to good use!
I mean, she said that I couldn't go trick-or-treating...
ZAM
...but she never said anything about them!
TRICK OR TREAT

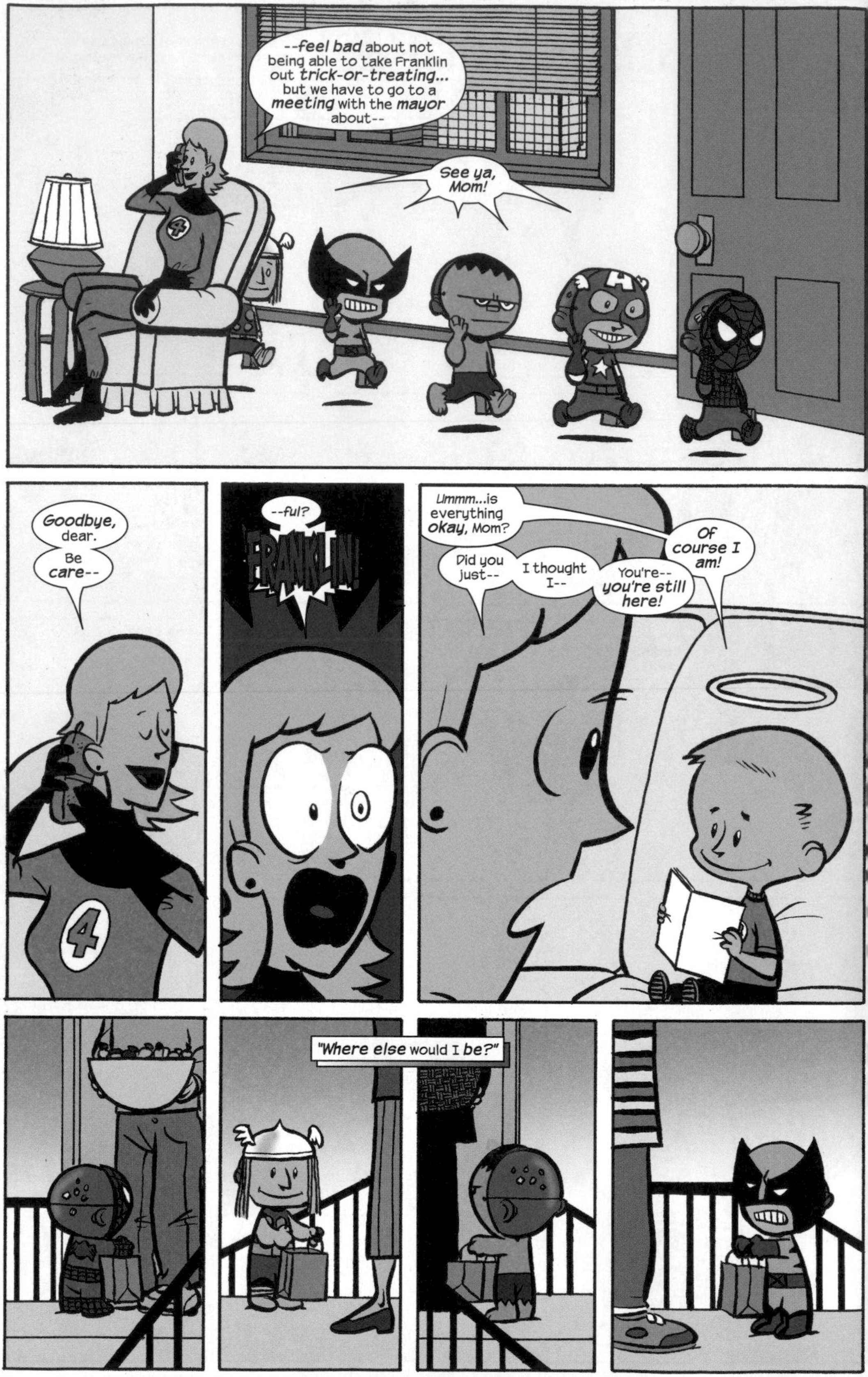
--feel bad about not being able to take Franklin out trick-or-treating... but we have to go to a meeting with the mayor about--
See ya, Mom!
Goodbye, dear.
Be care--
--ful?
FRANKLIN!
Ummm...is everything okay, Mom?
Of course I am!
Did you just--
I thought I--
You're-- you're still here!
"Where else would I be?"

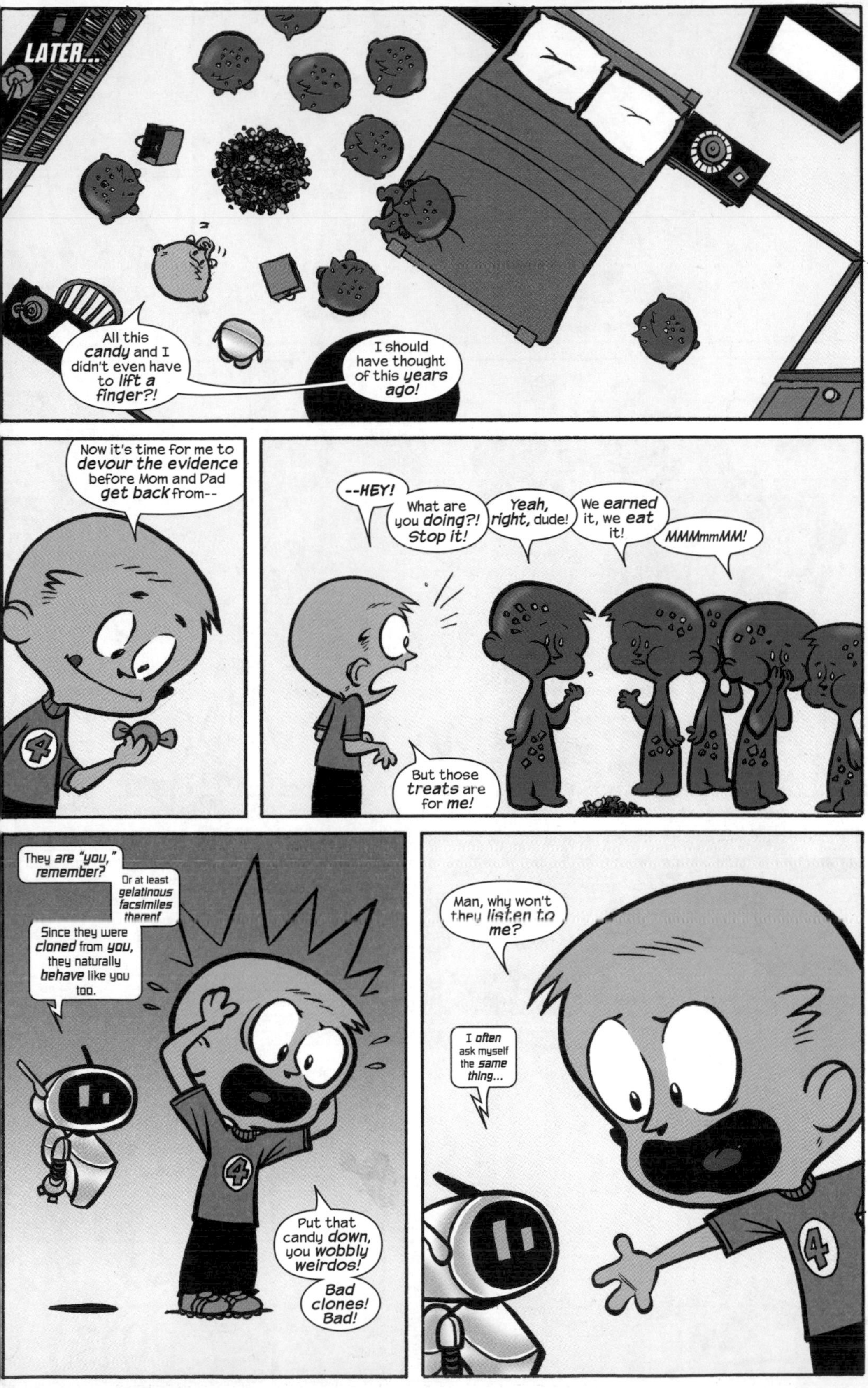
LATER...
All this candy and I didn't even have to lift a finger?!
I should have thought of this years ago!
Now it's time for me to devour the evidence before Mom and Dad get back from--
--HEY!
What are you doing?! Stop it!
Yeah, right, dude!
We earned it, we eat it!
MMMmmMM!
But those treats are for me!
They are "you," remember?
Or at least gelatinous facsimiles thereof.
Since they were cloned from you, they naturally behave like you too.
Put that candy down, you wobbly weirdos!
Bad clones! Bad!
Man, why won't they listen to me?
I often ask myself the same thing...

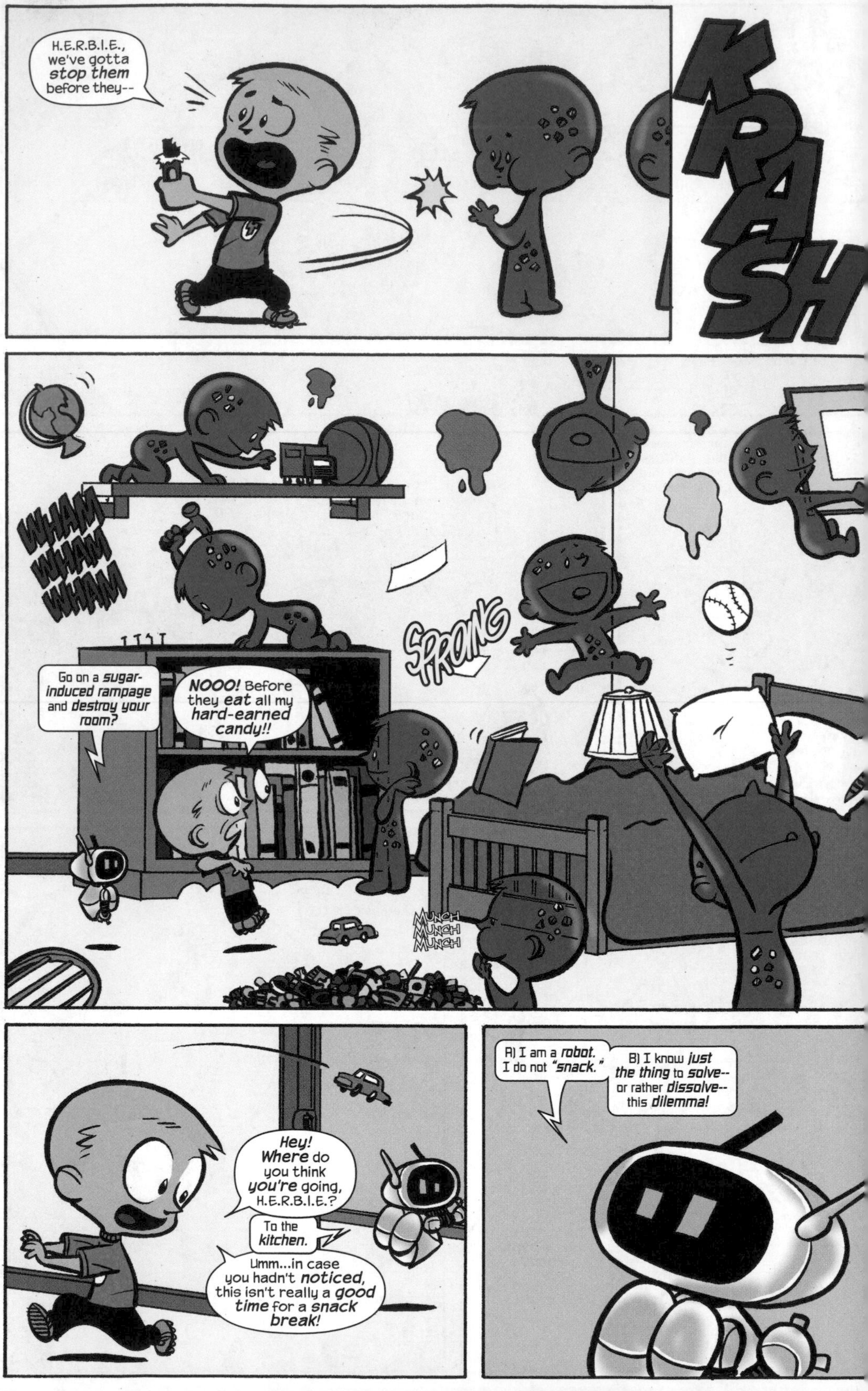
H.E.R.B.I.E., we've gotta stop them before they--
KRASH
WHAM WHAM WHAM
SPROING
Go on a sugar-induced rampage and destroy your room?
NOOO! Before they eat all my hard-earned candy!!
MUNCH MUNCH MUNCH
Hey! Where do you think you're going, H.E.R.B.I.E.?
To the kitchen.
Umm...in case you hadn't noticed, this isn't really a good time for a snack break!
A) I am a robot. I do not "snack."
B) I know just the thing to solve-- or rather dissolve-- this dilemma!

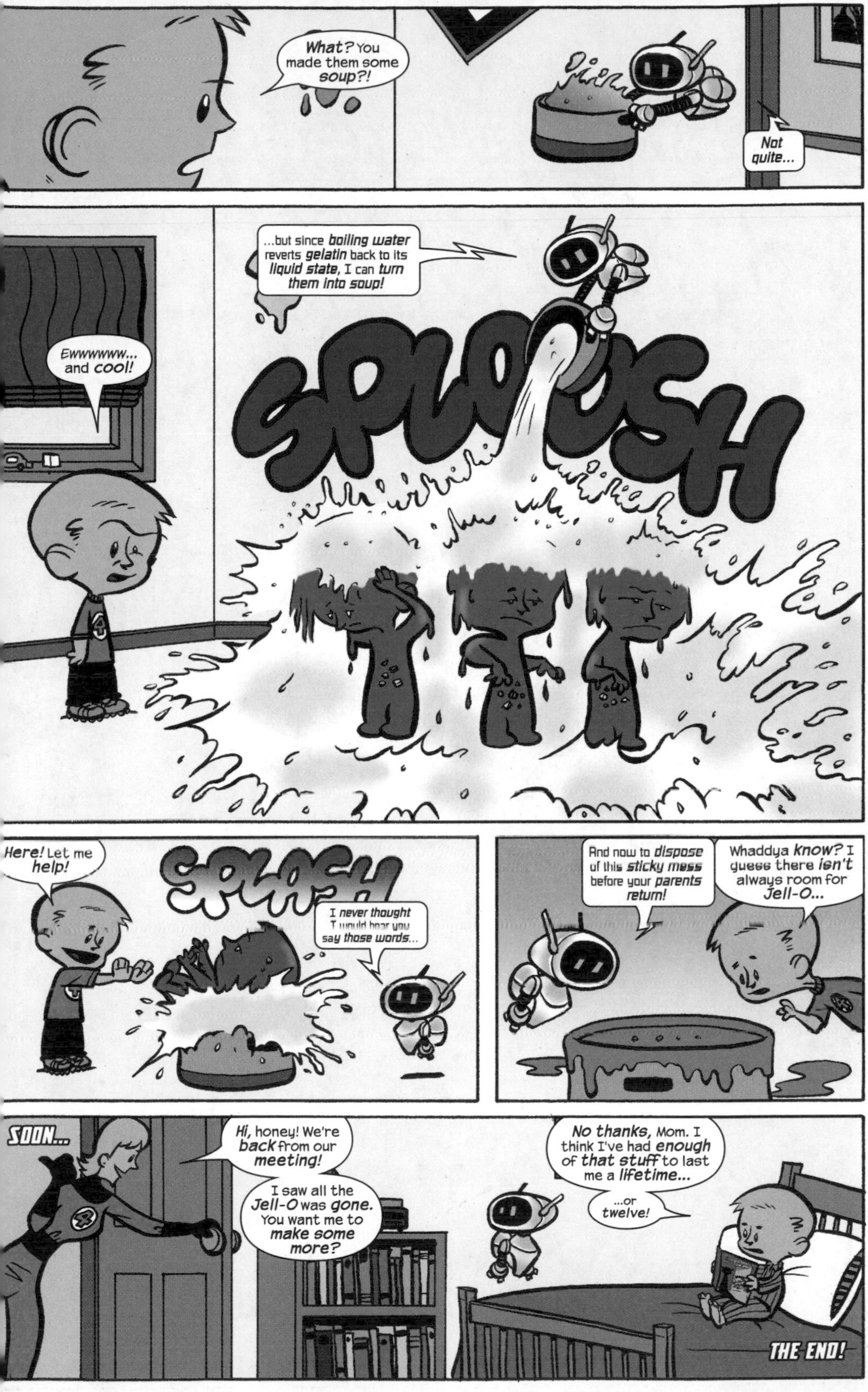
What? You made them some soup?!
Not quite...
...but since boiling water reverts gelatin back to its liquid state, I can turn them into soup!
Ewwwwww... and cool!
SPLOOSH
Here! Let me help!
SPLASH
I never thought I would hear you say those words...
And now to dispose of this sticky mess before your parents return!
Whaddya know? I guess there isn't always room for Jell-O...
SOON...
Hi, honey! We're back from our meeting!
I saw all the Jell-O was gone. You want me to make some more?
No thanks, Mom. I think I've had enough of that stuff to last me a lifetime...
...or twelve!
THE END!

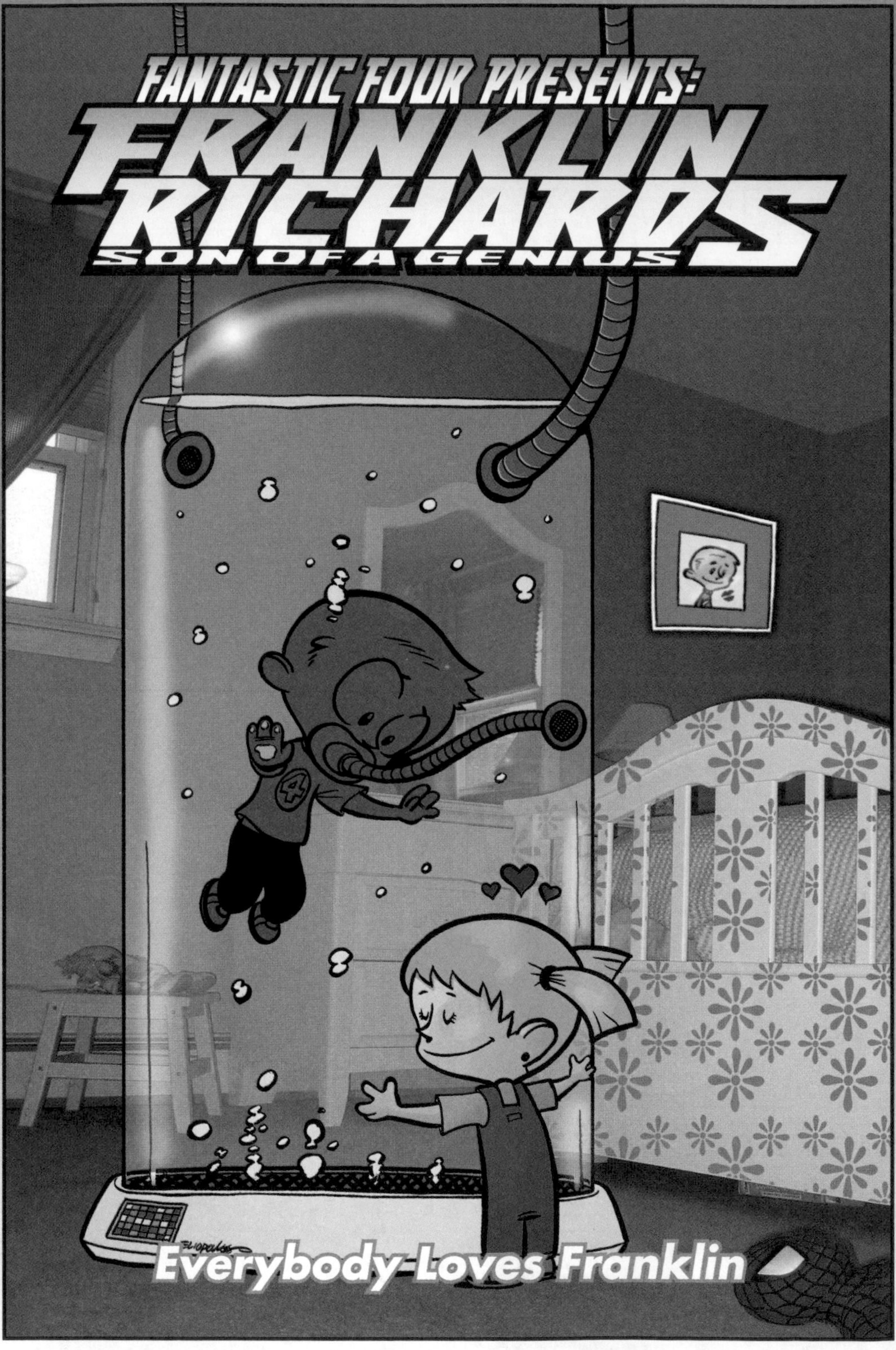

FANTASTIC FOUR PRESENTS:
FRANKLIN RICHARDS
SON OF A GENIUS
Everybody Loves Franklin

FANTASTIC FOUR PRESENTS:
FRANKLIN RICHARDS
SON OF A GENIUS
EVERYBODY LOVES FRANKLIN

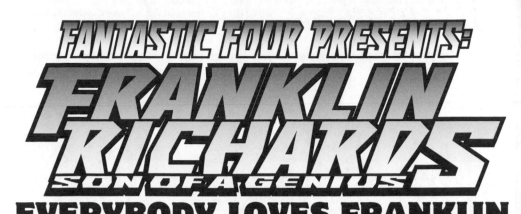

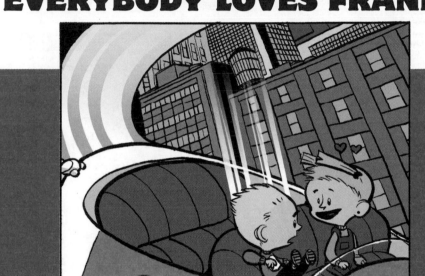

CHRIS ELIOPOULOS AND MARC SUMERAK
STORY

MARC SUMERAK — SCRIPT
CHRIS ELIOPOULOS — ART & LETTERS
GURIHIRU — COLOR

VALENTE & TAVERAS — PRODUCTION
NATHAN COSBY — ASST. EDITOR
MARK PANICCIA — CONSULTING EDITOR
MACKENZIE CADENHEAD — EDITOR
JOE QUESADA — EDITOR IN CHIEF
DAN BUCKLEY — PUBLISHER

STORY ONE
CHRISTMAS TIME WARP

STORY TWO
MY DINNER WITH DOOM(BOTS)!

STORY THREE
FRANKIE, MY DEAR...

STORY FOUR
NOW YOU SEE ME...

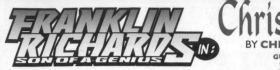

FRANKLIN RICHARDS SON OF A GENIUS IN:

Christmas Time Warp!

BY CHRIS ELIOPOULOS & MARC SUMERAK

GURIHIRU COLORS · NATHAN COSBY ASSISTANT EDITOR · TOM VALENTE PRODUCTION

MARK PANICCIA CONSULTING EDITOR · MACKENZIE CADENHEAD EDITOR

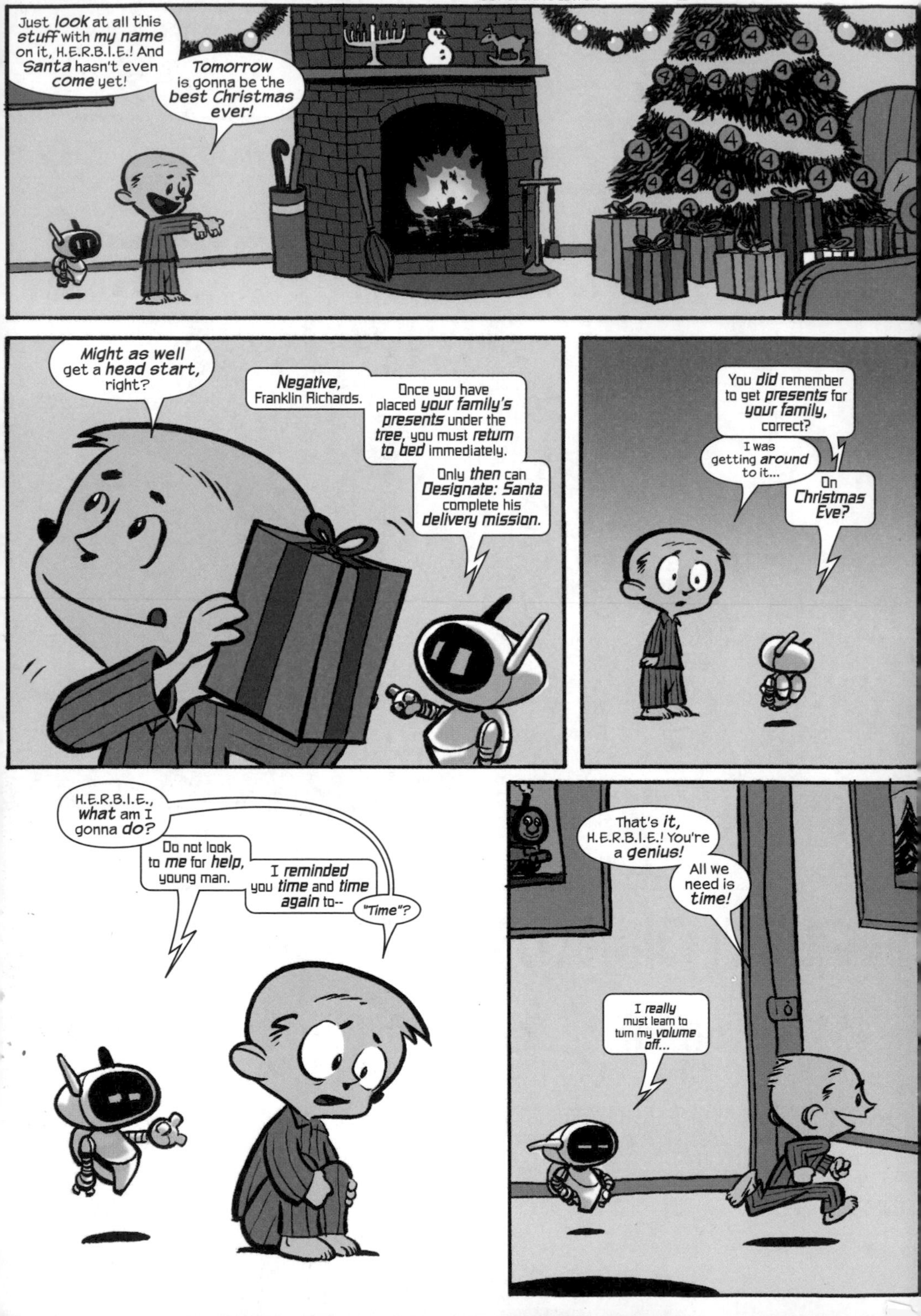

Just look at all this stuff with my name on it, H.E.R.B.I.E.! And Santa hasn't even come yet!
Tomorrow is gonna be the best Christmas ever!
Might as well get a head start, right?
Negative, Franklin Richards.
Once you have placed your family's presents under the tree, you must return to bed immediately.
Only then can Designate: Santa complete his delivery mission.
You did remember to get presents for your family, correct?
I was getting around to it...
On Christmas Eve?
H.E.R.B.I.E., what am I gonna do?
Do not look to me for help, young man.
I reminded you time and time again to--
"Time"?
That's it, H.E.R.B.I.E.! You're a genius!
All we need is time!
I really must learn to turn my volume off...

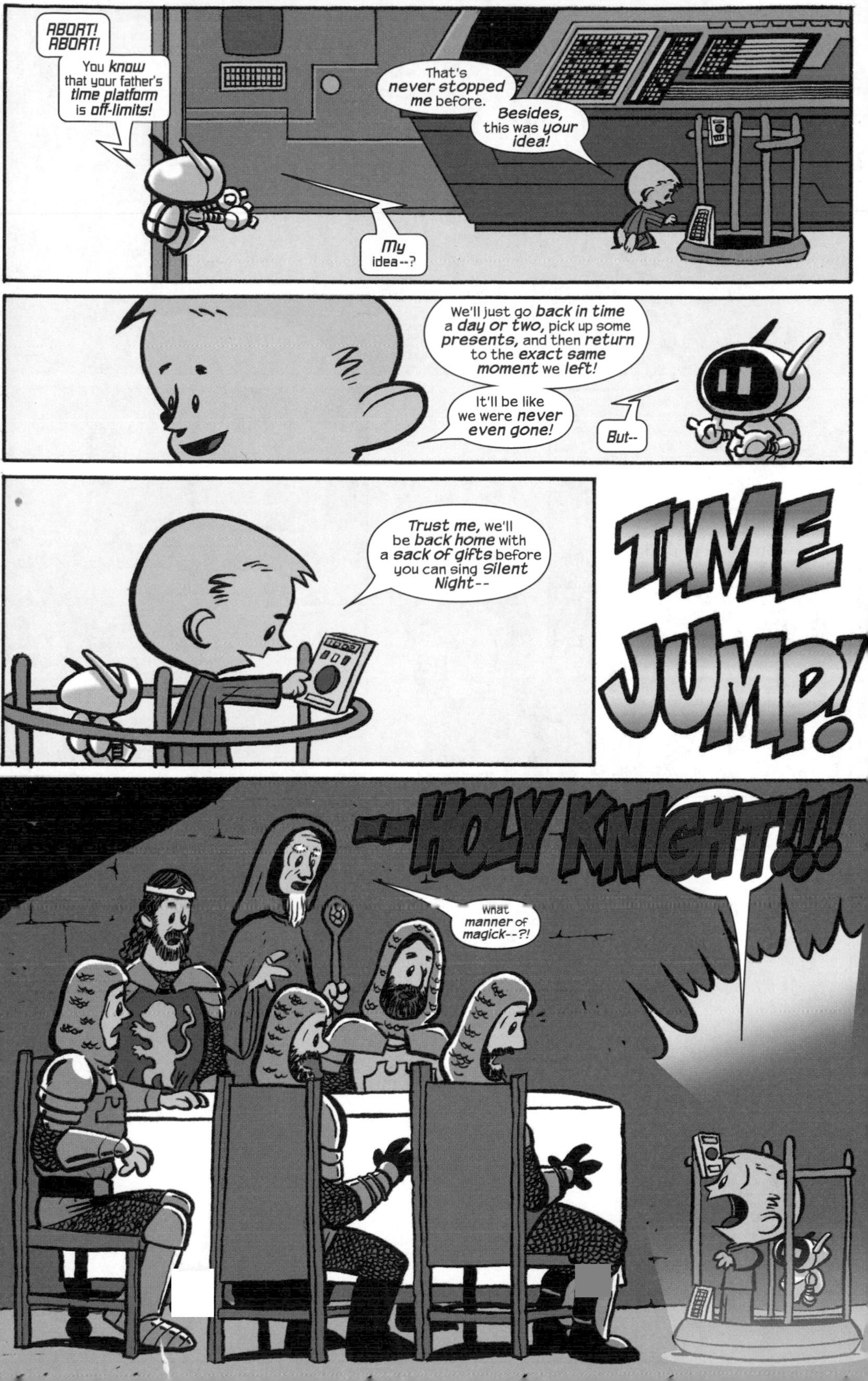

ABORT! ABORT!
You know that your father's time platform is off-limits!
That's never stopped me before.
Besides, this was your idea!
My idea--?
We'll just go back in time a day or two, pick up some presents, and then return to the exact same moment we left!
It'll be like we were never even gone!
But--
Trust me, we'll be back home with a sack of gifts before you can sing Silent Night--
TIME JUMP!
--HOLY KNIGHT!!!
What manner of magick--?!

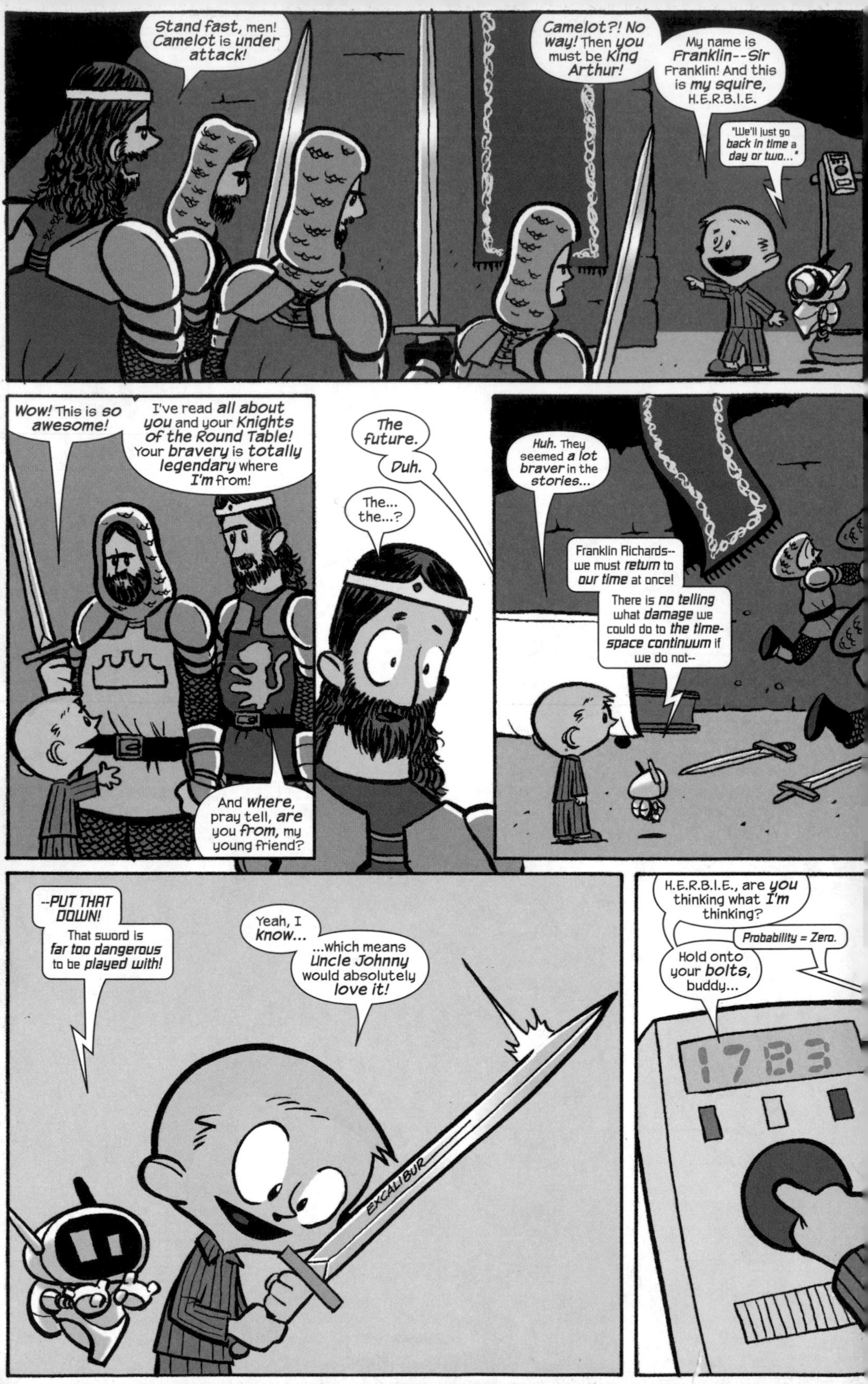

Stand fast, men! Camelot is under attack!
Camelot?! No way! Then you must be King Arthur!
My name is Franklin--Sir Franklin! And this is my squire, H.E.R.B.I.E.
"We'll just go back in time a day or two..."
Wow! This is so awesome!
I've read all about you and your Knights of the Round Table! Your bravery is totally legendary where I'm from!
And where, pray tell, are you from, my young friend?
The future.
Duh.
The... the...?
Huh. They seemed a lot braver in the stories...
Franklin Richards-- we must return to our time at once!
There is no telling what damage we could do to the time-space continuum if we do not--
--PUT THAT DOWN!
That sword is far too dangerous to be played with!
Yeah, I know...
...which means Uncle Johnny would absolutely love it!
EXCALIBUR
H.E.R.B.I.E., are you thinking what I'm thinking?
Probability = Zero.
Hold onto your bolts, buddy...
1783

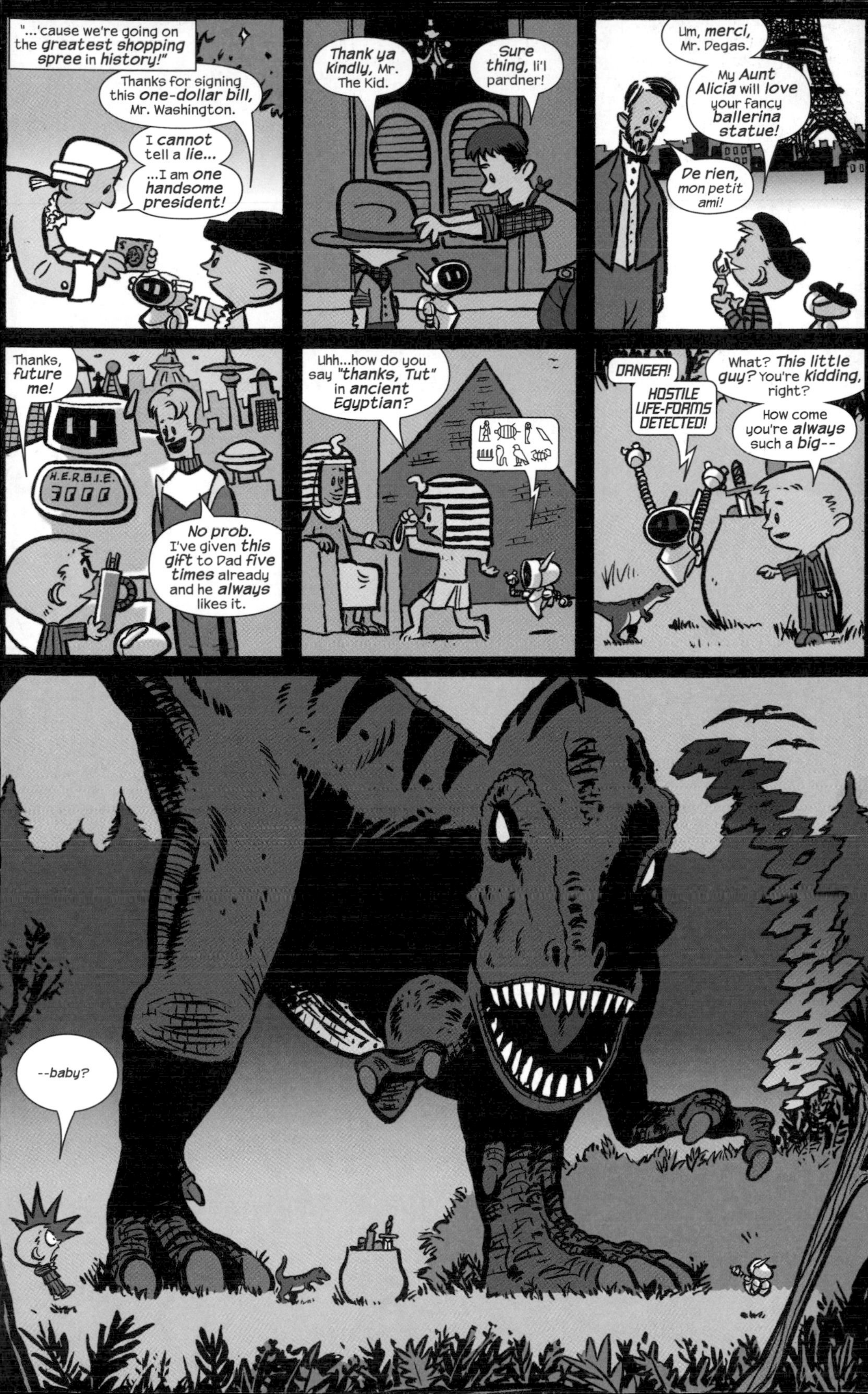
"...'cause we're going on the greatest shopping spree in history!"
Thanks for signing this one-dollar bill, Mr. Washington.
I cannot tell a lie...
...I am one handsome president!
Thank ya kindly, Mr. The Kid.
Sure thing, li'l pardner!
Um, merci, Mr. Degas.
My Aunt Alicia will love your fancy ballerina statue!
De rien, mon petit ami!
Thanks, future me!
H.E.R.B.I.E. 3000
No prob. I've given this gift to Dad five times already and he always likes it.
Uhh...how do you say "thanks, Tut" in ancient Egyptian?
DANGER!
HOSTILE LIFE-FORMS DETECTED!
What? This little guy? You're kidding, right?
How come you're always such a big--
--baby?

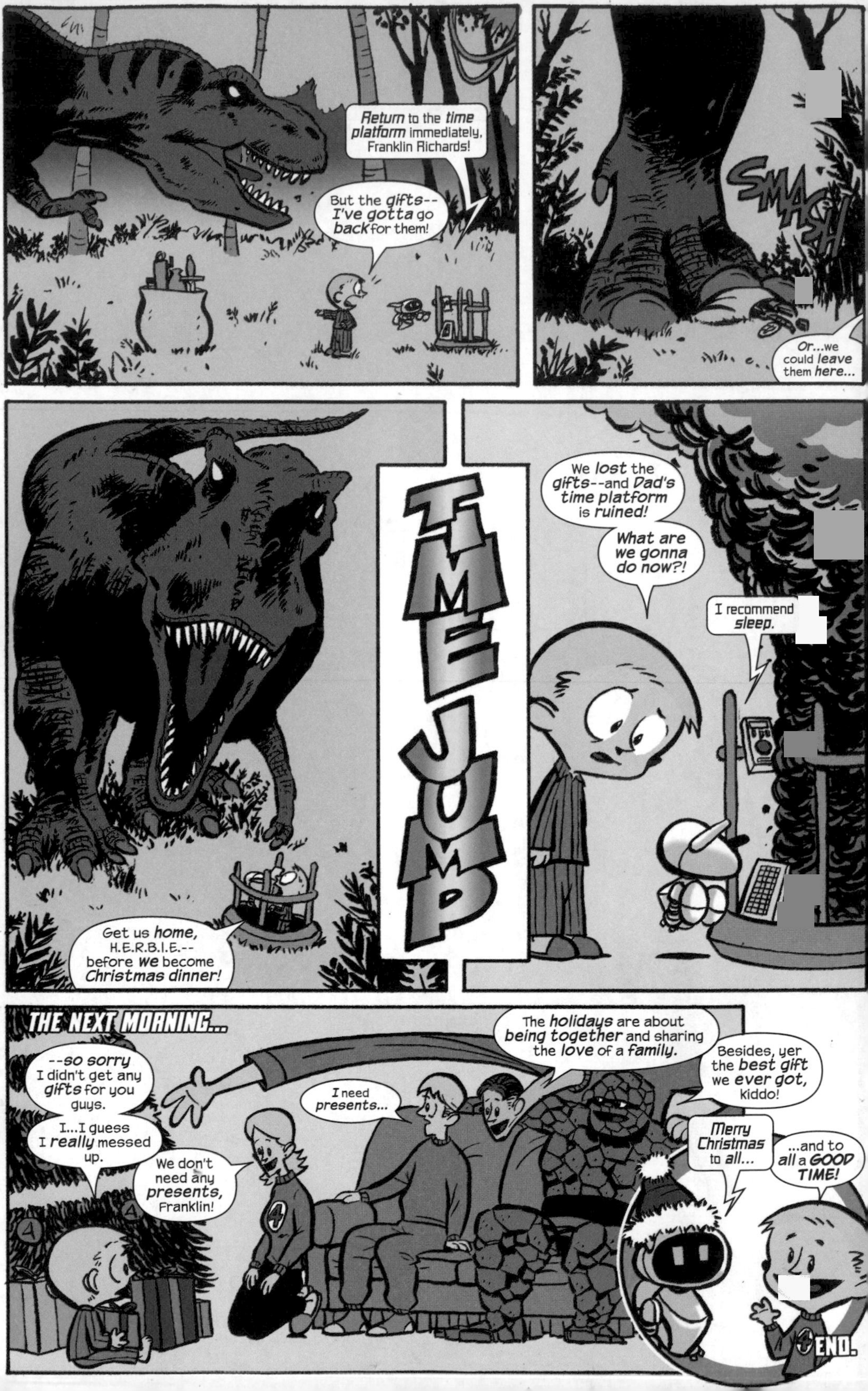

Return to the time platform immediately, Franklin Richards!
But the gifts-- I've gotta go back for them!
SMASH
Or...we could leave them here...
TIME JUMP
Get us home, H.E.R.B.I.E.-- before we become Christmas dinner!
We lost the gifts--and Dad's time platform is ruined!
What are we gonna do now?!
I recommend sleep.
THE NEXT MORNING...
--so sorry I didn't get any gifts for you guys.
I...I guess I really messed up.
We don't need any presents, Franklin!
I need presents...
The holidays are about being together and sharing the love of a family.
Besides, yer the best gift we ever got, kiddo!
Merry Christmas to all...
...and to all a GOOD TIME!
END.

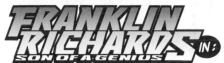

FRANKLIN RICHARDS SON OF A GENIUS IN: MY DINNER WITH DOOM(BOTS)!

BY CHRIS ELIOPOULOS & MARC SUMERAK

GURIHIRU COLORS

SPECIAL THANKS FOR BUBBLE BOMBS **JEREMY & JUSTIN ELIOPOULOS**

TOM VALENTE PRODUCTION

NATHAN COSBY ASSISTANT EDITOR

MARK PANICCIA CONSULTING EDITOR

MACKENZIE CADENHEAD EDITOR

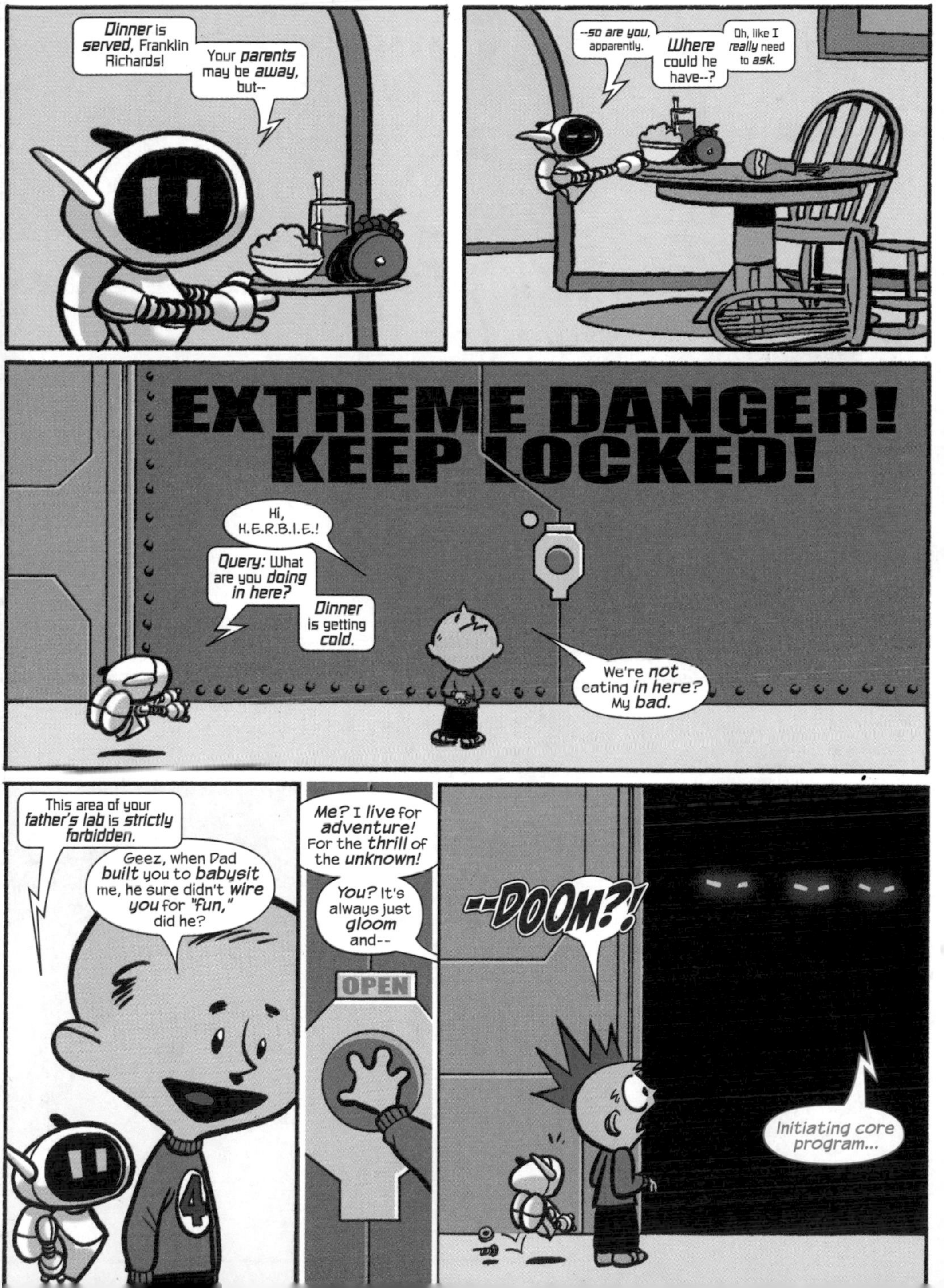
Dinner is *served*, Franklin Richards!
Your *parents* may be *away*, but--
--*so are you*, apparently.
Where could he have--?
Oh, like I *really* need to *ask*.
EXTREME DANGER! KEEP LOCKED!
Hi, H.E.R.B.I.E.!
Query: What are you *doing in here?*
Dinner is getting *cold*.
We're *not* eating *in here?* My *bad*.
This area of your *father's lab* is *strictly forbidden*.
Geez, when Dad *built* you to *babysit* me, he sure didn't *wire you* for *"fun,"* did he?
Me? I *live* for *adventure!* For the *thrill* of the *unknown!*
You? It's always just *gloom* and--
OPEN
--DOOM?!
Initiating core program...

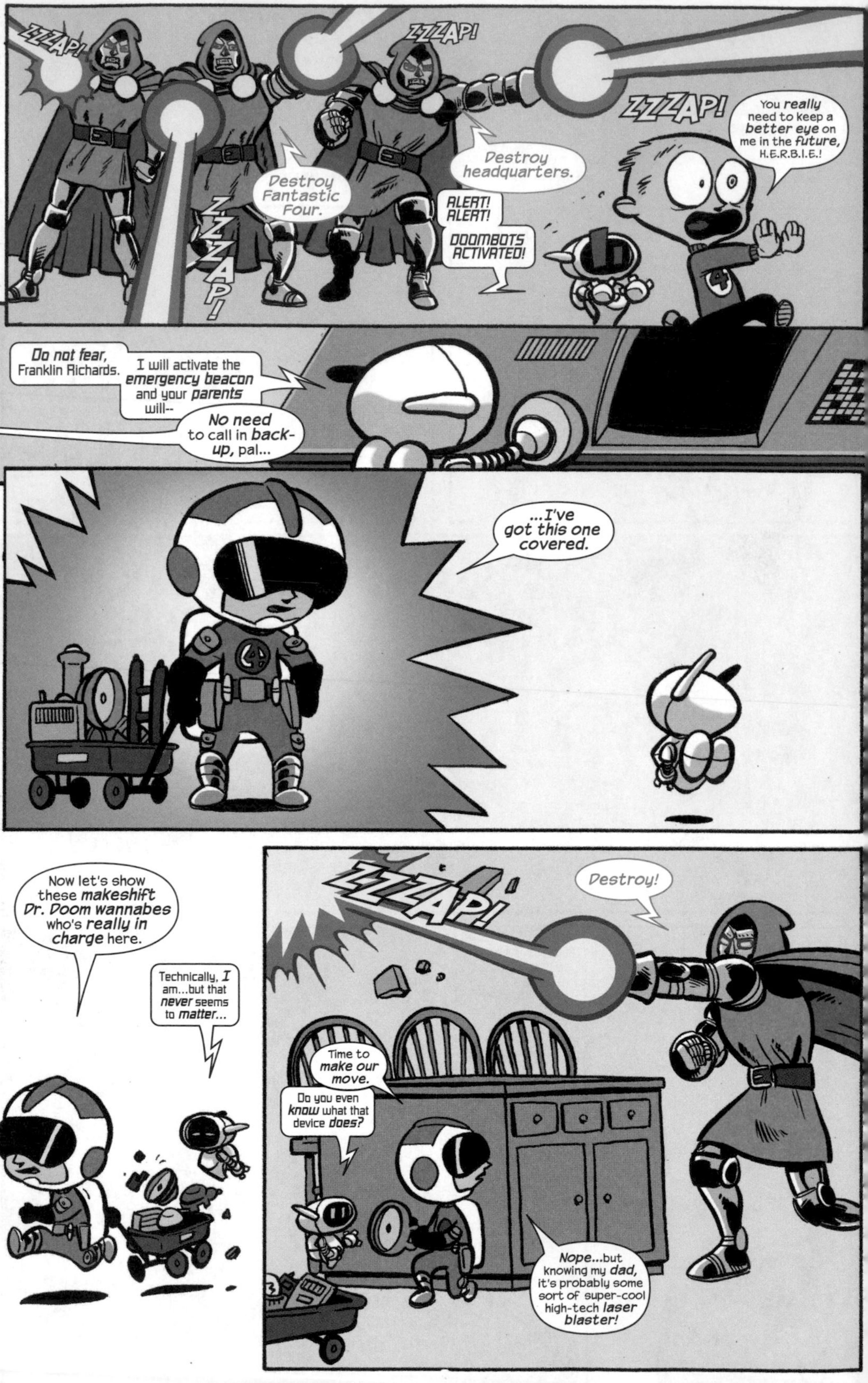

ZZZAP!
ZZZAP!
Destroy Fantastic Four.
ZZZAP!
Destroy headquarters.
ALERT! ALERT!
DOOMBOTS ACTIVATED!
ZZZAP!
You really need to keep a better eye on me in the future, H.E.R.B.I.E.!
Do not fear, Franklin Richards.
I will activate the emergency beacon and your parents will--
No need to call in back-up, pal...
...I've got this one covered.
Now let's show these makeshift Dr. Doom wannabes who's really in charge here.
Technically, I am...but that never seems to matter...
ZZZAP!
Destroy!
Time to make our move.
Do you even know what that device does?
Nope...but knowing my dad, it's probably some sort of super-cool high-tech laser blaster!

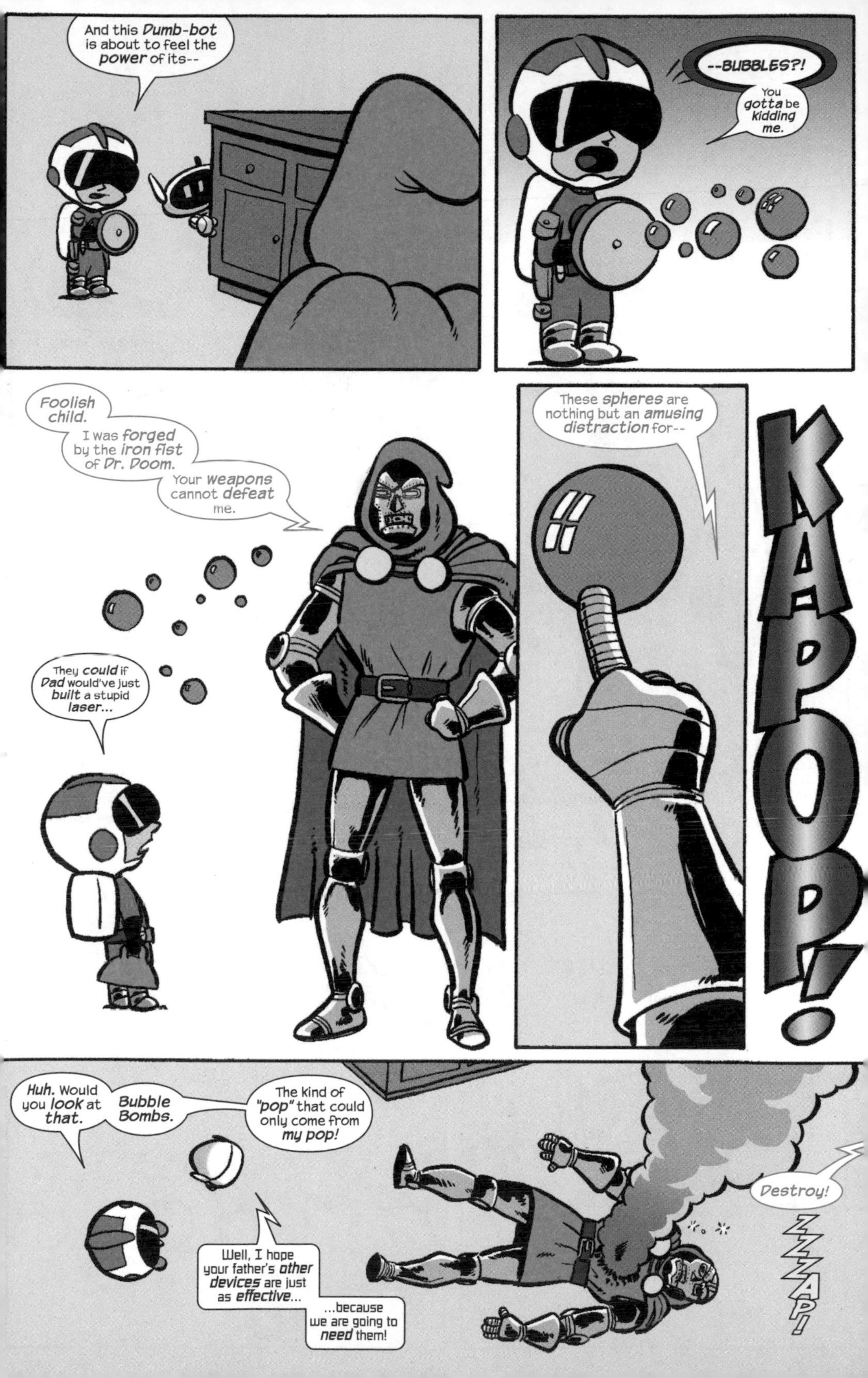
And this Dumb-bot is about to feel the power of its--
--BUBBLES?!
You gotta be kidding me.
Foolish child.
I was forged by the iron fist of Dr. Doom.
Your weapons cannot defeat me.
They could if Dad would've just built a stupid laser...
These spheres are nothing but an amusing distraction for--
KAPOP!
Huh. Would you look at that.
Bubble Bombs.
The kind of "pop" that could only come from my pop!
Destroy!
ZZZAP!
Well, I hope your father's other devices are just as effective...
...because we are going to need them!

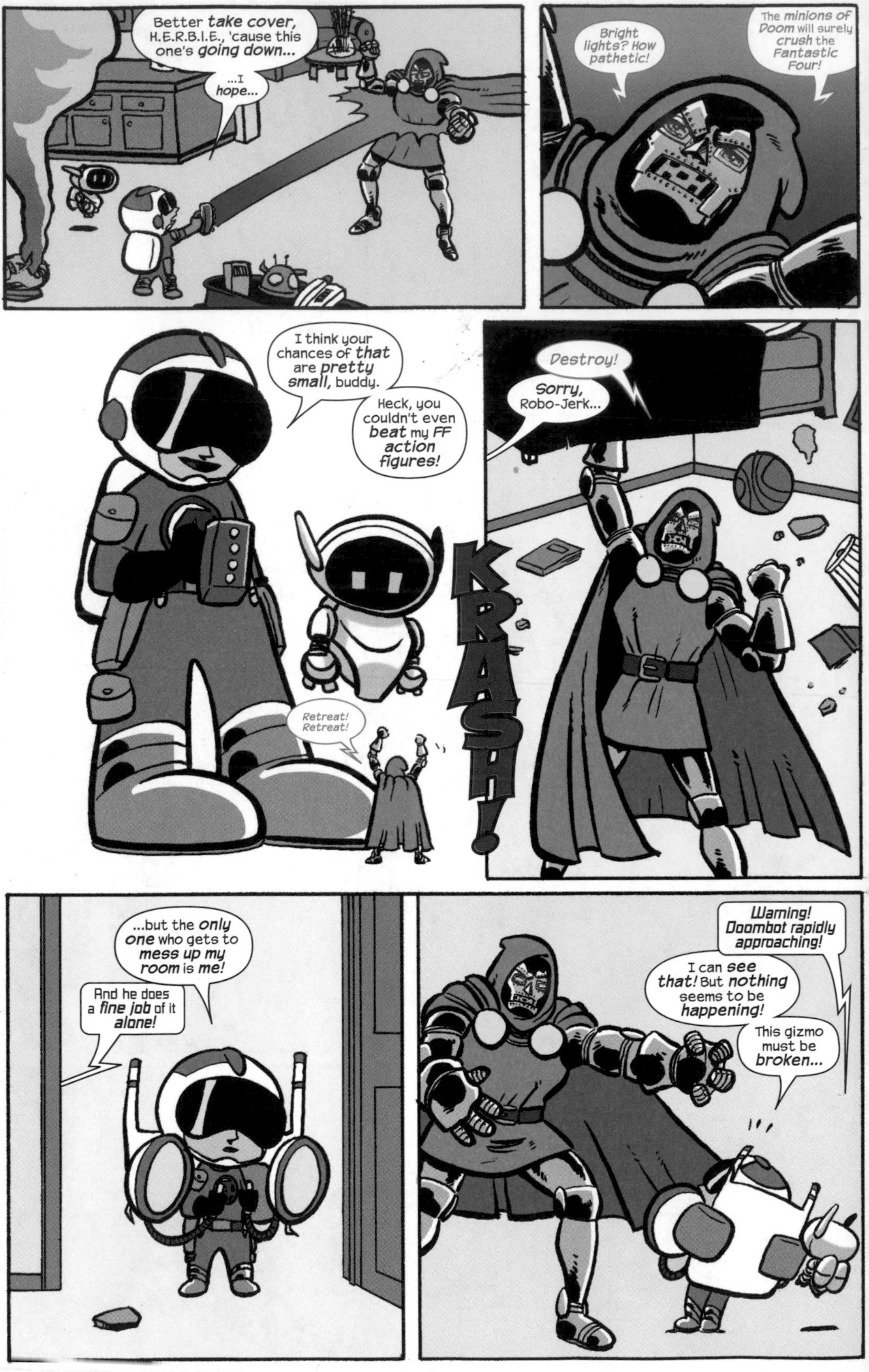
Better take cover, H.E.R.B.I.E., 'cause this one's going down...
...I hope...
Bright lights? How pathetic!
The minions of Doom will surely crush the Fantastic Four!
I think your chances of that are pretty small, buddy.
Heck, you couldn't even beat my FF action figures!
Retreat! Retreat!
KRASH!
Destroy!
Sorry, Robo-Jerk...
...but the only one who gets to mess up my room is me!
And he does a fine job of it alone!
Warning! Doombot rapidly approaching!
I can see that! But nothing seems to be happening!
This gizmo must be broken...

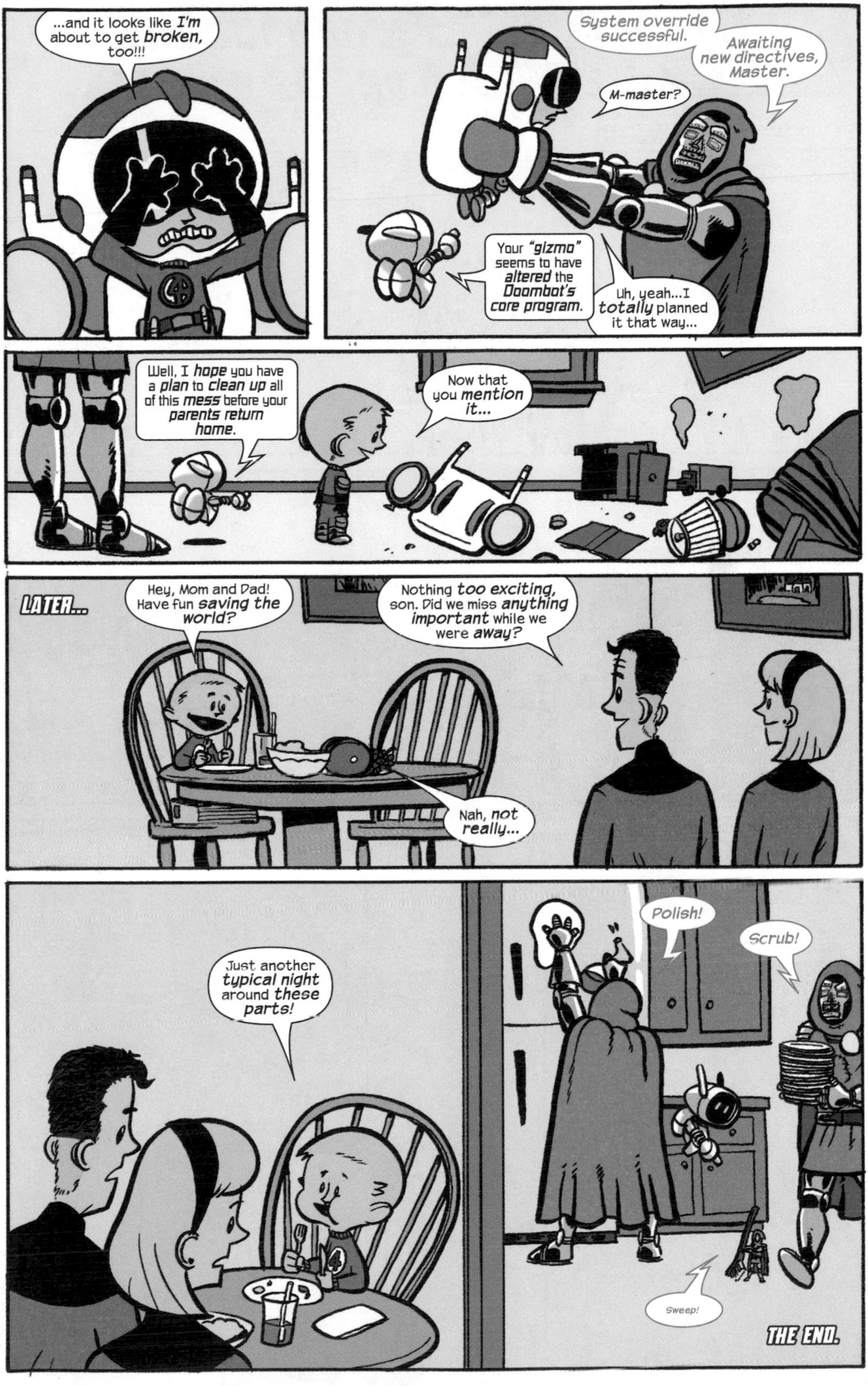
...and it looks like I'm about to get broken, too!!!
System override successful.
Awaiting new directives, Master.
M-master?
Your "gizmo" seems to have altered the Doombot's core program.
Uh, yeah...I totally planned it that way...
Well, I hope you have a plan to clean up all of this mess before your parents return home.
Now that you mention it...
LATER...
Hey, Mom and Dad! Have fun saving the world?
Nothing too exciting, son. Did we miss anything important while we were away?
Nah, not really...
Just another typical night around these parts!
Polish!
Scrub!
Sweep!
THE END.

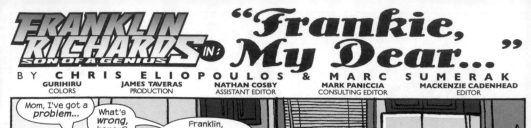

FRANKLIN RICHARDS SON OF A GENIUS IN: "Frankie, My Dear..."

BY CHRIS ELIOPOULOS & MARC SUMERAK

GURIHIRU
COLORS

JAMES TAVERAS
PRODUCTION

NATHAN COSBY
ASSISTANT EDITOR

MARK PANICCIA
CONSULTING EDITOR

MACKENZIE CADENHEAD
EDITOR

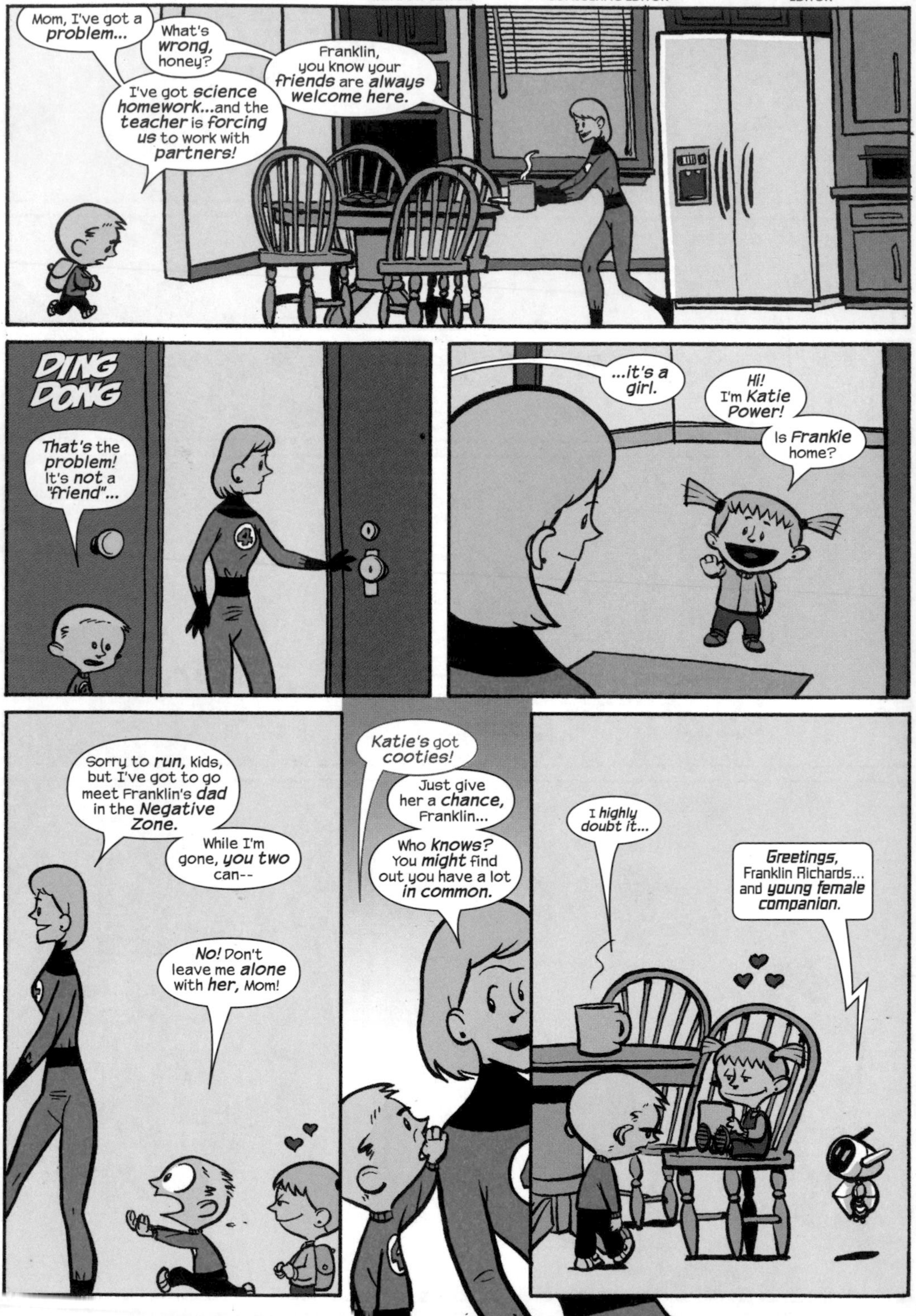
Mom, I've got a problem...
What's wrong, honey?
I've got science homework...and the teacher is forcing us to work with partners!
Franklin, you know your friends are always welcome here.
DING DONG
That's the problem! It's not a "friend"...
...it's a girl.
Hi! I'm Katie Power!
Is Frankie home?
Sorry to run, kids, but I've got to go meet Franklin's dad in the Negative Zone.
While I'm gone, you two can--
No! Don't leave me alone with her, Mom!
Katie's got cooties!
Just give her a chance, Franklin...
Who knows? You might find out you have a lot in common.
I highly doubt it...
Greetings, Franklin Richards... and young female companion.

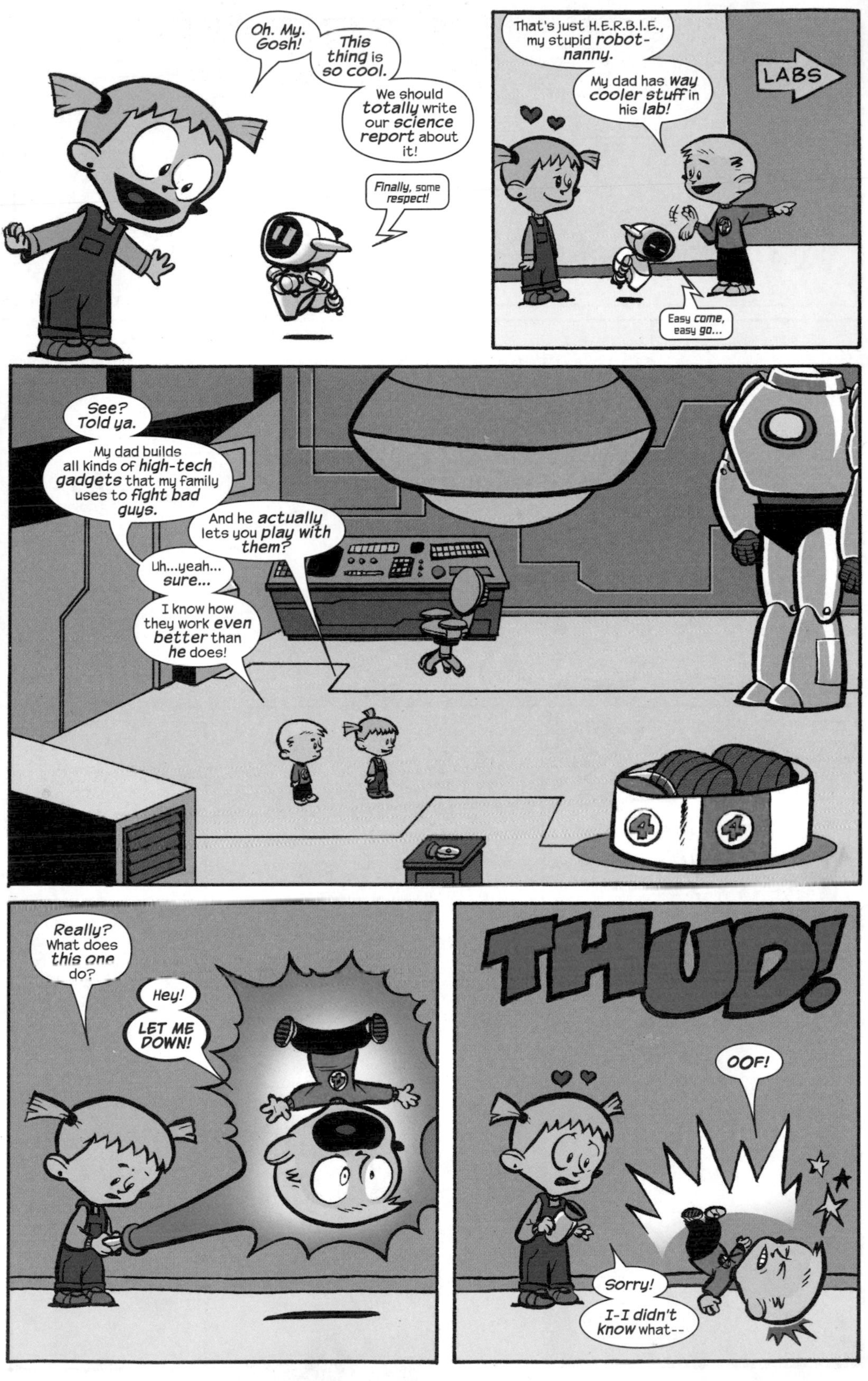
Oh. My. Gosh!
This thing is so cool.
We should totally write our science report about it!
Finally, some respect!
That's just H.E.R.B.I.E., my stupid robot-nanny.
My dad has way cooler stuff in his lab!
LABS
Easy come, easy go...
See? Told ya.
My dad builds all kinds of high-tech gadgets that my family uses to fight bad guys.
And he actually lets you play with them?
Uh...yeah... sure...
I know how they work even better than he does!
Really? What does this one do?
Hey!
LET ME DOWN!
THUD!
OOF!
Sorry!
I-I didn't know what--

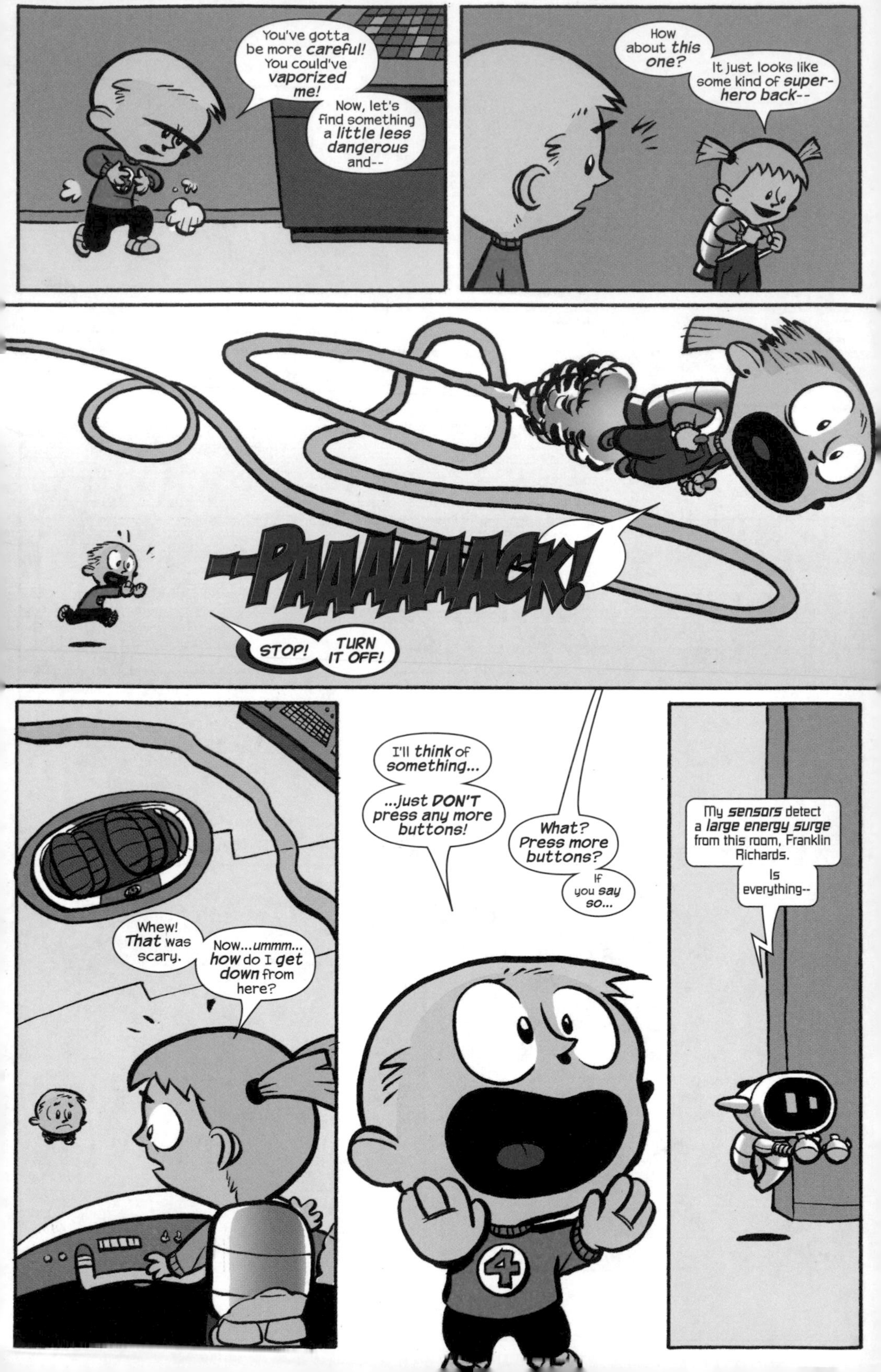
You've gotta be more careful! You could've vaporized me!
Now, let's find something a little less dangerous and--
How about this one?
It just looks like some kind of super-hero back--
--PAAAAAACK!
STOP!
TURN IT OFF!
Whew! That was scary.
Now...ummm... how do I get down from here?
I'll think of something...
...just DON'T press any more buttons!
What? Press more buttons?
If you say so...
My sensors detect a large energy surge from this room, Franklin Richards.
Is everything--

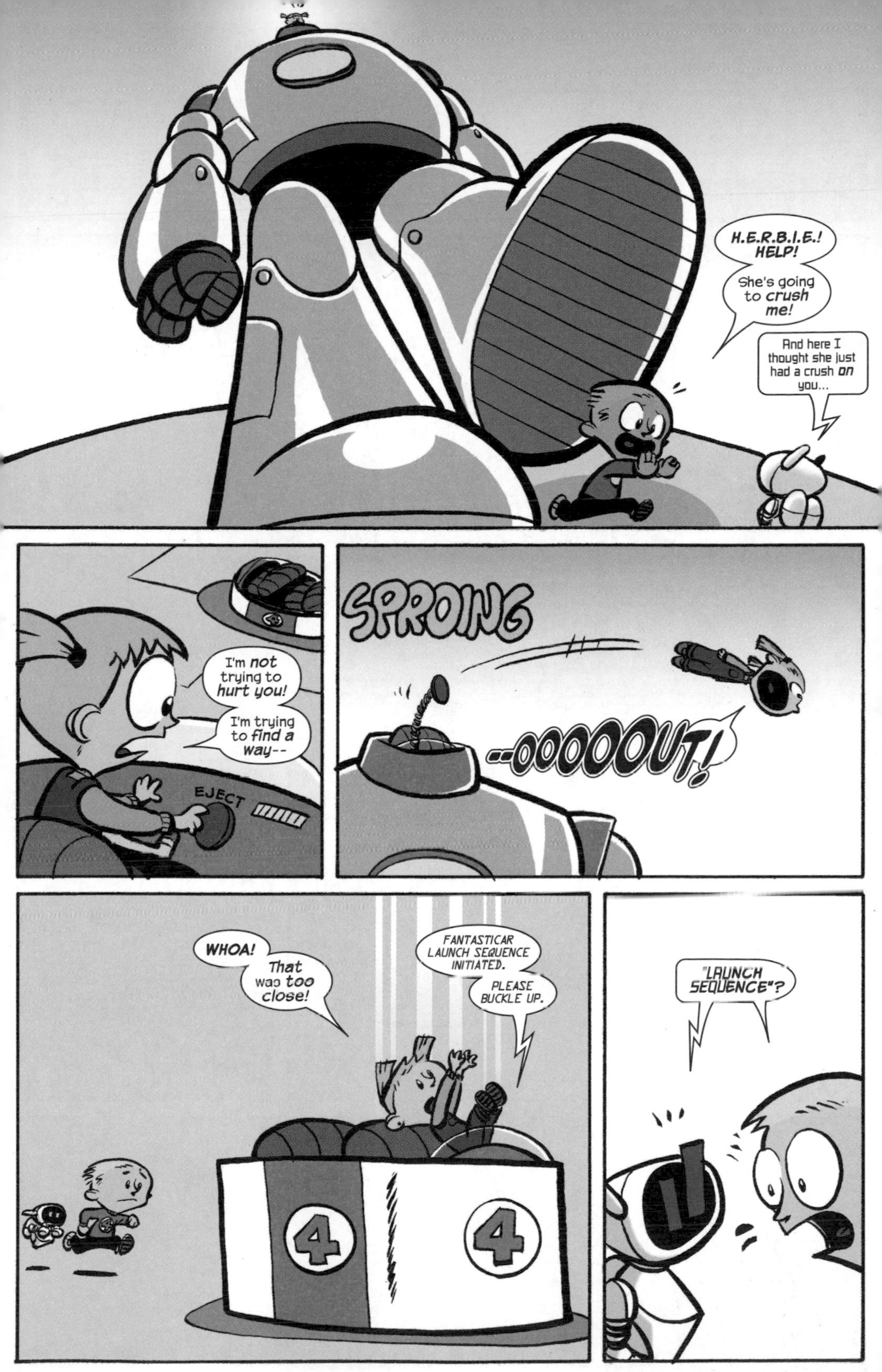
H.E.R.B.I.E.! HELP!
She's going to crush me!
And here I thought she just had a crush on you...
I'm not trying to hurt you!
I'm trying to find a way--
EJECT
SPROING
--OOOOOOUT!
WHOA!
That was too close!
FANTASTICAR LAUNCH SEQUENCE INITIATED.
PLEASE BUCKLE UP.
4
4
"LAUNCH SEQUENCE"?

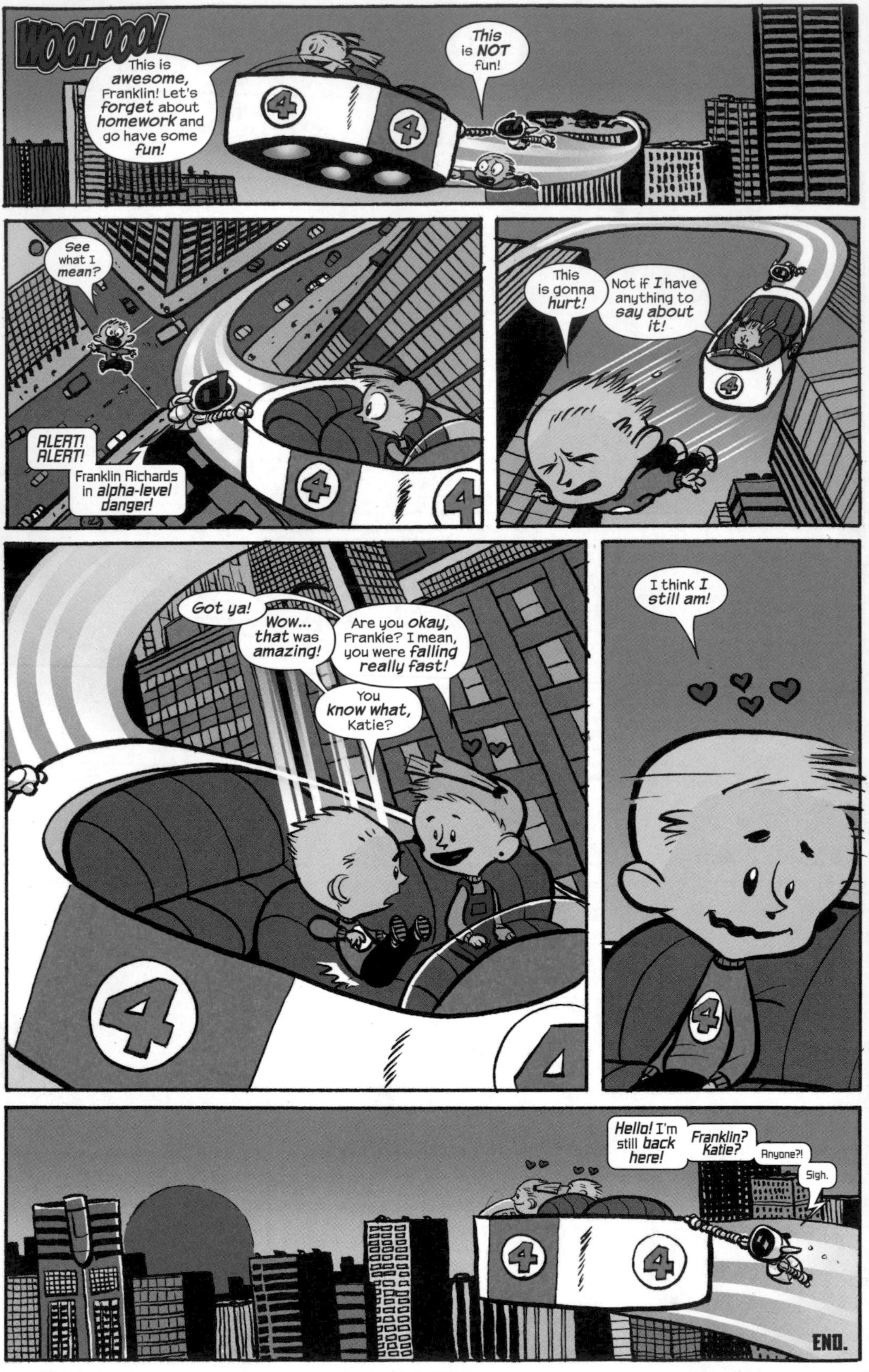

WOOHOOO!
This is awesome, Franklin! Let's forget about homework and go have some fun!
This is NOT fun!
See what I mean?
ALERT! ALERT!
Franklin Richards in alpha-level danger!
This is gonna hurt!
Not if I have anything to say about it!
Got ya!
Wow... that was amazing!
Are you okay, Frankie? I mean, you were falling really fast!
You know what, Katie?
I think I still am!
Hello! I'm still back here!
Franklin? Katie?
Anyone?!
Sigh.
END.

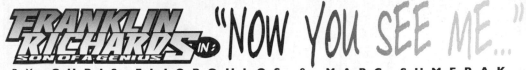

FRANKLIN RICHARDS SON OF A GENIUS IN: "NOW YOU SEE ME..."

BY CHRIS ELIOPOULOS & MARC SUMERAK

GURIHIRU COLORS
JAMES TAVERAS PRODUCTION
NATHAN COSBY ASSISTANT EDITOR
MARK PANICCIA CONSULTING EDITOR
MACKENZIE CADENHEAD EDITOR

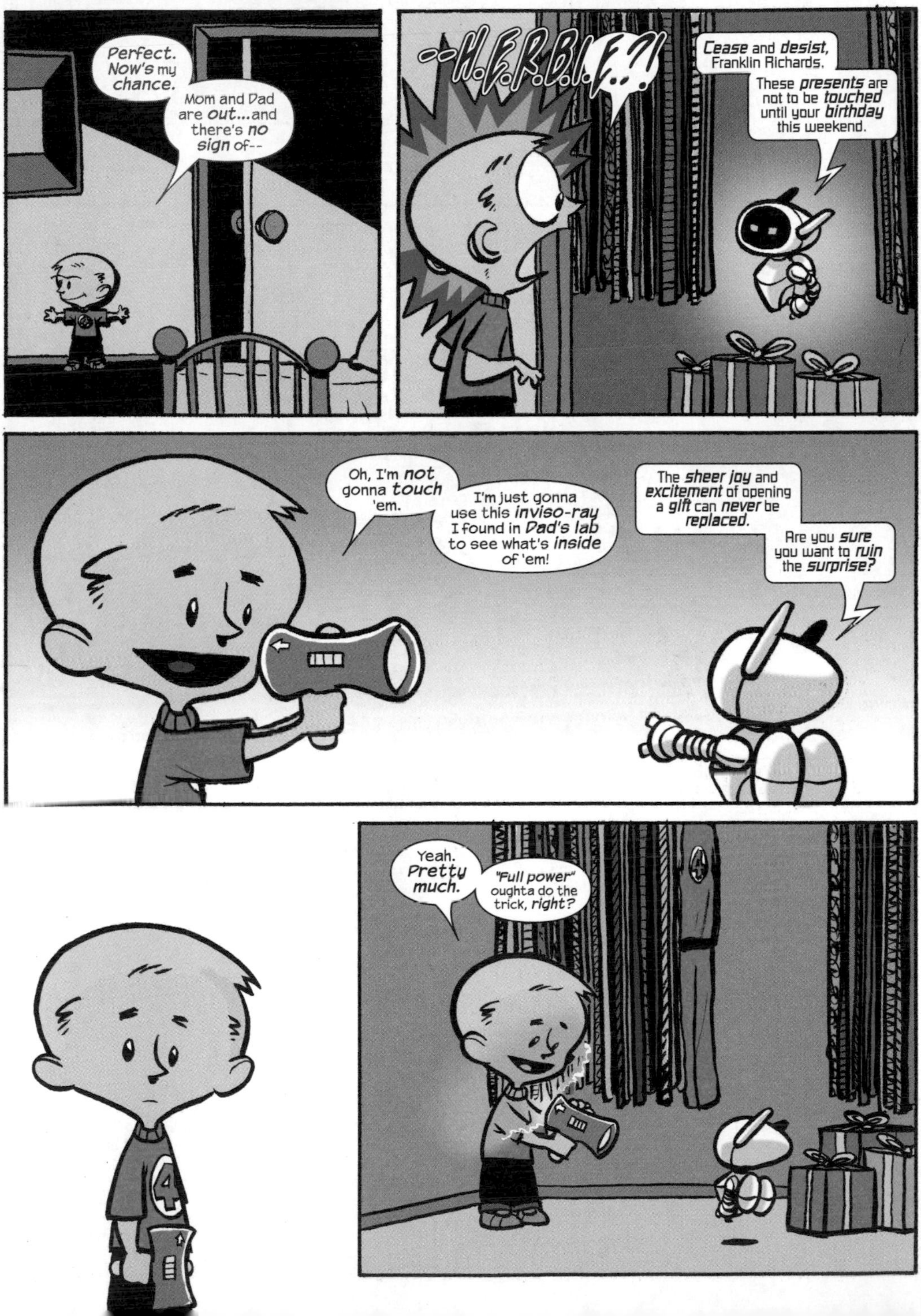

Perfect. Now's my chance.
Mom and Dad are out...and there's no sign of--
--H.E.R.B.I.E.?!
Cease and desist, Franklin Richards.
These presents are not to be touched until your birthday this weekend.
Oh, I'm not gonna touch 'em.
I'm just gonna use this inviso-ray I found in Dad's lab to see what's inside of 'em!
The sheer joy and excitement of opening a gift can never be replaced.
Are you sure you want to ruin the surprise?
Yeah. Pretty much.
"Full power" oughta do the trick, right?

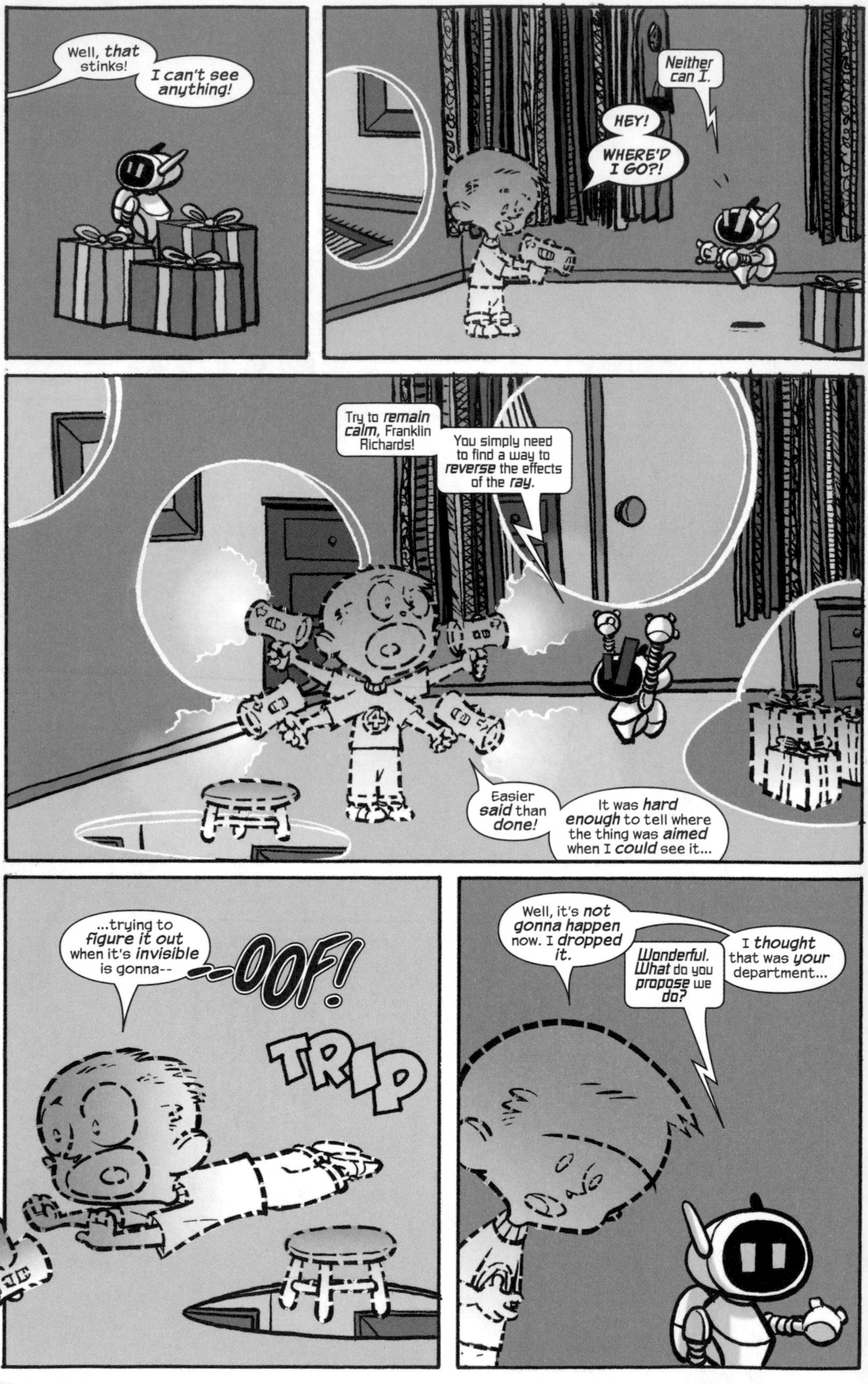

Well, *that* stinks!
I can't see anything!
Neither can I.
HEY!
WHERE'D I GO?!
Try to ***remain calm***, Franklin Richards!
You simply need to find a way to ***reverse*** the effects of the ***ray***.
Easier ***said*** than ***done!***
It was ***hard enough*** to tell where the thing was ***aimed*** when I ***could*** see it...
...trying to ***figure it out*** when it's ***invisible*** is gonna--
--OOF!
TRIP
Well, it's ***not gonna happen*** now. I ***dropped it.***
I ***thought*** that was ***your*** department...
Wonderful. What do you ***propose*** we ***do?***

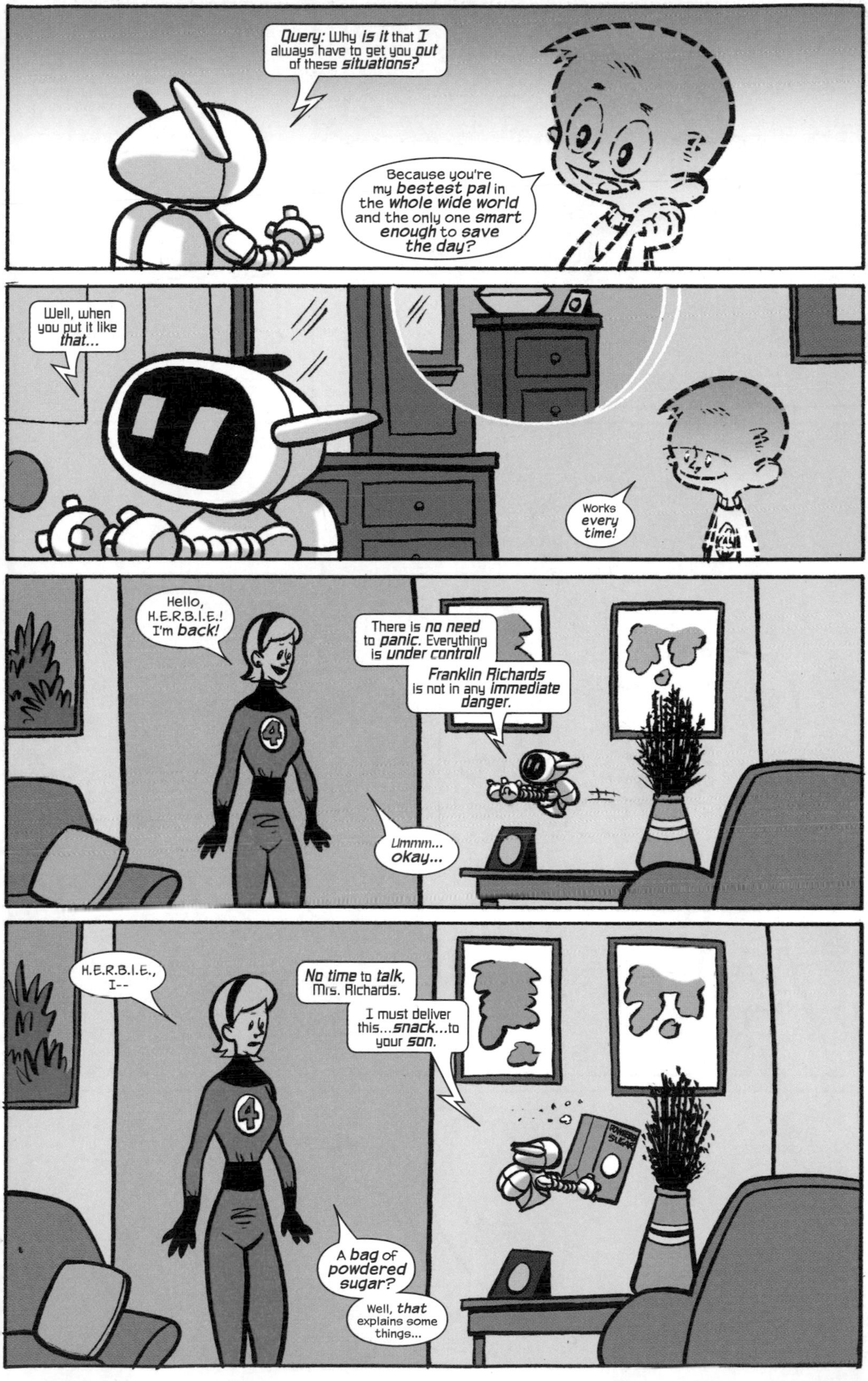
Query: Why is it that I always have to get you out of these situations?
Because you're my bestest pal in the whole wide world and the only one smart enough to save the day?
Well, when you put it like that...
Works every time!
Hello, H.E.R.B.I.E.! I'm back!
There is no need to panic. Everything is under control!
Franklin Richards is not in any immediate danger.
Ummm... okay...
H.E.R.B.I.E., I--
No time to talk, Mrs. Richards.
I must deliver this...snack...to your son.
A bag of powdered sugar?
Well, that explains some things...

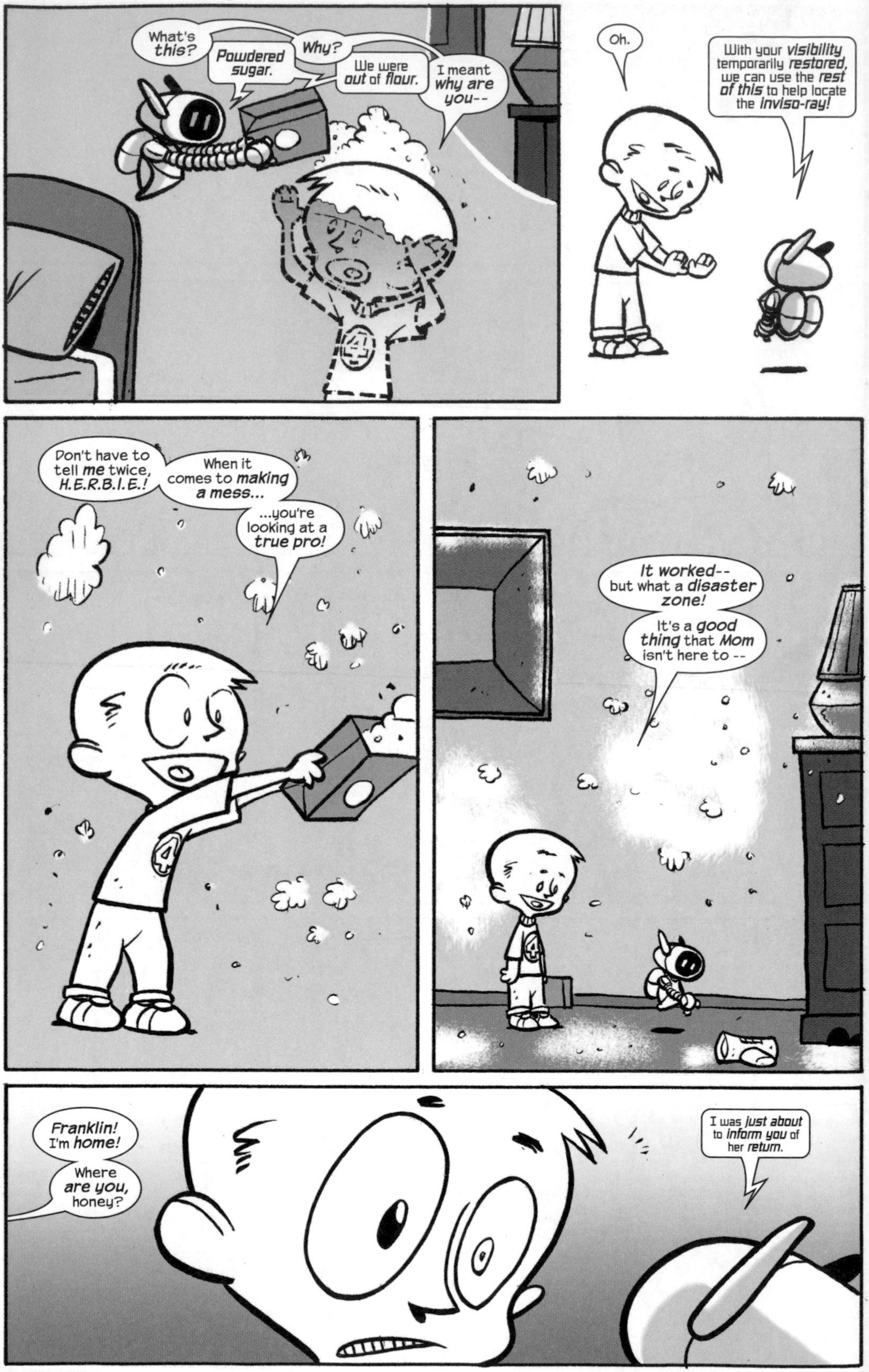
What's this?
Powdered sugar.
Why?
We were out of flour.
I meant why are you--
Oh.
With your visibility temporarily restored, we can use the rest of this to help locate the inviso-ray!
Don't have to tell me twice, H.E.R.B.I.E.!
When it comes to making a mess...
...you're looking at a true pro!
It worked-- but what a disaster zone!
It's a good thing that Mom isn't here to --
Franklin! I'm home!
Where are you, honey?
I was just about to inform you of her return.

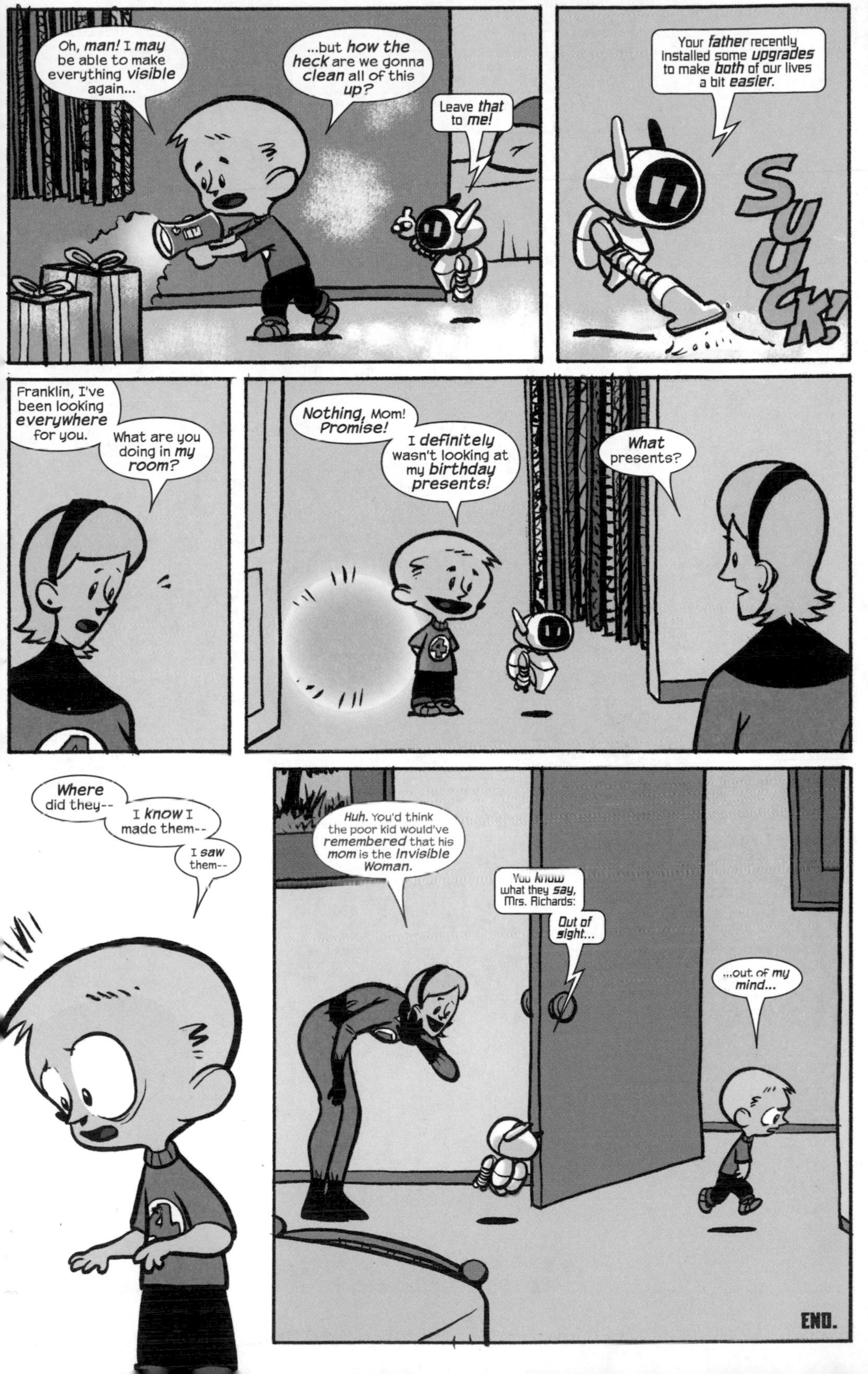
Oh, man! I may be able to make everything visible again...
...but how the heck are we gonna clean all of this up?
Leave that to me!
Your father recently installed some upgrades to make both of our lives a bit easier.
SUUUCK!
Franklin, I've been looking everywhere for you.
What are you doing in my room?
Nothing, Mom! Promise!
I definitely wasn't looking at my birthday presents!
What presents?
Where did they--
I know I made them--
I saw them--
Huh. You'd think the poor kid would've remembered that his mom is the Invisible Woman.
You know what they say, Mrs. Richards:
Out of sight...
...out of my mind...
END.

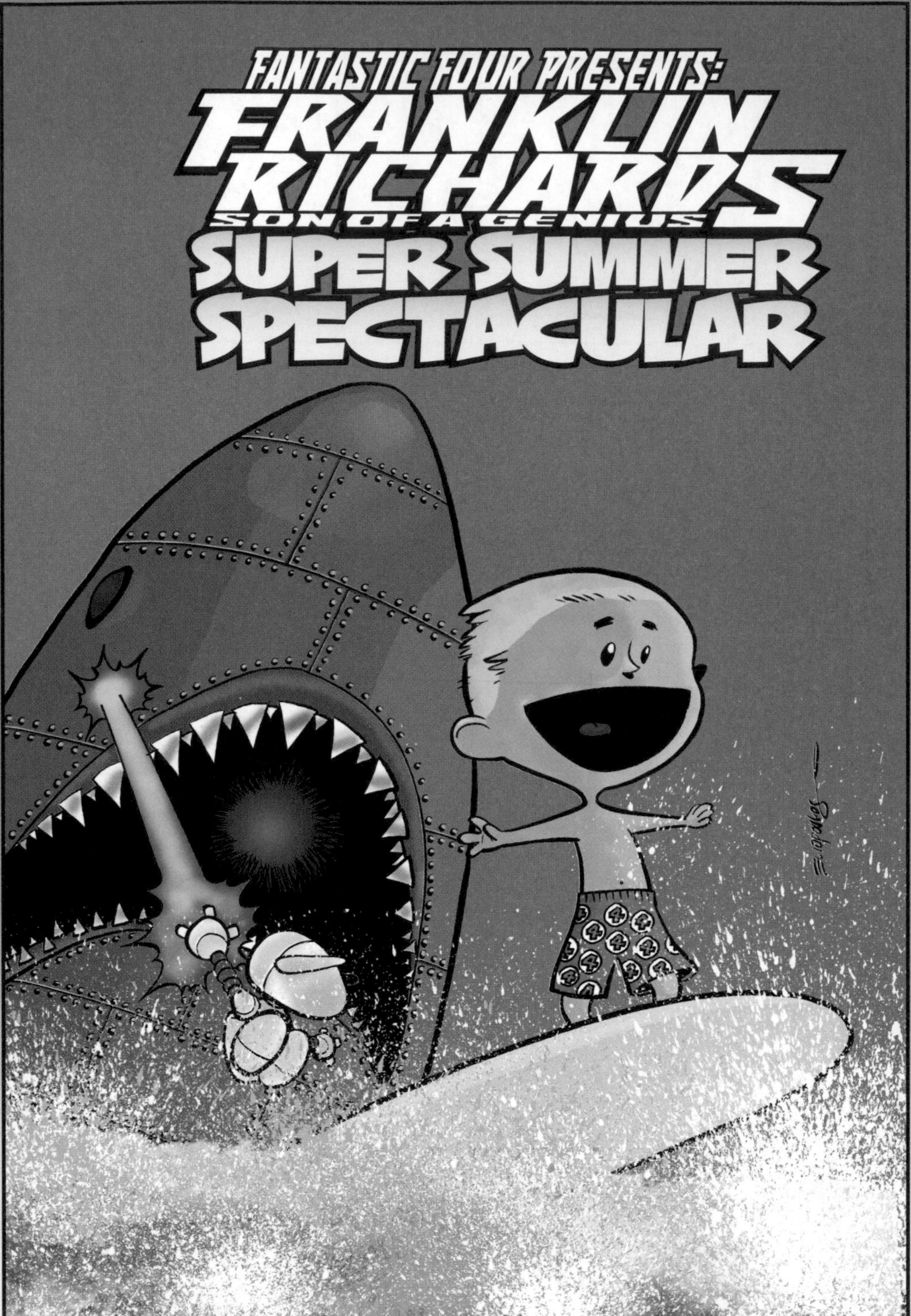
FANTASTIC FOUR PRESENTS:
FRANKLIN RICHARDS
SON OF A GENIUS
SUPER SUMMER SPECTACULAR

FANTASTIC FOUR PRESENTS:
FRANKLIN RICHARDS
SON OF A GENIUS
SUPER SUMMER SPECTACULAR

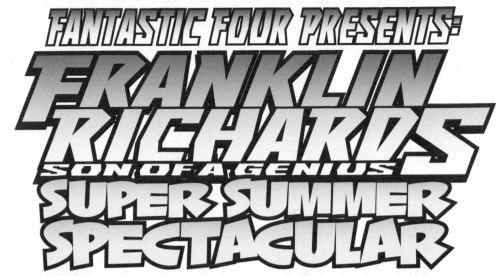

CHRIS ELIOPOULOS AND MARC SUMERAK
STORY

MARC SUMERAK
SCRIPT

CHRIS ELIOPOULOS
ART & LETTERS

LOVERN KINDZIERSKI
COLOR

BRAD JOHANSEN
PRODUCTION

NATHAN COSBY
ASSISTANT EDITOR

MARK PANICCIA
EDITOR

MACKENZIE CADENHEAD
EDITOR EMERITUS

JOE QUESADA
EDITOR IN CHIEF

DAN BUCKLEY
PUBLISHER

DEDICATED TO THE MEMORY OF **JAMES J. VERDE**, MY FATHER-IN-LAW AND FRIEND--CHRIS

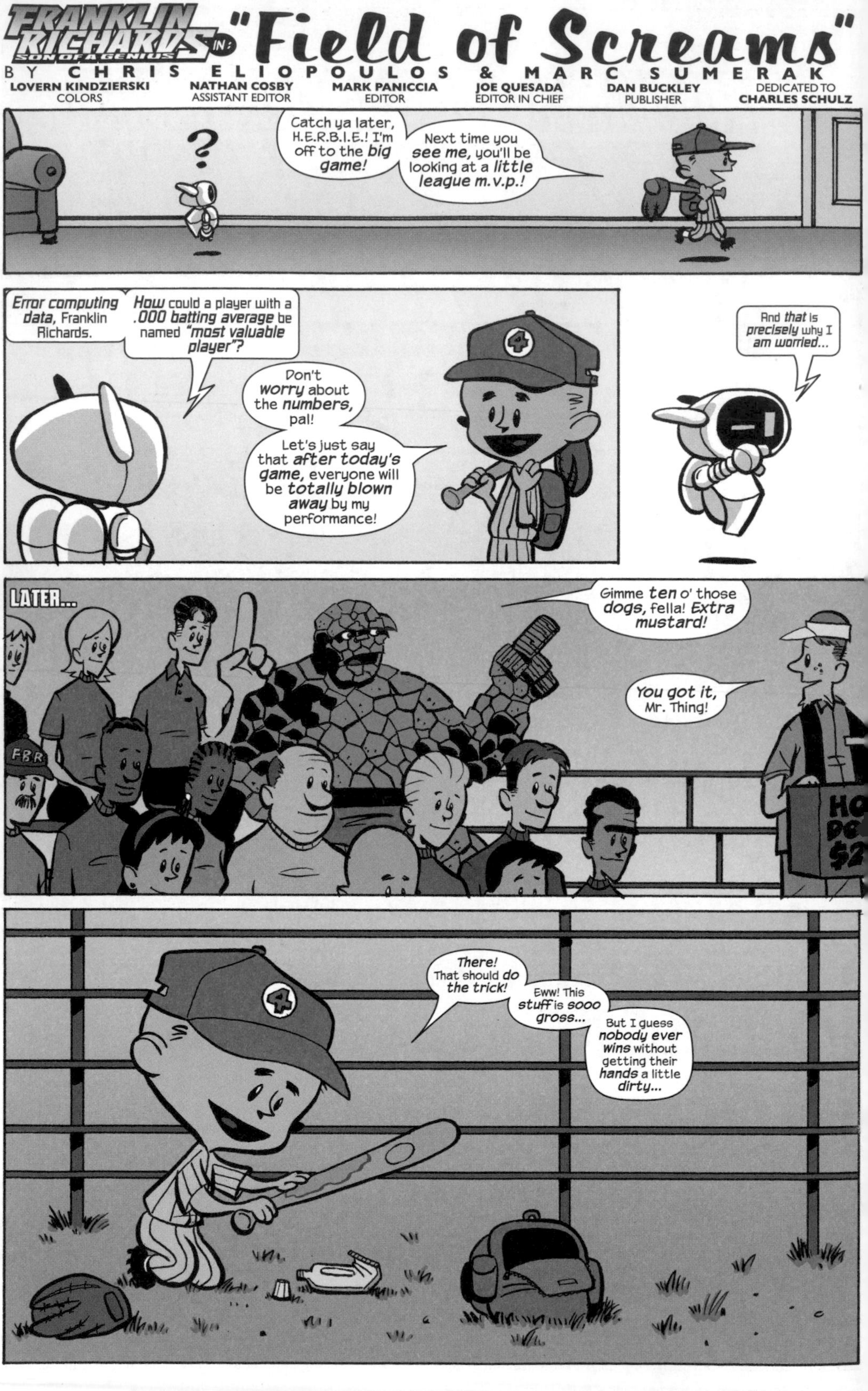
FRANKLIN RICHARDS SON OF A GENIUS IN: "Field of Screams"
BY CHRIS ELIOPOULOS & MARC SUMERAK
LOVERN KINDZIERSKI COLORS
NATHAN COSBY ASSISTANT EDITOR
MARK PANICCIA EDITOR
JOE QUESADA EDITOR IN CHIEF
DAN BUCKLEY PUBLISHER
DEDICATED TO CHARLES SCHULZ
Catch ya later, H.E.R.B.I.E.! I'm off to the big game!
Next time you see me, you'll be looking at a little league m.v.p.!
Error computing data, Franklin Richards.
How could a player with a .000 batting average be named "most valuable player"?
Don't worry about the numbers, pal!
Let's just say that after today's game, everyone will be totally blown away by my performance!
And that is precisely why I am worried...
LATER...
Gimme ten o' those dogs, fella! Extra mustard!
You got it, Mr. Thing!
There! That should do the trick!
Eww! This stuff is sooo gross...
But I guess nobody ever wins without getting their hands a little dirty...

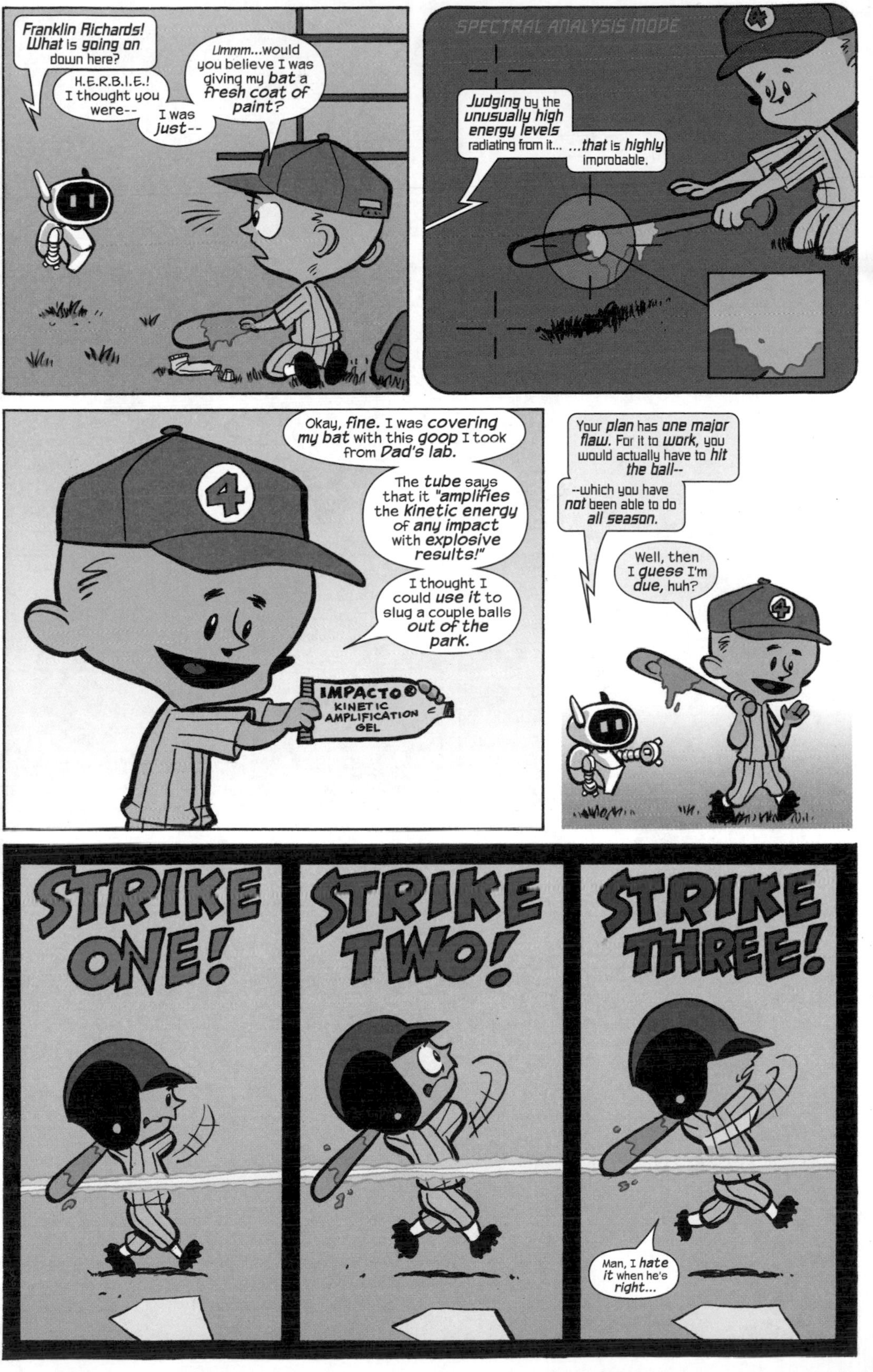

Franklin Richards! What is going on down here?
H.E.R.B.I.E.! I thought you were--
I was just--
Ummm...would you believe I was giving my bat a fresh coat of paint?
SPECTRAL ANALYSIS MODE
Judging by the unusually high energy levels radiating from it...
...that is highly improbable.
Okay, fine. I was covering my bat with this goop I took from Dad's lab.
The tube says that it "amplifies the kinetic energy of any impact with explosive results!"
I thought I could use it to slug a couple balls out of the park.
IMPACTO® KINETIC AMPLIFICATION GEL
Your plan has one major flaw. For it to work, you would actually have to hit the ball--
--which you have not been able to do all season.
Well, then I guess I'm due, huh?
STRIKE ONE!
STRIKE TWO!
STRIKE THREE!
Man, I hate it when he's right...

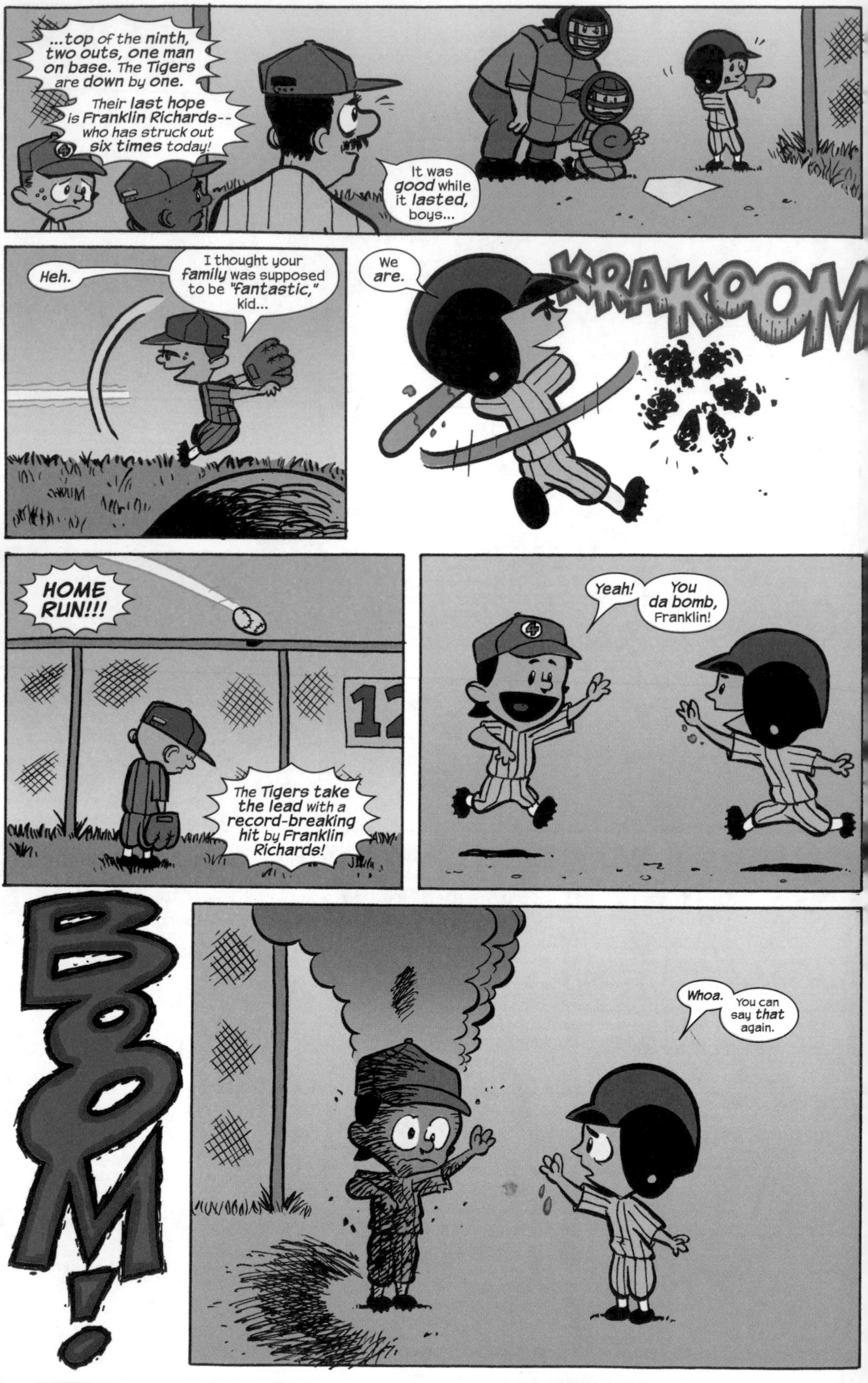
...top of the ninth, two outs, one man on base. The Tigers are down by one.
Their last hope is Franklin Richards-- who has struck out six times today!
It was good while it lasted, boys...
Heh.
I thought your family was supposed to be "fantastic," kid...
We are.
KRAKOOM
HOME RUN!!!
12
The Tigers take the lead with a record-breaking hit by Franklin Richards!
Yeah!
You da bomb, Franklin!
BOOM!
Whoa.
You can say that again.

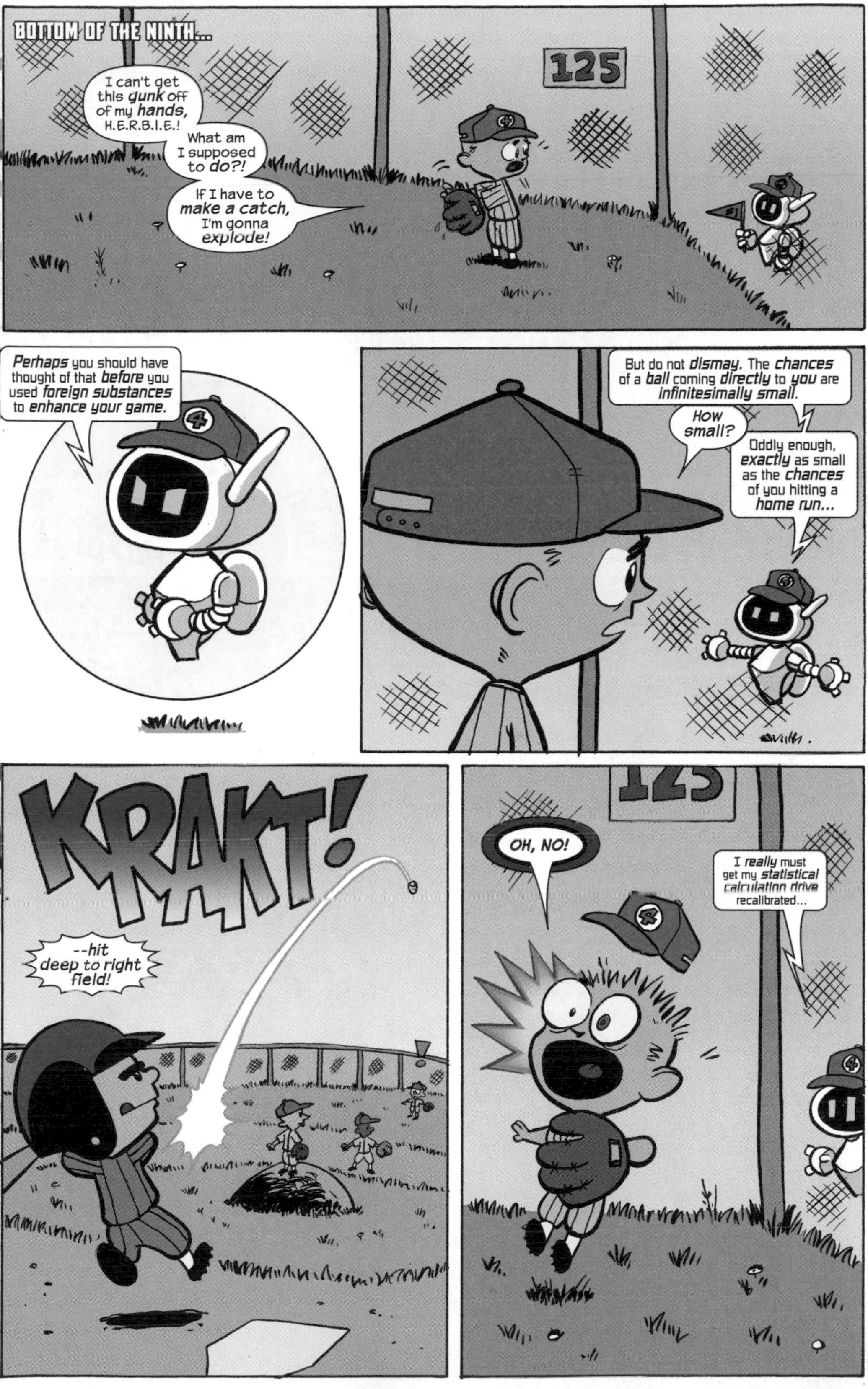
BOTTOM OF THE NINTH...
I can't get this gunk off of my hands, H.E.R.B.I.E.!
What am I supposed to do?!
If I have to make a catch, I'm gonna explode!
125
Perhaps you should have thought of that before you used foreign substances to enhance your game.
But do not dismay. The chances of a ball coming directly to you are infinitesimally small.
How small?
Oddly enough, exactly as small as the chances of you hitting a home run...
KRAKT!
--hit deep to right field!
OH, NO!
I really must get my statistical calculation drive recalibrated...

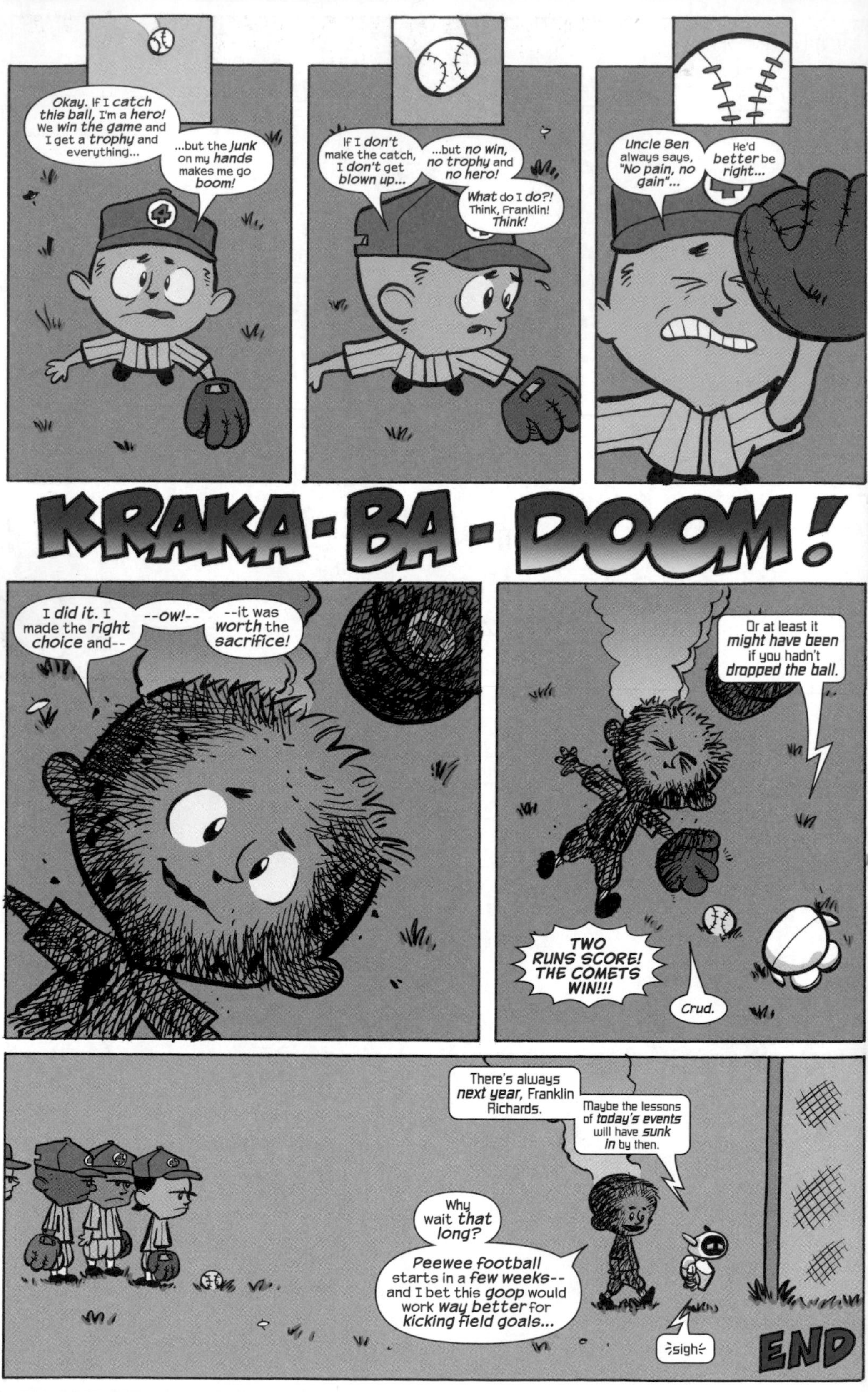
Okay. If I catch this ball, I'm a hero! We win the game and I get a trophy and everything...
...but the junk on my hands makes me go boom!
If I don't make the catch, I don't get blown up...
...but no win, no trophy and no hero!
What do I do?! Think, Franklin! Think!
Uncle Ben always says, "No pain, no gain"...
He'd better be right...
KRAKA-BA-DOOM!
I did it. I made the right choice and--
--OW!--
--it was worth the sacrifice!
Or at least it might have been if you hadn't dropped the ball.
TWO RUNS SCORE! THE COMETS WIN!!!
Crud.
There's always next year, Franklin Richards.
Maybe the lessons of today's events will have sunk in by then.
Why wait that long?
Peewee football starts in a few weeks--and I bet this goop would work way better for kicking field goals...
sigh
END

FRANKLIN RICHARDS SON OF A GENIUS IN: "SQUID KID!"

BY CHRIS ELIOPOULOS & MARC SUMERAK

LOVERN KINDZIERSKI COLORS | NATHAN COSBY ASSISTANT EDITOR | MARK PANICCIA EDITOR | JOE QUESADA EDITOR IN CHIEF | DAN BUCKLEY PUBLISHER

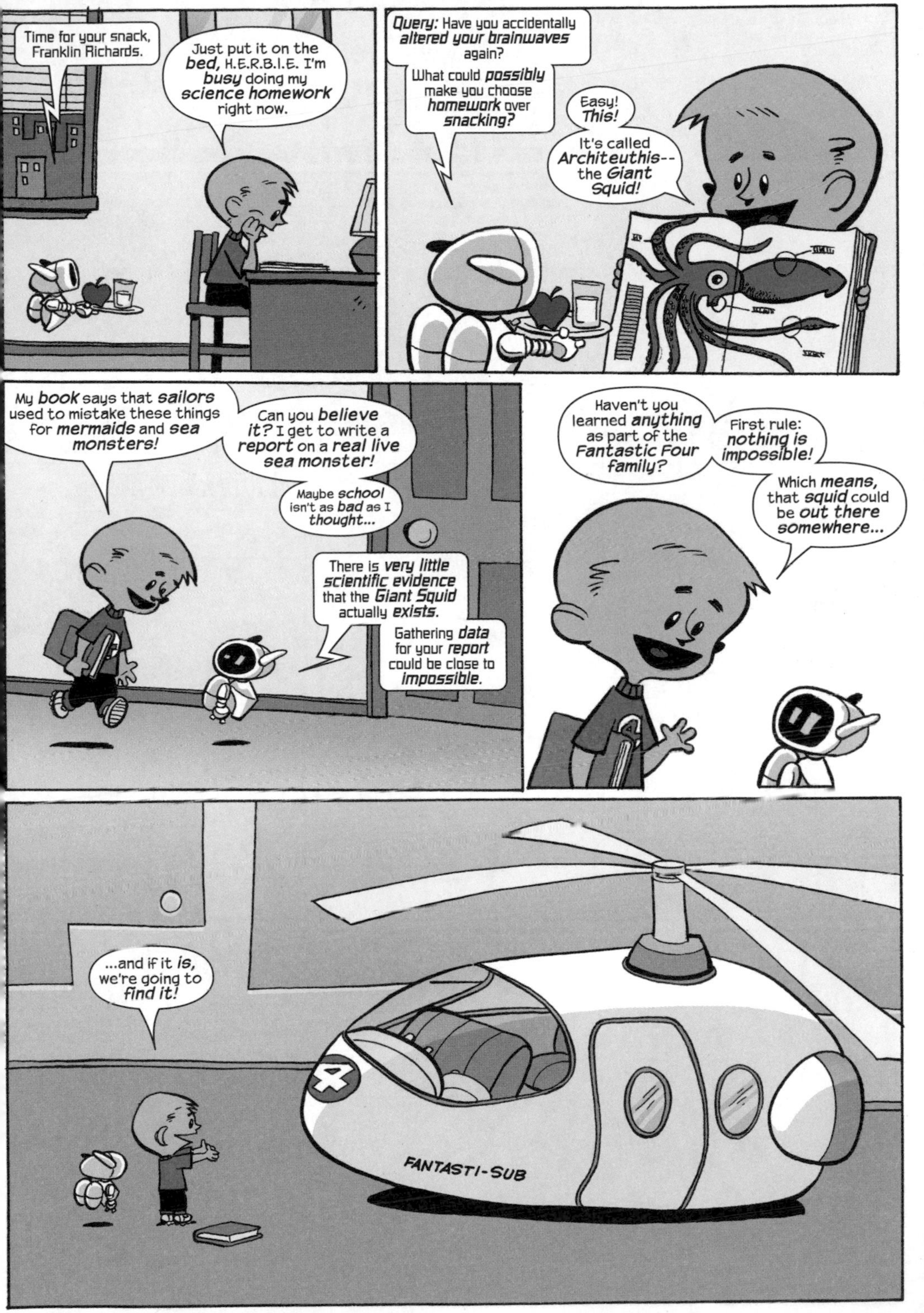
Time for your snack, Franklin Richards.
Just put it on the bed, H.E.R.B.I.E. I'm busy doing my science homework right now.
Query: Have you accidentally altered your brainwaves again?
What could possibly make you choose homework over snacking?
Easy! This!
It's called Architeuthis-- the Giant Squid!
My book says that sailors used to mistake these things for mermaids and sea monsters!
Can you believe it? I get to write a report on a real live sea monster!
Maybe school isn't as bad as I thought...
There is very little scientific evidence that the Giant Squid actually exists.
Gathering data for your report could be close to impossible.
Haven't you learned anything as part of the Fantastic Four family?
First rule: nothing is impossible!
Which means, that squid could be out there somewhere...
...and if it is, we're going to find it!
FANTASTI-SUB

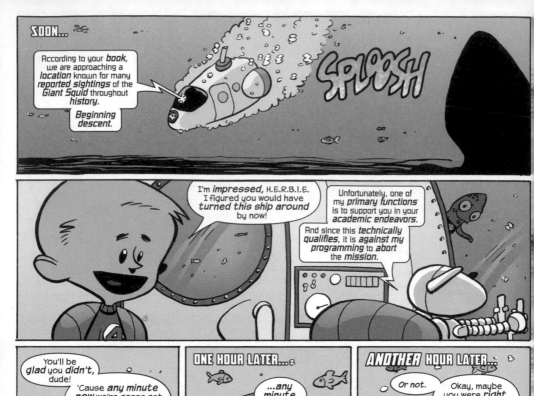

SOON...

According to your *book*, we are approaching a *location* known for many *reported sightings* of the *Giant Squid* throughout history.

Beginning descent.

SPLOOSH

I'm *impressed*, H.E.R.B.I.E. I figured you would have *turned this ship around* by now!

Unfortunately, one of my *primary functions* is to support you in your *academic endeavors*.

And since this *technically qualifies*, it is against my programming to *abort* the *mission*.

You'll be *glad* you *didn't*, dude!

'Cause *any minute now* we're gonna get a *look* at the *most awesomest creature on Earth...*

ONE HOUR LATER...

...any minute now...

ANOTHER HOUR LATER...

Or not.

Okay, maybe you were *right*, H.E.R.B.I.E. Maybe there *is no such thing* as a--

BOOM!

--GIANT SQUID?!

ALERT! ALERT!

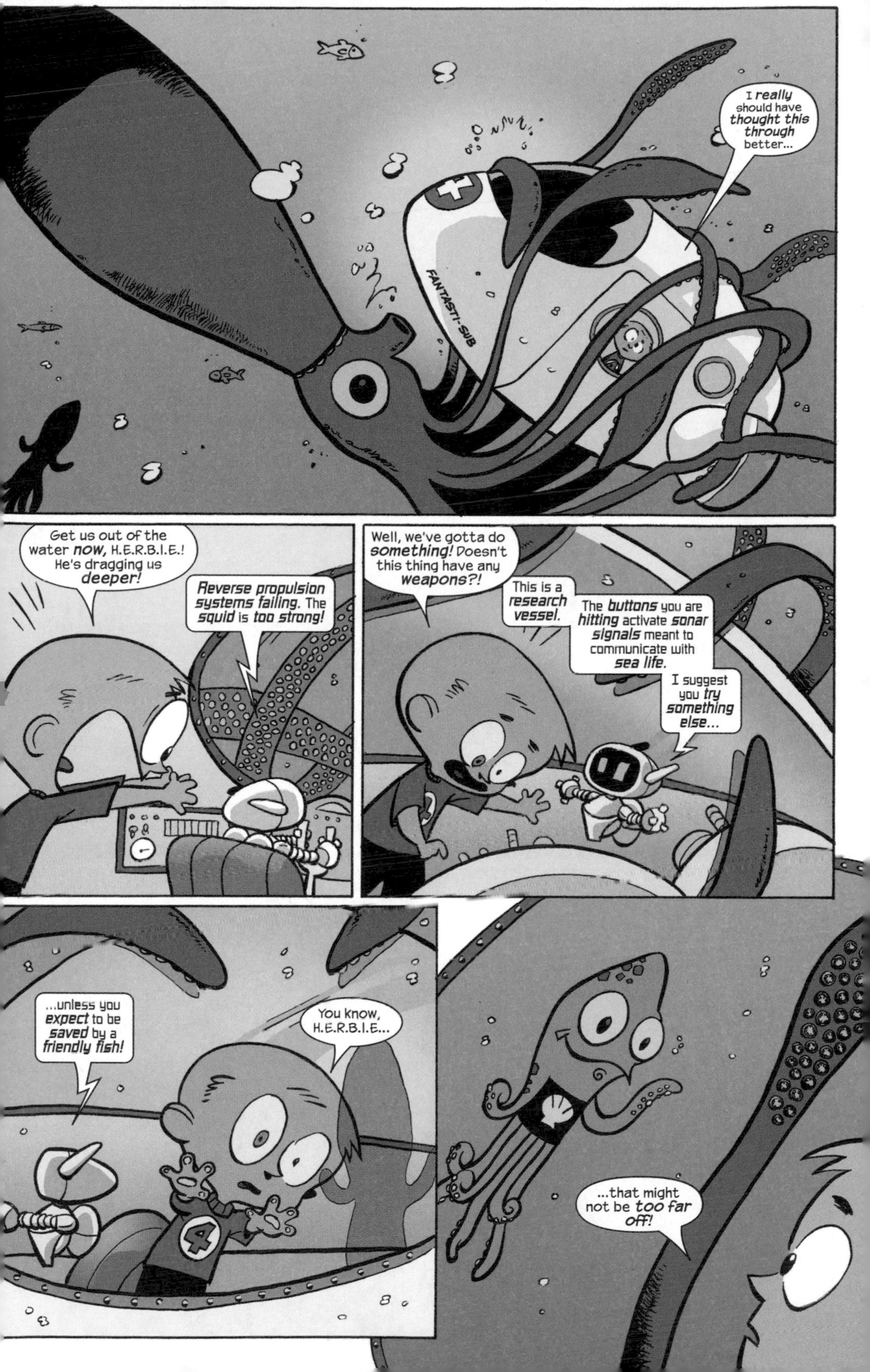
I really should have thought this through better...
FANTASTI-SUB
Get us out of the water now, H.E.R.B.I.E.! He's dragging us deeper!
Reverse propulsion systems failing. The squid is too strong!
Well, we've gotta do something! Doesn't this thing have any weapons?!
This is a research vessel.
The buttons you are hitting activate sonar signals meant to communicate with sea life.
I suggest you try something else...
...unless you expect to be saved by a friendly fish!
You know, H.E.R.B.I.E...
...that might not be too far off!

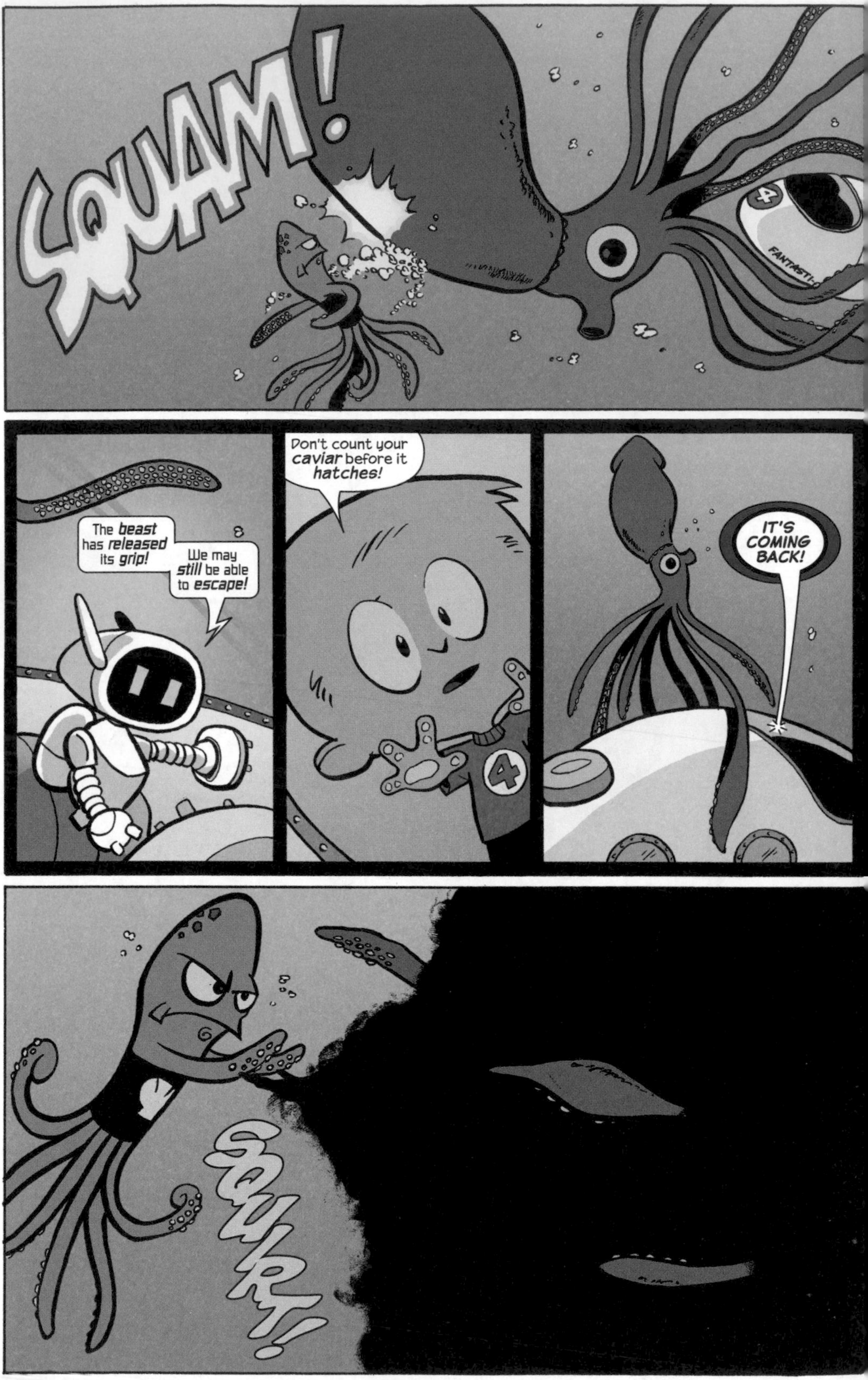
SQUAM!
FANTASTI-
The beast has released its grip!
We may still be able to escape!
Don't count your caviar before it hatches!
IT'S COMING BACK!
SQUIRT!

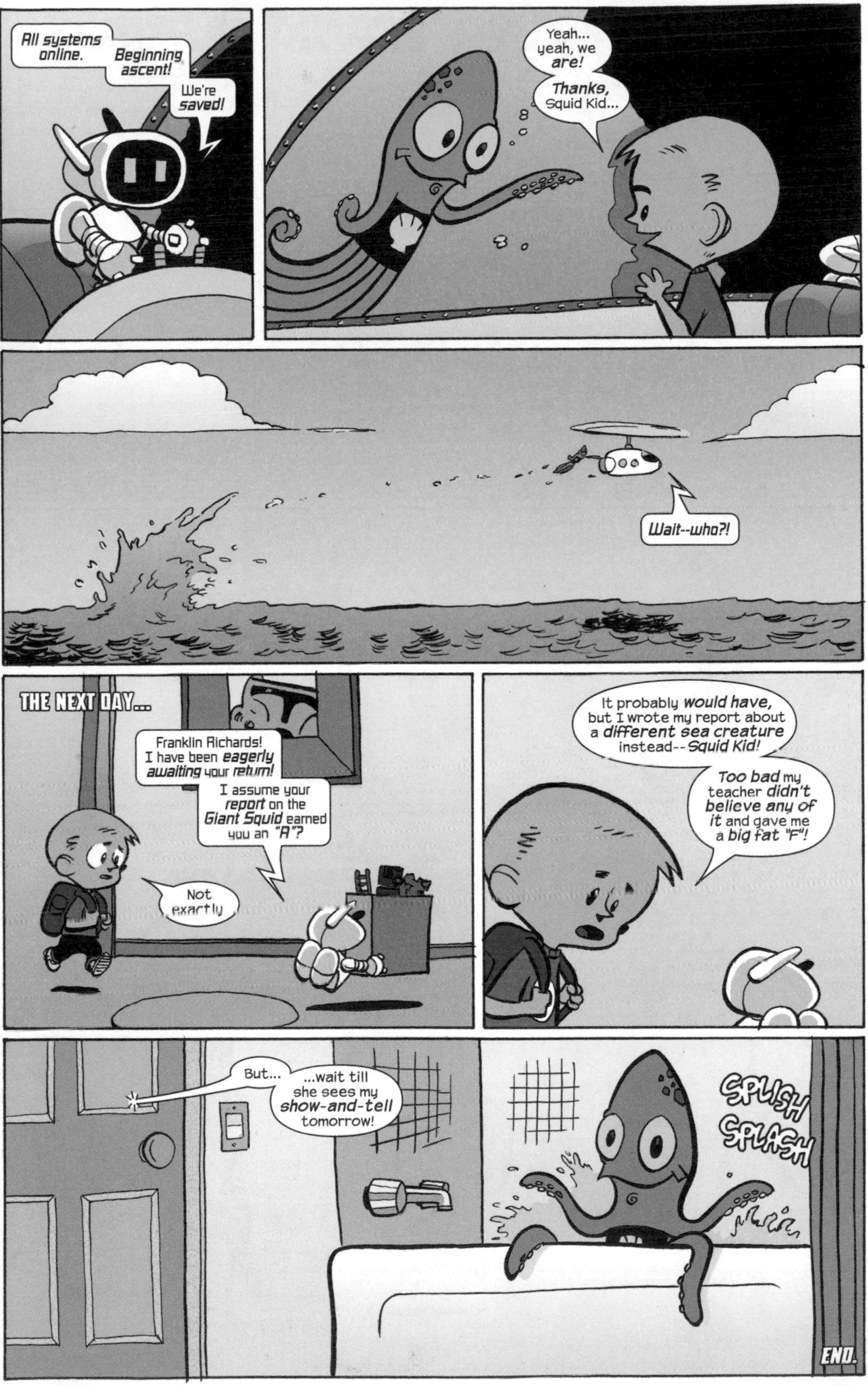
All systems online.
Beginning ascent!
We're saved!
Yeah... yeah, we are!
Thanks, Squid Kid...
Wait--who?!
THE NEXT DAY...
Franklin Richards! I have been eagerly awaiting your return!
I assume your report on the Giant Squid earned you an "A"?
Not exactly
It probably would have, but I wrote my report about a different sea creature instead--Squid Kid!
Too bad my teacher didn't believe any of it and gave me a big fat "F"!
But...
...wait till she sees my show-and-tell tomorrow!
SPLISH
SPLASH
END.

FRANKLIN RICHARDS SON OF A GENIUS IN: "FREAKY FRANKLIN FRIDAY!"

BY CHRIS ELIOPOULOS & MARC SUMERAK

LOVERN KINDZIERSKI COLORS · NATHAN COSBY ASSISTANT EDITOR · MARK PANICCIA EDITOR · JOE QUESADA EDITOR IN CHIEF · DAN BUCKLEY PUBLISHER

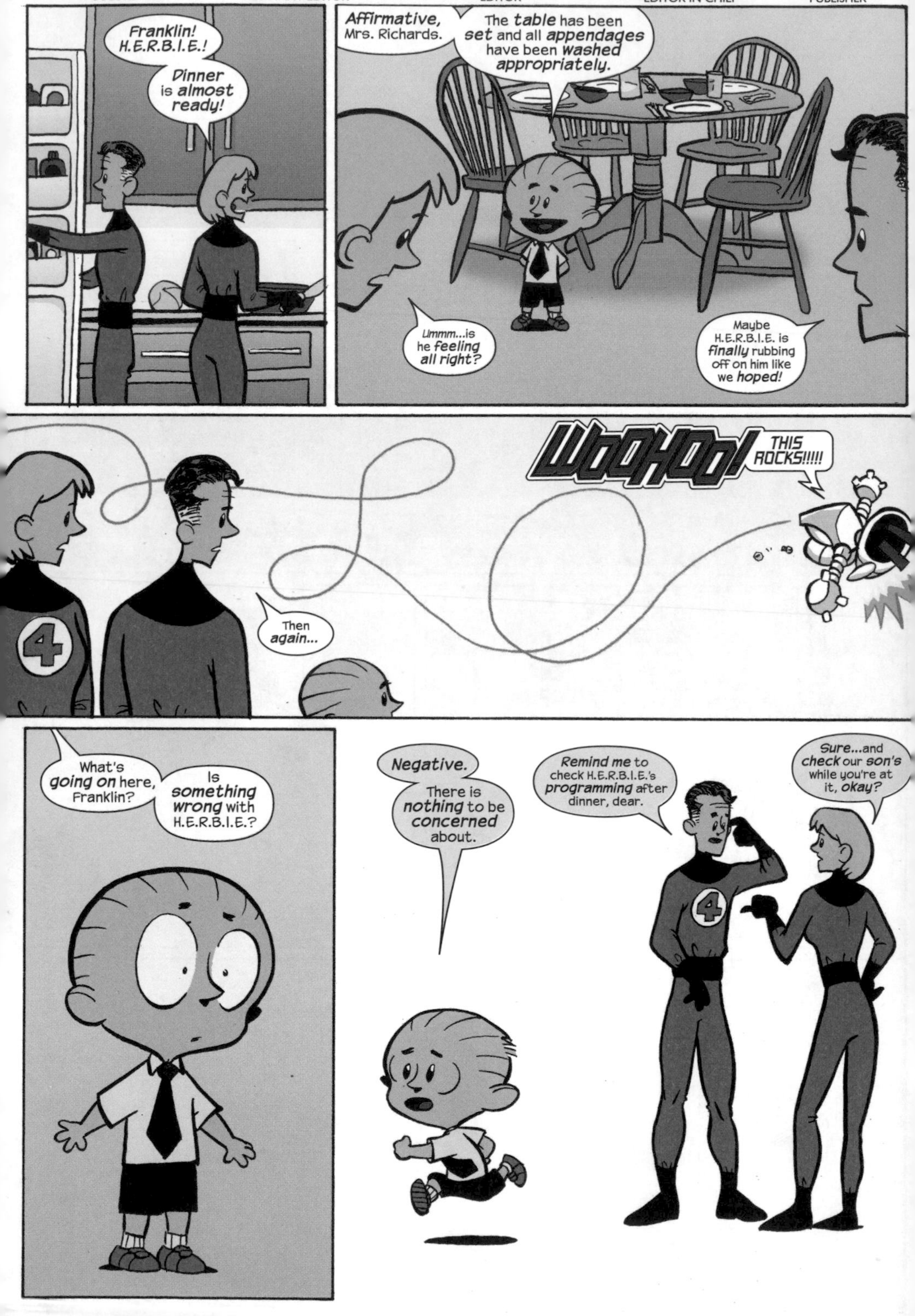

Franklin! H.E.R.B.I.E.!
Dinner is almost ready!
Affirmative, Mrs. Richards.
The table has been set and all appendages have been washed appropriately.
Ummm...is he feeling all right?
Maybe H.E.R.B.I.E. is finally rubbing off on him like we hoped!
WOOHOO!
THIS ROCKS!!!!!
Then again...
What's going on here, Franklin?
Is something wrong with H.E.R.B.I.E.?
Negative.
There is nothing to be concerned about.
Remind me to check H.E.R.B.I.E.'s programming after dinner, dear.
Sure...and check our son's while you're at it, okay?

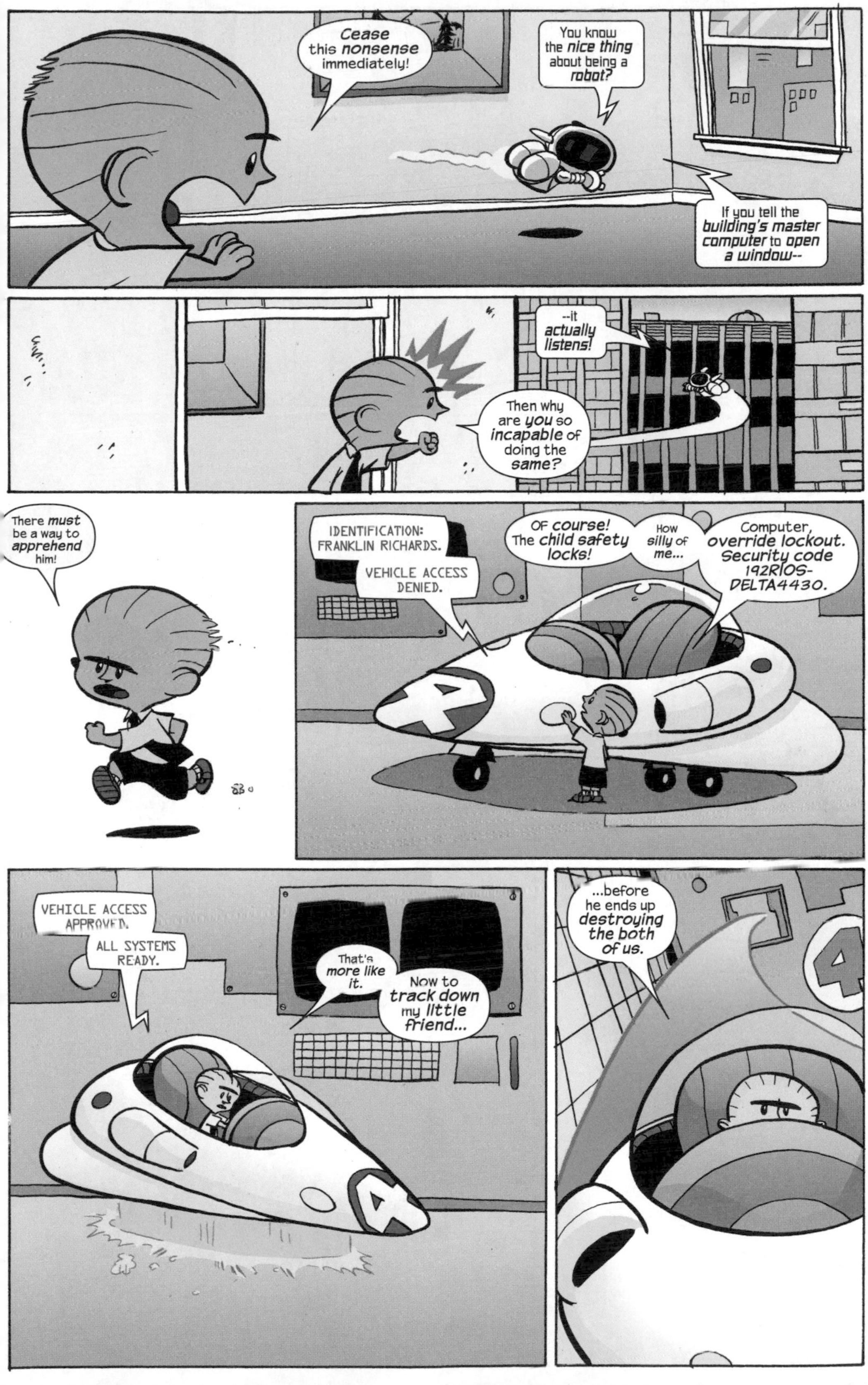
Cease this nonsense immediately!
You know the nice thing about being a robot?
If you tell the building's master computer to open a window--
--it actually listens!
Then why are you so incapable of doing the same?
There must be a way to apprehend him!
IDENTIFICATION: FRANKLIN RICHARDS.
VEHICLE ACCESS DENIED.
Of course! The child safety locks!
How silly of me...
Computer, override lockout. Security code 192RIOS-DELTA4430.
VEHICLE ACCESS APPROVED.
ALL SYSTEMS READY.
That's more like it.
Now to track down my little friend...
...before he ends up destroying the both of us.

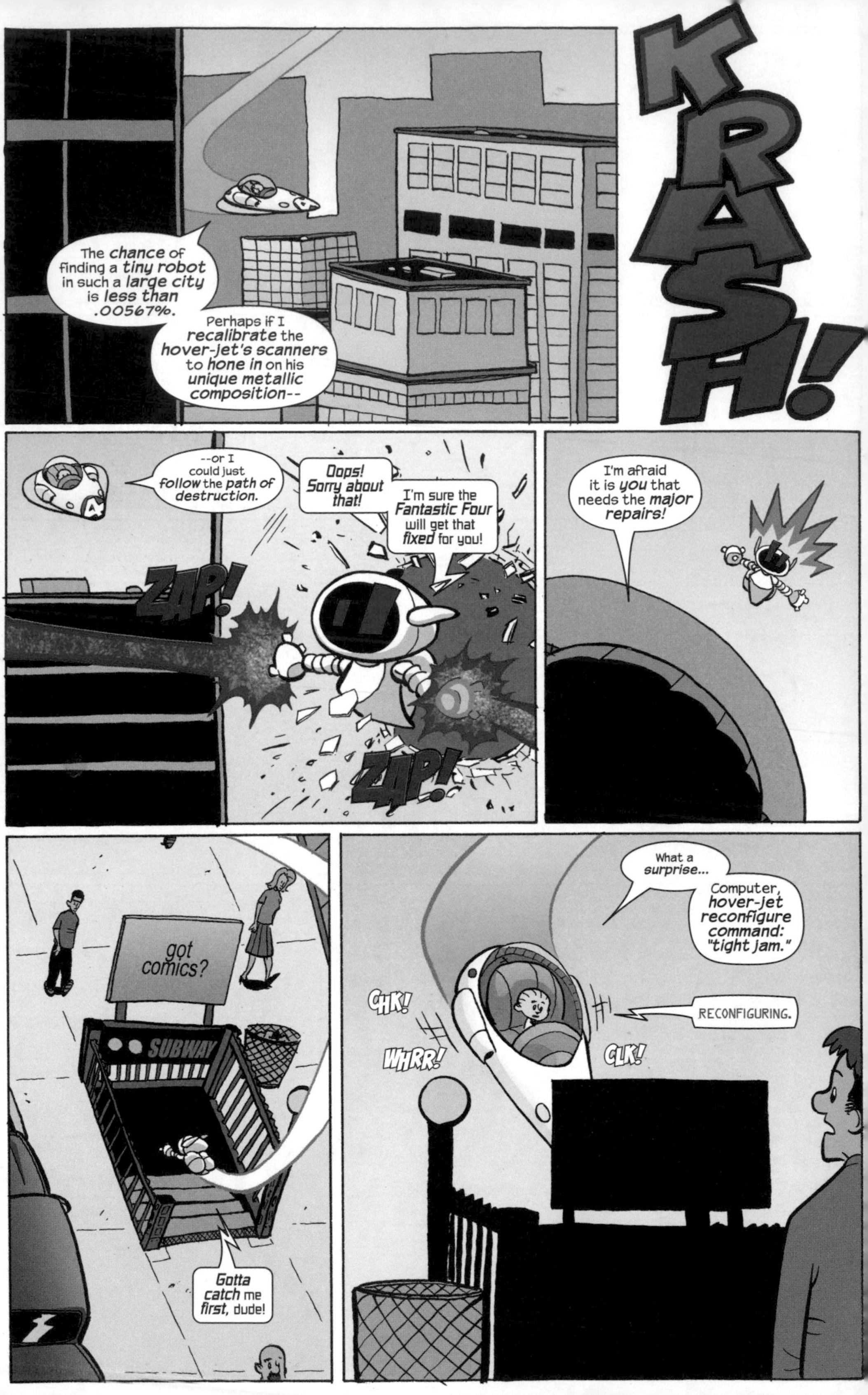
The chance of finding a tiny robot in such a large city is less than .00567%.
Perhaps if I recalibrate the hover-jet's scanners to hone in on his unique metallic composition--
KRASH!
--or I could just follow the path of destruction.
Oops! Sorry about that!
I'm sure the Fantastic Four will get that fixed for you!
ZAP!
ZAP!
I'm afraid it is you that needs the major repairs!
got comics?
SUBWAY
Gotta catch me first, dude!
What a surprise...
Computer, hover-jet reconfigure command: "tight jam."
CHK!
WHRR!
CLK!
RECONFIGURING.

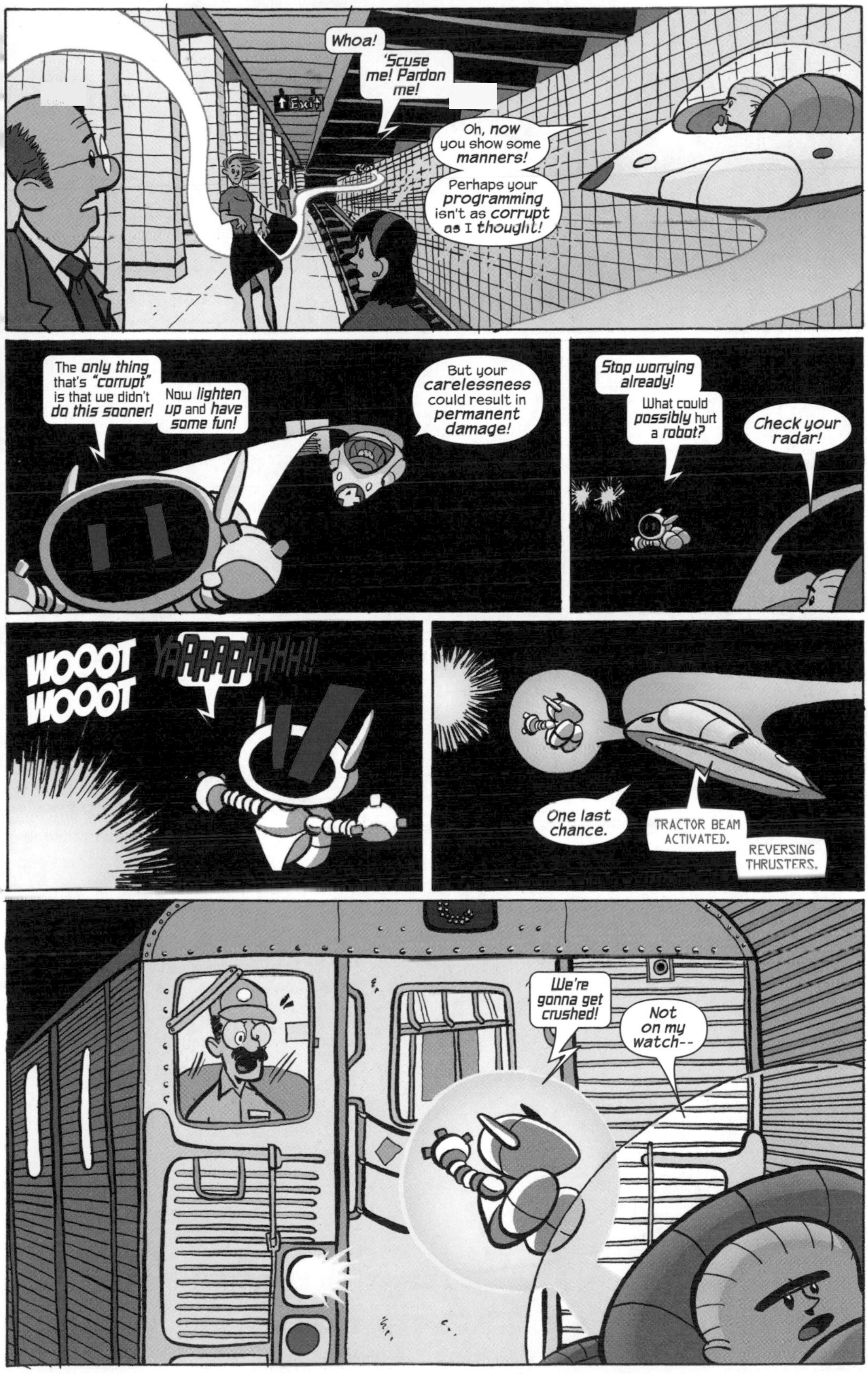
Exit
Whoa!
'Scuse me! Pardon me!
Oh, now you show some manners!
Perhaps your programming isn't as corrupt as I thought!
The only thing that's "corrupt" is that we didn't do this sooner!
Now lighten up and have some fun!
But your carelessness could result in permanent damage!
Stop worrying already!
What could possibly hurt a robot?
Check your radar!
WOOOT WOOOT
YAAAAAHHHH!!
One last chance.
TRACTOR BEAM ACTIVATED.
REVERSING THRUSTERS.
We're gonna get crushed!
Not on my watch--

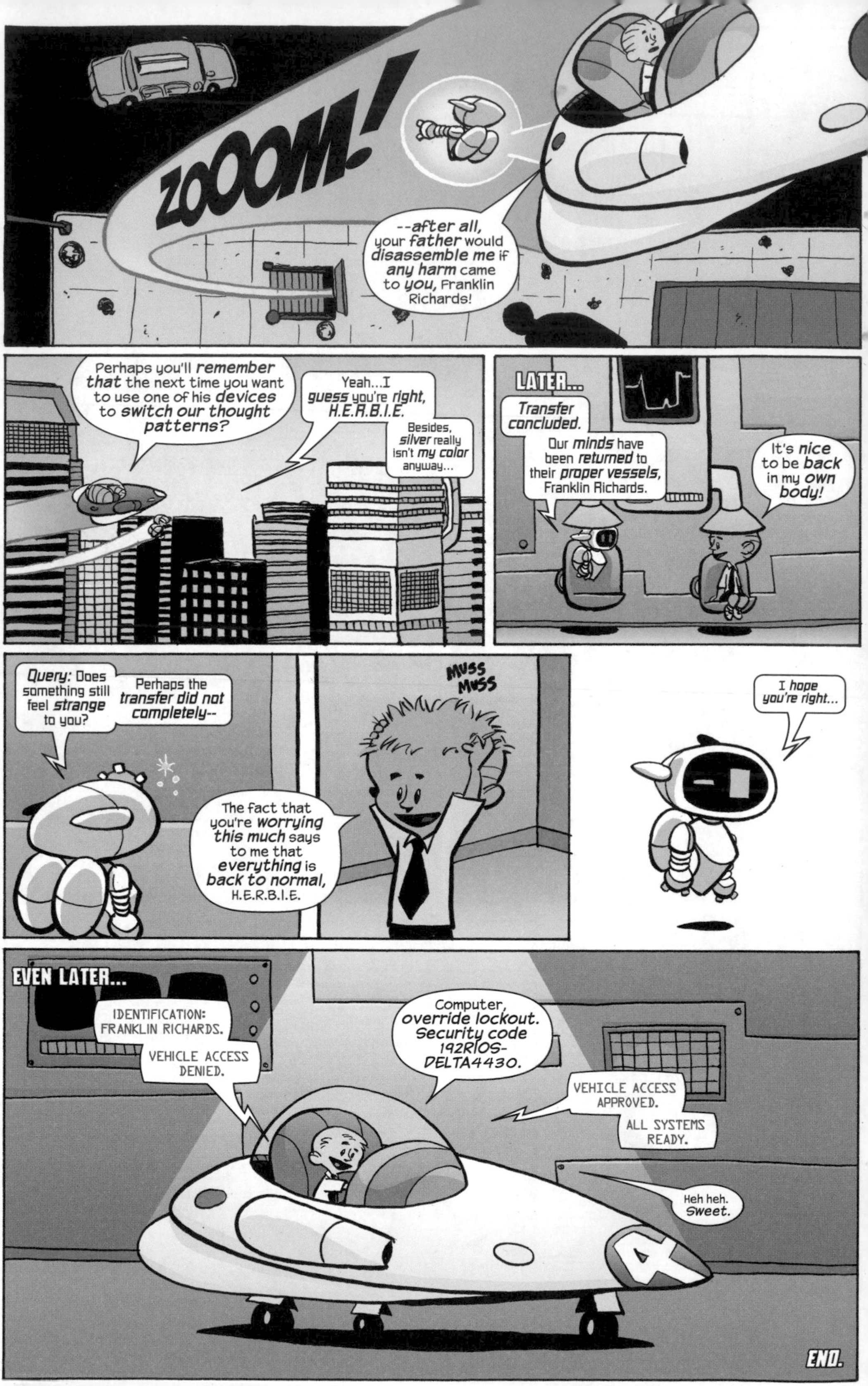
ZOOOM!
--after all, your father would disassemble me if any harm came to you, Franklin Richards!
Perhaps you'll remember that the next time you want to use one of his devices to switch our thought patterns?
Yeah...I guess you're right, H.E.R.B.I.E.
Besides, silver really isn't my color anyway...
LATER...
Transfer concluded.
Our minds have been returned to their proper vessels, Franklin Richards.
It's nice to be back in my own body!
Query: Does something still feel strange to you?
Perhaps the transfer did not completely--
MUSS MUSS
The fact that you're worrying this much says to me that everything is back to normal, H.E.R.B.I.E.
I hope you're right...
EVEN LATER...
IDENTIFICATION: FRANKLIN RICHARDS.
VEHICLE ACCESS DENIED.
Computer, override lockout. Security code 192RIOS-DELTA4430.
VEHICLE ACCESS APPROVED.
ALL SYSTEMS READY.
Heh heh. Sweet.
END.

FRANKLIN RICHARDS SON OF A GENIUS IN: "BOUNCING BABY BOY!"

BY CHRIS ELIOPOULOS & MARC SUMERAK

LOVERN KINDZIERSKI COLORS | NATHAN COSBY ASSISTANT EDITOR | MARK PANICCIA EDITOR | JOE QUESADA EDITOR IN CHIEF | DAN BUCKLEY PUBLISHER

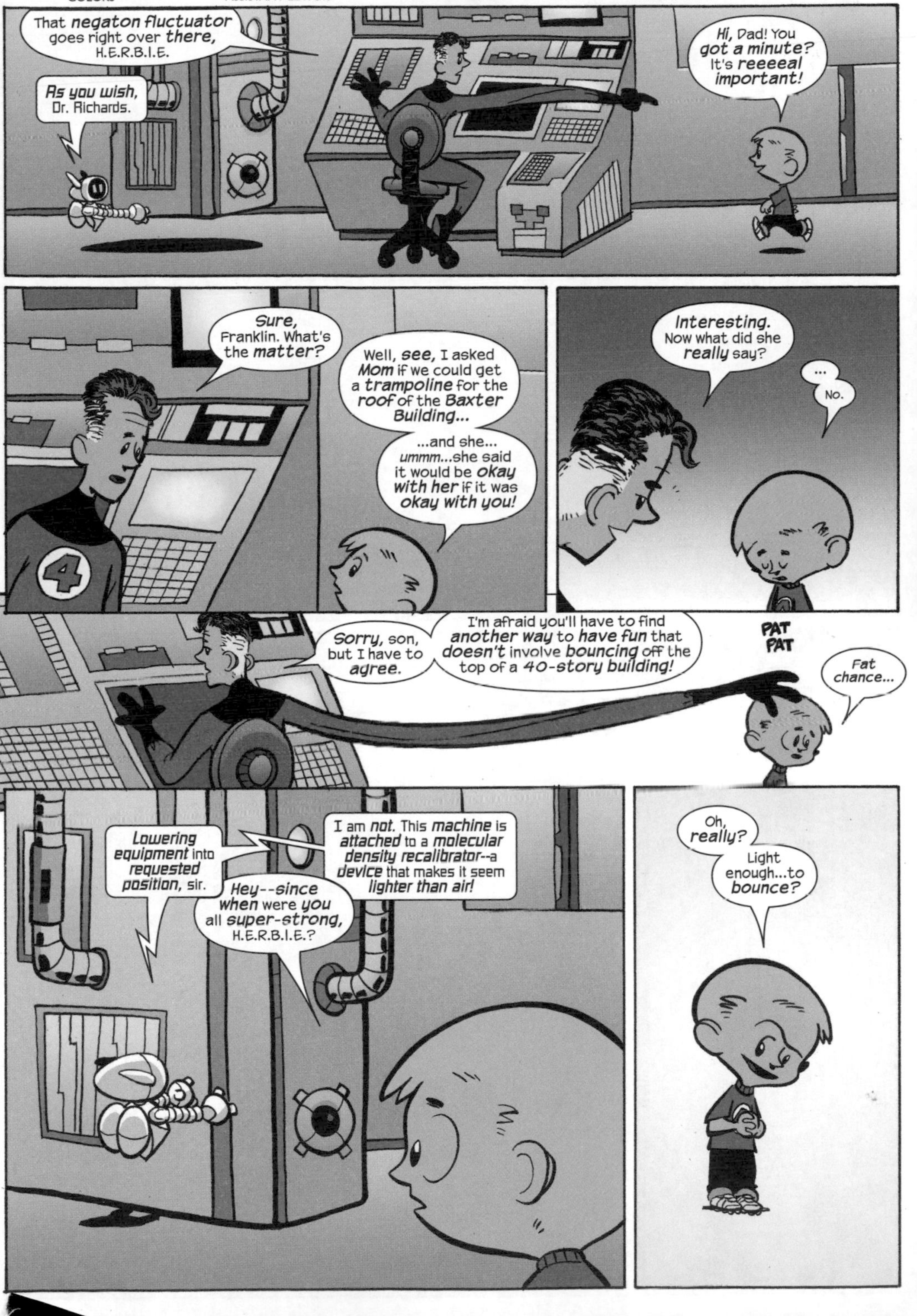
That negaton fluctuator goes right over there, H.E.R.B.I.E.
As you wish, Dr. Richards.
Hi, Dad! You got a minute? It's reeeeal important!
Sure, Franklin. What's the matter?
Well, see, I asked Mom if we could get a trampoline for the roof of the Baxter Building...
...and she... ummm...she said it would be okay with her if it was okay with you!
Interesting. Now what did she really say?
...
No.
Sorry, son, but I have to agree.
I'm afraid you'll have to find another way to have fun that doesn't involve bouncing off the top of a 40-story building!
PAT PAT
Fat chance...
Lowering equipment into requested position, sir.
Hey--since when were you all super-strong, H.E.R.B.I.E.?
I am not. This machine is attached to a molecular density recalibrator--a device that makes it seem lighter than air!
Oh, really?
Light enough...to bounce?

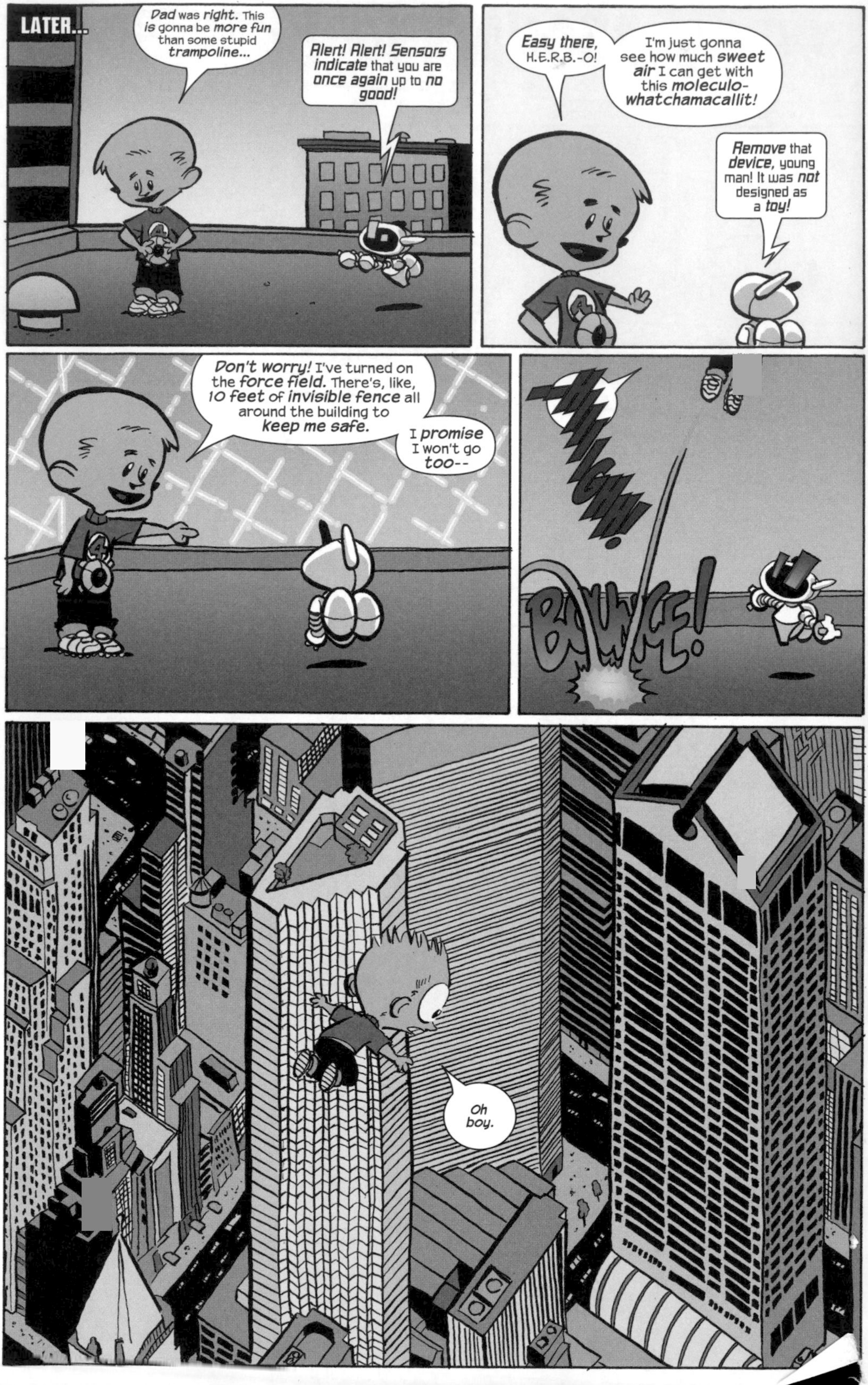
LATER...
Dad was right. This is gonna be more fun than some stupid trampoline...
Alert! Alert! Sensors indicate that you are once again up to no good!
Easy there, H.E.R.B.-O!
I'm just gonna see how much sweet air I can get with this moleculo-whatchamacallit!
Remove that device, young man! It was not designed as a toy!
Don't worry! I've turned on the force field. There's, like, 10 feet of invisible fence all around the building to keep me safe.
I promise I won't go too--
AAAAGH!
BOUNCE!
Oh boy.

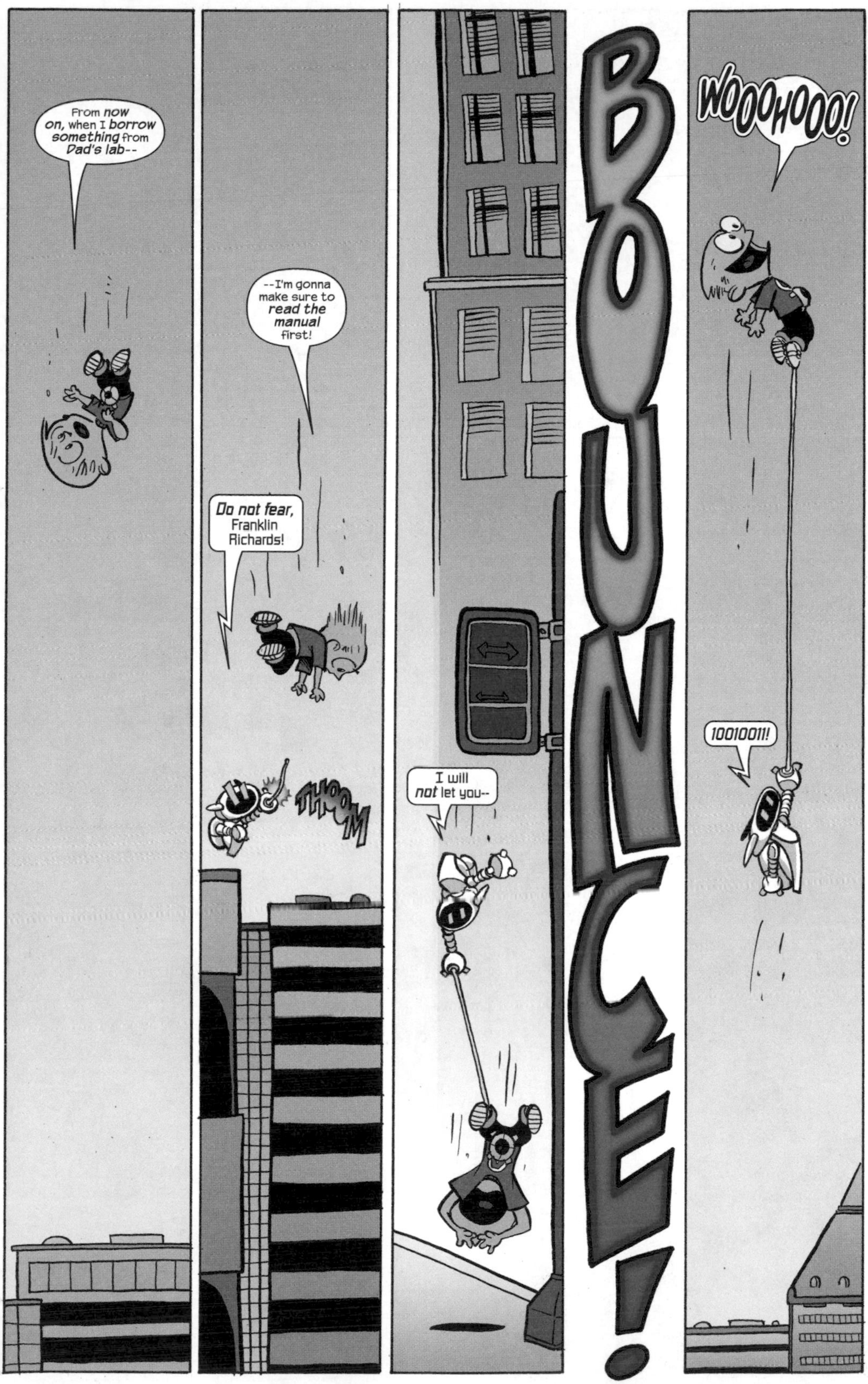
From now on, when I borrow something from Dad's lab--
--I'm gonna make sure to read the manual first!
Do not fear, Franklin Richards!
THOOM
I will not let you--
BOUNCE!
WOOOHOOO!
10010011!

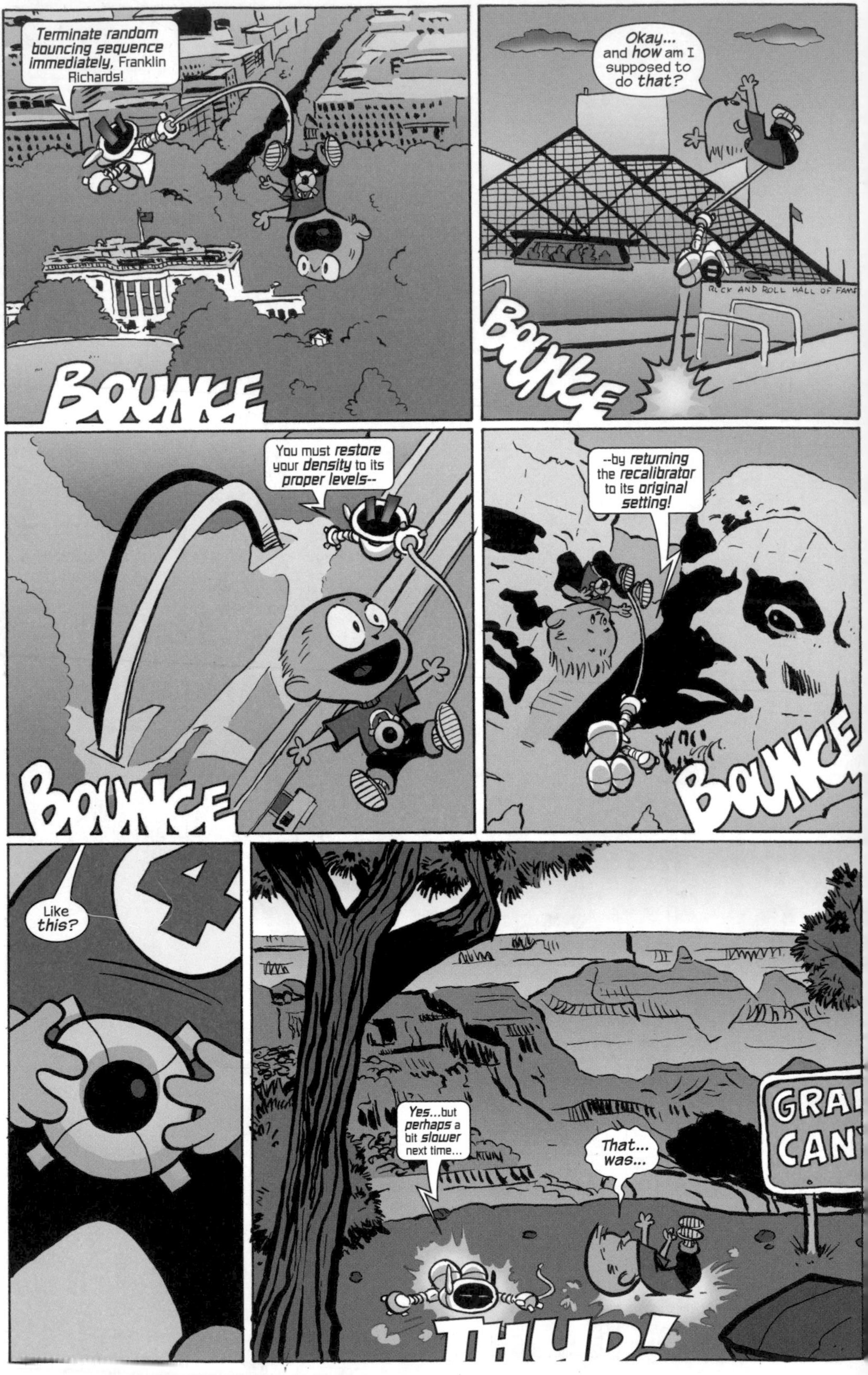

Terminate random bouncing sequence immediately, Franklin Richards!
BOUNCE
Okay... and how am I supposed to do that?
ROCK AND ROLL HALL OF FAME
BOUNCE
You must restore your density to its proper levels--
BOUNCE
--by returning the recalibrator to its original setting!
BOUNCE
Like this?
Yes...but perhaps a bit slower next time...
That... was...
THUD!

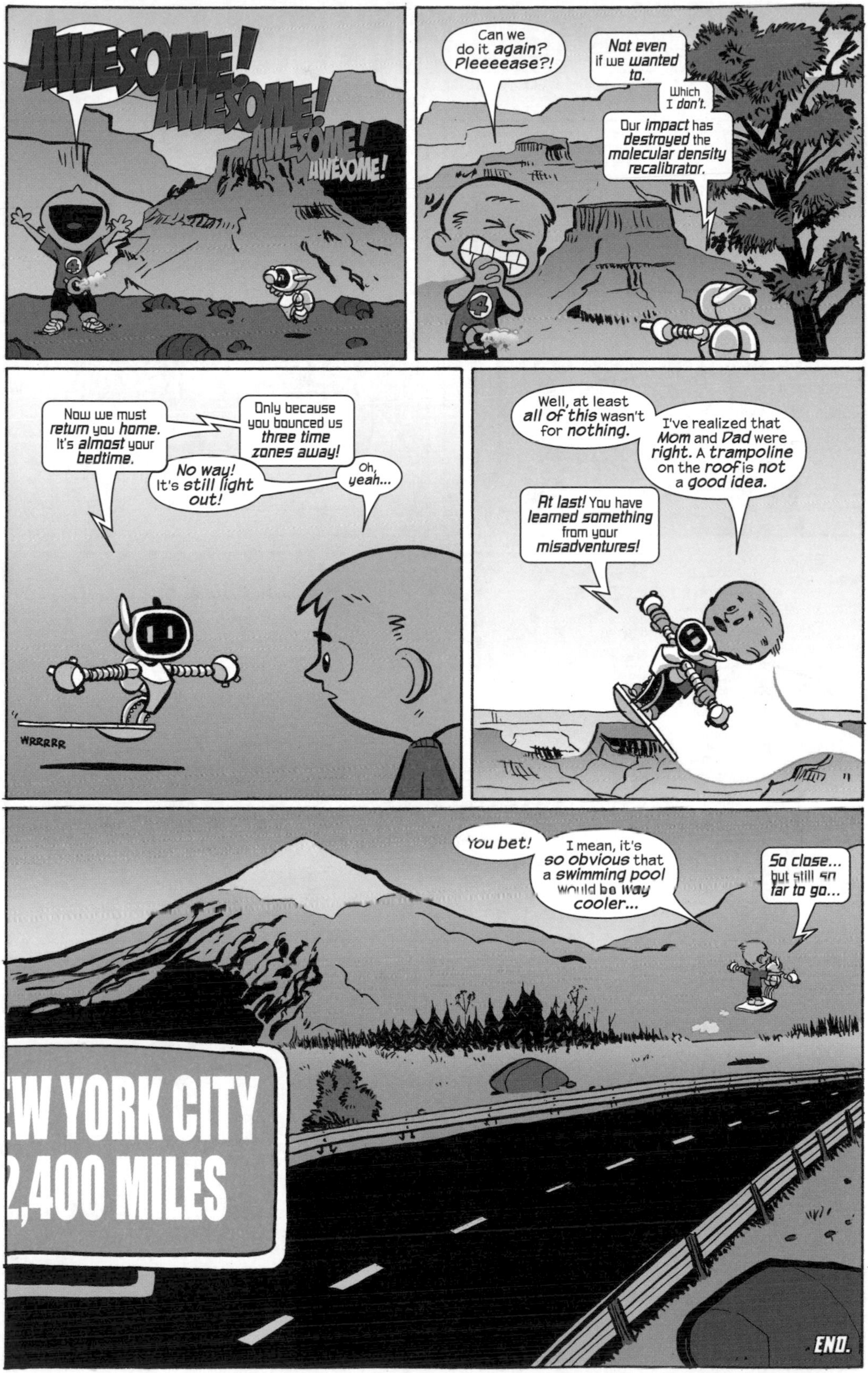
AWESOME! AWESOME! AWESOME! AWESOME!
Can we do it again? Pleeeease?!
Not even if we wanted to.
Which I don't.
Our impact has destroyed the molecular density recalibrator.
Now we must return you home. It's almost your bedtime.
Only because you bounced us three time zones away!
No way! It's still light out!
Oh, yeah...
WRRRRR
Well, at least all of this wasn't for nothing.
I've realized that Mom and Dad were right. A trampoline on the roof is not a good idea.
At last! You have learned something from your misadventures!
You bet!
I mean, it's so obvious that a swimming pool would be way cooler...
So close... but still so far to go...
EW YORK CITY
2,400 MILES
END.

FRANKLIN RICHARDS SON OF A GENIUS IN: "COMIC BOOK FREE-FOR-ALL!"

BY CHRIS ELIOPOULOS & MARC SUMERAK

LOVERN KINDZIERSKI, COLORS — NATHAN COSBY, ASSISTANT EDITOR — MARK PANICCIA, CONSULTING EDITOR — MACKENZIE CADENHEAD, EDITOR

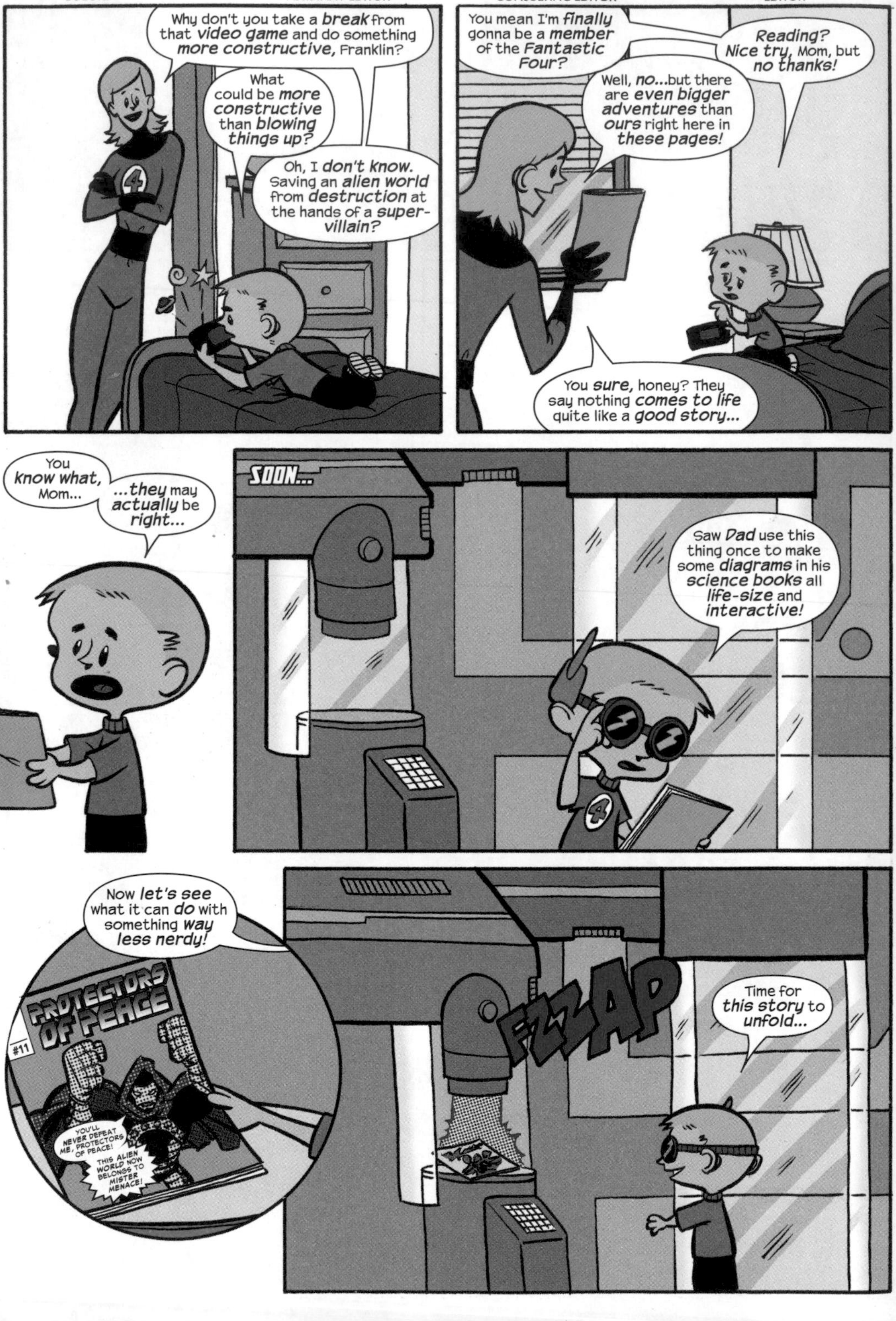

Why don't you take a break from that video game and do something more constructive, Franklin?
What could be more constructive than blowing things up?
Oh, I don't know. Saving an alien world from destruction at the hands of a super-villain?
You mean I'm finally gonna be a member of the Fantastic Four?
Well, no...but there are even bigger adventures than ours right here in these pages!
Reading? Nice try, Mom, but no thanks!
You sure, honey? They say nothing comes to life quite like a good story...
You know what, Mom...
...they may actually be right...
SOON...
Saw Dad use this thing once to make some diagrams in his science books all life-size and interactive!
Now let's see what it can do with something way less nerdy!
PROTECTORS OF PEACE
#11
YOU'LL NEVER DEFEAT ME, PROTECTORS OF PEACE!
THIS ALIEN WORLD NOW BELONGS TO MISTER MENACE!
FZZAP
Time for this story to unfold...

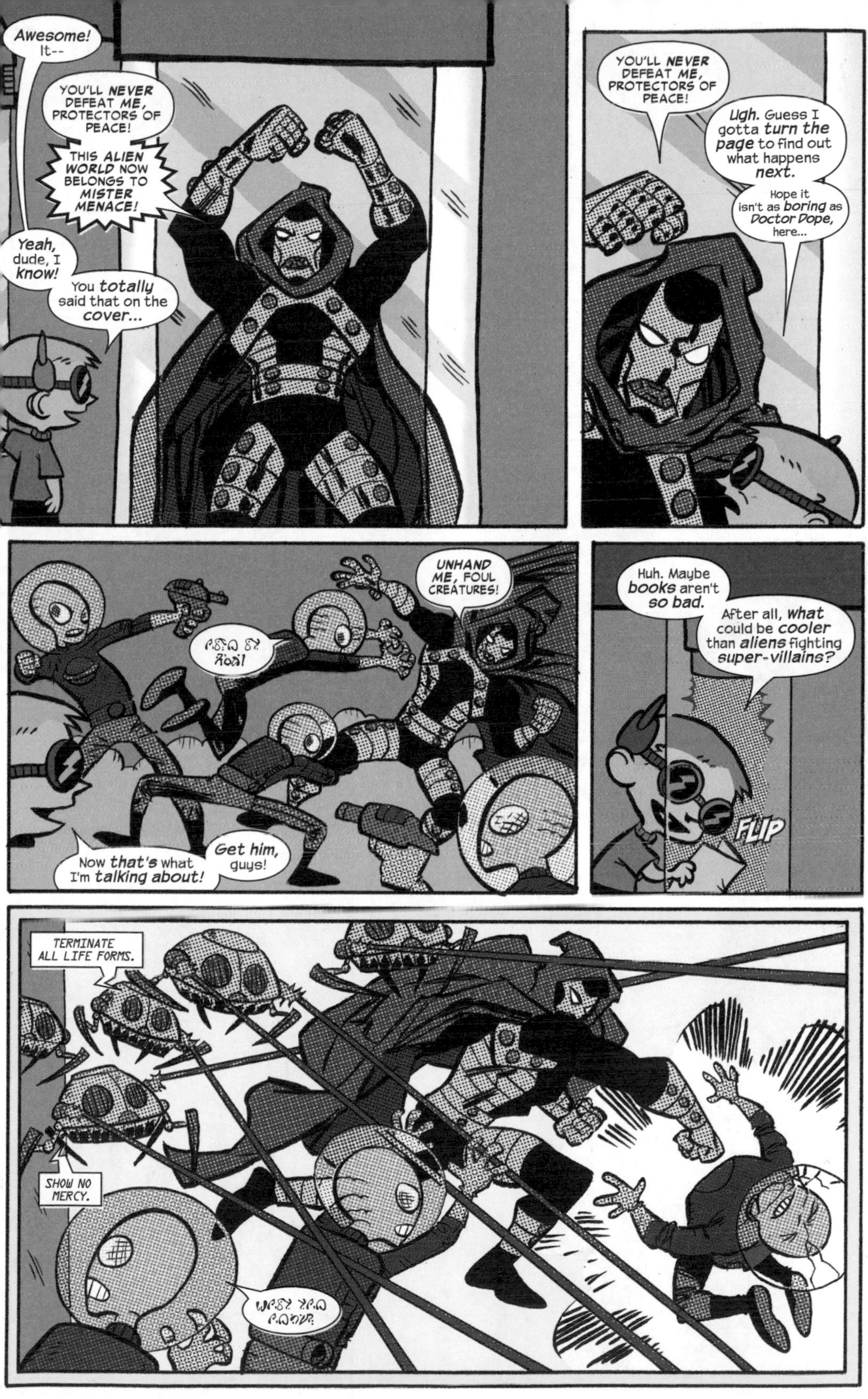
Awesome! It--
YOU'LL NEVER DEFEAT ME, PROTECTORS OF PEACE!
THIS ALIEN WORLD NOW BELONGS TO MISTER MENACE!
Yeah, dude, I know!
You totally said that on the cover...
YOU'LL NEVER DEFEAT ME, PROTECTORS OF PEACE!
Ugh. Guess I gotta turn the page to find out what happens next.
Hope it isn't as boring as Doctor Dope, here...
UNHAND ME, FOUL CREATURES!
Get him, guys!
Now that's what I'm talking about!
Huh. Maybe books aren't so bad.
After all, what could be cooler than aliens fighting super-villains?
FLIP
TERMINATE ALL LIFE FORMS.
SHOW NO MERCY.

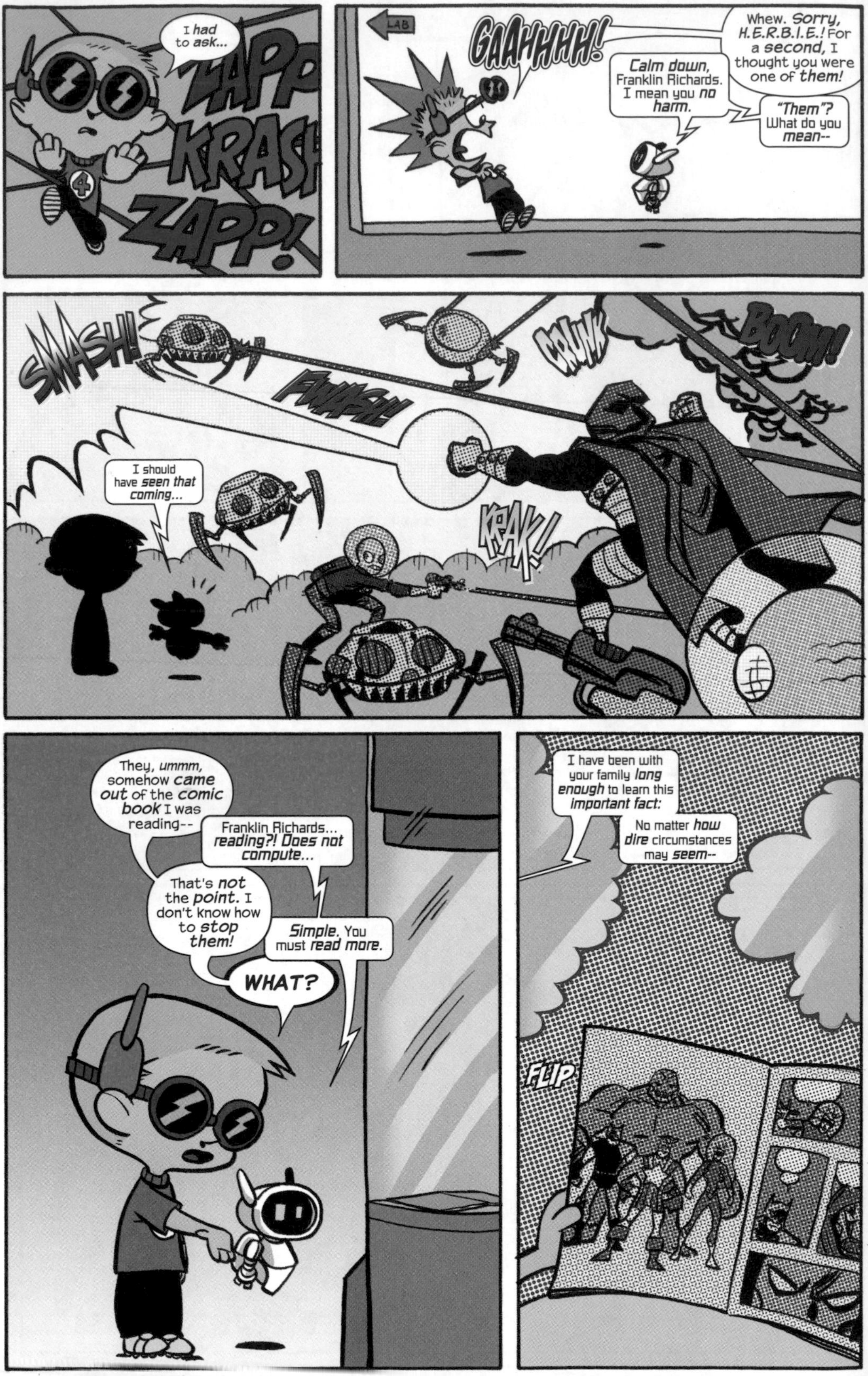
I had to ask...
ZAPP
KRASH
ZAPP!
LAB
GAAHHHH!
Calm down, Franklin Richards. I mean you no harm.
Whew. Sorry, H.E.R.B.I.E.! For a second, I thought you were one of them!
"Them"? What do you mean--
SMASH!
CRUNK
BOOM!
FWASH!
I should have seen that coming...
KRAK!
They, ummm, somehow came out of the comic book I was reading--
Franklin Richards... reading?! Does not compute...
That's not the point. I don't know how to stop them!
Simple. You must read more.
WHAT?
I have been with your family long enough to learn this important fact:
No matter how dire circumstances may seem--
FLIP

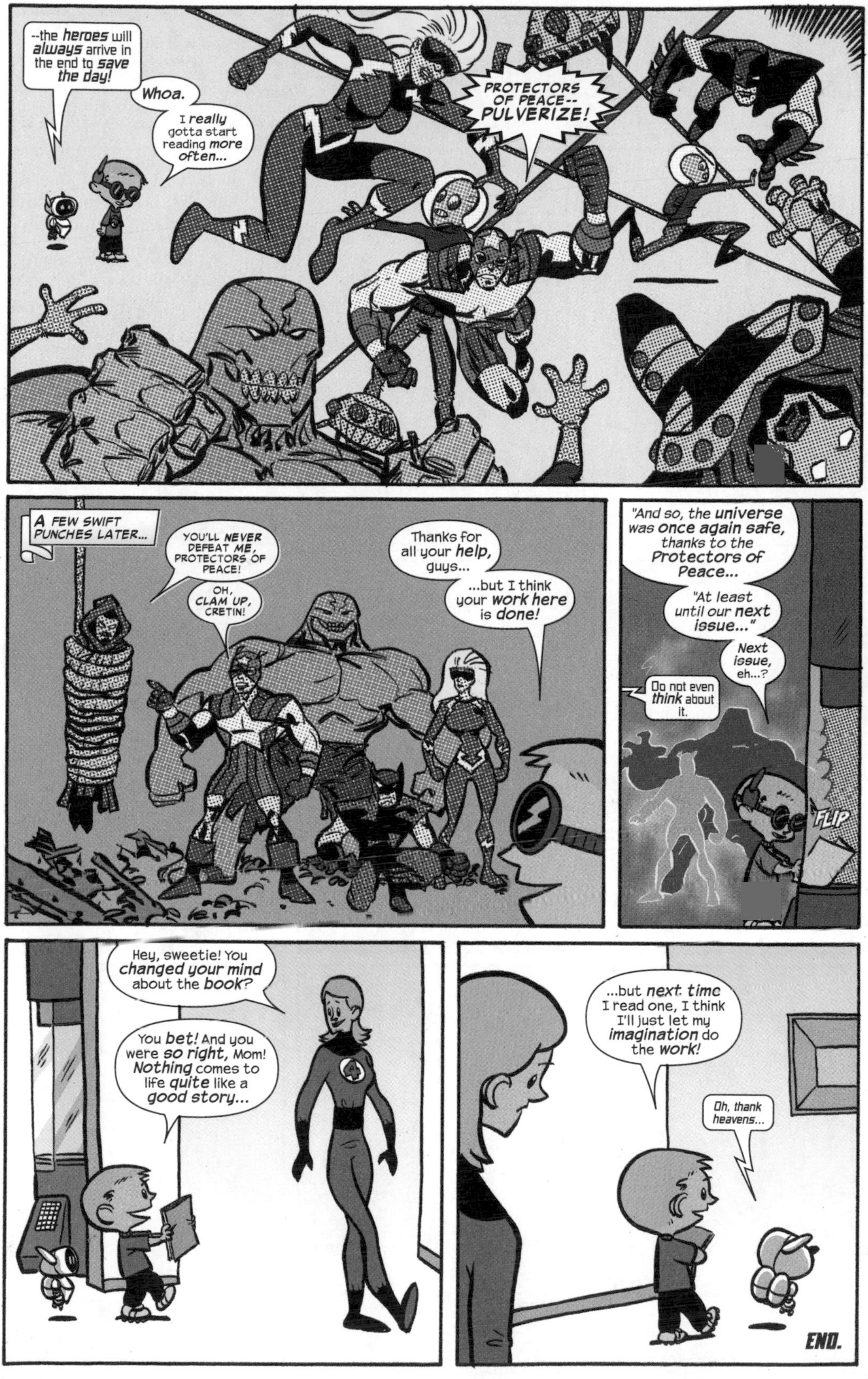
--the heroes will always arrive in the end to save the day!
Whoa.
I really gotta start reading more often...
PROTECTORS OF PEACE-- PULVERIZE!
A FEW SWIFT PUNCHES LATER...
YOU'LL NEVER DEFEAT ME, PROTECTORS OF PEACE!
OH, CLAM UP, CRETIN!
Thanks for all your help, guys...
...but I think your work here is done!
"And so, the universe was once again safe, thanks to the Protectors of Peace...
"At least until our next issue..."
Next issue, eh...?
Do not even think about it.
FLIP
Hey, sweetie! You changed your mind about the book?
You bet! And you were so right, Mom! Nothing comes to life quite like a good story...
...but next time I read one, I think I'll just let my imagination do the work!
Oh, thank heavens...
END.

FRANKLIN RICHARDS' ROBOT, H.E.R.B.I.E. IN: "H.E.R.B.I.E.'S DAY OFF"

BY CHRIS ELIOPOULOS & MARC SUMERAK

GURIHIRU COLORS · **TOM VALENTE** PRODUCTION · **NATHAN COSBY** ASSISTANT EDITOR · **MARK PANICCIA** CONSULTING EDITOR · **MACKENZIE CADENHEAD** EDITOR

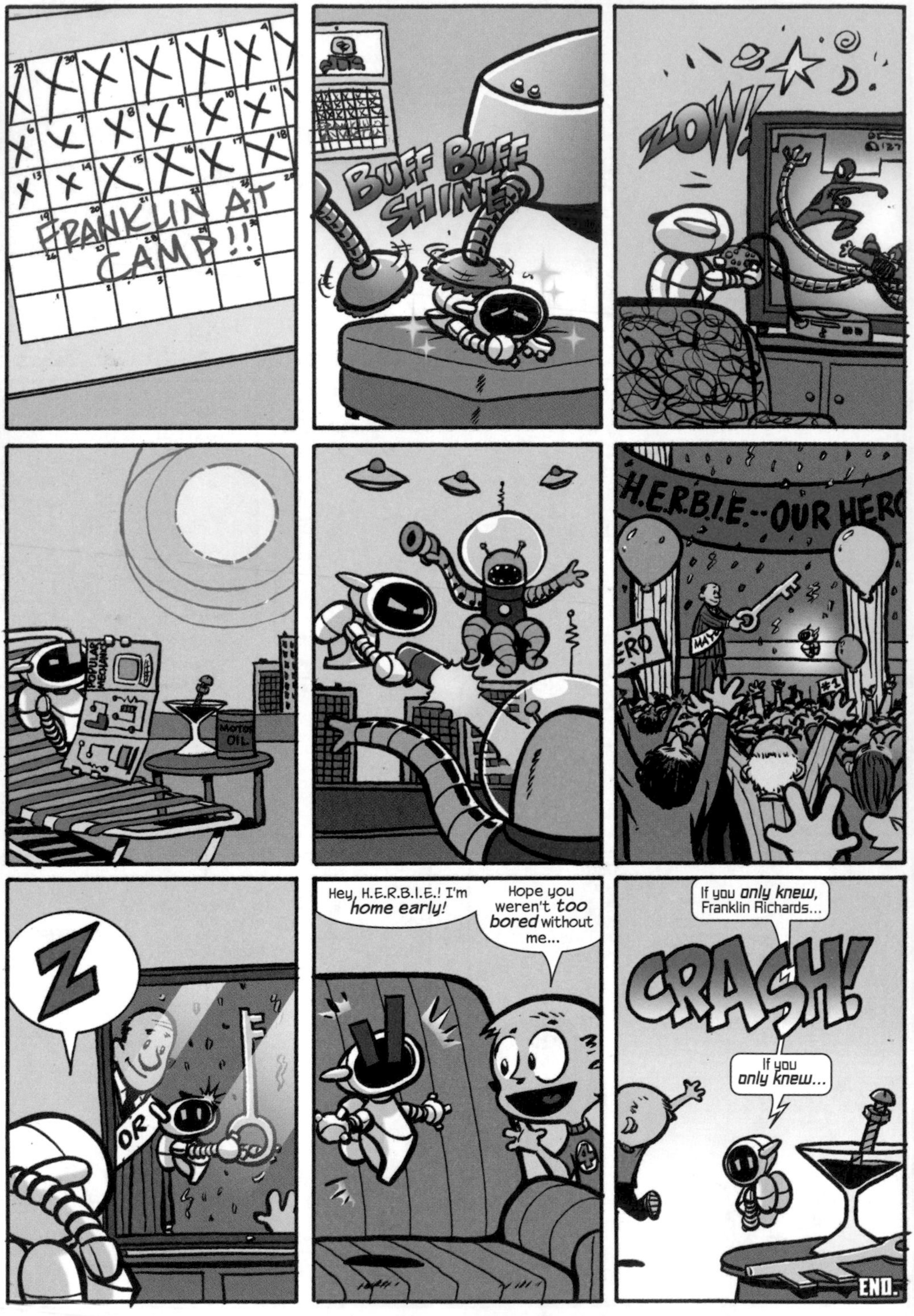

FRANKLIN AT CAMP!!
BUFF BUFF SHINE
ZOW!
MOTOR OIL
H.E.R.B.I.E.--OUR HERO
HERO
#1
Z
OR
Hey, H.E.R.B.I.E.! I'm *home early!*
Hope you weren't *too bored* without me...
If you *only knew*, Franklin Richards...
CRASH!
If you *only knew*...
END.

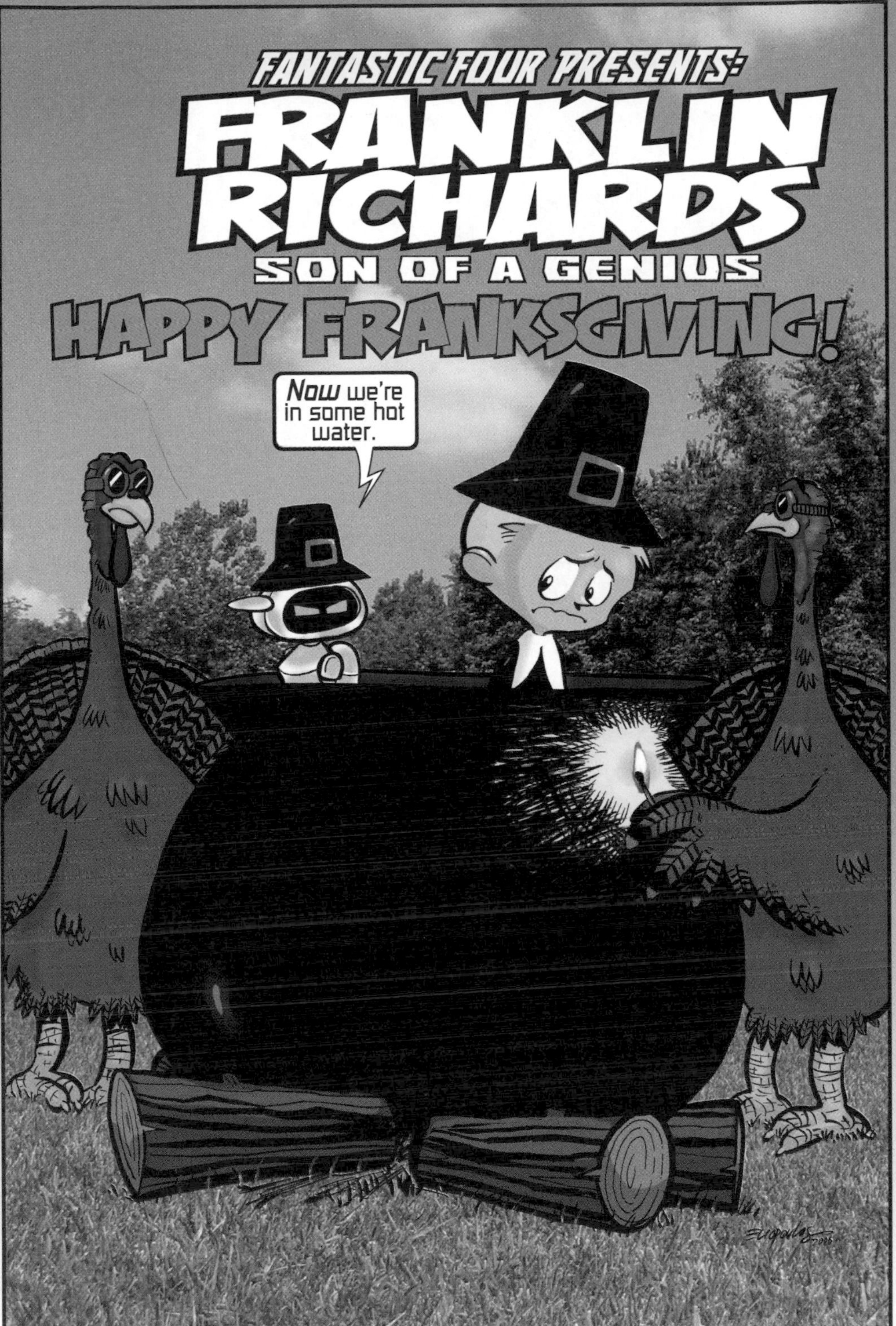
FANTASTIC FOUR PRESENTS:
FRANKLIN RICHARDS
SON OF A GENIUS
HAPPY FRANKSGIVING!
Now we're in some hot water.

FANTASTIC FOUR PRESENTS:
FRANKLIN RICHARDS
SON OF A GENIUS
HAPPY FRANKSGIVING!

CHRIS ELIOPOULOS and MARC SUMERAK
STORY

MARC SUMERAK
SCRIPT

CHRIS ELIOPOULOS
ART & LETTERS

BRAD ANDERSON
COLOR

NATHAN COSBY
ASSISTANT EDITOR

MARK PANICCIA
EDITOR

MACKENZIE CADENHEAD
EDITOR EMERITUS

JOE QUESADA
EDITOR IN CHIEF

DAN BUCKLEY
PUBLISHER

STORY ONE
HAMSTER HAVOC!

STORY TWO
TELEPATHY TERROR!

STORY THREE
SPEED DEMON!

STORY FOUR
OCEAN-APE ESCAPE!

STORY FIVE
TURKEY TROUBLE!

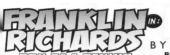

FRANKLIN RICHARDS SON OF A GENIUS IN: HAMSTER HAVOC!

BY CHRIS ELIOPOULOS & MARC SUMERAK
BRAD ANDERSON COLORS
NATHAN COSBY ASSISTANT EDITOR
MARK PANICCIA EDITOR

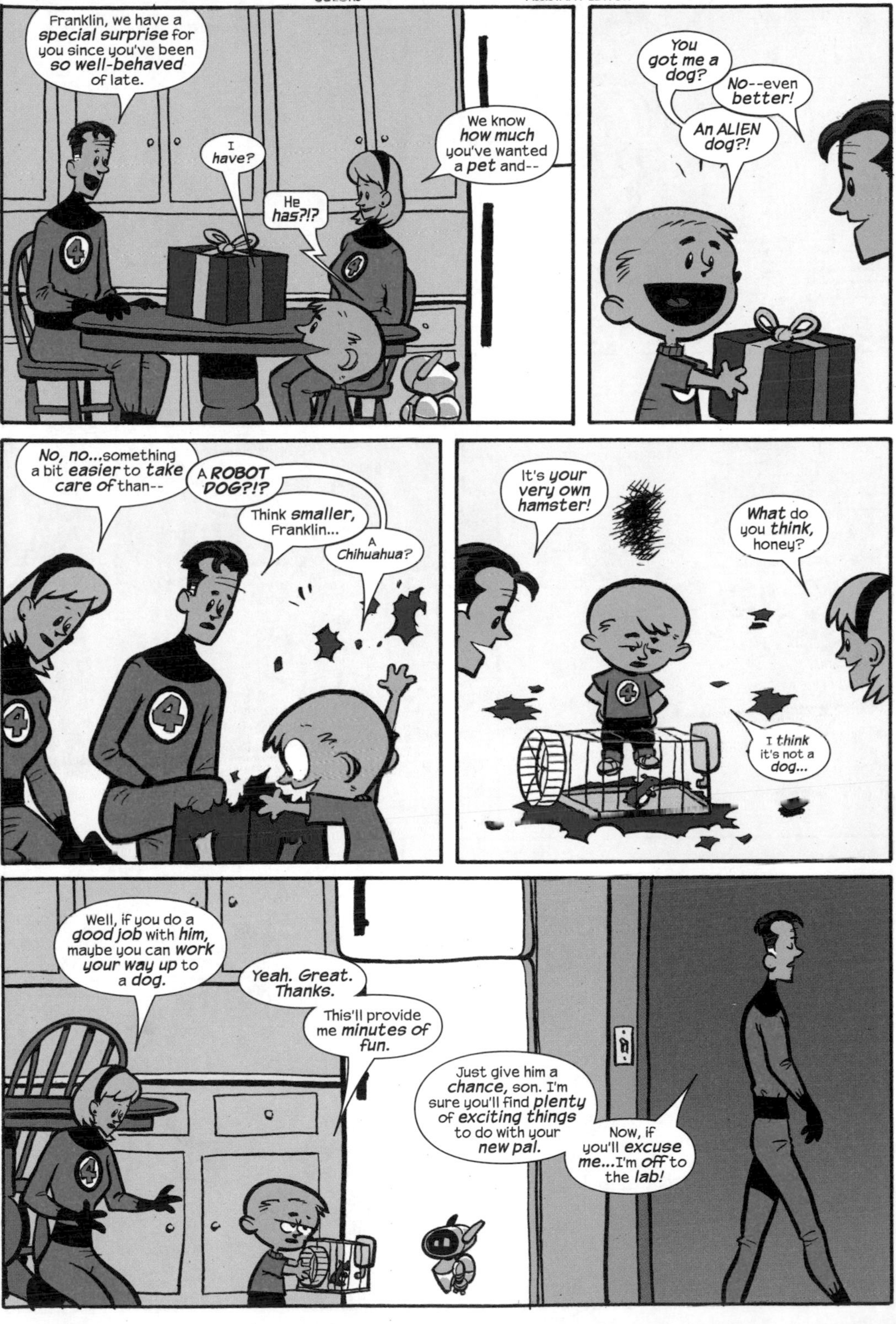
Franklin, we have a special surprise for you since you've been so well-behaved of late.
I have?
He has?!?
We know how much you've wanted a pet and--
You got me a dog?
No--even better!
An ALIEN dog?!
No, no...something a bit easier to take care of than--
A ROBOT DOG?!?
Think smaller, Franklin...
A Chihuahua?
It's your very own hamster!
What do you think, honey?
I think it's not a dog...
Well, if you do a good job with him, maybe you can work your way up to a dog.
Yeah. Great. Thanks.
This'll provide me minutes of fun.
Just give him a chance, son. I'm sure you'll find plenty of exciting things to do with your new pal.
Now, if you'll excuse me...I'm off to the lab!

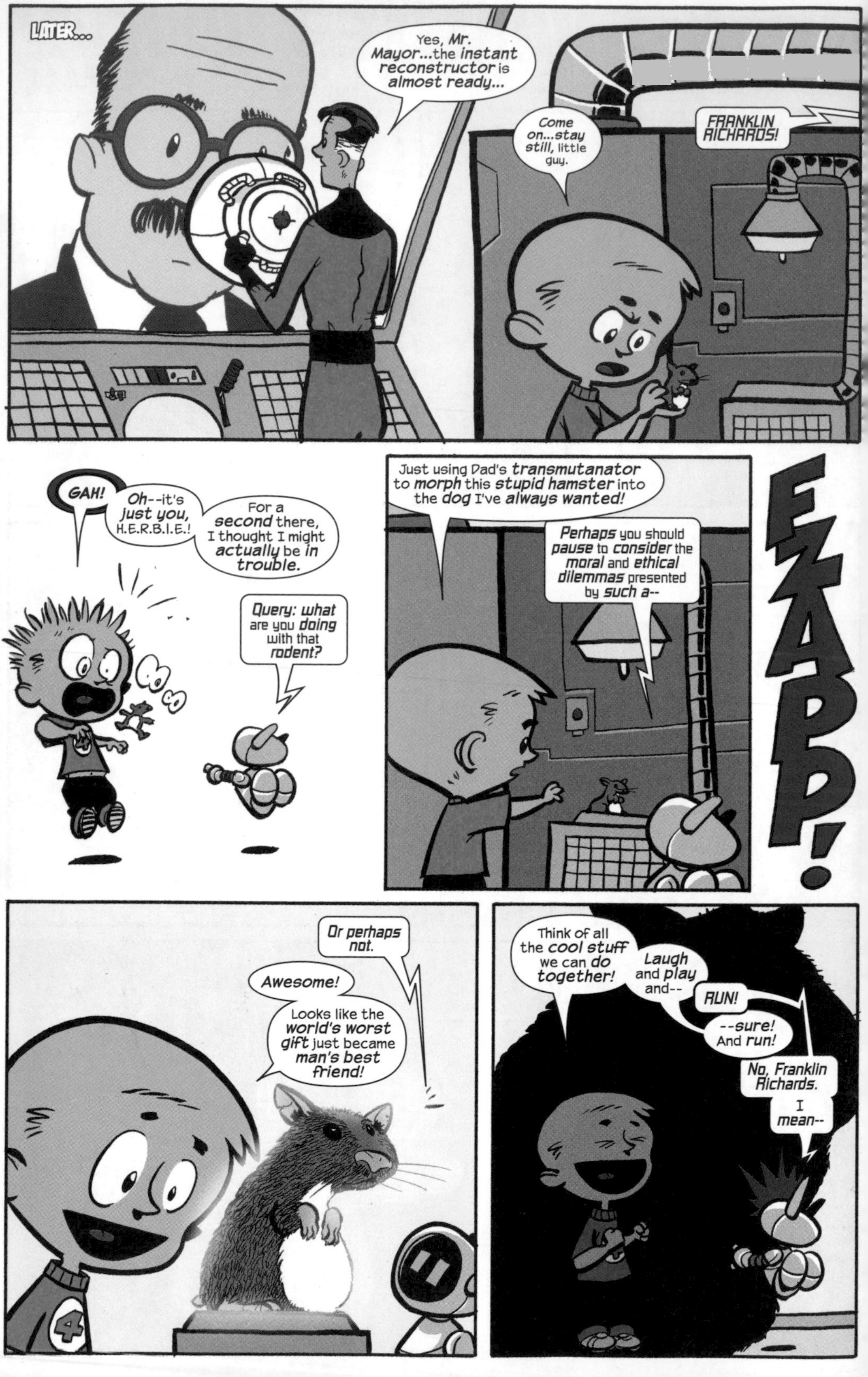
LATER...
Yes, Mr. Mayor...the instant reconstructor is almost ready...
Come on...stay still, little guy.
FRANKLIN RICHARDS!
GAH!
Oh--it's just you, H.E.R.B.I.E.!
For a second there, I thought I might actually be in trouble.
Query: what are you doing with that rodent?
Just using Dad's transmutanator to morph this stupid hamster into the dog I've always wanted!
Perhaps you should pause to consider the moral and ethical dilemmas presented by such a--
ZZAPP!
Or perhaps not.
Awesome!
Looks like the world's worst gift just became man's best friend!
Think of all the cool stuff we can do together!
Laugh and play and--
RUN!
--sure! And run!
No, Franklin Richards.
I mean--

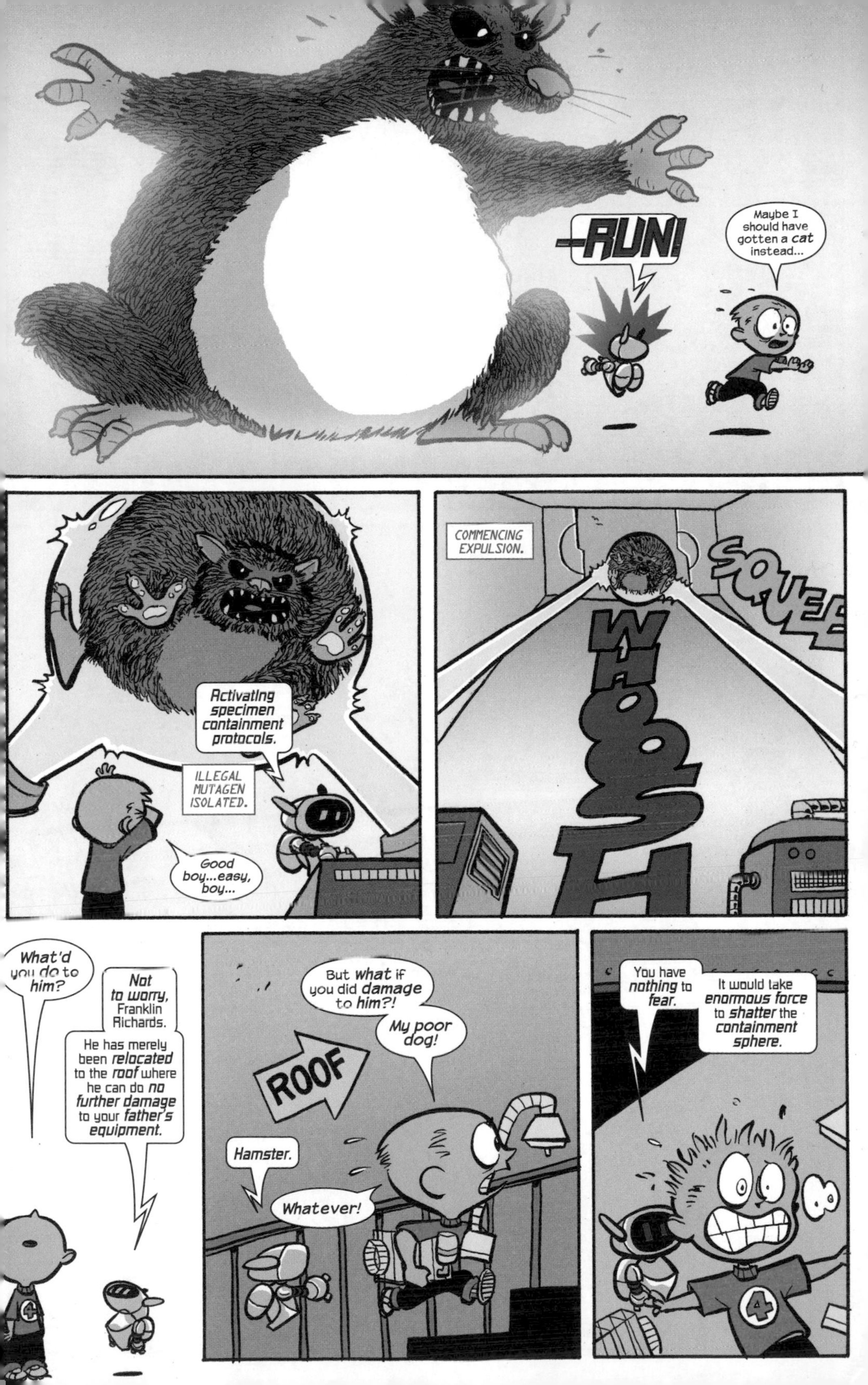
-RUN!
Maybe I should have gotten a *cat* instead...
Activating specimen containment protocols.
ILLEGAL MUTAGEN ISOLATED.
Good boy...easy, boy...
COMMENCING EXPULSION.
SQUEE
WHOOOSH
What'd you do to him?
Not to worry, Franklin Richards.
He has merely been *relocated* to the *roof* where he can do *no further damage* to your *father's equipment.*
But *what* if you did *damage* to *him?!*
My poor dog!
ROOF
Hamster.
Whatever!
You have *nothing* to *fear.*
It would take *enormous force* to *shatter* the *containment sphere.*

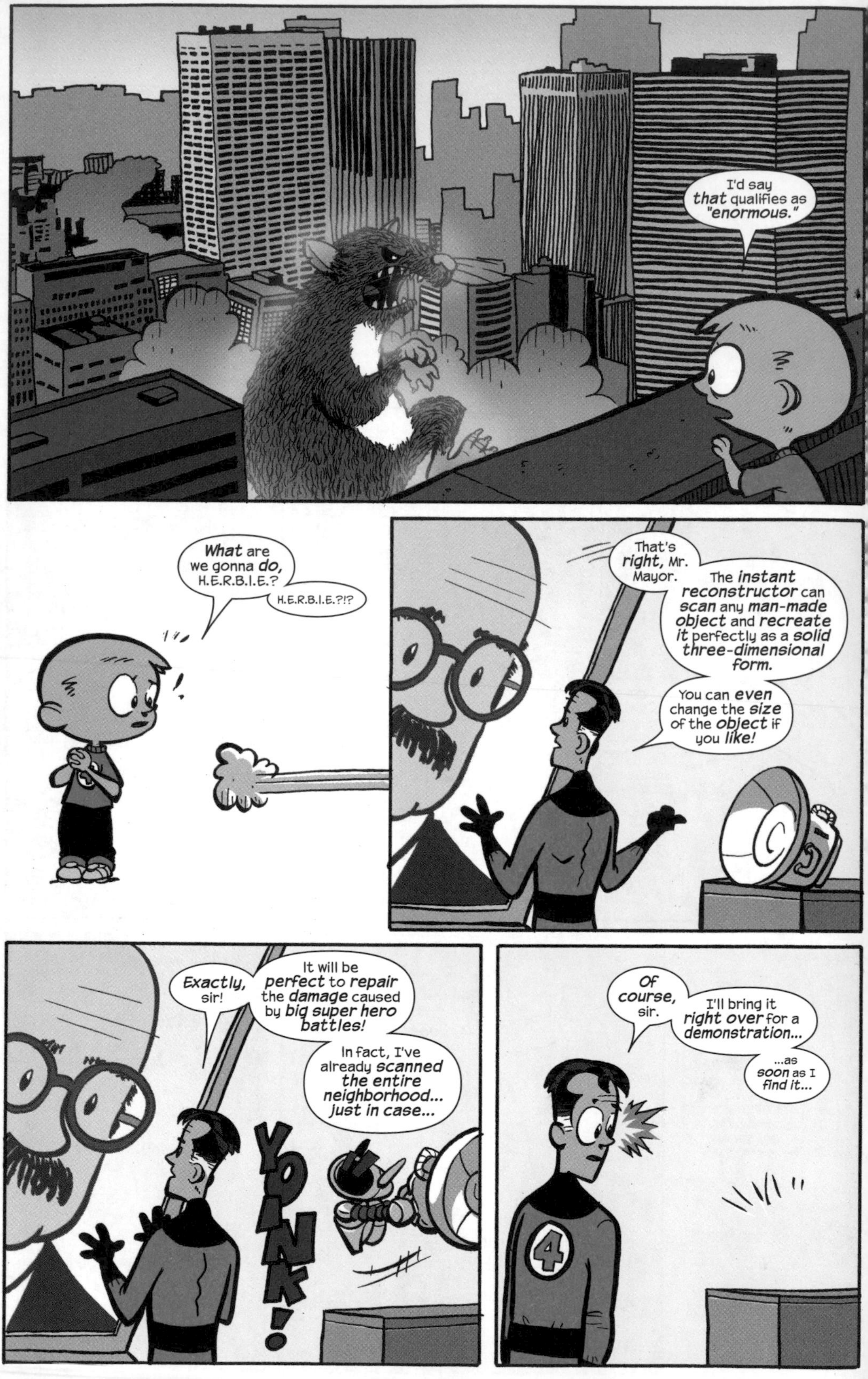
I'd say *that* qualifies as *"enormous."*
What are we gonna *do,* H.E.R.B.I.E.?
H.E.R.B.I.E.?!?
That's *right,* Mr. Mayor.
The *instant reconstructor* can *scan* any *man-made object* and *recreate it* perfectly as a *solid three-dimensional form.*
You can *even* change the *size* of the *object* if you *like!*
Exactly, sir!
It will be *perfect* to *repair* the *damage* caused by *big super hero battles!*
In fact, I've already *scanned the entire neighborhood... just in case...*
YOINK!
Of course, sir.
I'll bring it *right over* for a *demonstration...*
...as *soon* as I *find it...*

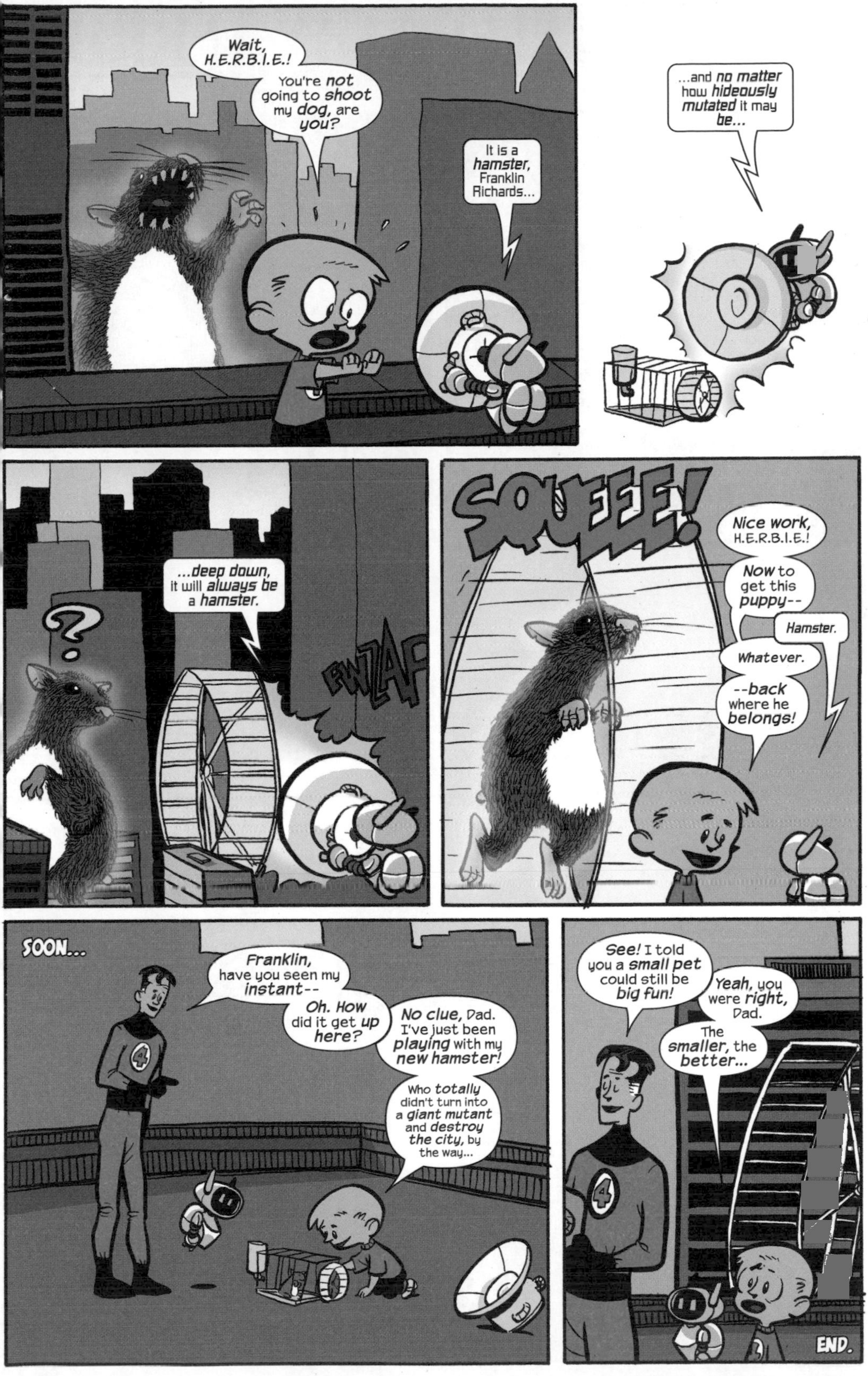
Wait, H.E.R.B.I.E.!
You're not going to shoot my dog, are you?
It is a hamster, Franklin Richards...
...and no matter how hideously mutated it may be...
...deep down, it will always be a hamster.
?
FWZAP
SQUEEE!
Nice work, H.E.R.B.I.E.!
Now to get this puppy--
Hamster.
Whatever.
--back where he belongs!
SOON...
Franklin, have you seen my instant--
Oh. How did it get up here?
No clue, Dad. I've just been playing with my new hamster!
Who totally didn't turn into a giant mutant and destroy the city, by the way...
See! I told you a small pet could still be big fun!
Yeah, you were right, Dad.
The smaller, the better...
END.

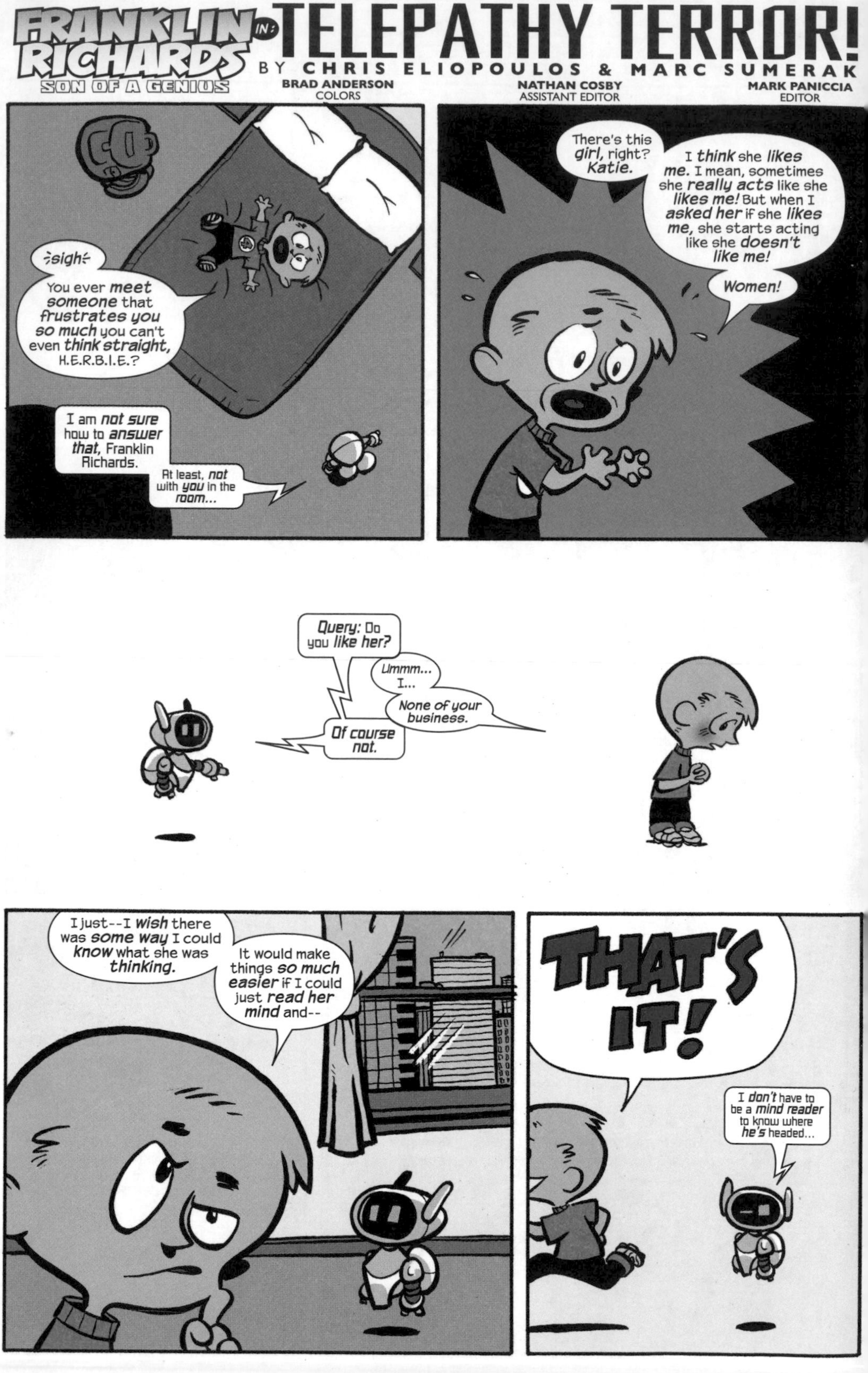
FRANKLIN RICHARDS SON OF A GENIUS IN: TELEPATHY TERROR!
BY CHRIS ELIOPOULOS & MARC SUMERAK
BRAD ANDERSON COLORS
NATHAN COSBY ASSISTANT EDITOR
MARK PANICCIA EDITOR
sigh
You ever meet someone that frustrates you so much you can't even think straight, H.E.R.B.I.E.?
I am not sure how to answer that, Franklin Richards.
At least, not with you in the room...
There's this girl, right? Katie.
I think she likes me. I mean, sometimes she really acts like she likes me! But when I asked her if she likes me, she starts acting like she doesn't like me!
Women!
Query: Do you like her?
Ummm... I...
None of your business.
Of course not.
I just--I wish there was some way I could know what she was thinking.
It would make things so much easier if I could just read her mind and--
THAT'S IT!
I don't have to be a mind reader to know where he's headed...

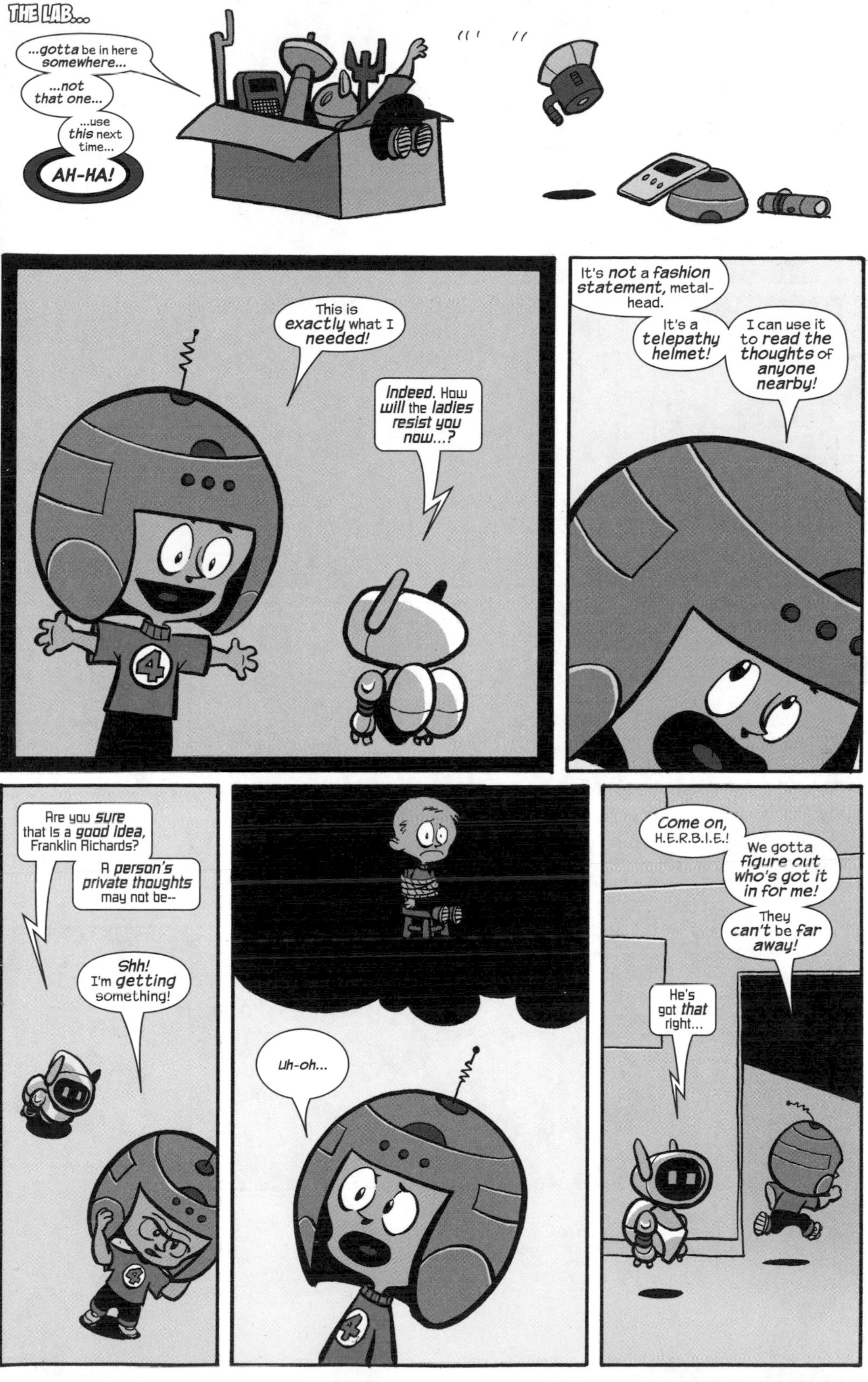
THE LAB...
...gotta be in here somewhere...
...not that one...
...use this next time...
AH-HA!
This is exactly what I needed!
Indeed. How will the ladies resist you now...?
It's not a fashion statement, metal-head.
It's a telepathy helmet!
I can use it to read the thoughts of anyone nearby!
Are you sure that is a good idea, Franklin Richards?
A person's private thoughts may not be--
Shh! I'm getting something!
Uh-oh...
Come on, H.E.R.B.I.E.!
We gotta figure out who's got it in for me!
They can't be far away!
He's got that right...

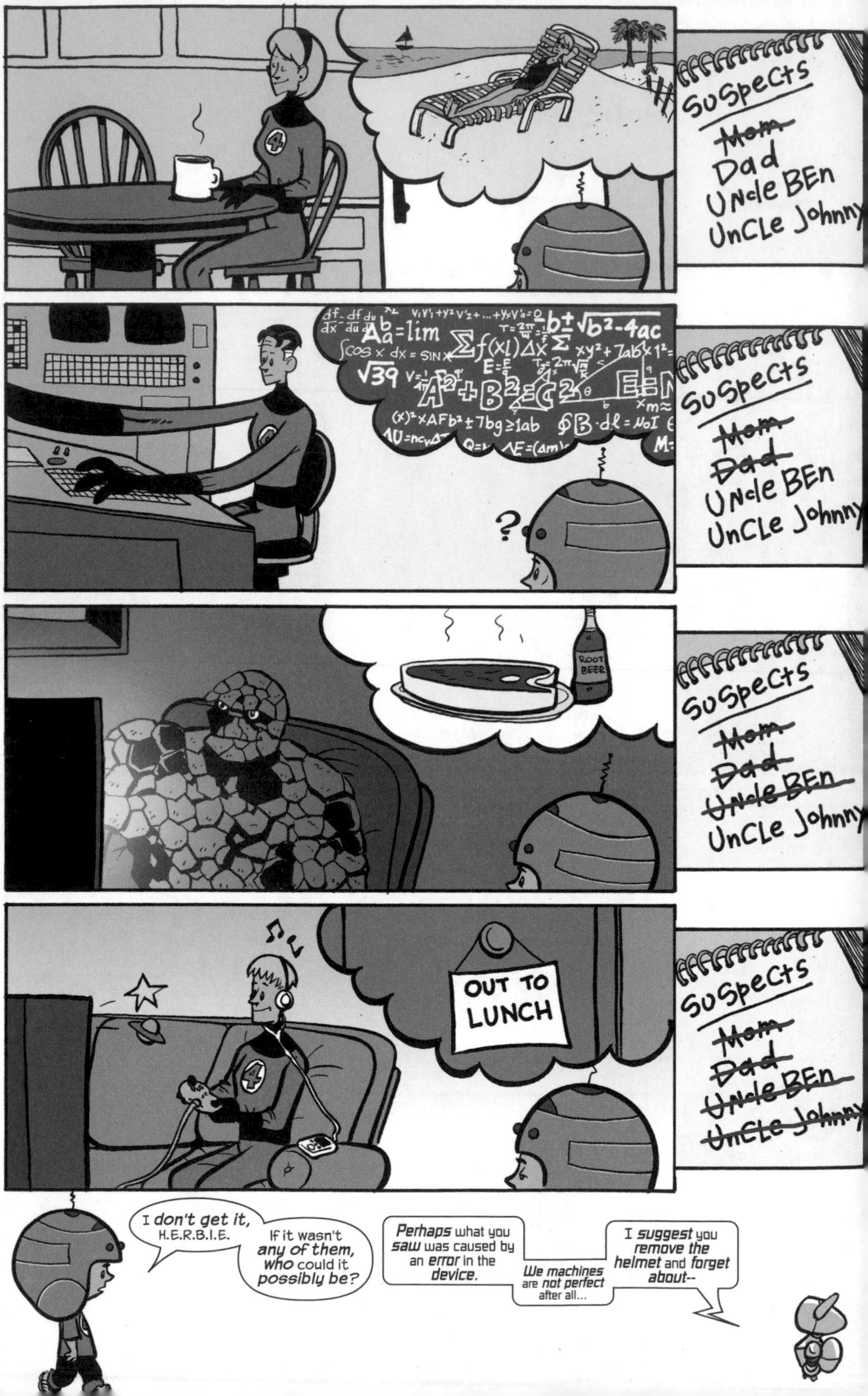

SUSPECTS
~~Mom~~
Dad
Uncle BEn
Uncle Johnny
SUSPECTS
~~Mom~~
~~Dad~~
Uncle BEn
Uncle Johnny
ROOT BEER
SUSPECTS
~~Mom~~
~~Dad~~
~~Uncle BEn~~
Uncle Johnny
OUT TO LUNCH
SUSPECTS
~~Mom~~
~~Dad~~
~~Uncle BEn~~
~~Uncle Johnny~~
I *don't get it*, H.E.R.B.I.E.
If it wasn't *any of them*, *who* could it *possibly be?*
Perhaps what you *saw* was caused by an *error* in the *device*.
We machines are *not perfect* after all...
I *suggest* you *remove the helmet* and *forget about--*

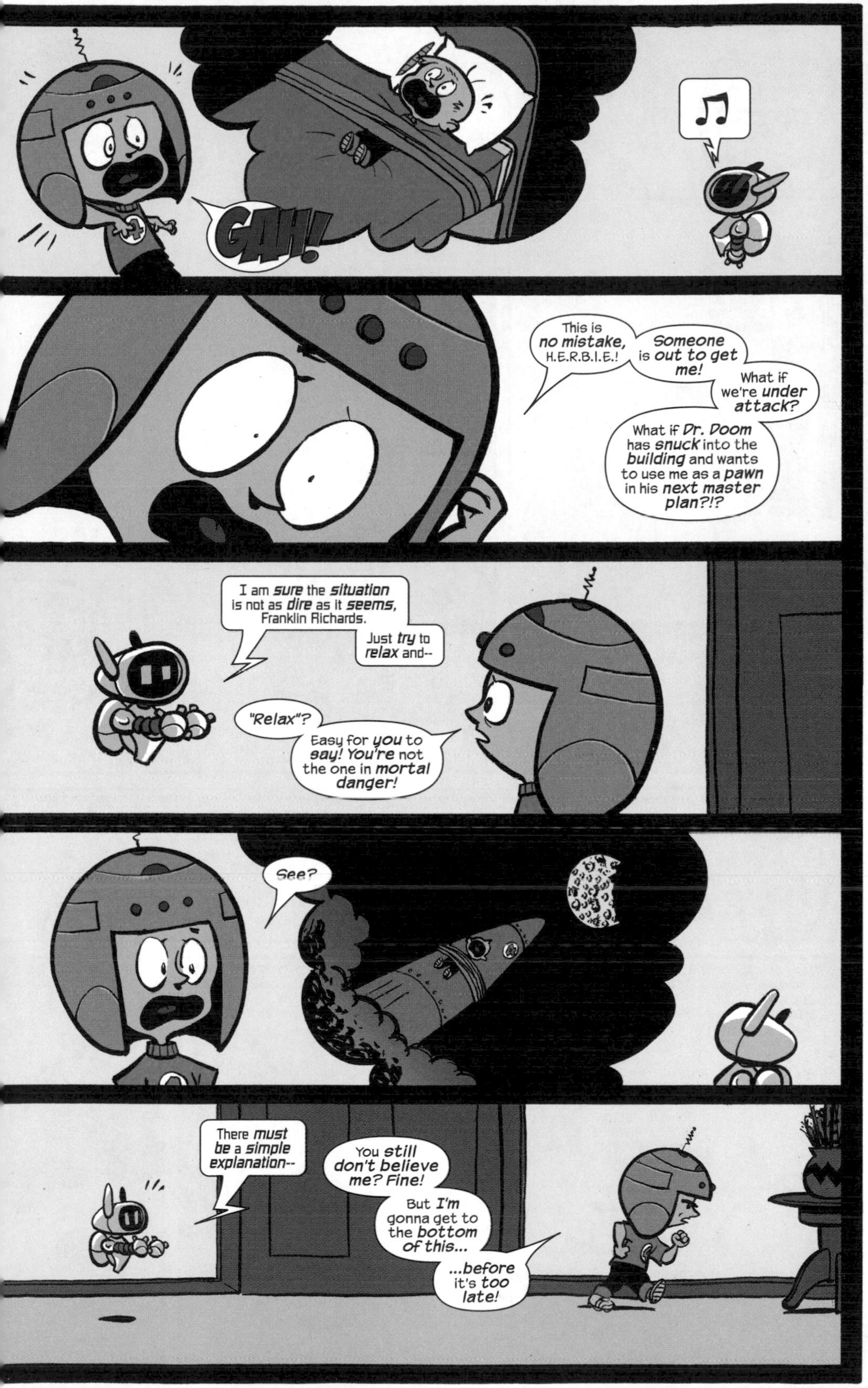

♫
GAH!
This is no mistake, H.E.R.B.I.E.!
Someone is out to get me!
What if we're under attack?
What if Dr. Doom has snuck into the building and wants to use me as a pawn in his next master plan?!?
I am sure the situation is not as dire as it seems, Franklin Richards.
Just try to relax and--
"Relax"?
Easy for you to say! You're not the one in mortal danger!
See?
There must be a simple explanation--
You still don't believe me? Fine!
But I'm gonna get to the bottom of this...
...before it's too late!

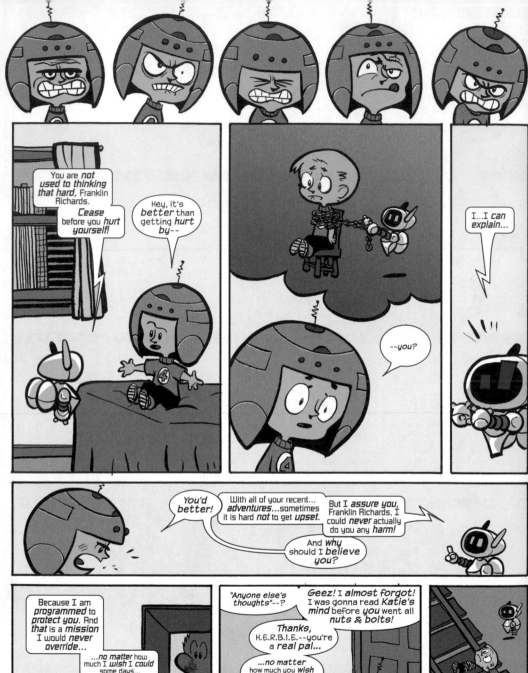

You are *not used to* thinking that *hard,* Franklin Richards. *Cease* before you *hurt yourself!*

Hey, it's *better* than getting *hurt by*--

I...I *can* explain...

--*you?*

You'd *better!*

With all of your recent... *adventures*...sometimes it is hard *not* to get *upset.* But I *assure you,* Franklin Richards, I could *never* actually do you any *harm!*

And *why* should I *believe you?*

Because I am *programmed* to *protect you.* And *that* is a *mission* I would *never* override...

...no matter how much I *wish* I *could* some days...

But now *maybe* you'll *think twice* before *reading* anyone else's *thoughts.*

"Anyone else's thoughts"--?

Geez! I almost forgot! I was gonna read *Katie's mind* before *you* went all *nuts & bolts!*

Thanks, H.E.R.B.I.E.--you're a *real pal...*

...no matter how much you *wish* you *weren't* some days...

END.

FRANKLIN RICHARDS SON OF A GENIUS IN: SPEED DEMON

BY CHRIS ELIOPOULOS & MARC SUMERAK

BRAD ANDERSON COLORS
NATHAN COSBY ASSISTANT EDITOR
MARK PANICCIA EDITOR

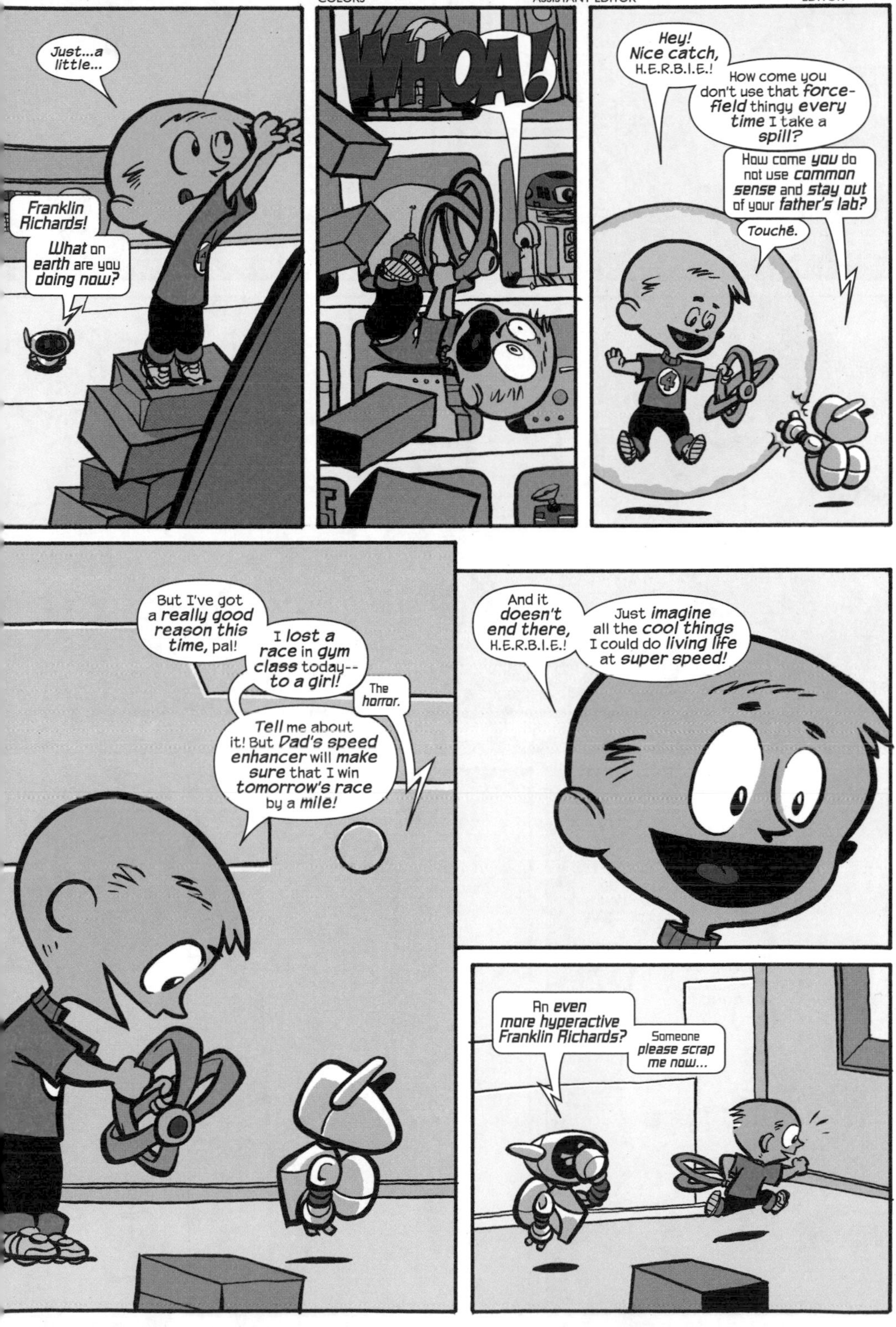

Just...a little...
Franklin Richards!
What on earth are you doing now?
WHOA!
Hey! Nice catch, H.E.R.B.I.E.!
How come you don't use that force-field thingy every time I take a spill?
How come you do not use common sense and stay out of your father's lab?
Touché.
But I've got a really good reason this time, pal!
I lost a race in gym class today--to a girl!
The horror.
Tell me about it! But Dad's speed enhancer will make sure that I win tomorrow's race by a mile!
And it doesn't end there, H.E.R.B.I.E.!
Just imagine all the cool things I could do living life at super speed!
An even more hyperactive Franklin Richards?
Someone please scrap me now...

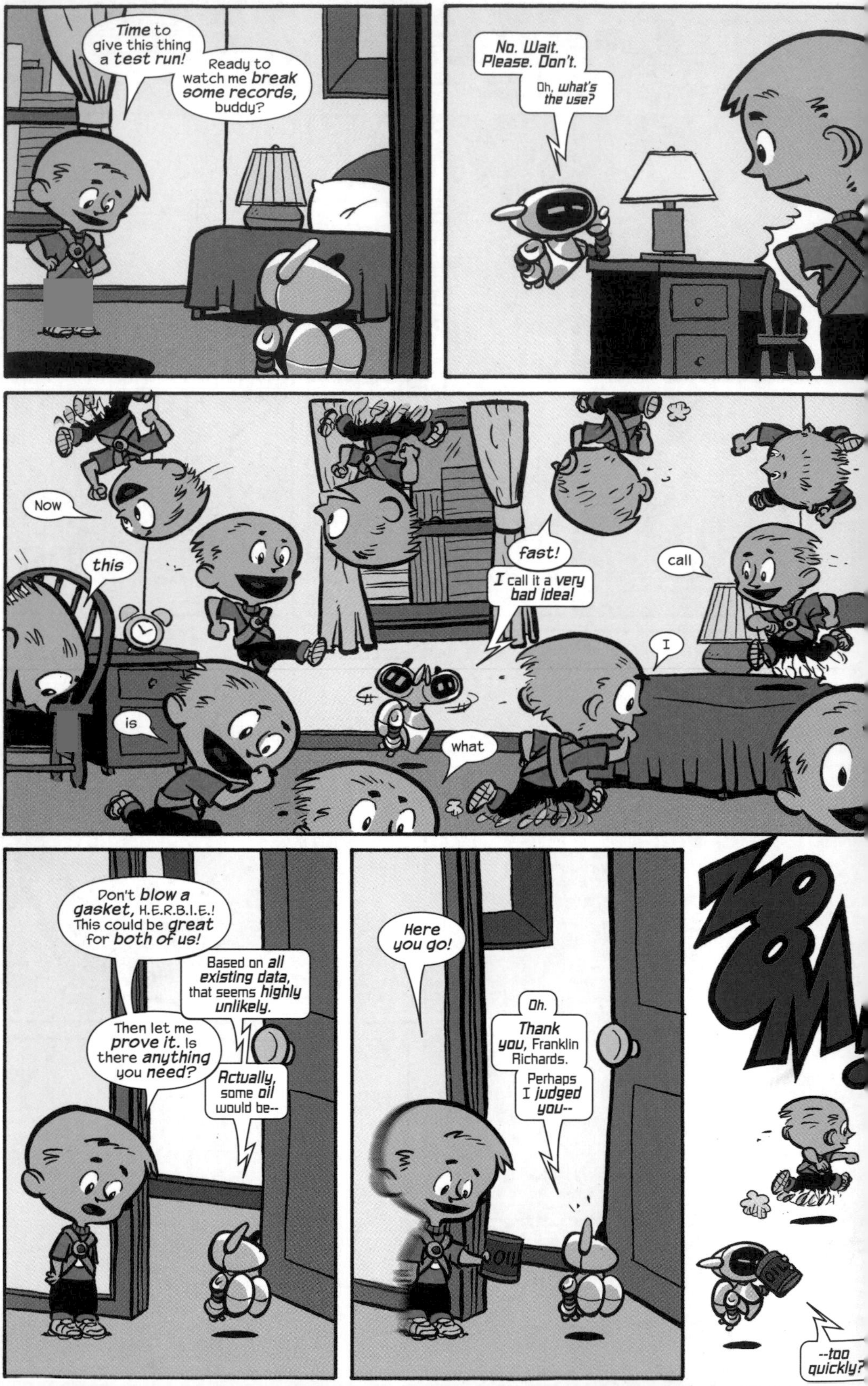

Time to give this thing a test run!
Ready to watch me break some records, buddy?
No. Wait. Please. Don't.
Oh, what's the use?
Now
this
is
what
I
call
fast!
I call it a very bad idea!
Don't blow a gasket, H.E.R.B.I.E.! This could be great for both of us!
Based on all existing data, that seems highly unlikely.
Then let me prove it. Is there anything you need?
Actually, some oil would be--
Here you go!
Oh.
Thank you, Franklin Richards.
Perhaps I judged you--
ZOOM!
OIL
--too quickly?

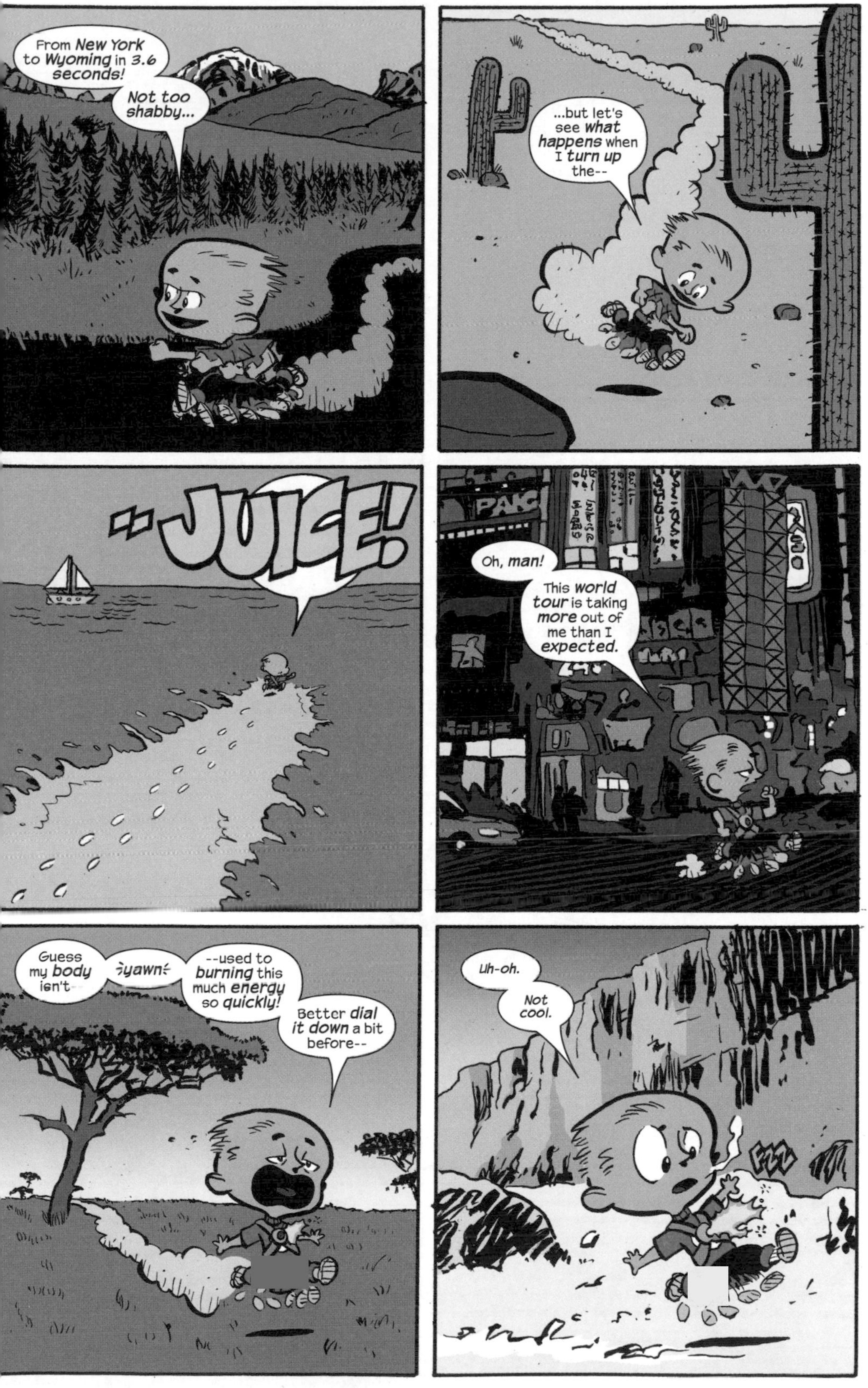

From New York to Wyoming in 3.6 seconds!
Not too shabby...
...but let's see what happens when I turn up the--
--JUICE!
Oh, man!
This world tour is taking more out of me than I expected.
Guess my body isn't--
yawn
--used to burning this much energy so quickly!
Better dial it down a bit before--
Uh-oh.
Not cool.

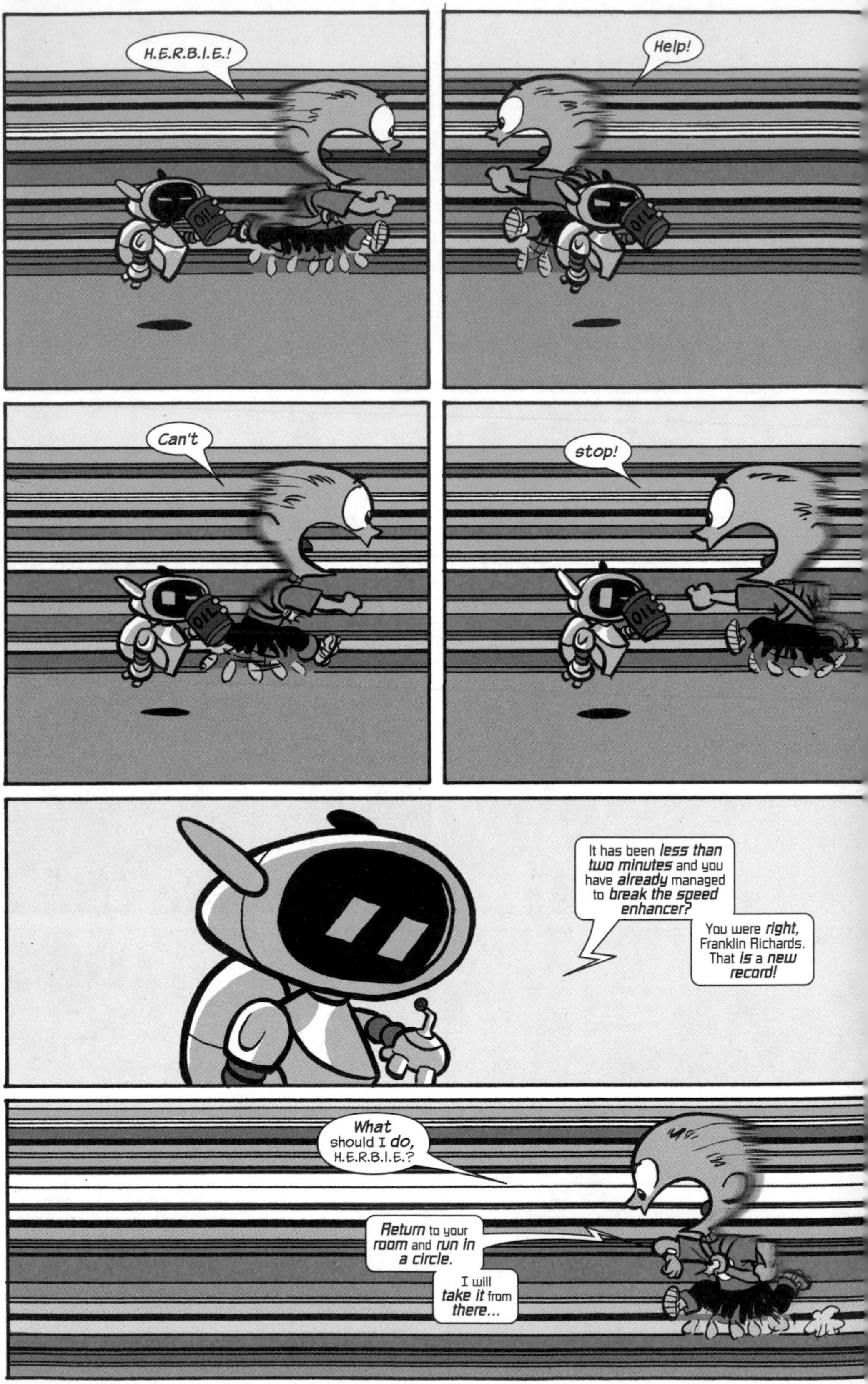
H.E.R.B.I.E.!
Help!
Can't
stop!
It has been less than two minutes and you have already managed to break the speed enhancer?
You were right, Franklin Richards. That is a new record!
What should I do, H.E.R.B.I.E.?
Return to your room and run in a circle.
I will take it from there...

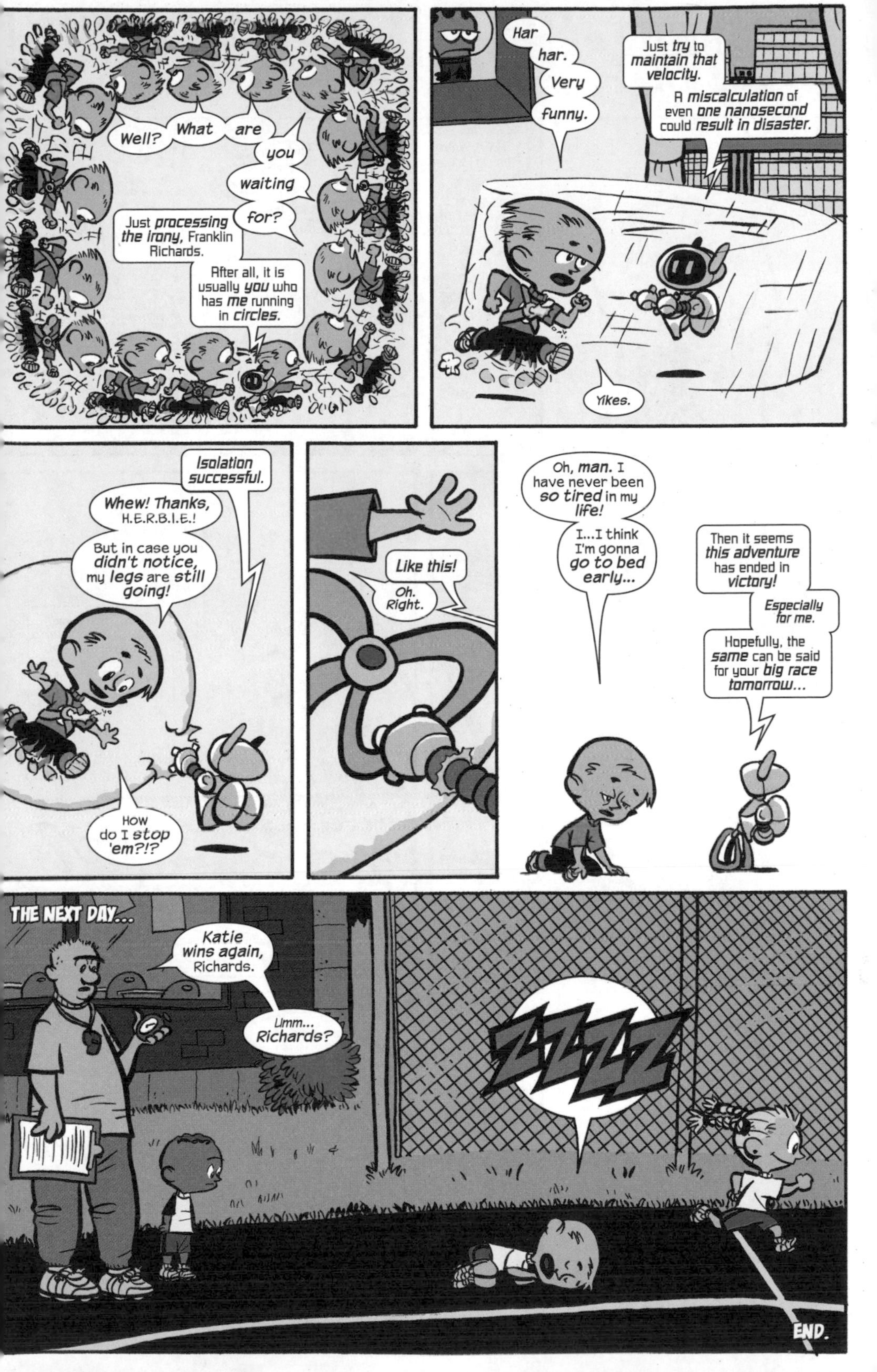
Well?
What
are
you
waiting
for?
Just processing the irony, Franklin Richards.
After all, it is usually you who has me running in circles.
Har
har.
Very
funny.
Just try to maintain that velocity.
A miscalculation of even one nanosecond could result in disaster.
Yikes.
Isolation successful.
Whew! Thanks, H.E.R.B.I.E.!
But in case you didn't notice, my legs are still going!
How do I stop 'em?!?
Like this!
Oh. Right.
Oh, man. I have never been so tired in my life!
I...I think I'm gonna go to bed early...
Then it seems this adventure has ended in victory!
Especially for me.
Hopefully, the same can be said for your big race tomorrow...
THE NEXT DAY...
Katie wins again, Richards.
Umm... Richards?
ZZZZ
END.

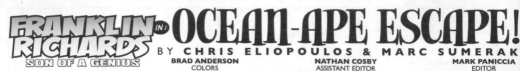

FRANKLIN RICHARDS SON OF A GENIUS IN: OCEAN-APE ESCAPE!

BY CHRIS ELIOPOULOS & MARC SUMERAK

BRAD ANDERSON COLORS · NATHAN COSBY ASSISTANT EDITOR · MARK PANICCIA EDITOR

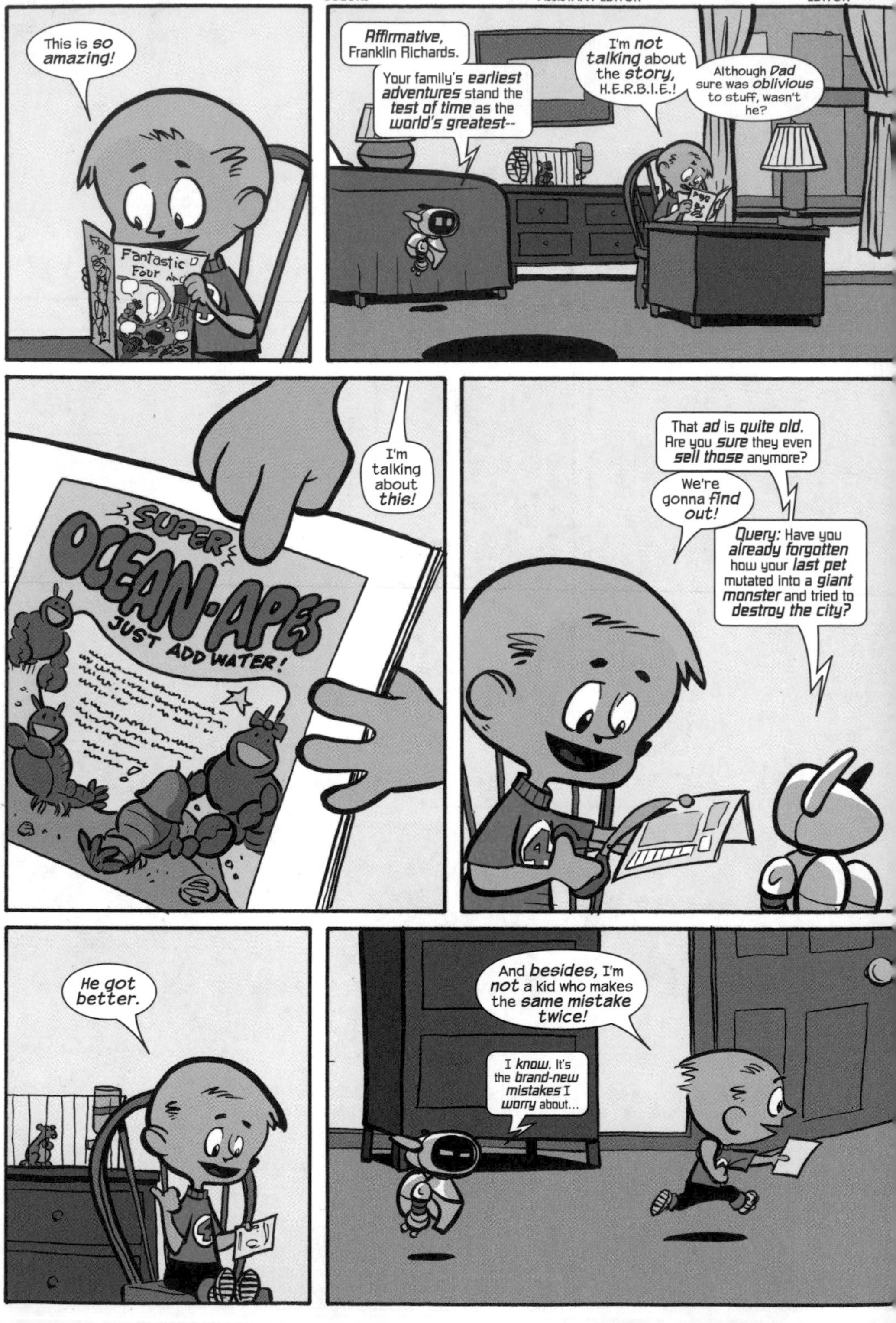

This is so amazing!
Fantastic Four
Affirmative, Franklin Richards.
Your family's earliest adventures stand the test of time as the world's greatest--
I'm not talking about the story, H.E.R.B.I.E.!
Although Dad sure was oblivious to stuff, wasn't he?
I'm talking about this!
SUPER OCEAN-APES JUST ADD WATER!
That ad is quite old. Are you sure they even sell those anymore?
We're gonna find out!
Query: Have you already forgotten how your last pet mutated into a giant monster and tried to destroy the city?
He got better.
And besides, I'm not a kid who makes the same mistake twice!
I know. It's the brand-new mistakes I worry about...

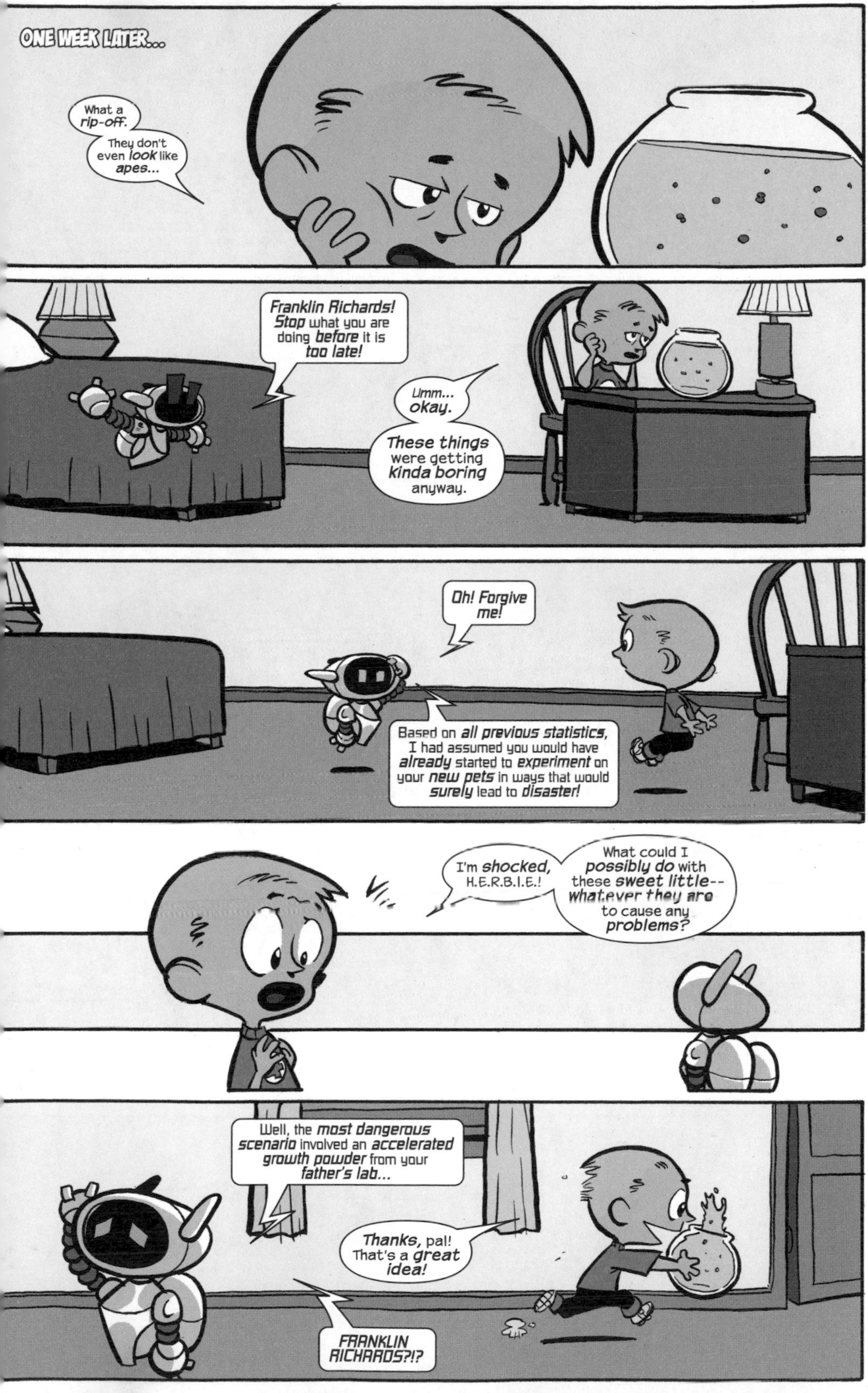
ONE WEEK LATER...
What a rip-off. They don't even look like apes...
Franklin Richards! Stop what you are doing before it is too late!
Umm... okay.
These things were getting kinda boring anyway.
Oh! Forgive me!
Based on all previous statistics, I had assumed you would have already started to experiment on your new pets in ways that would surely lead to disaster!
I'm shocked, H.E.R.B.I.E.!
What could I possibly do with these sweet little--whatever they are to cause any problems?
Well, the most dangerous scenario involved an accelerated growth powder from your father's lab...
Thanks, pal! That's a great idea!
FRANKLIN RICHARDS?!?

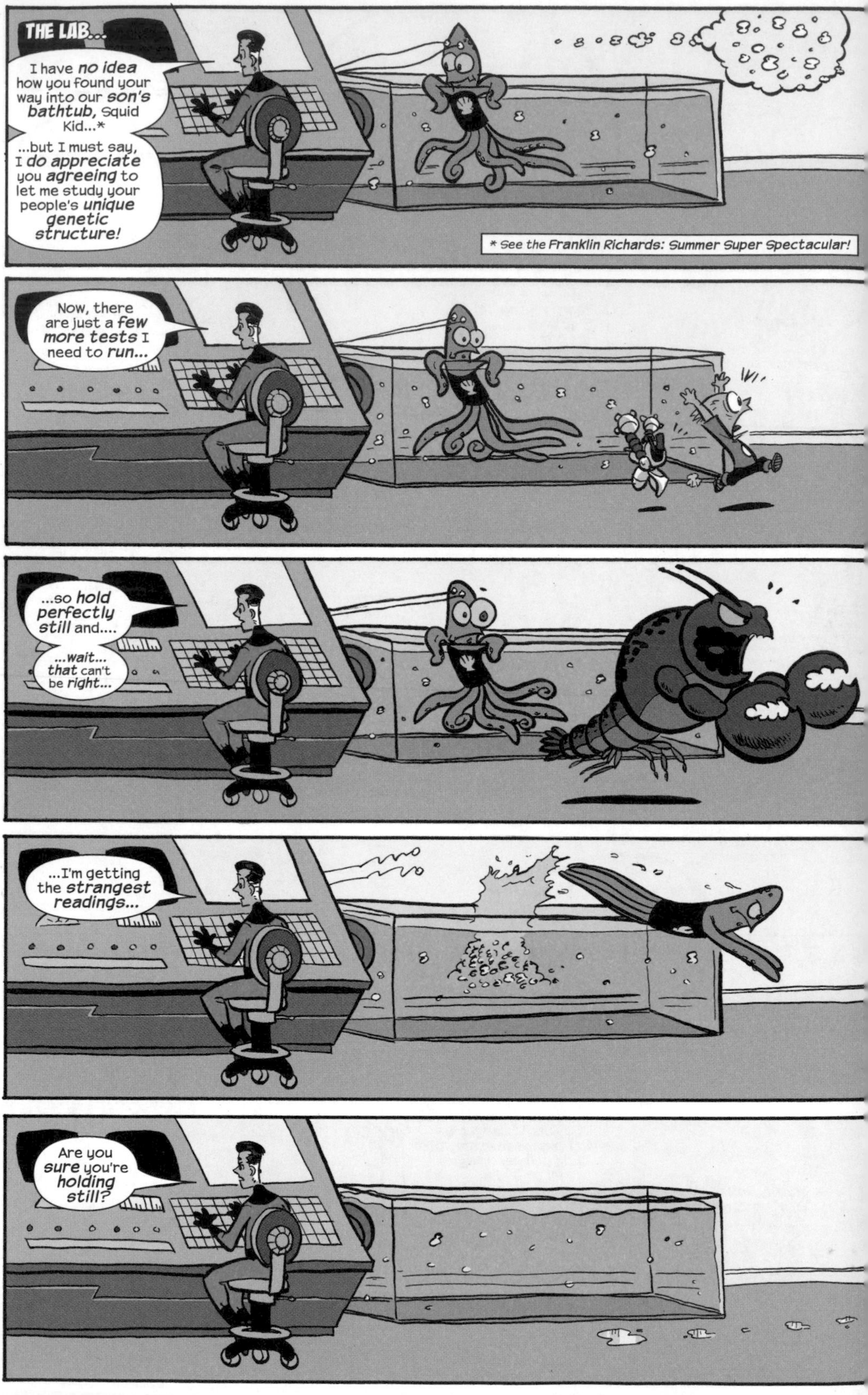
THE LAB...
I have no idea how you found your way into our son's bathtub, Squid Kid...*
...but I must say, I do appreciate you agreeing to let me study your people's unique genetic structure!
* See the Franklin Richards: Summer Super Spectacular!
Now, there are just a few more tests I need to run...
...so hold perfectly still and....
...wait... that can't be right...
...I'm getting the strangest readings...
Are you sure you're holding still?

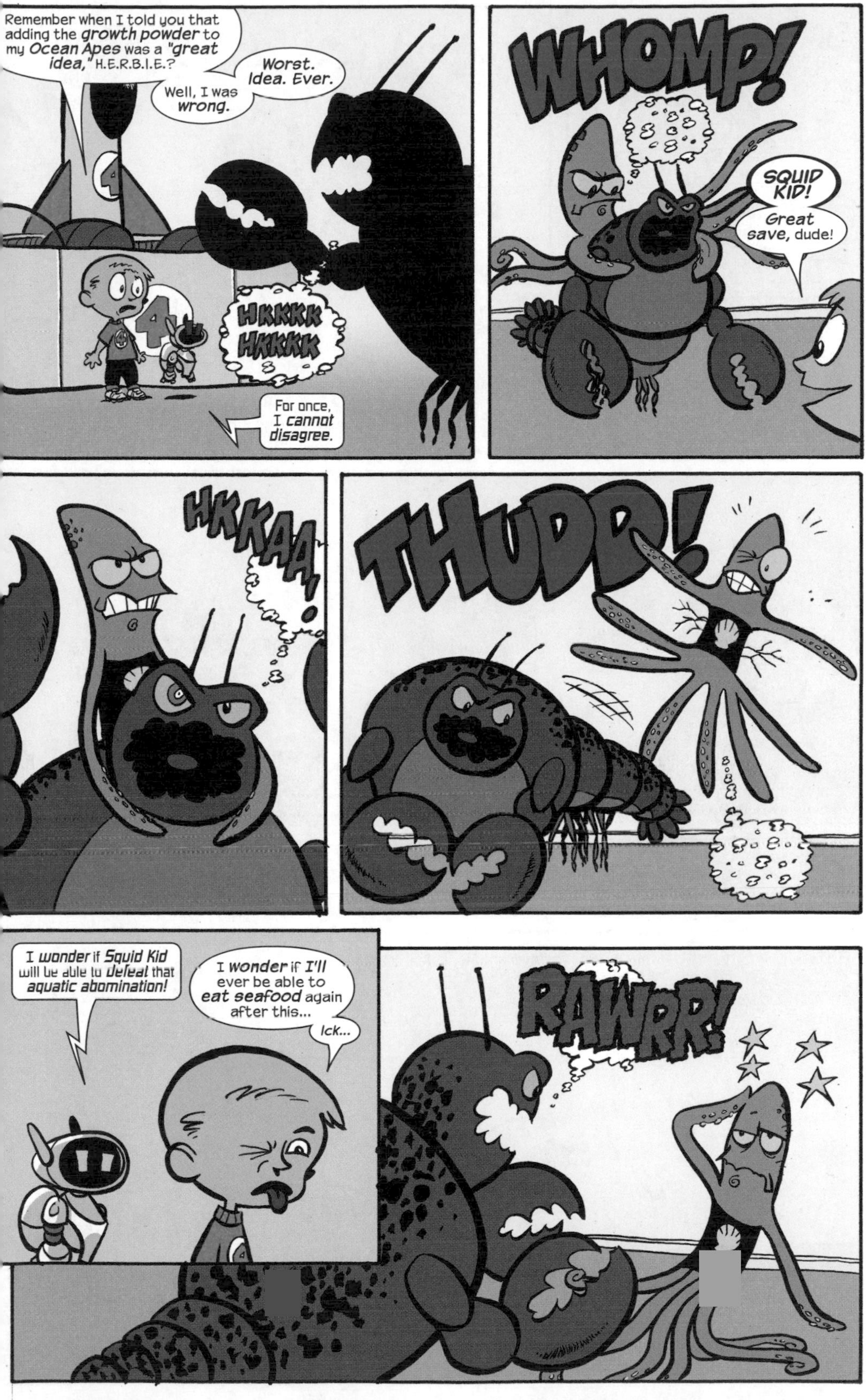

Remember when I told you that adding the growth powder to my Ocean Apes was a "great idea," H.E.R.B.I.E.?
Well, I was wrong.
Worst. Idea. Ever.
HKKKK HKKKK
For once, I cannot disagree.
WHOMP!
SQUID KID!
Great save, dude!
HKKAA!
THUDD!
I wonder if Squid Kid will be able to defeat that aquatic abomination!
I wonder if I'll ever be able to eat seafood again after this...
Ick...
RAWRR!

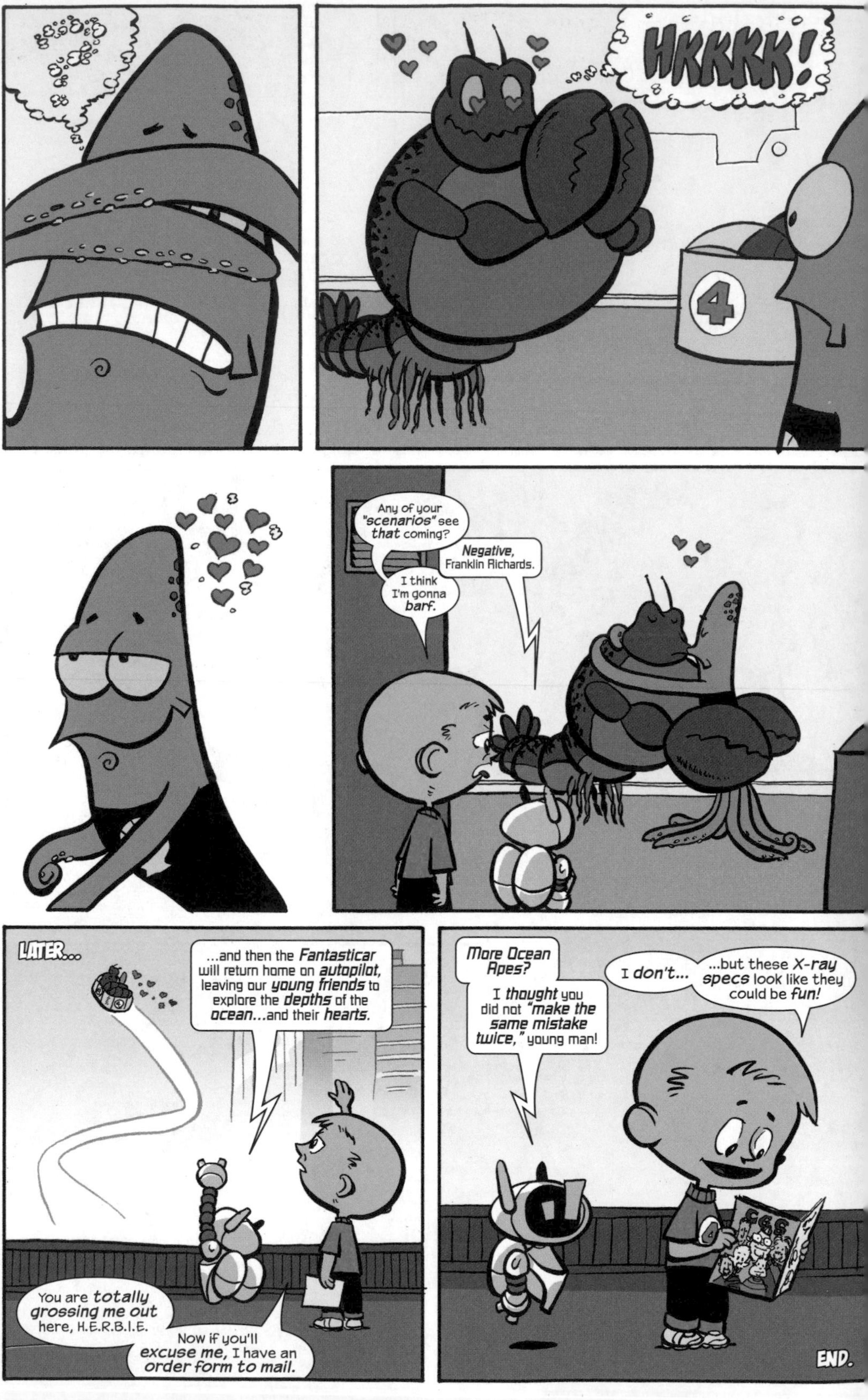
HKKKK!
Any of your "scenarios" see that coming?
Negative, Franklin Richards.
I think I'm gonna barf.
LATER...
...and then the Fantasticar will return home on autopilot, leaving our young friends to explore the depths of the ocean...and their hearts.
You are totally grossing me out here, H.E.R.B.I.E.
Now if you'll excuse me, I have an order form to mail.
More Ocean Apes?
I thought you did not "make the same mistake twice," young man!
I don't...
...but these X-ray specs look like they could be fun!
END.

FRANKLIN RICHARDS SON OF A GENIUS IN: TURKEY TROUBLE!

BY CHRIS ELIOPOULOS & MARC SUMERAK

BRAD ANDERSON COLORS

NATHAN COSBY ASSISTANT EDITOR

MARK PANICCIA EDITOR

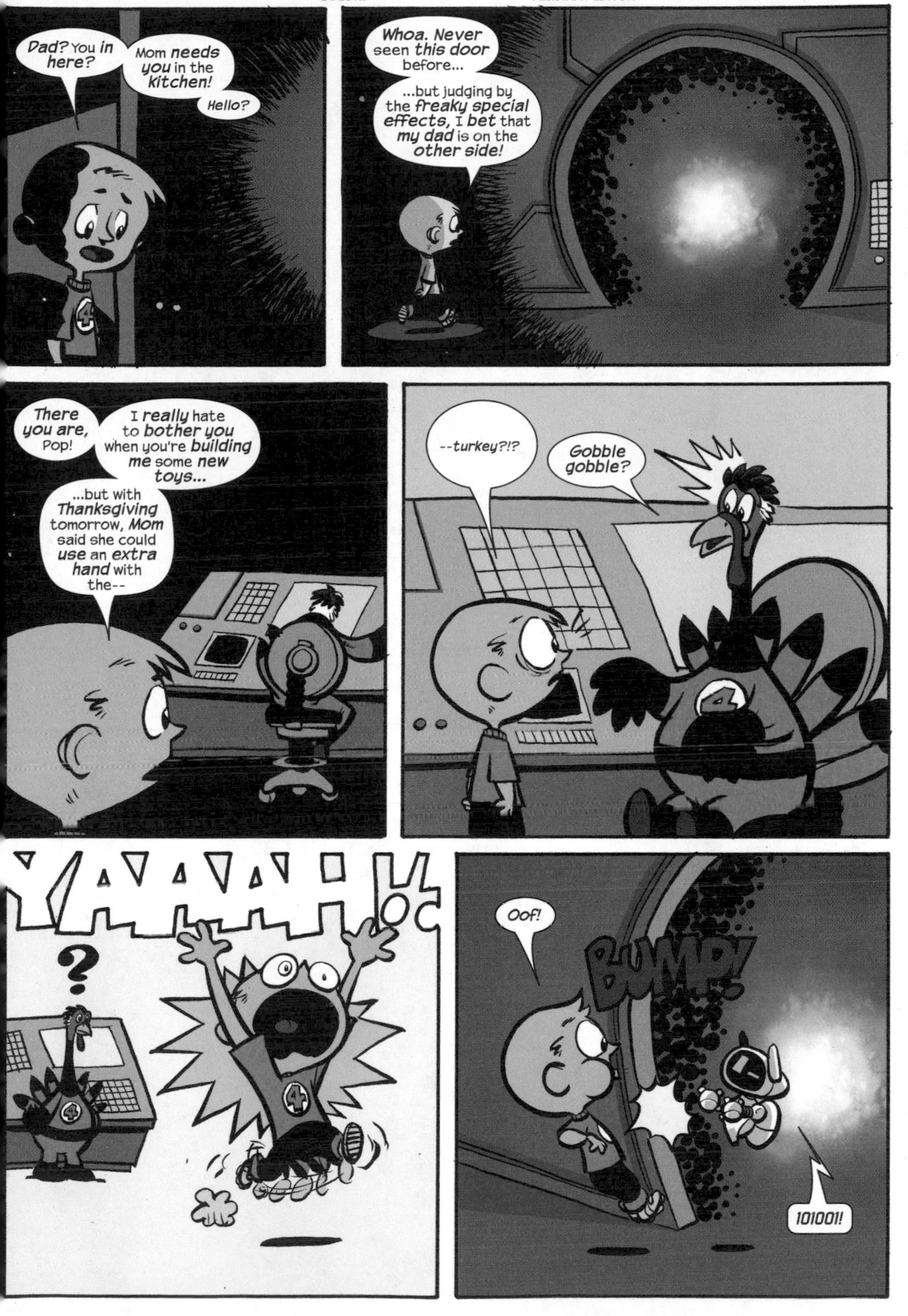

Dad? You in here?
Mom needs you in the kitchen!
Hello?
Whoa. Never seen this door before...
...but judging by the freaky special effects, I bet that my dad is on the other side!
There you are, Pop!
I really hate to bother you when you're building me some new toys...
...but with Thanksgiving tomorrow, Mom said she could use an extra hand with the--
--turkey?!?
Gobble gobble?
?
Oof!
BUMP!
101001!

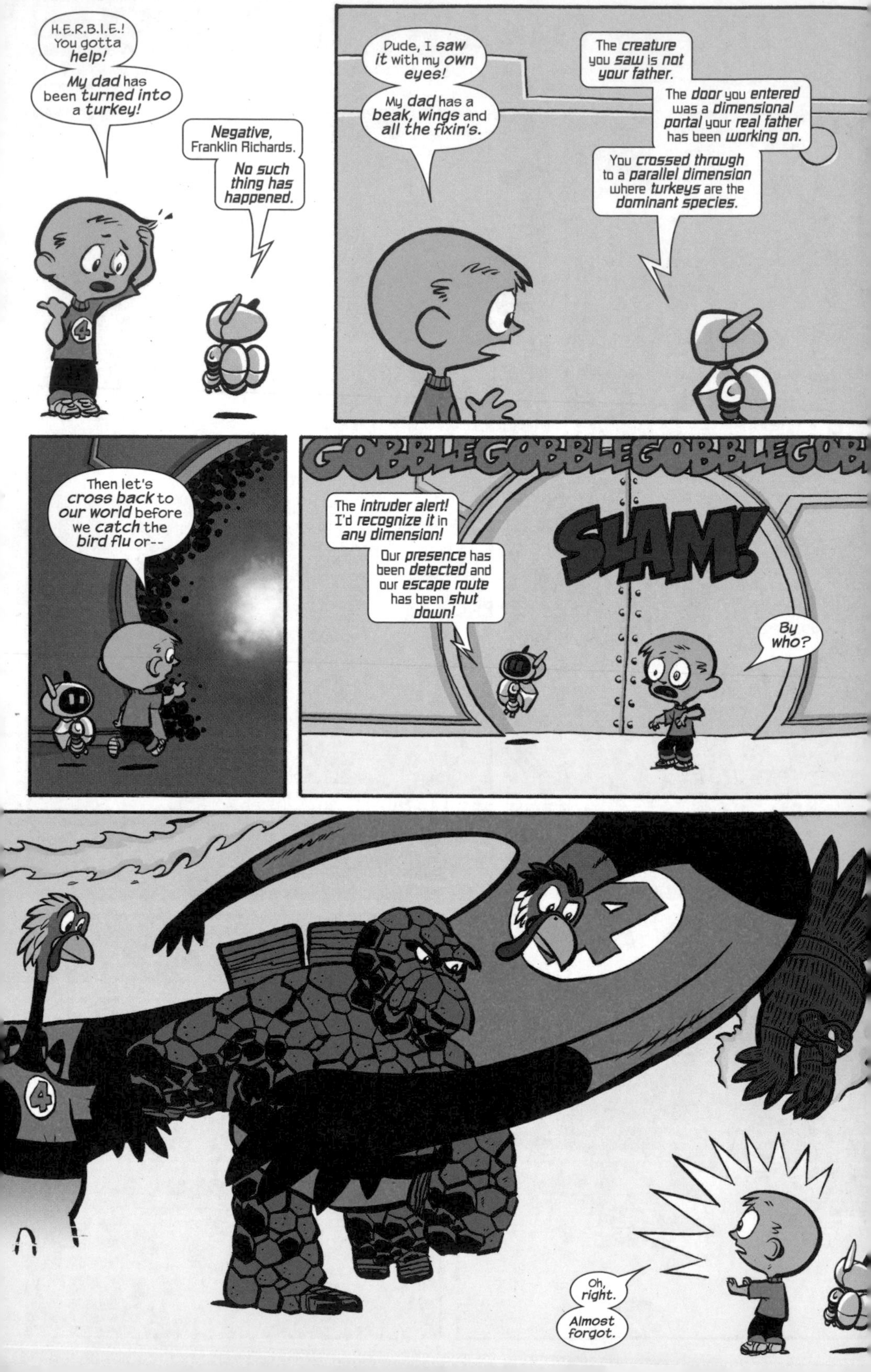
H.E.R.B.I.E.! You gotta help!
My dad has been turned into a turkey!
Negative, Franklin Richards.
No such thing has happened.
Dude, I saw it with my own eyes!
My dad has a beak, wings and all the fixin's.
The creature you saw is not your father.
The door you entered was a dimensional portal your real father has been working on.
You crossed through to a parallel dimension where turkeys are the dominant species.
Then let's cross back to our world before we catch the bird flu or--
GOBBLEGOBBLEGOBBLEGOB
The intruder alert! I'd recognize it in any dimension!
SLAM!
Our presence has been detected and our escape route has been shut down!
By who?
Oh, right.
Almost forgot.

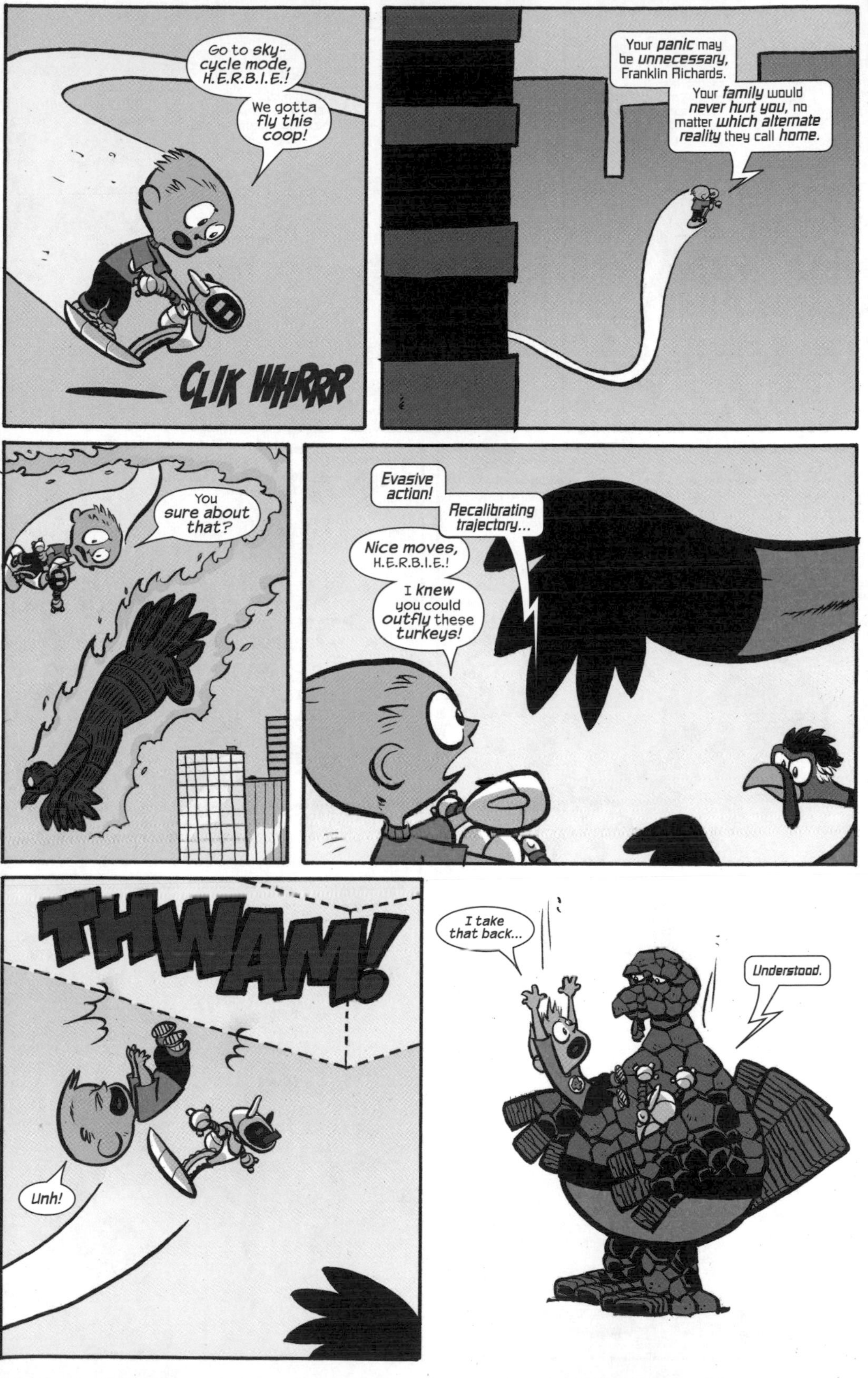

Go to sky-cycle mode, H.E.R.B.I.E.!
We gotta fly this coop!
CLIK WHRRR
Your panic may be unnecessary, Franklin Richards.
Your family would never hurt you, no matter which alternate reality they call home.
You sure about that?
Evasive action!
Recalibrating trajectory...
Nice moves, H.E.R.B.I.E.!
I knew you could outfly these turkeys!
THWAM!
Unh!
I take that back...
Understood.

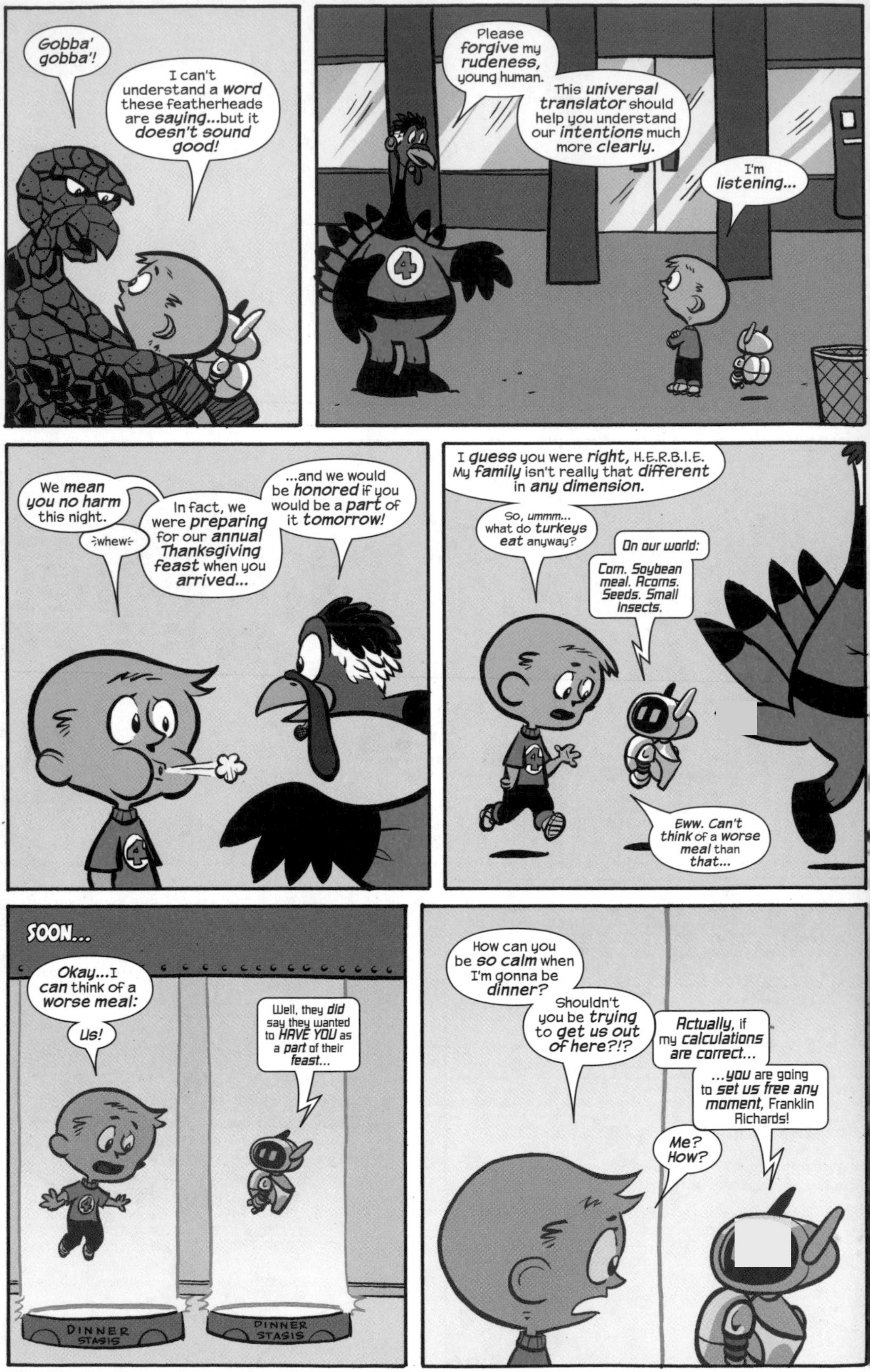
Gobba' gobba'!
I can't understand a word these featherheads are saying...but it doesn't sound good!
Please forgive my rudeness, young human.
This universal translator should help you understand our intentions much more clearly.
I'm listening...
We mean you no harm this night.
In fact, we were preparing for our annual Thanksgiving feast when you arrived...
...and we would be honored if you would be a part of it tomorrow!
whew
I guess you were right, H.E.R.B.I.E. My family isn't really that different in any dimension.
So, ummm... what do turkeys eat anyway?
On our world:
Corn. Soybean meal. Acorns. Seeds. Small insects.
Eww. Can't think of a worse meal than that...
SOON...
Okay...I can think of a worse meal:
Us!
Well, they did say they wanted to HAVE YOU as a part of their feast...
DINNER STASIS
DINNER STASIS
How can you be so calm when I'm gonna be dinner?
Shouldn't you be trying to get us out of here?!?
Actually, if my calculations are correct...
...you are going to set us free any moment, Franklin Richards!
Me? How?

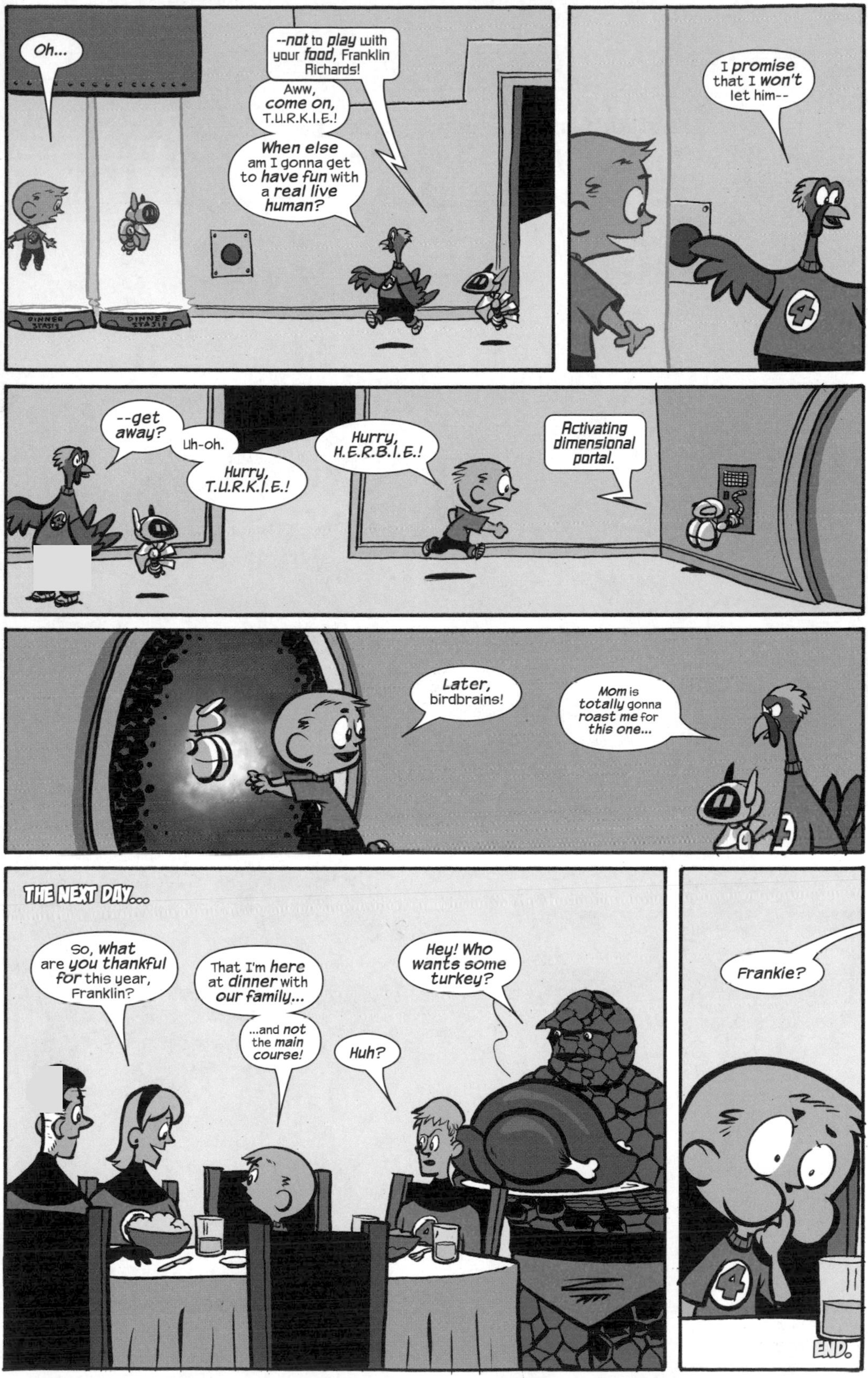

Oh...
--not to play with your food, Franklin Richards!
Aww, come on, T.U.R.K.I.E.!
When else am I gonna get to have fun with a real live human?
DINNER STASIS
DINNER STASIS
I promise that I won't let him--
--get away?
Uh-oh.
Hurry, T.U.R.K.I.E.!
Hurry, H.E.R.B.I.E.!
Activating dimensional portal.
Later, birdbrains!
Mom is totally gonna roast me for this one...
THE NEXT DAY...
So, what are you thankful for this year, Franklin?
That I'm here at dinner with our family...
...and not the main course!
Huh?
Hey! Who wants some turkey?
Frankie?
END.

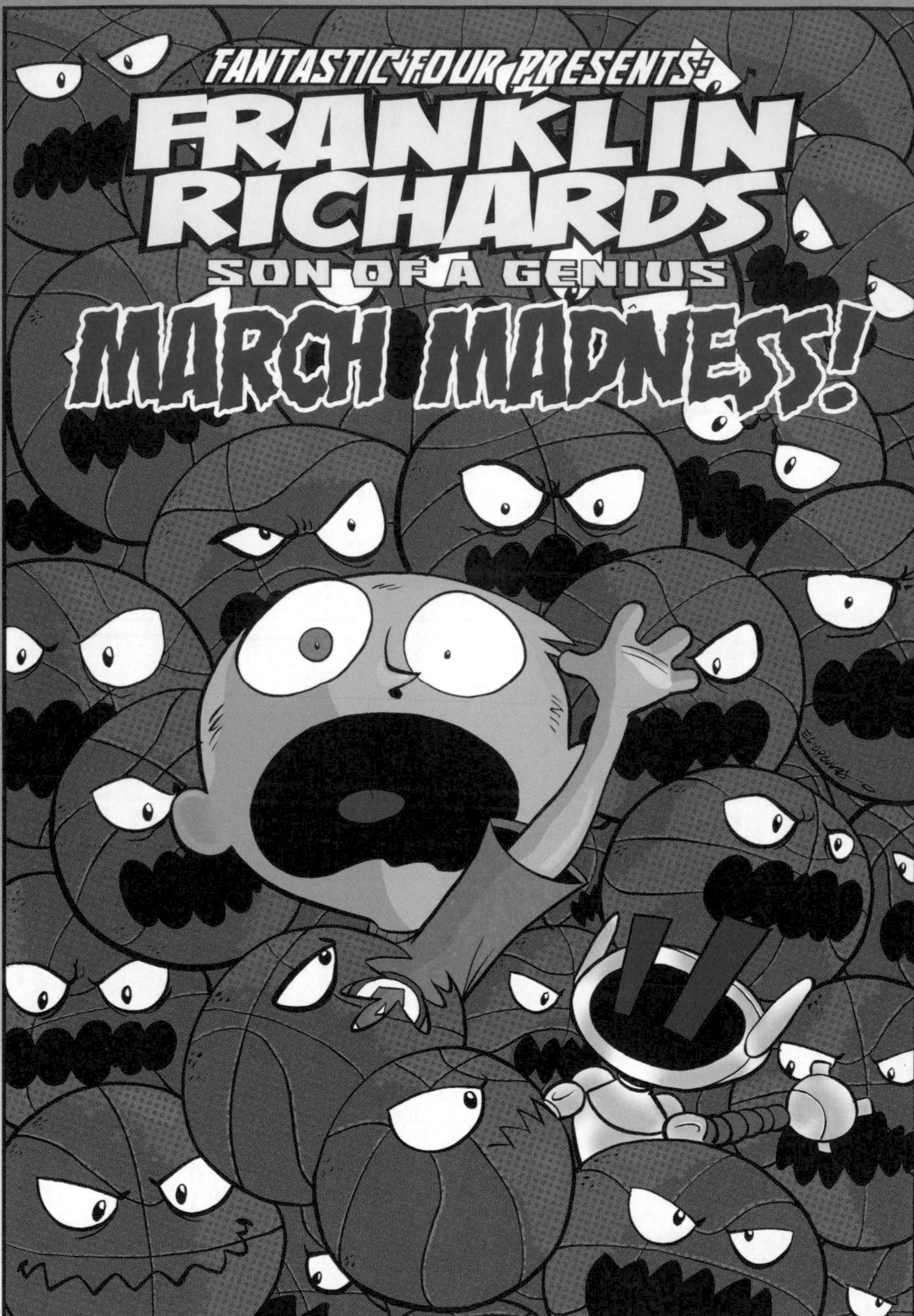
FANTASTIC FOUR PRESENTS:
FRANKLIN RICHARDS
SON OF A GENIUS
MARCH MADNESS!

FANTASTIC FOUR PRESENTS: FRANKLIN RICHARDS
SON OF A GENIUS
MARCH MADNESS!

CHRIS ELIOPOULOS AND MARC SUMERAK
STORY

MARC SUMERAK
SCRIPT

CHRIS ELIOPOULOS
ART & LETTERS

BRAD ANDERSON
COLOR

BRAD JOHANSEN
PRODUCTION

NATHAN COSBY
ASSISTANT EDITOR

MARK PANICCIA
EDITOR

JOE QUESADA
EDITOR IN CHIEF

DAN BUCKLEY
PUBLISHER

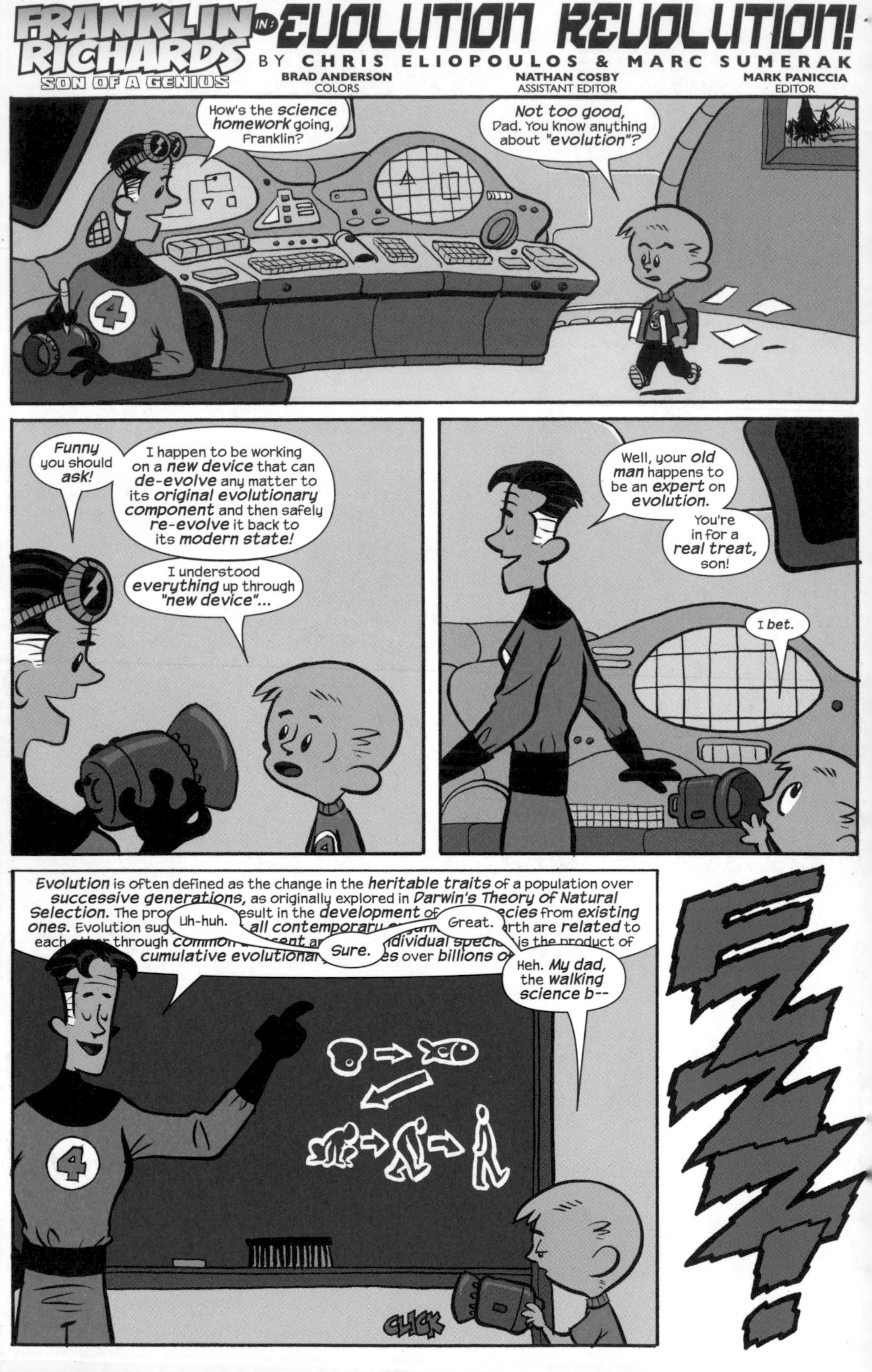

FRANKLIN RICHARDS SON OF A GENIUS
IN: EVOLUTION REVOLUTION!
BY CHRIS ELIOPOULOS & MARC SUMERAK
BRAD ANDERSON COLORS
NATHAN COSBY ASSISTANT EDITOR
MARK PANICCIA EDITOR
How's the science homework going, Franklin?
Not too good, Dad. You know anything about "evolution"?
Funny you should ask!
I happen to be working on a new device that can de-evolve any matter to its original evolutionary component and then safely re-evolve it back to its modern state!
I understood everything up through "new device"...
Well, your old man happens to be an expert on evolution.
You're in for a real treat, son!
I bet.
Evolution is often defined as the change in the heritable traits of a population over successive generations, as originally explored in Darwin's Theory of Natural Selection. The proc esult in the development of ecies from existing ones. Evolution sug all contemporary arth are related to each other through common scent an ndividual specie is the product of cumulative evolutiona es over billions o
Uh-huh.
Great.
Sure.
Heh. My dad, the walking science b--
CLICK
ZZZZT!

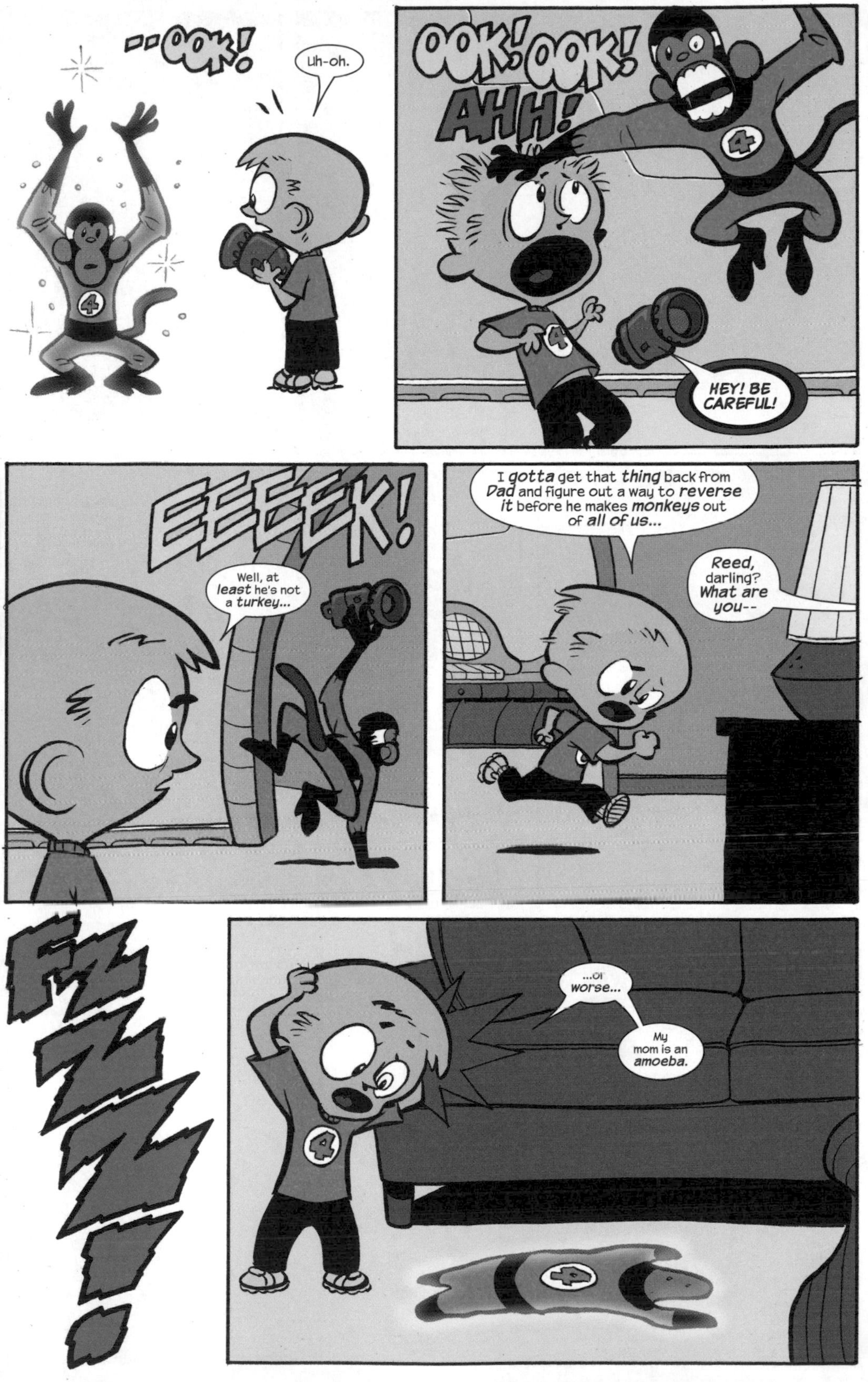
--OOK!
Uh-oh.
OOK! OOK!
AHH!
HEY! BE CAREFUL!
EEEEK!
Well, at least he's not a turkey...
I gotta get that thing back from Dad and figure out a way to reverse it before he makes monkeys out of all of us...
Reed, darling? What are you--
FZZZ!!
...or worse...
My mom is an amoeba.

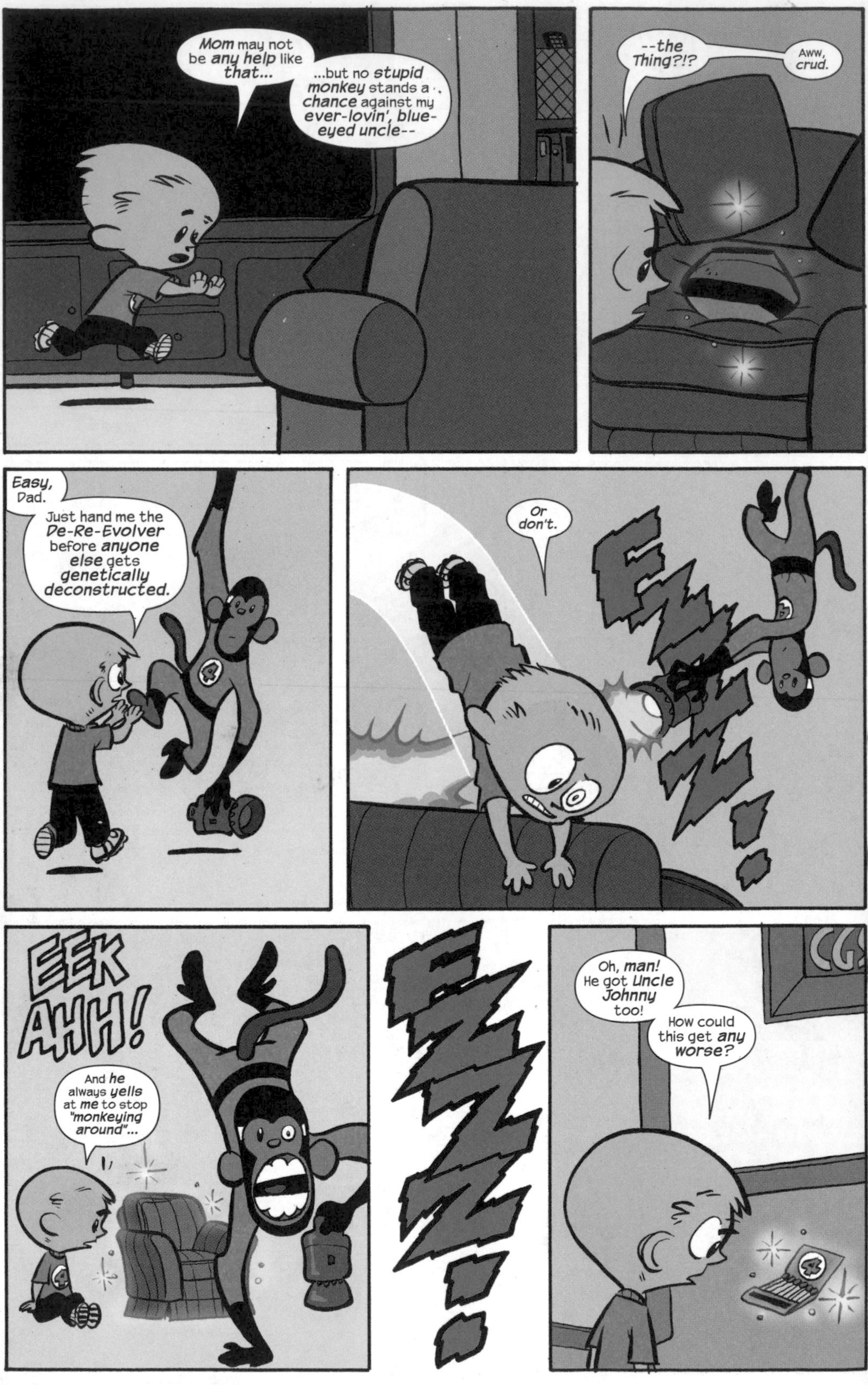

Mom may not be any help like that...
...but no stupid monkey stands a chance against my ever-lovin', blue-eyed uncle--
--the Thing?!?
Aww, crud.
Easy, Dad.
Just hand me the De-Re-Evolver before anyone else gets genetically deconstructed.
Or don't.
FZZZ!
EEK AHH!
And he always yells at me to stop "monkeying around"...
FZZZ!
Oh, man! He got Uncle Johnny too!
How could this get any worse?

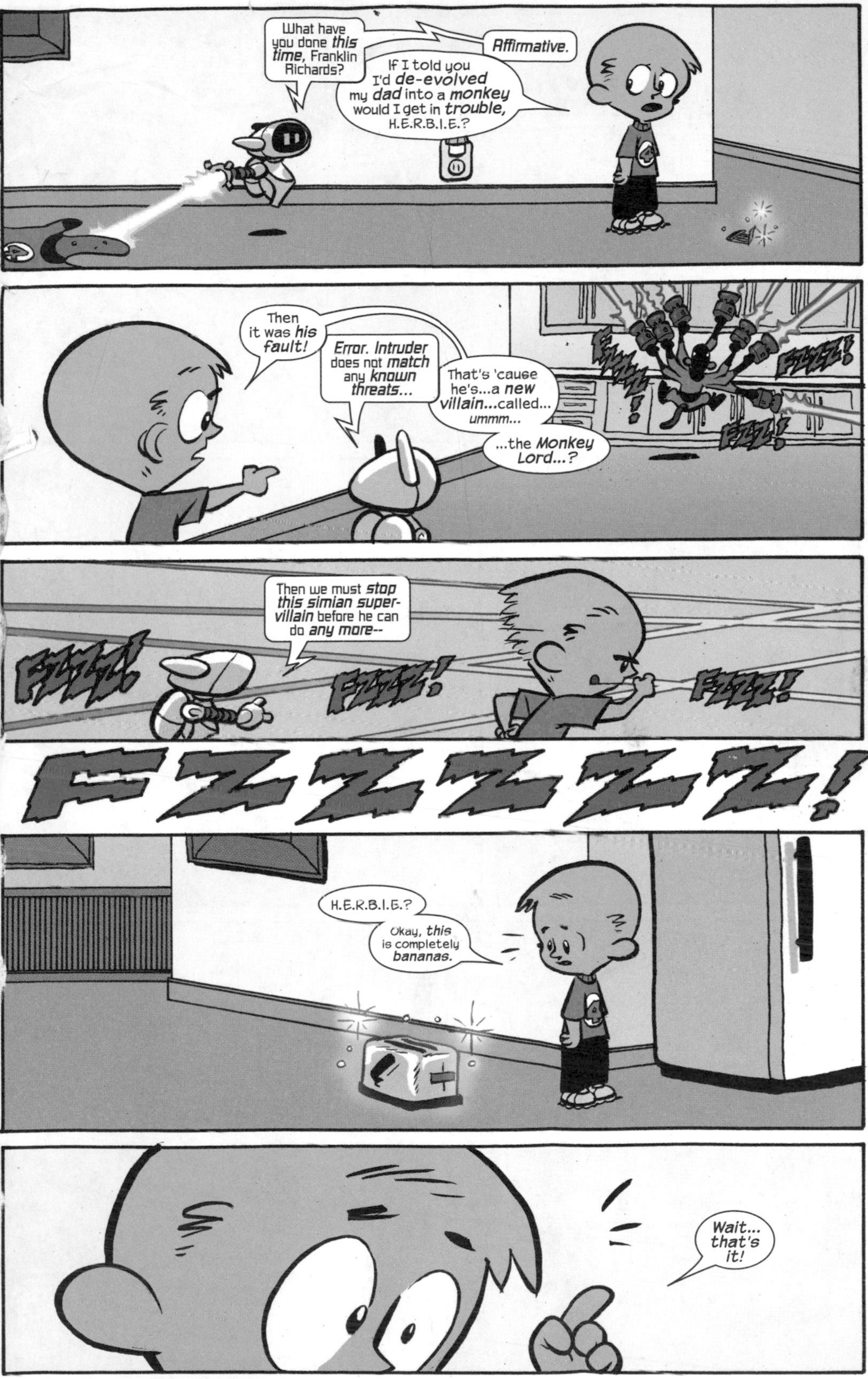
What have you done this time, Franklin Richards?
Affirmative.
If I told you I'd de-evolved my dad into a monkey would I get in trouble, H.E.R.B.I.E.?
Then it was his fault!
Error. Intruder does not match any known threats...
That's 'cause he's...a new villain...called... ummm...
...the Monkey Lord...?
FZZZZ!
FZZZ!
FZZZZ!
Then we must stop this simian super-villain before he can do any more--
FZZZZ!
FZZZZ!
FZZZZ!
FZZZZZ!
H.E.R.B.I.E.?
Okay, this is completely bananas.
Wait... that's it!

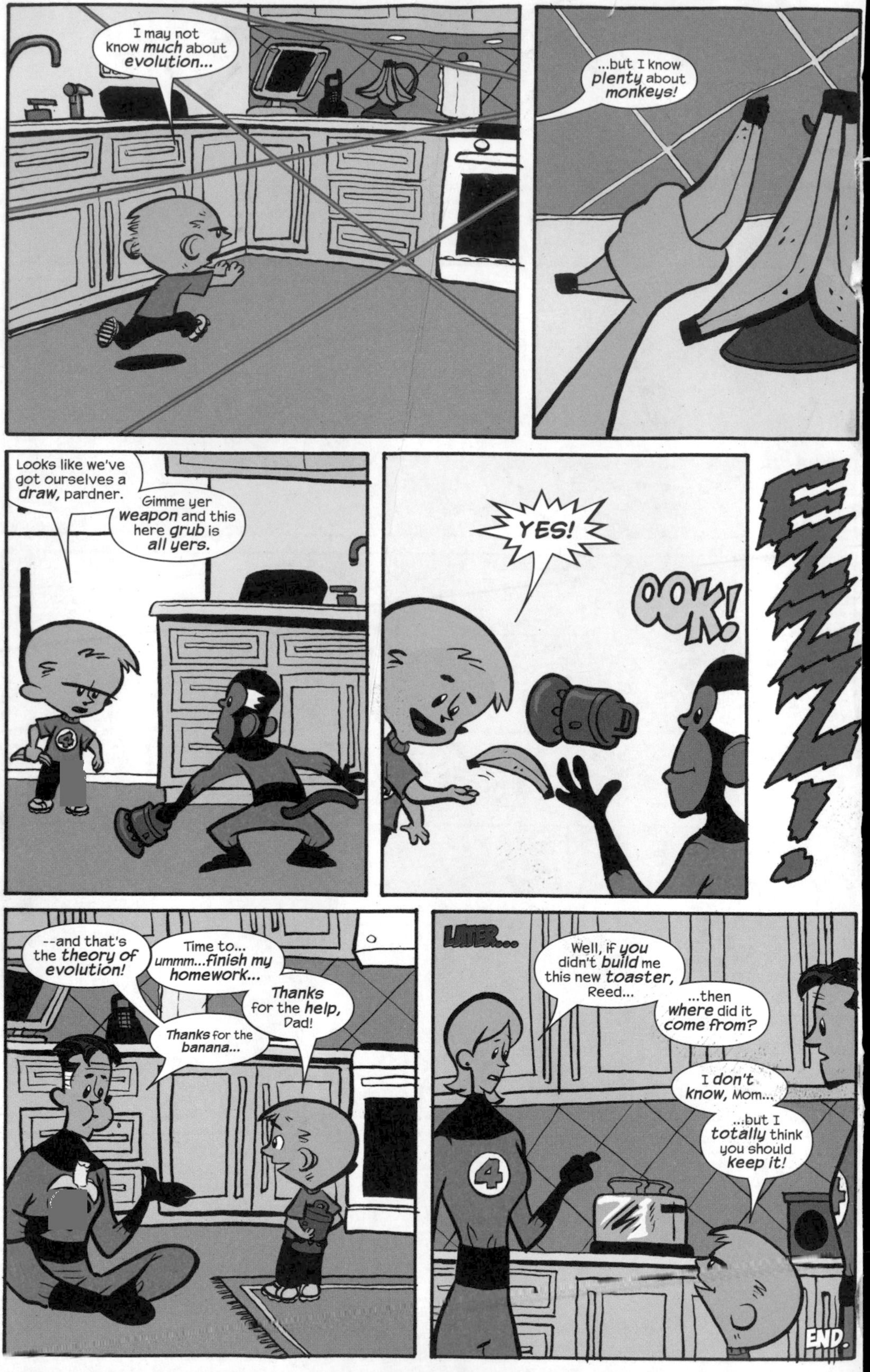

I may not know much about evolution...
...but I know plenty about monkeys!
Looks like we've got ourselves a draw, pardner.
Gimme yer weapon and this here grub is all yers.
YES!
OOK!
ZZZZ!
--and that's the theory of evolution!
Time to... ummm...finish my homework...
Thanks for the help, Dad!
Thanks for the banana...
LATER...
Well, if you didn't build me this new toaster, Reed...
...then where did it come from?
I don't know, Mom...
...but I totally think you should keep it!
END.

FRANKLIN RICHARDS: SON OF A GENIUS IN: MOLECULAR MAYHEM

BY CHRIS ELIOPOULOS & MARC SUMERAK

BRAD ANDERSON COLORS
NATHAN COSBY ASSISTANT EDITOR
MARK PANICCIA EDITOR

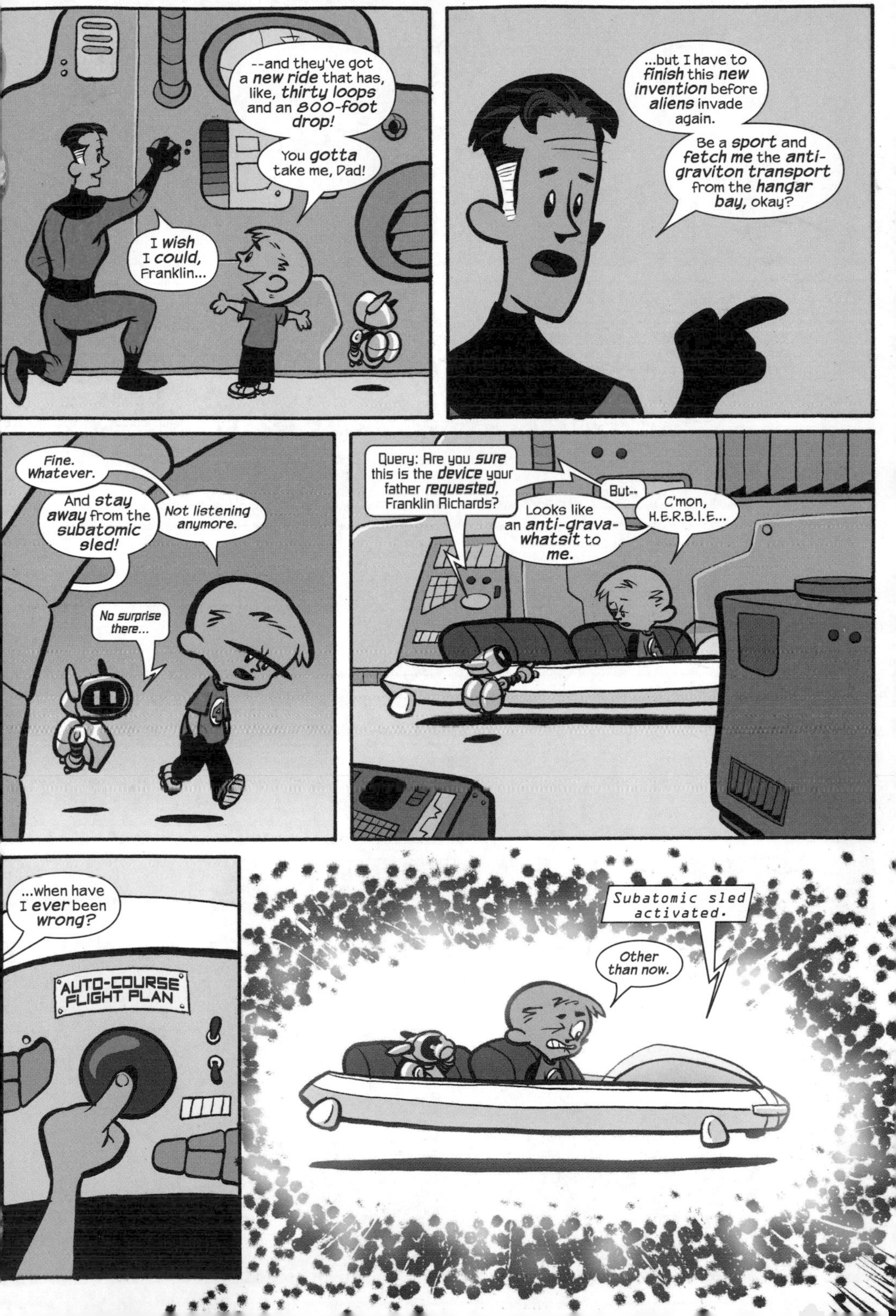

--and they've got a new ride that has, like, thirty loops and an 800-foot drop!
You gotta take me, Dad!
I wish I could, Franklin...
...but I have to finish this new invention before aliens invade again.
Be a sport and fetch me the anti-graviton transport from the hangar bay, okay?
Fine. Whatever.
And stay away from the subatomic sled!
Not listening anymore.
No surprise there...
Query: Are you sure this is the device your father requested, Franklin Richards?
But--
Looks like an anti-grava-whatsit to me.
C'mon, H.E.R.B.I.E...
...when have I ever been wrong?
AUTO-COURSE FLIGHT PLAN
Subatomic sled activated.
Other than now.

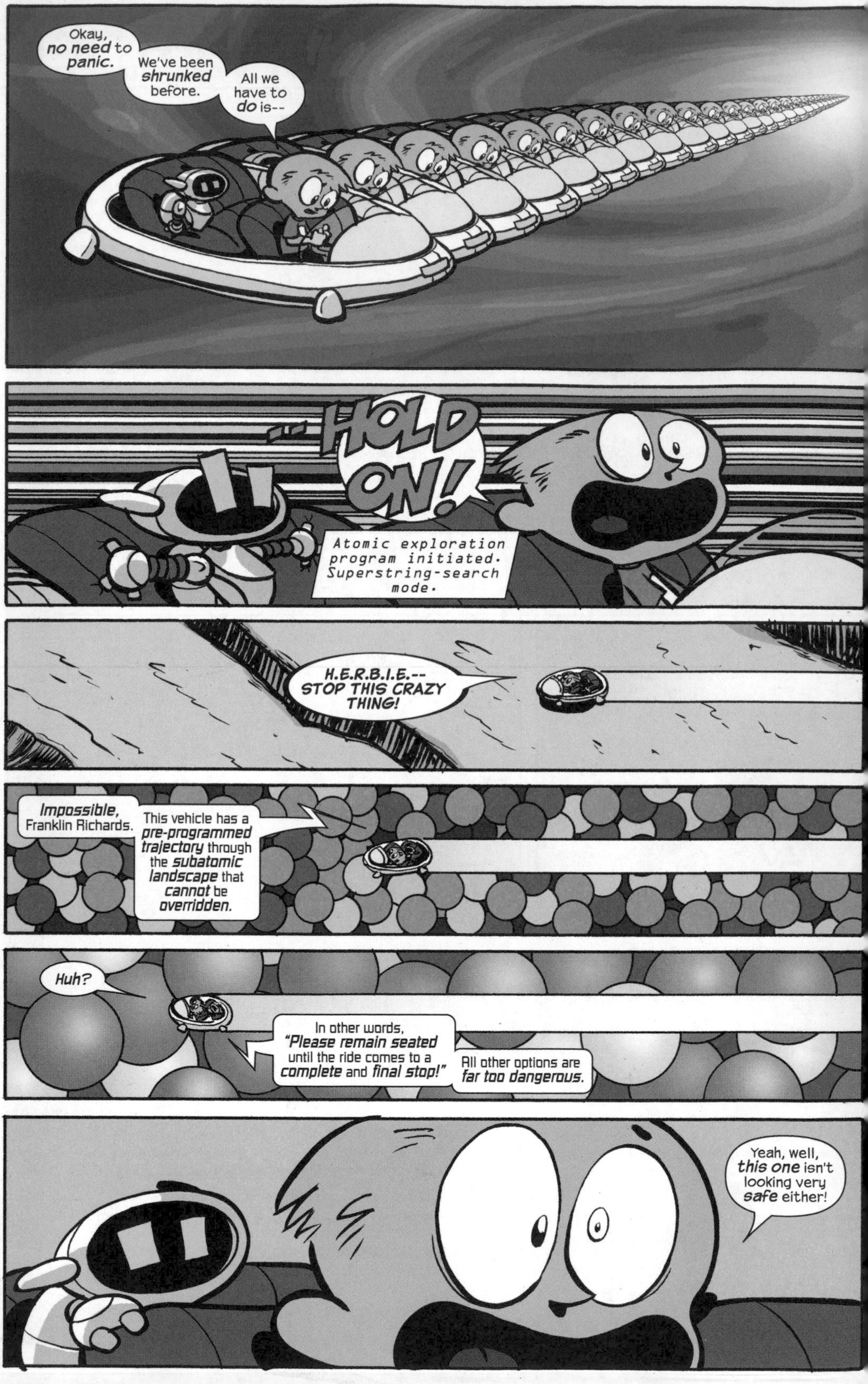

Okay, no need to panic.
We've been shrunked before.
All we have to do is--
--HOLD ON!
Atomic exploration program initiated. Superstring-search mode.
H.E.R.B.I.E.--STOP THIS CRAZY THING!
Impossible, Franklin Richards.
This vehicle has a pre-programmed trajectory through the subatomic landscape that cannot be overridden.
Huh?
In other words, "Please remain seated until the ride comes to a complete and final stop!"
All other options are far too dangerous.
Yeah, well, this one isn't looking very safe either!

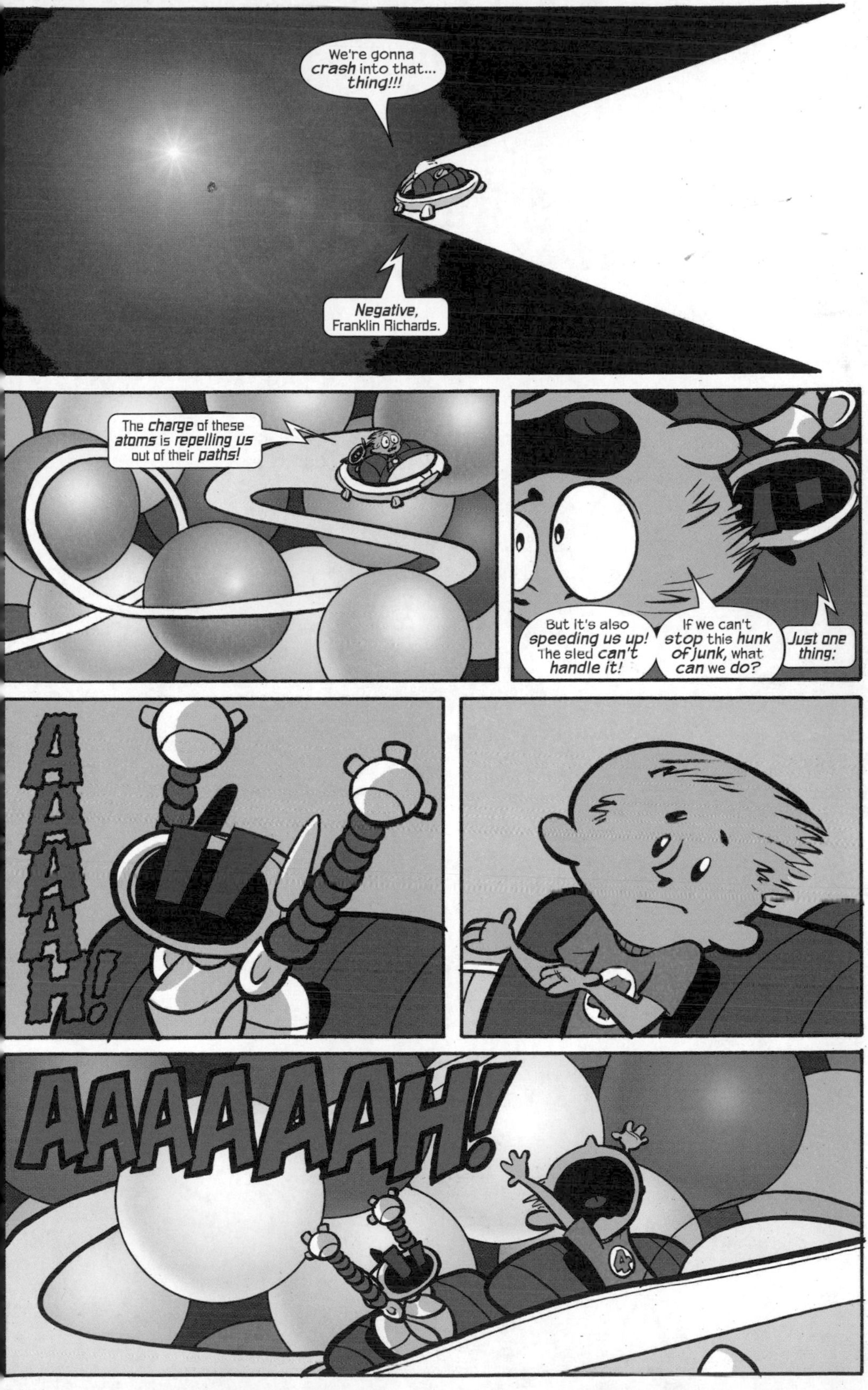
We're gonna crash into that... thing!!!
Negative, Franklin Richards.
The charge of these atoms is repelling us out of their paths!
But it's also speeding us up! The sled can't handle it!
If we can't stop this hunk of junk, what can we do?
Just one thing:
AAAAAH!
AAAAAAH!

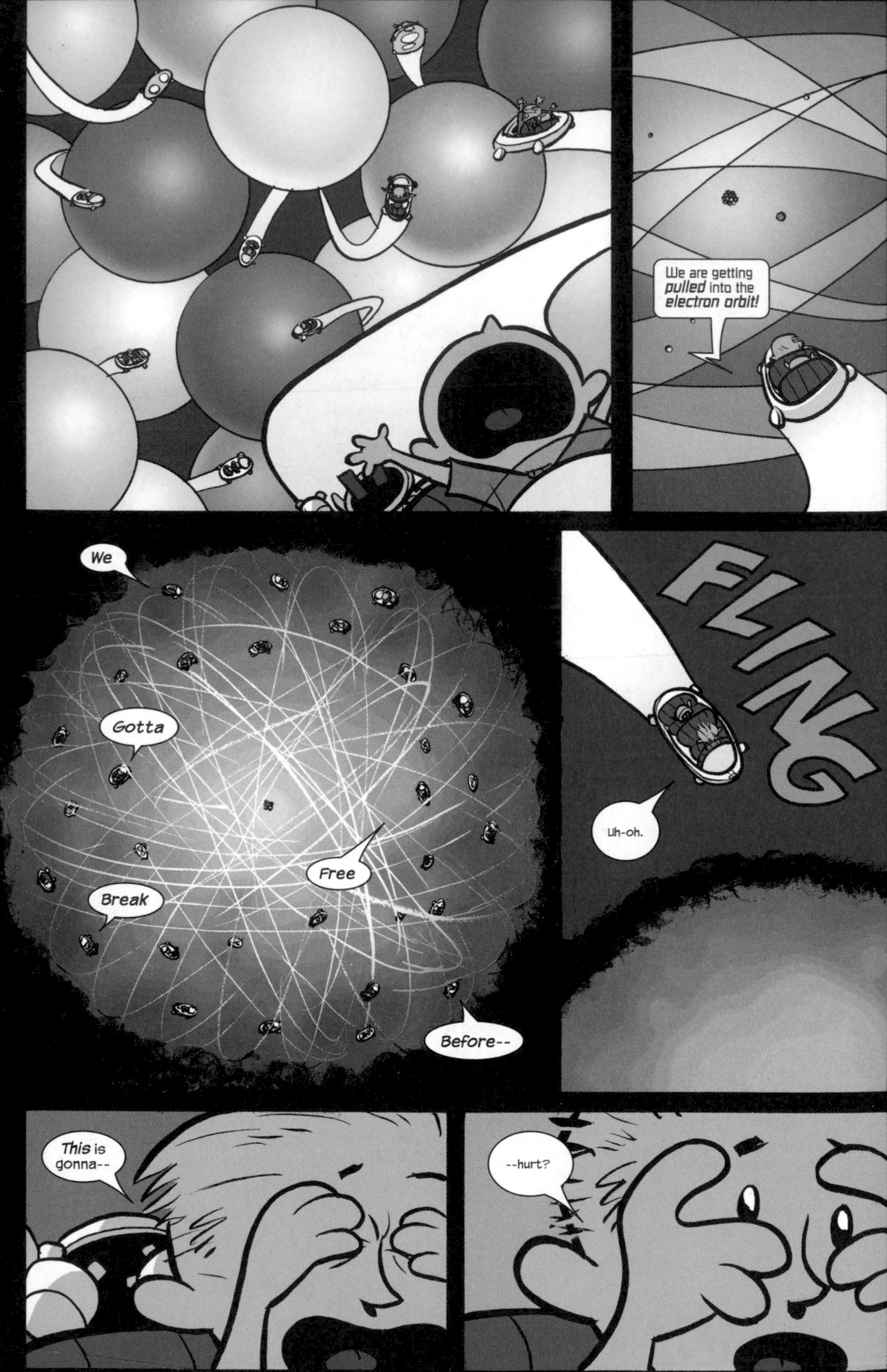
We are getting *pulled* into the *electron orbit!*
We
Gotta
Break
Free
Before--
FLING
Uh-oh.
This is gonna--
--hurt?

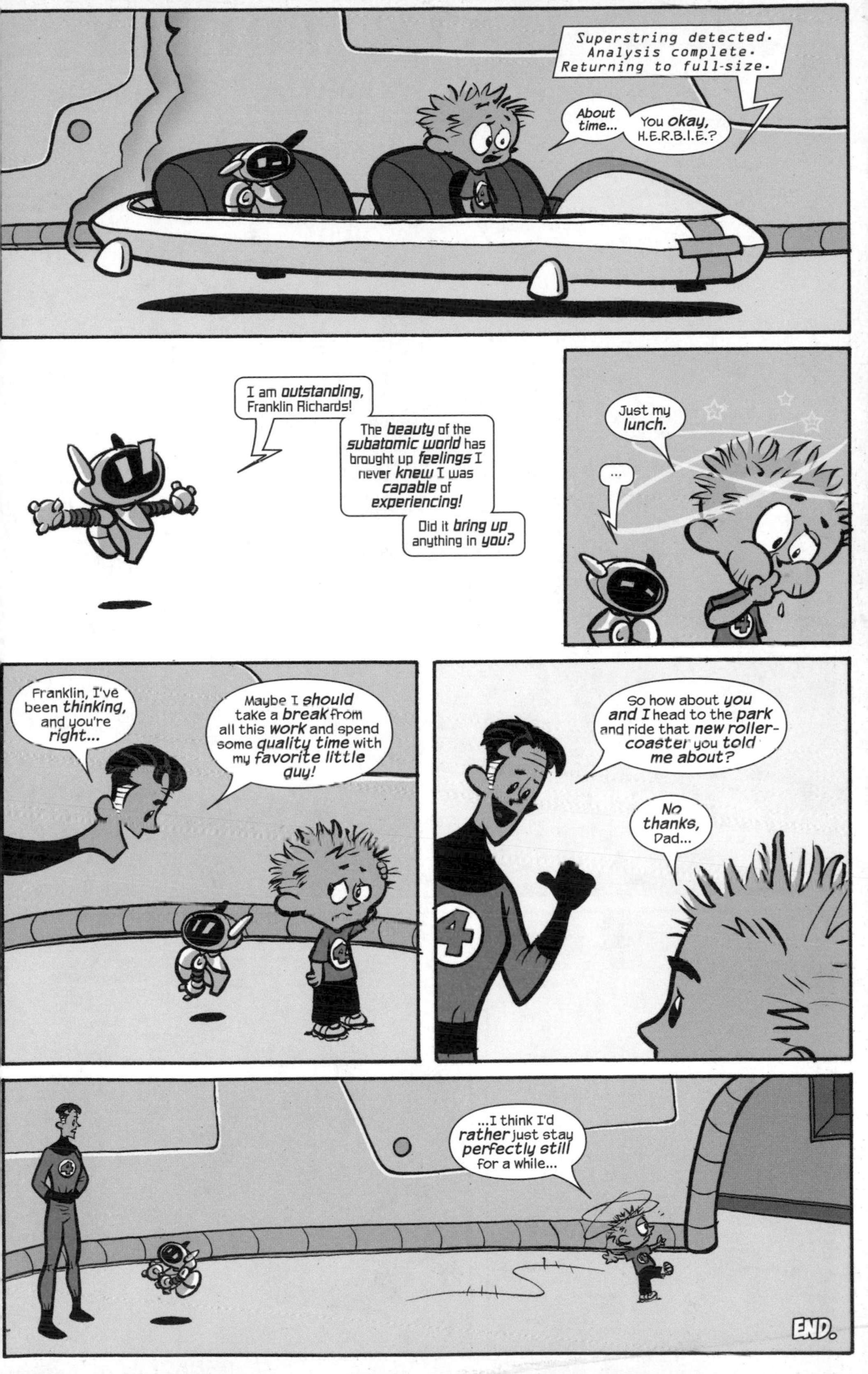
Superstring detected. Analysis complete. Returning to full-size.
About time...
You okay, H.E.R.B.I.E.?
I am outstanding, Franklin Richards!
The beauty of the subatomic world has brought up feelings I never knew I was capable of experiencing!
Did it bring up anything in you?
Just my lunch.
...
Franklin, I've been thinking, and you're right...
Maybe I should take a break from all this work and spend some quality time with my favorite little guy!
So how about you and I head to the park and ride that new roller-coaster you told me about?
No thanks, Dad...
...I think I'd rather just stay perfectly still for a while...
END.

FRANKLIN RICHARDS SON OF A GENIUS IN: HAIR TODAY...

BY CHRIS ELIOPOULOS & MARC SUMERAK

BRAD ANDERSON COLORS
NATHAN COSBY ASSISTANT EDITOR
MARK PANICCIA EDITOR

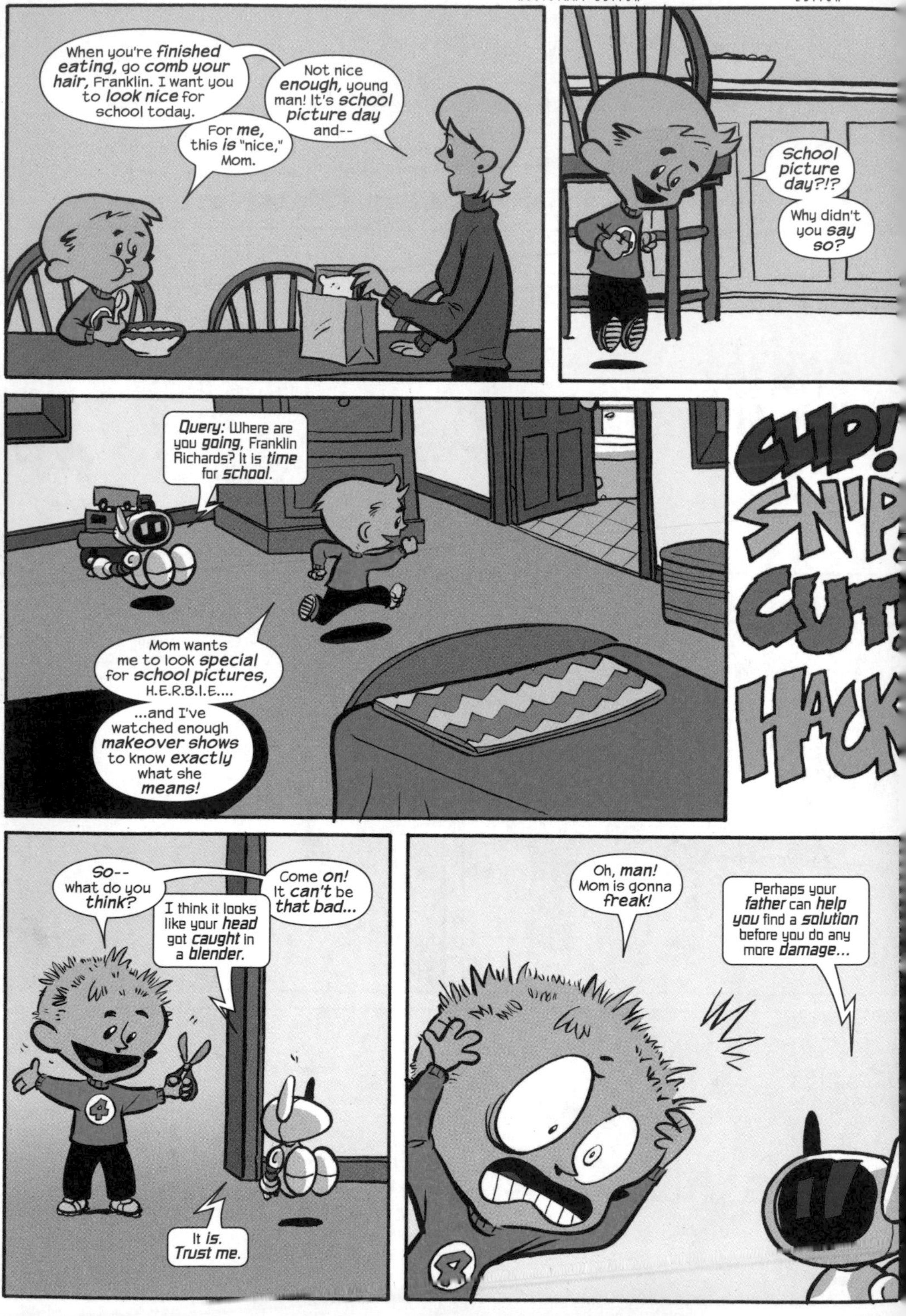

When you're finished eating, go comb your hair, Franklin. I want you to look nice for school today.
For me, this is "nice," Mom.
Not nice enough, young man! It's school picture day and--
School picture day?!?
Why didn't you say so?
Query: Where are you going, Franklin Richards? It is time for school.
Mom wants me to look special for school pictures, H.E.R.B.I.E....
...and I've watched enough makeover shows to know exactly what she means!
CLIP!
CUT
So-- what do you think?
I think it looks like your head got caught in a blender.
Come on! It can't be that bad...
It is. Trust me.
Oh, man! Mom is gonna freak!
Perhaps your father can help you find a solution before you do any more damage...

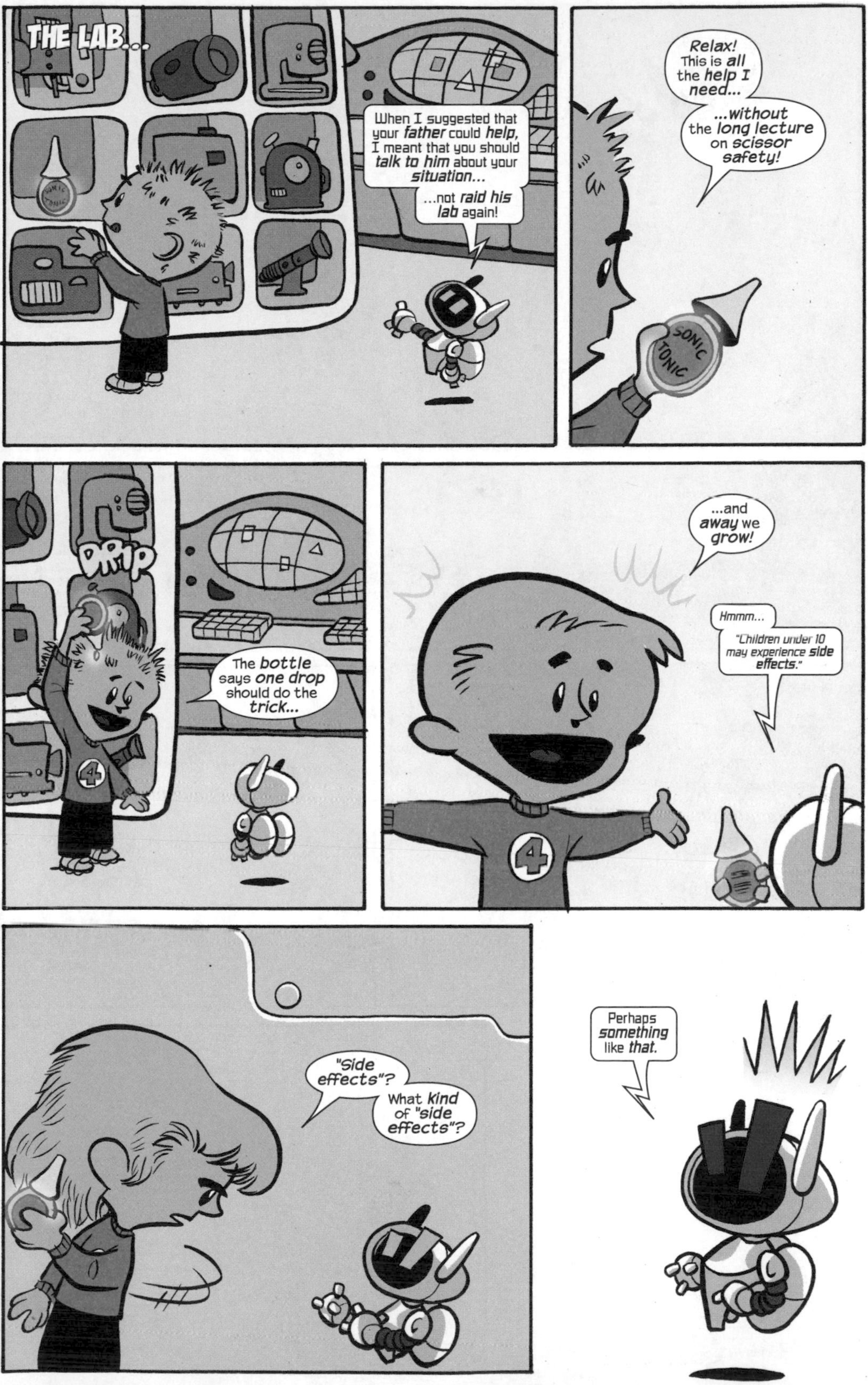
THE LAB...
When I suggested that your father could help, I meant that you should talk to him about your situation...
...not raid his lab again!
Relax! This is all the help I need...
...without the long lecture on scissor safety!
SONIC TONIC
DRIP
The bottle says one drop should do the trick...
...and away we grow!
Hmmm...
"Children under 10 may experience side effects."
"Side effects"?
What kind of "side effects"?
Perhaps something like that.

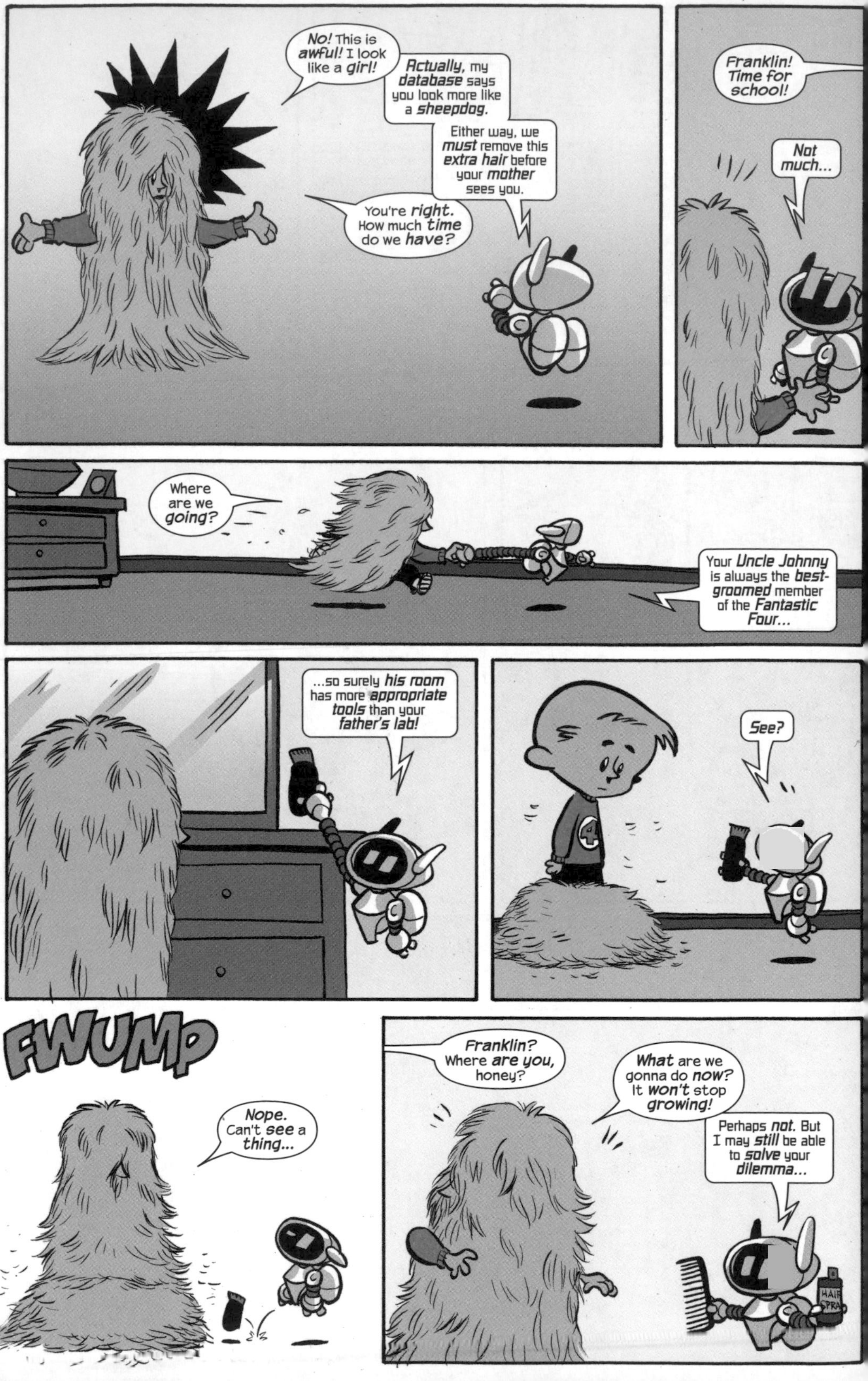
No! This is awful! I look like a girl!
Actually, my database says you look more like a sheepdog.
Either way, we must remove this extra hair before your mother sees you.
You're right. How much time do we have?
Franklin! Time for school!
Not much...
Where are we going?
Your Uncle Johnny is always the best-groomed member of the Fantastic Four...
...so surely his room has more appropriate tools than your father's lab!
See?
FWUMP
Nope. Can't see a thing...
Franklin? Where are you, honey?
What are we gonna do now? It won't stop growing!
Perhaps not. But I may still be able to solve your dilemma...
HAIR SPRA

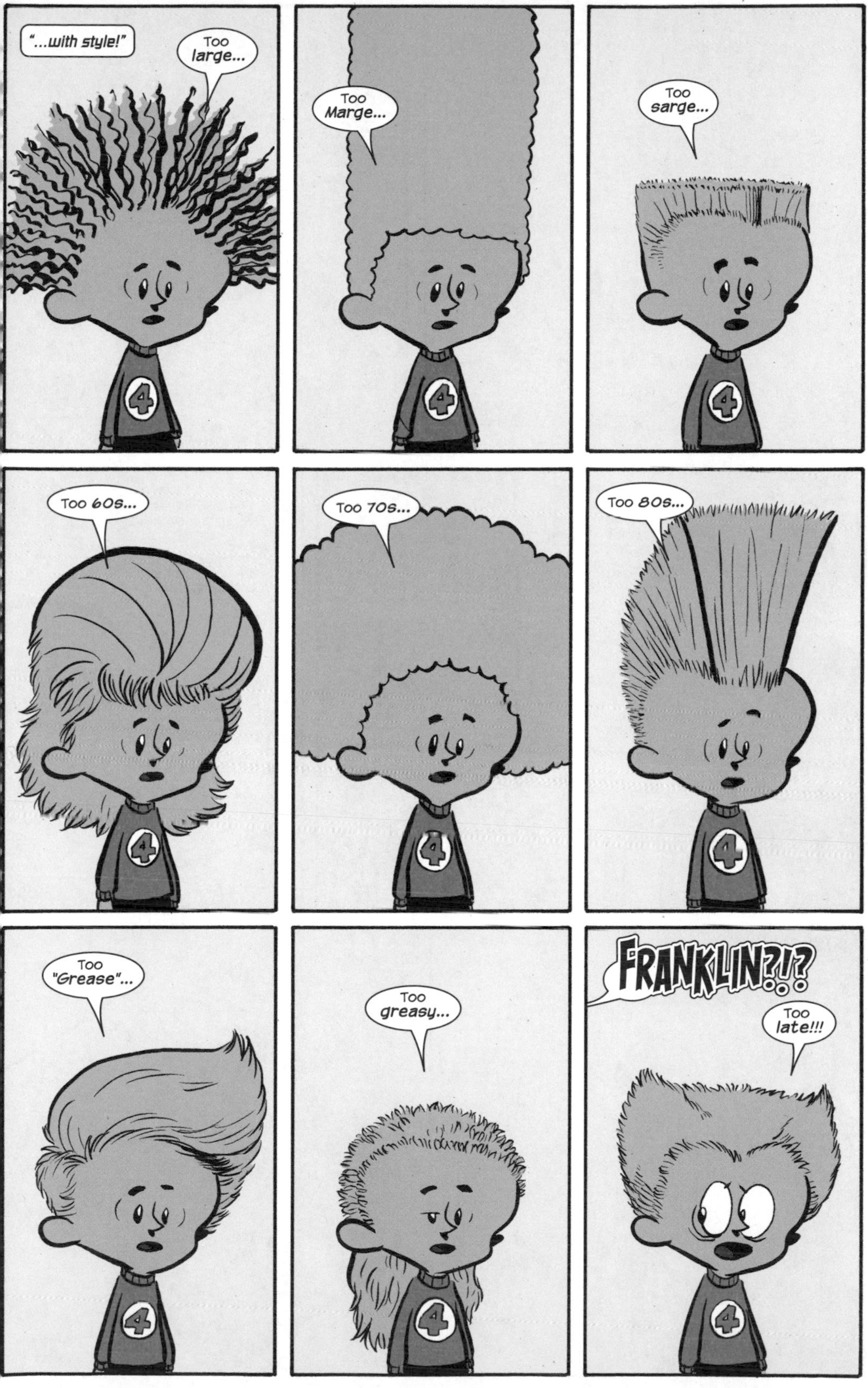
"...with style!"
Too large...
Too Marge...
Too sarge...
Too 60s...
Too 70s...
Too 80s...
Too "Grease"...
Too greasy...
FRANKLIN?!?
Too late!!!

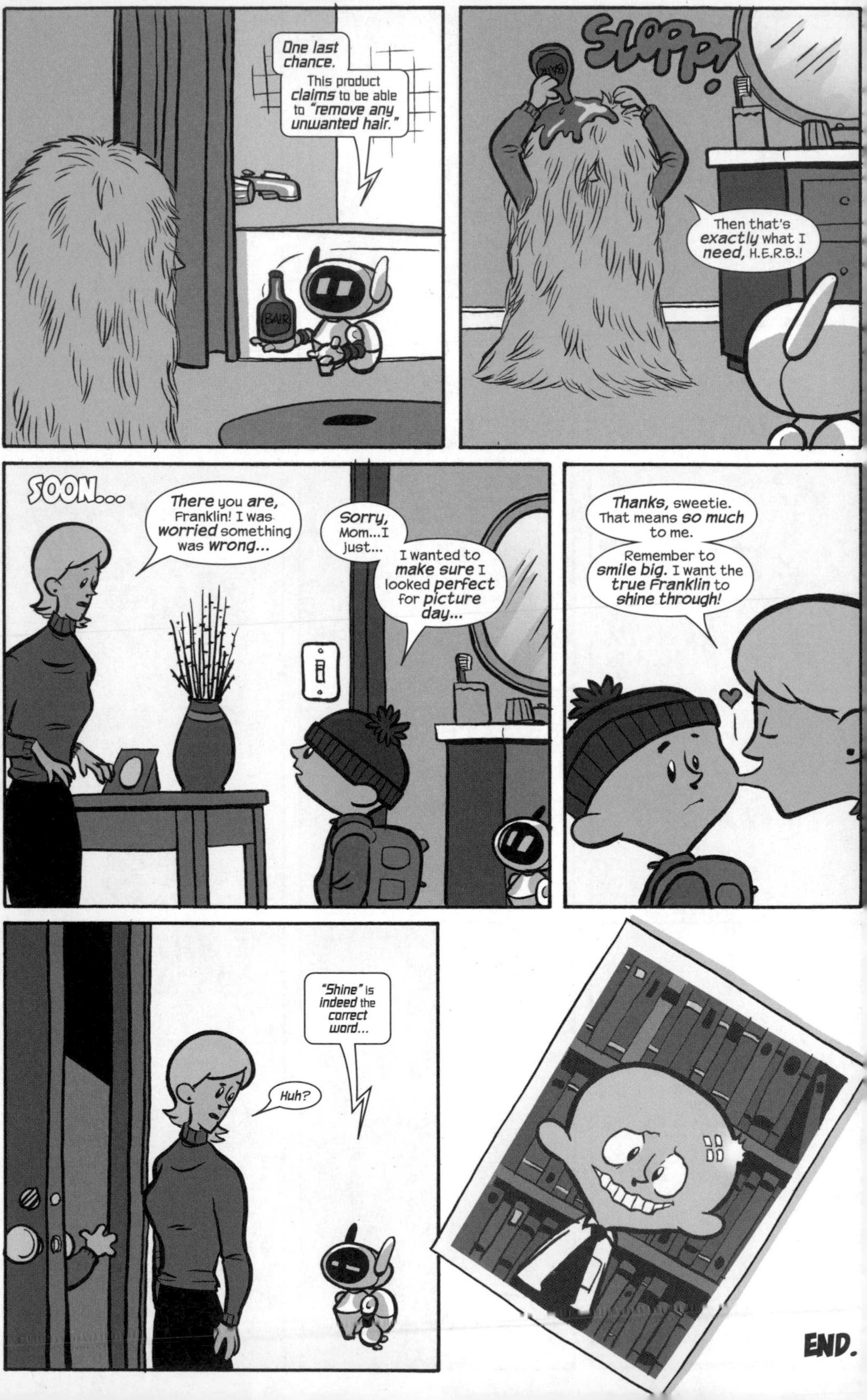
One last chance.
This product claims to be able to "remove any unwanted hair."
BAIR
SLOPP!
Then that's exactly what I need, H.E.R.B.!
SOON...
There you are, Franklin! I was worried something was wrong...
Sorry, Mom...I just...
I wanted to make sure I looked perfect for picture day...
Thanks, sweetie. That means so much to me.
Remember to smile big. I want the true Franklin to shine through!
"Shine" is indeed the correct word...
Huh?
END.

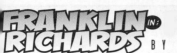

FRANKLIN RICHARDS in: ODENT'S REVENGE!

SON OF A GENIUS

BY CHRIS ELIOPOULOS & MARC SUMERAK

BRAD ANDERSON COLORS
NATHAN COSBY ASSISTANT EDITOR
MARK PANICCIA EDITOR

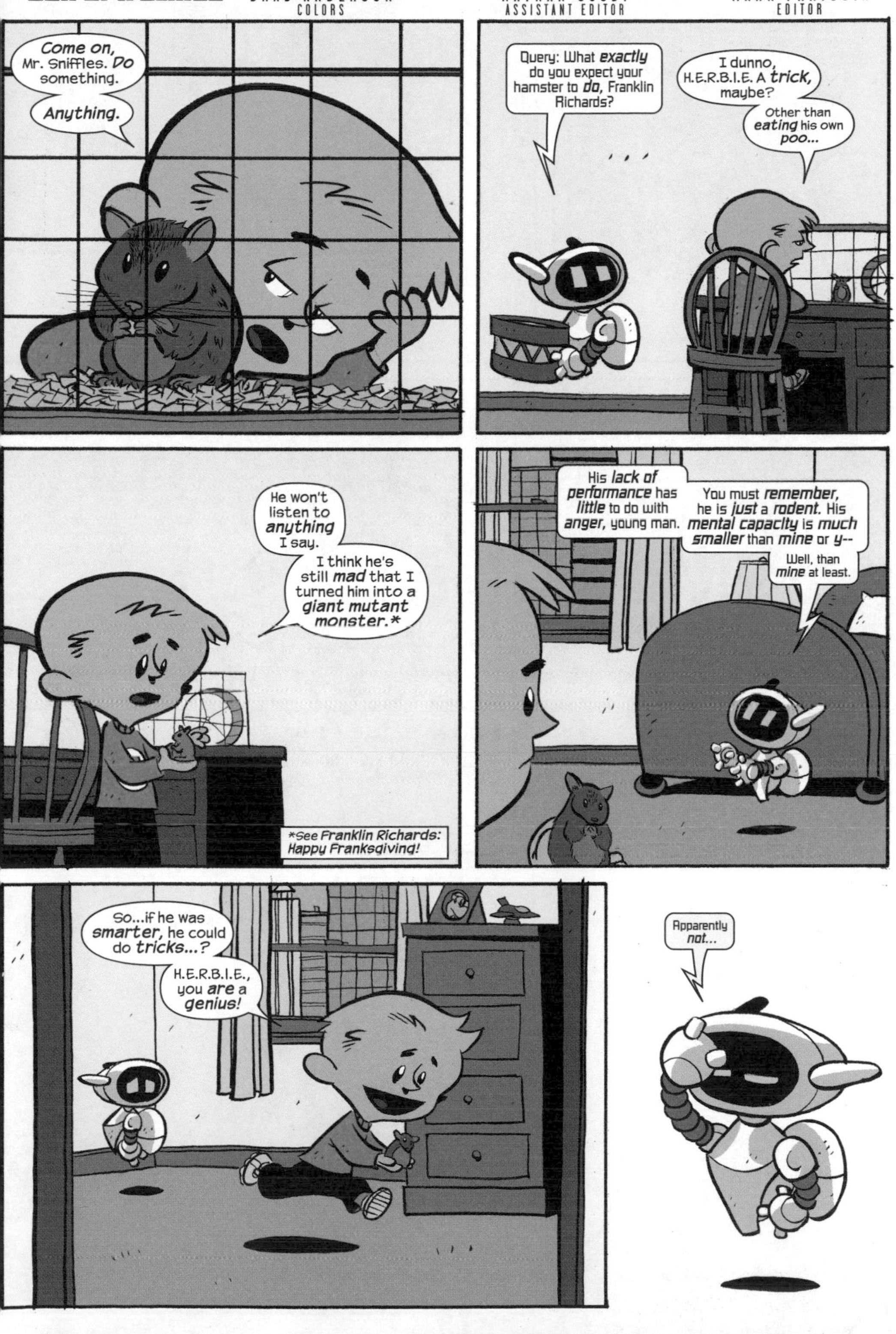

Come on, Mr. Sniffles. Do something.
Anything.
Query: What exactly do you expect your hamster to do, Franklin Richards?
I dunno, H.E.R.B.I.E. A trick, maybe?
Other than eating his own poo...
He won't listen to anything I say.
I think he's still mad that I turned him into a giant mutant monster.*
*See Franklin Richards: Happy Franksgiving!
His lack of performance has little to do with anger, young man.
You must remember, he is just a rodent. His mental capacity is much smaller than mine or y--
Well, than mine at least.
So...if he was smarter, he could do tricks...?
H.E.R.B.I.E., you are a genius!
Apparently not...

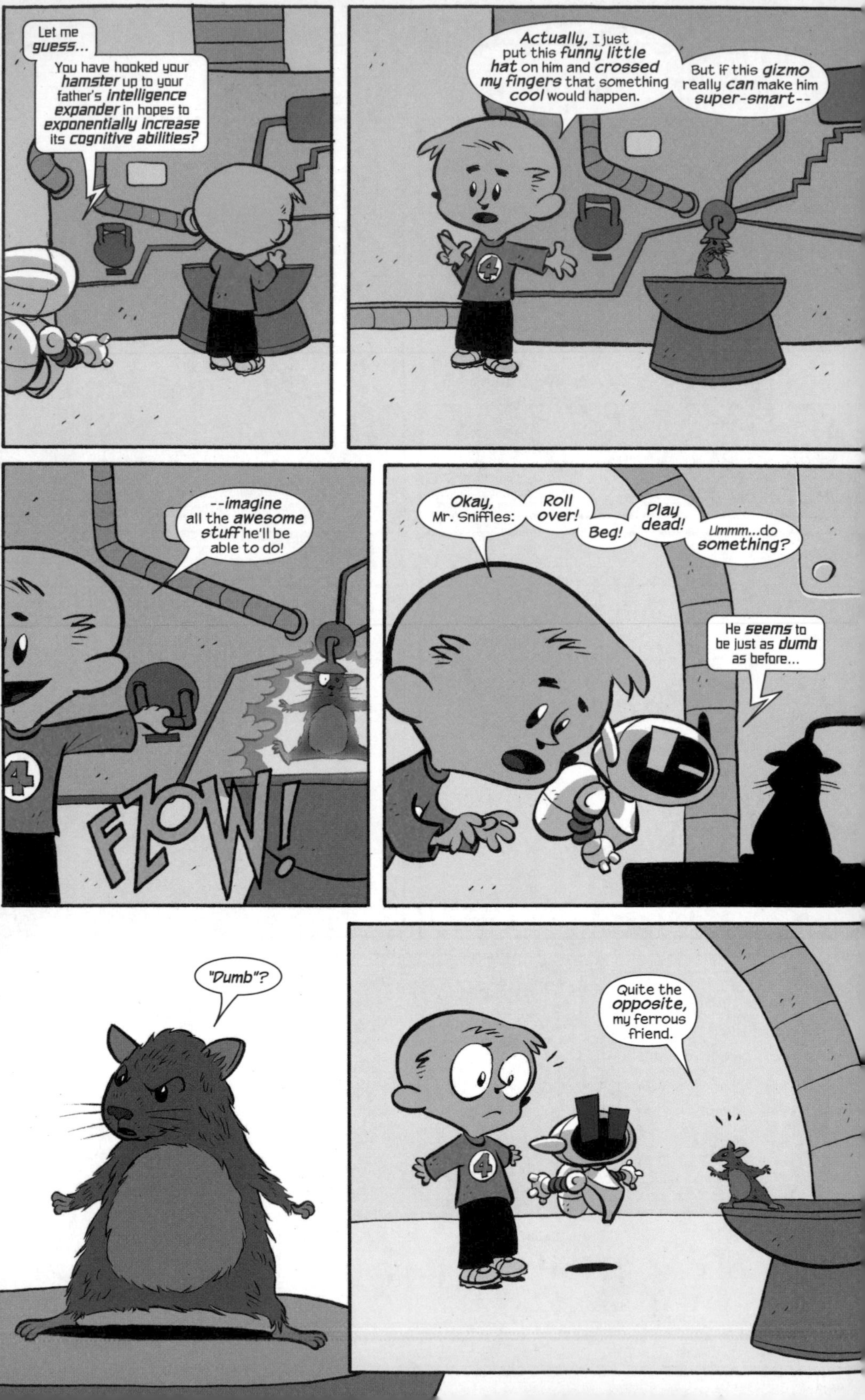
Let me guess...
You have hooked your hamster up to your father's intelligence expander in hopes to exponentially increase its cognitive abilities?
Actually, I just put this funny little hat on him and crossed my fingers that something cool would happen.
But if this gizmo really can make him super-smart--
--imagine all the awesome stuff he'll be able to do!
FZOW!
Okay, Mr. Sniffles:
Roll over!
Beg!
Play dead!
Ummm...do something?
He seems to be just as dumb as before...
"Dumb"?
Quite the opposite, my ferrous friend.

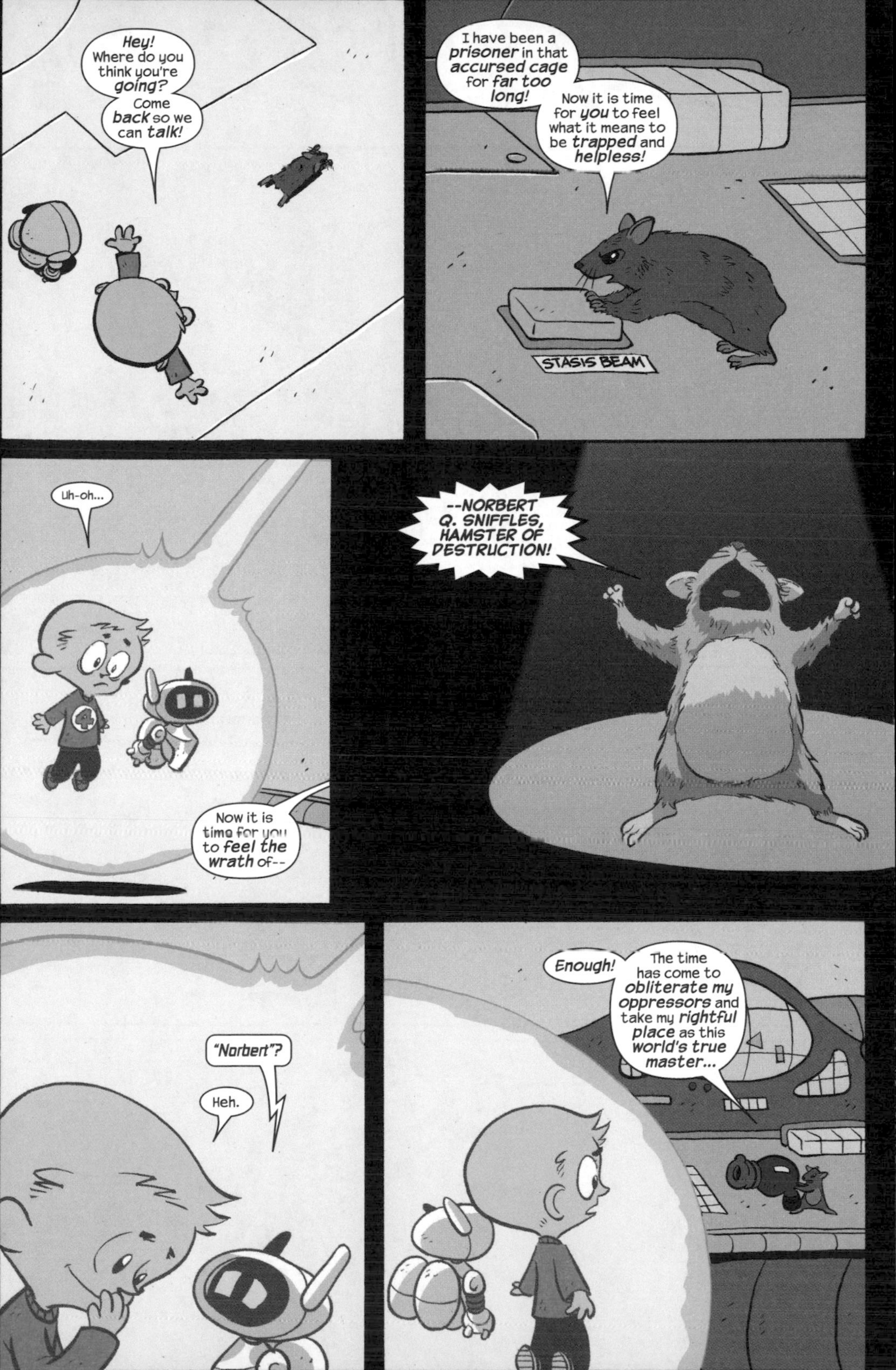
Hey! Where do you think you're going?
Come back so we can talk!
I have been a prisoner in that accursed cage for far too long!
Now it is time for you to feel what it means to be trapped and helpless!
STASIS BEAM
Uh-oh...
Now it is time for you to feel the wrath of--
--NORBERT Q. SNIFFLES, HAMSTER OF DESTRUCTION!
"Norbert"?
Heh.
Enough!
The time has come to obliterate my oppressors and take my rightful place as this world's true master...

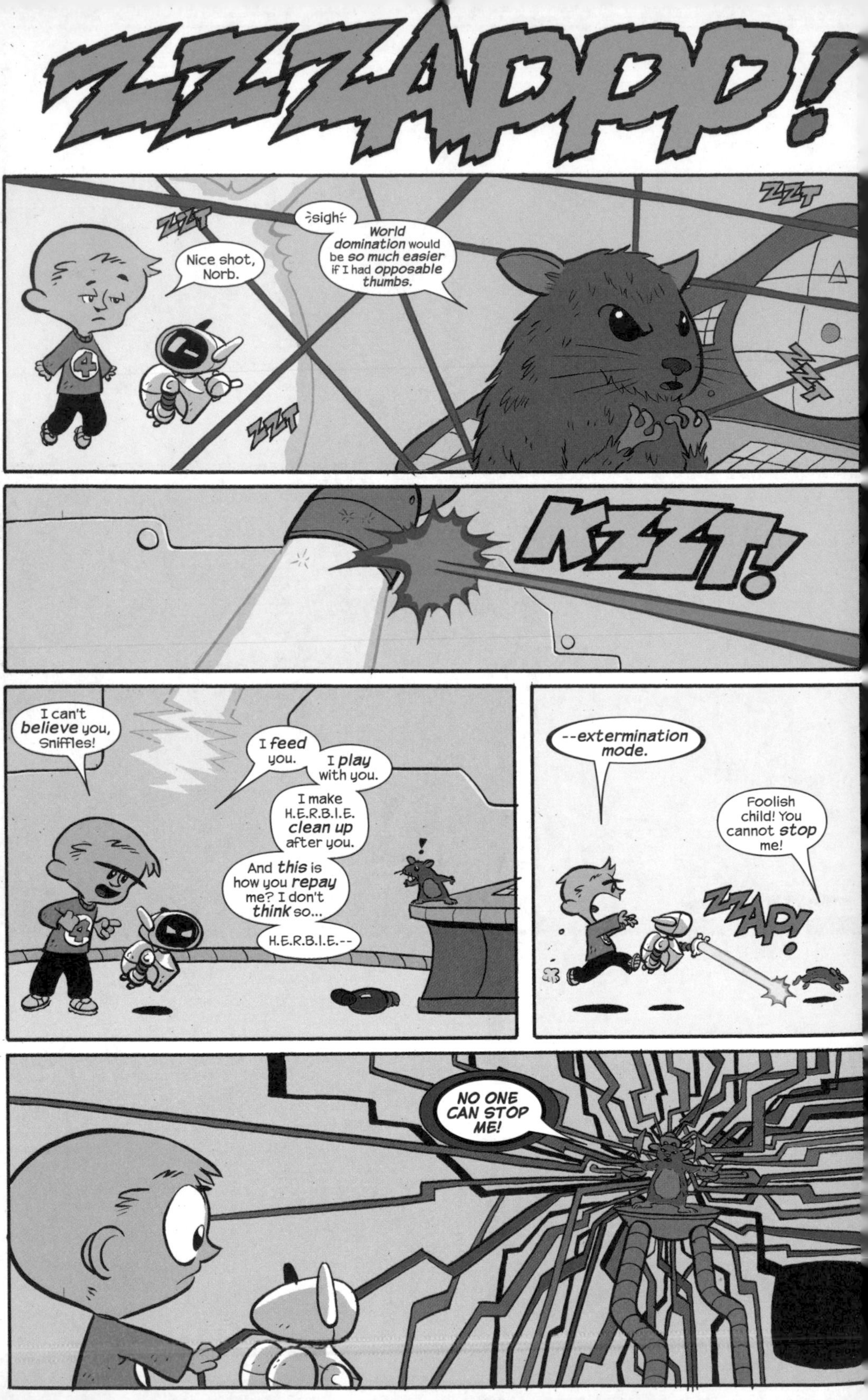
ZZZZAPPPP!
ZZZT
ZZZT
~sigh~
World domination would be so much easier if I had opposable thumbs.
Nice shot, Norb.
ZZZT
ZZZT
ZZZT
KZZT!
I can't believe you, Sniffles!
I feed you.
I play with you.
I make H.E.R.B.I.E. clean up after you.
And this is how you repay me? I don't think so...
H.E.R.B.I.E.--
--extermination mode.
Foolish child! You cannot stop me!
ZZAP!
NO ONE CAN STOP ME!

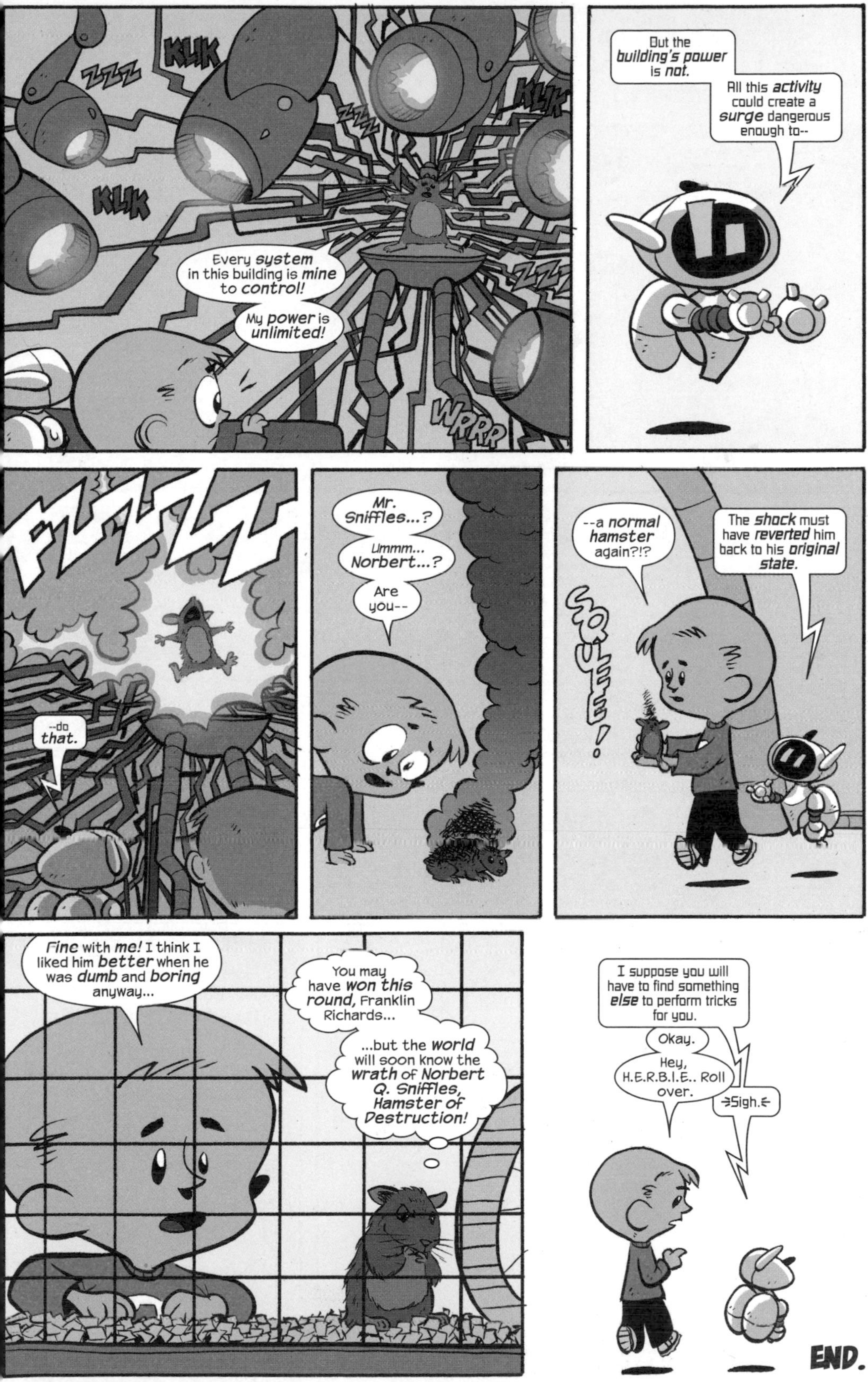
ZZZ
KLIK
KLIK
KLIK
ZZZ
Every system in this building is mine to control!
My power is unlimited!
ZZZ
WRRR
But the building's power is not.
All this activity could create a surge dangerous enough to--
FZZZ
--do that.
Mr. Sniffles...?
Ummm... Norbert...?
Are you--
--a normal hamster again?!?
The shock must have reverted him back to his original state.
SQUEEE!
Fine with me! I think I liked him better when he was dumb and boring anyway...
You may have won this round, Franklin Richards...
...but the world will soon know the wrath of Norbert Q. Sniffles, Hamster of Destruction!
I suppose you will have to find something else to perform tricks for you.
Okay.
Hey, H.E.R.B.I.E.. Roll over.
Sigh.
END.

FRANKLIN RICHARDS IN: BASKET-BRAWL!

SON OF A GENIUS

BY CHRIS ELIOPOULOS & MARC SUMERAK

BRAD ANDERSON
COLORS

NATHAN COSBY
ASSISTANT EDITOR

MARK PANICCIA
EDITOR

Franklin! Where **are** you, champ?

You're going to be **late** for your **first** game!

Just a **sec**, Dad...

...I'm just making **sure** I have all the right **equipment**...

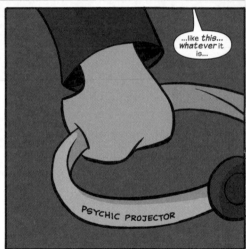

...like **this**... **whatever** it is...

PSYCHIC PROJECTOR

Time to **shoot** some hoops, H.E.R.B.I.E.!

I am **pleasantly surprised**, Franklin Richards.

After your last **disastrous attempt** at **playing sports**, I did not expect you to be so **eager** to try a **new game**.

It's just **basketball**, dude...

DANGER! SUPER-VILLAIN WEAPON STORAGE!

...how **bad** could it be?

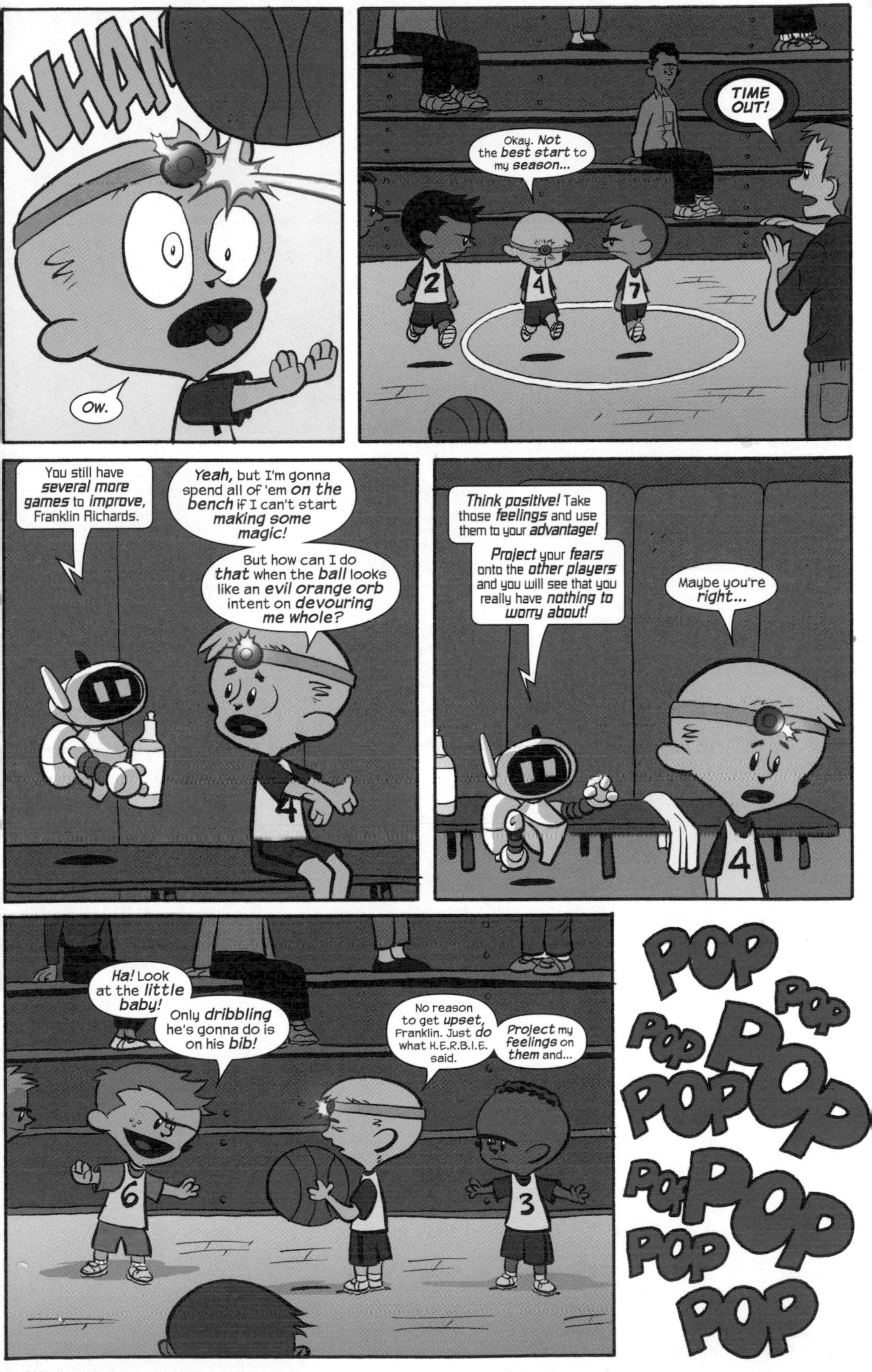
WHAM
Ow.
Okay. Not the best start to my season...
TIME OUT!
You still have several more games to improve, Franklin Richards.
Yeah, but I'm gonna spend all of 'em on the bench if I can't start making some magic!
But how can I do that when the ball looks like an evil orange orb intent on devouring me whole?
Think positive! Take those feelings and use them to your advantage!
Project your fears onto the other players and you will see that you really have nothing to worry about!
Maybe you're right...
Ha! Look at the little baby!
Only dribbling he's gonna do is on his bib!
No reason to get upset, Franklin. Just do what H.E.R.B.I.E. said.
Project my feelings on them and...
POP POP POP POP POP POP POP POP POP POP POP

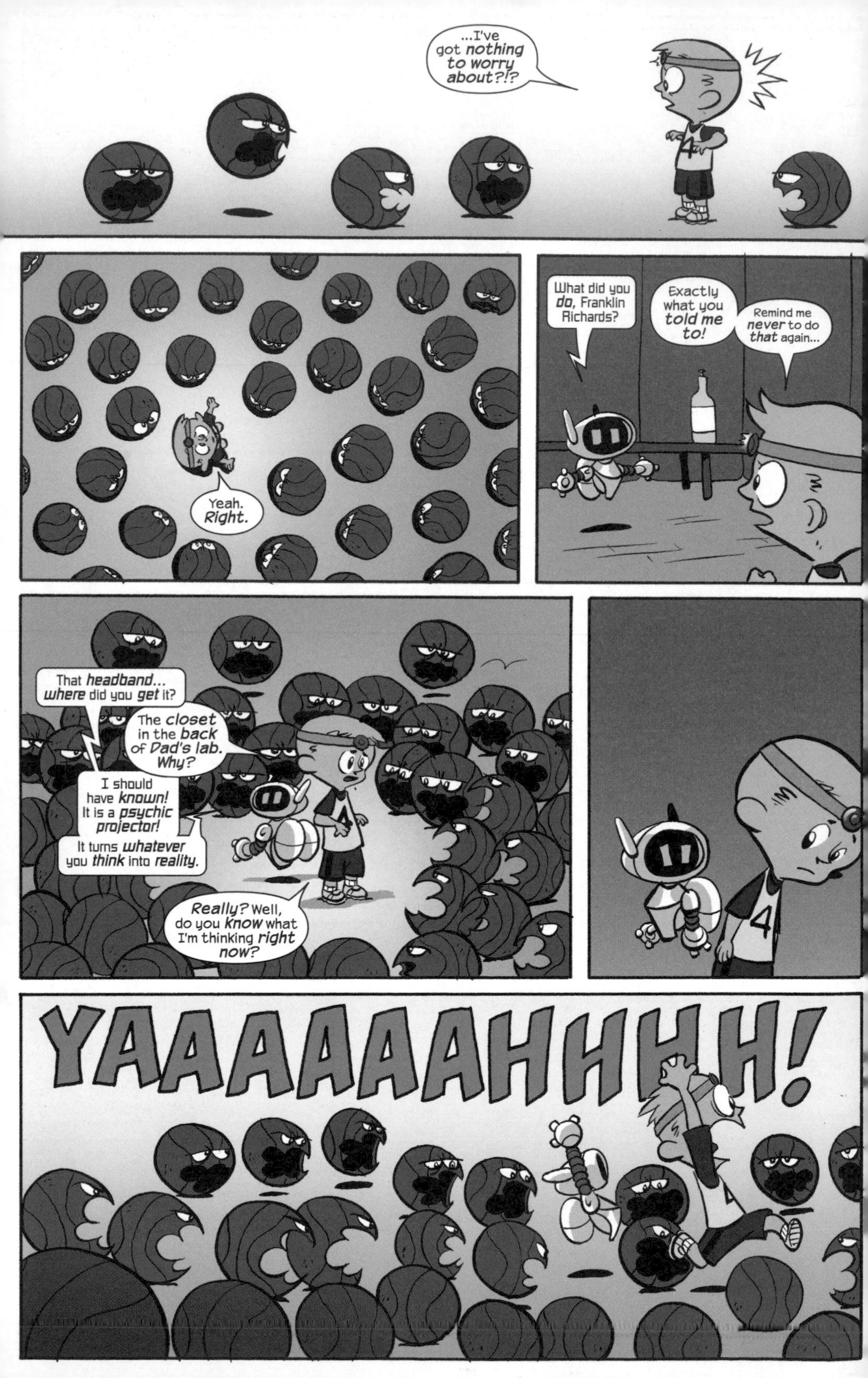

...I've got *nothing to worry about?!?*
Yeah. *Right.*
What did you *do,* Franklin Richards?
Exactly what you *told me to!*
Remind me *never* to do *that* again...
That *headband... where* did you *get* it?
The *closet* in the *back* of *Dad's lab. Why?*
I should have *known!* It is a *psychic projector!*
It turns *whatever* you *think* into *reality*.
Really? Well, do you *know* what I'm thinking *right now?*
YAAAAAAHHHH!

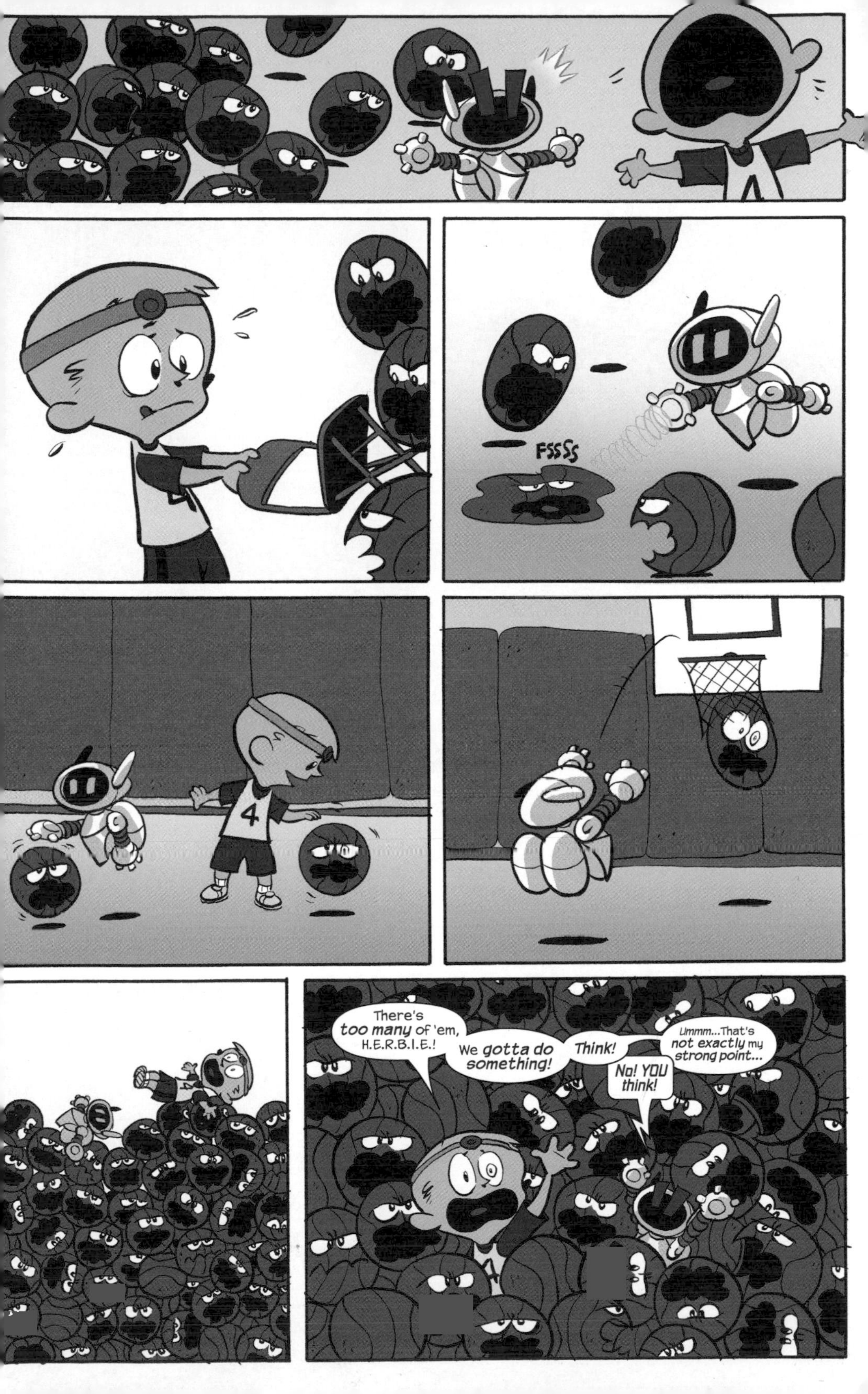
FSSSS
There's too many of 'em, H.E.R.B.I.E.!
We gotta do something!
Think!
Ummm...That's not exactly my strong point...
No! YOU think!

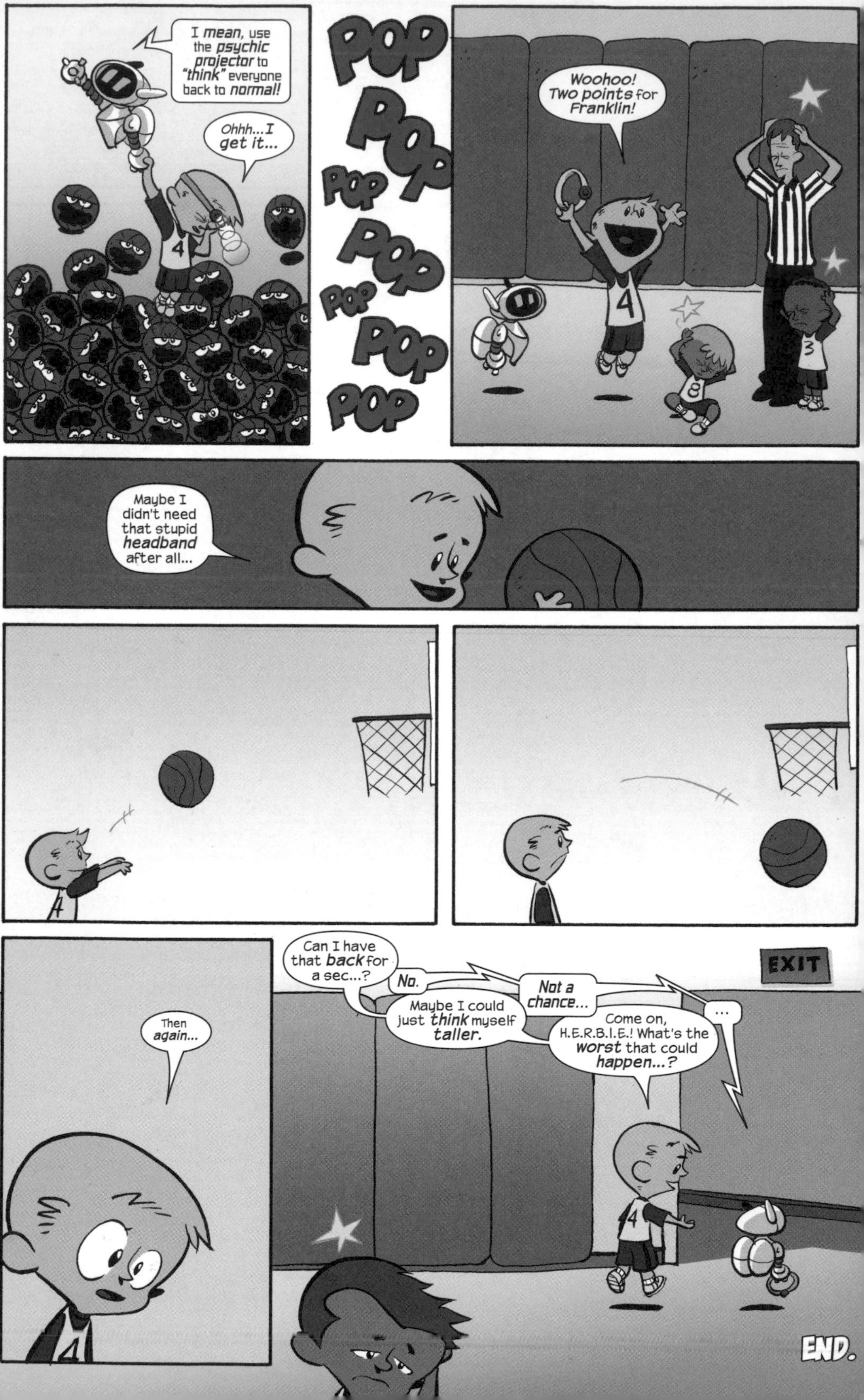
I mean, use the psychic projector to "think" everyone back to normal!
Ohhh...I get it...
POP POP POP POP POP POP POP
Woohoo! Two points for Franklin!
Maybe I didn't need that stupid headband after all...
Then again...
Can I have that back for a sec...?
No.
Not a chance...
Maybe I could just think myself taller.
...
Come on, H.E.R.B.I.E.! What's the worst that could happen...?
EXIT
END.

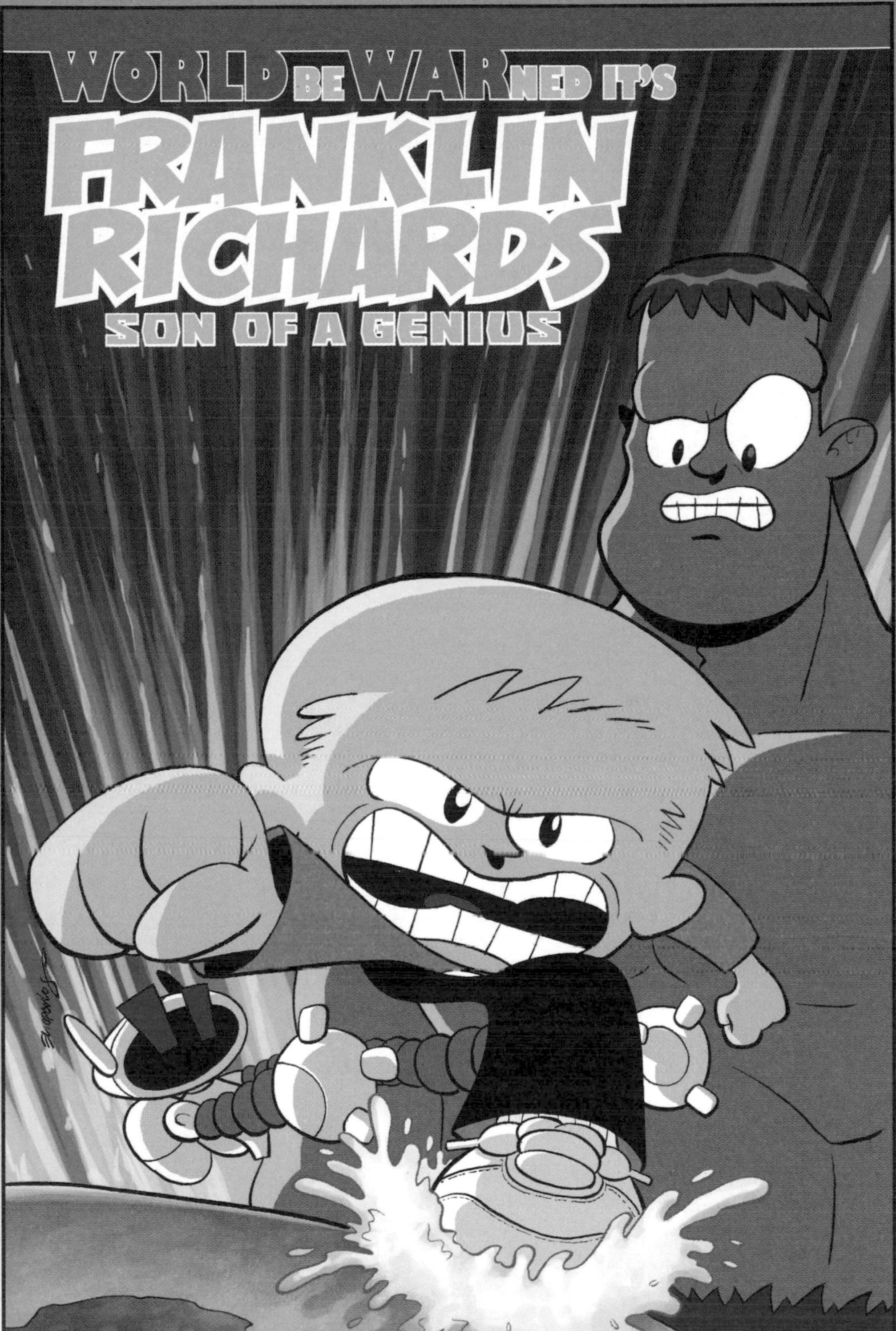
WORLD BE WARNED IT'S
FRANKLIN RICHARDS
SON OF A GENIUS

WORLD BE WARNED IT'S FRANKLIN RICHARDS
SON OF A GENIUS

CHRIS ELIOPOULOS AND MARC SUMERAK
STORY

MARC SUMERAK
SCRIPT

CHRIS ELIOPOULOS
ART & LETTERS

BRAD ANDERSON
COLORS

NATHAN COSBY
ASSISTANT EDITOR

MARK PANICCIA
EDITOR

JOE QUESADA
EDITOR IN CHIEF

DAN BUCKLEY
PUBLISHER

FRANKLIN RICHARDS SON OF A GENIUS IN: GRAVITY DEPRAVITY!

BY CHRIS ELIOPOULOS & MARC SUMERAK

BRAD ANDERSON COLORS · NATHAN COSBY ASSISTANT EDITOR · MARK PANICCIA EDITOR

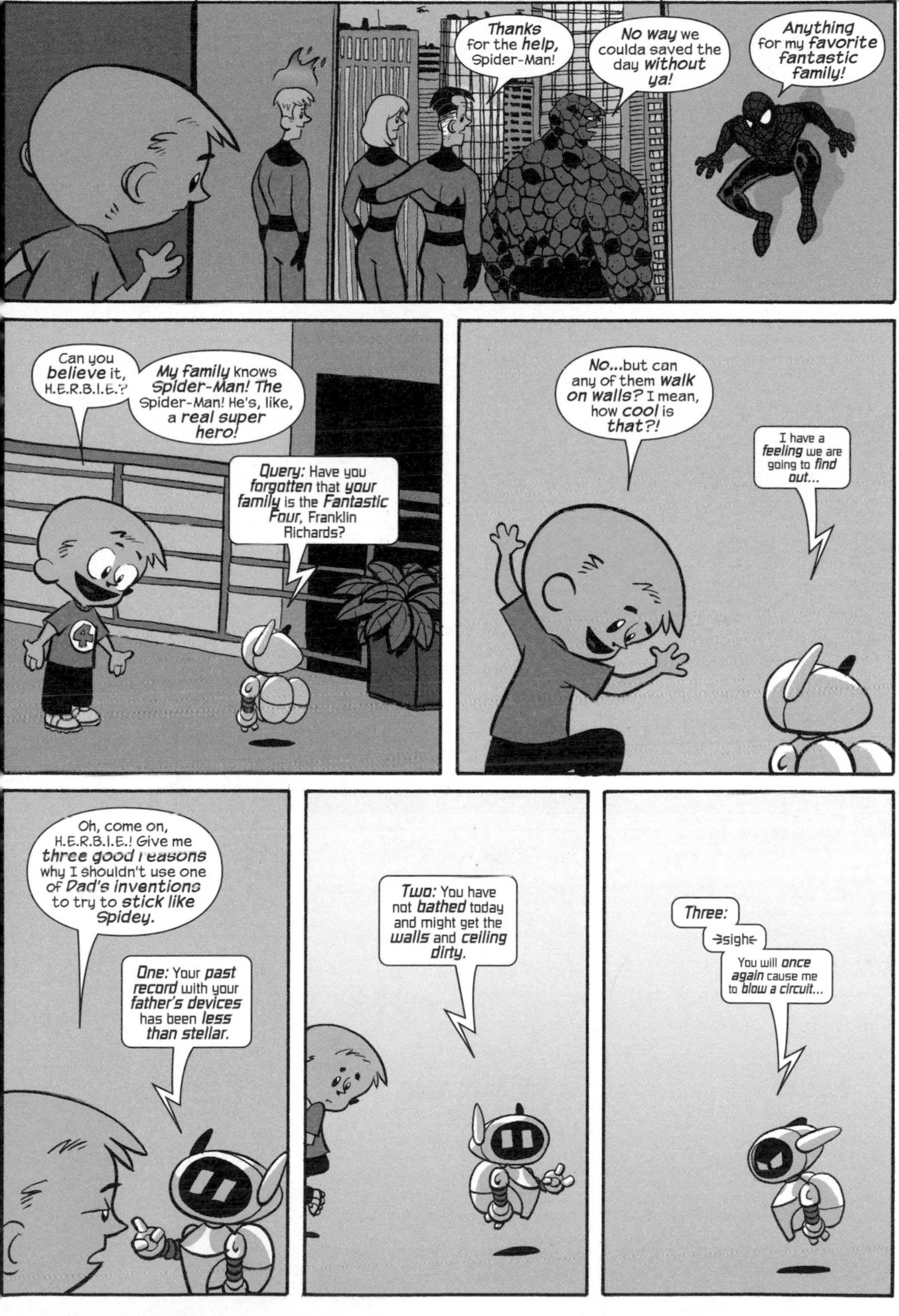

Thanks for the help, Spider-Man!
No way we coulda saved the day without ya!
Anything for my favorite fantastic family!
Can you believe it, H.E.R.B.I.E.?
My family knows Spider-Man! The Spider-Man! He's, like, a real super hero!
Query: Have you forgotten that your family is the Fantastic Four, Franklin Richards?
No...but can any of them walk on walls? I mean, how cool is that?!
I have a feeling we are going to find out...
Oh, come on, H.E.R.B.I.E.! Give me three good reasons why I shouldn't use one of Dad's inventions to try to stick like Spidey.
One: Your past record with your father's devices has been less than stellar.
Two: You have not bathed today and might get the walls and ceiling dirty.
Three:
sigh
You will once again cause me to blow a circuit...

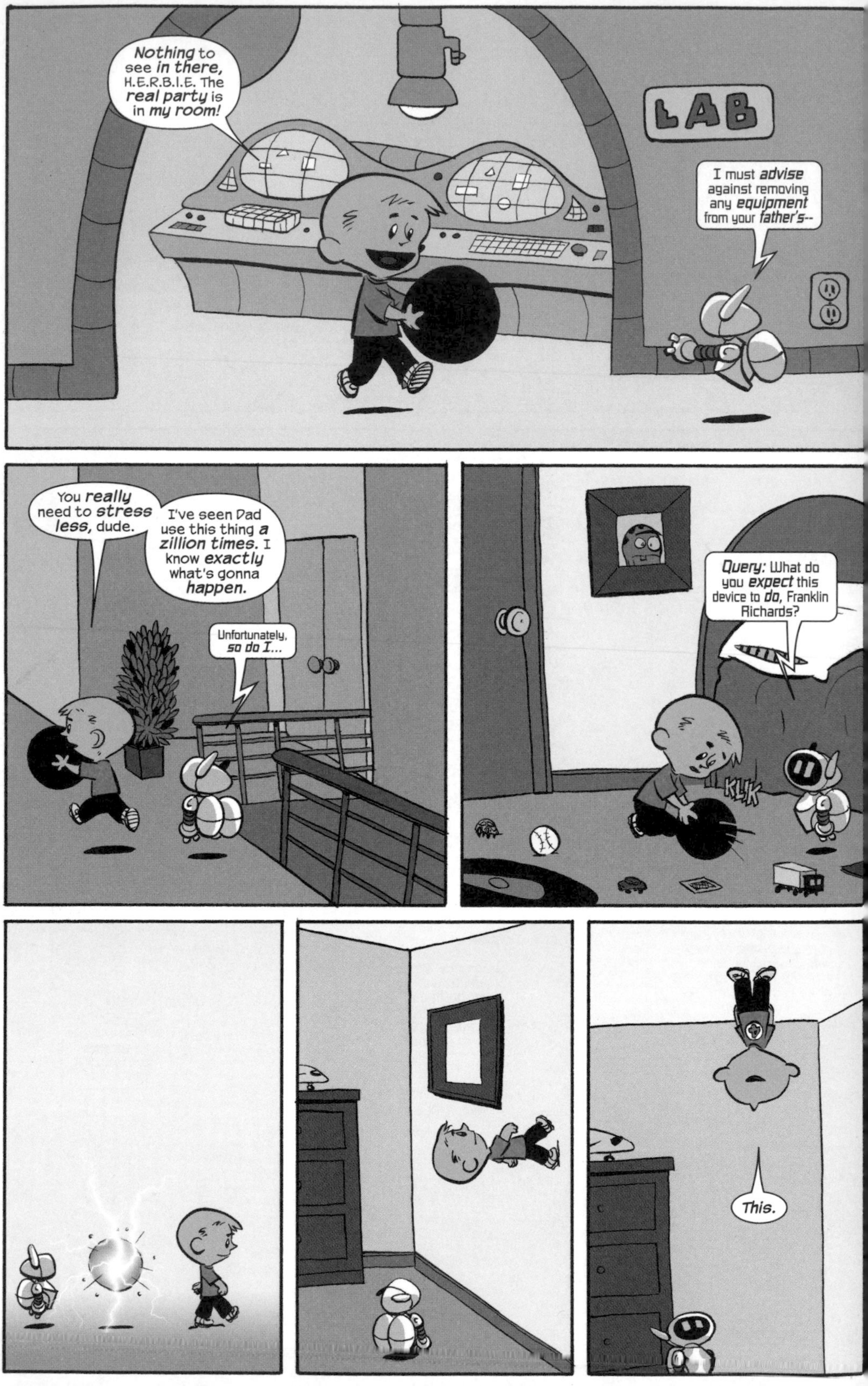
Nothing to see in there, H.E.R.B.I.E. The real party is in my room!
LAB
I must advise against removing any equipment from your father's--
You really need to stress less, dude.
I've seen Dad use this thing a zillion times. I know exactly what's gonna happen.
Unfortunately, so do I...
Query: What do you expect this device to do, Franklin Richards?
KLIK
This.

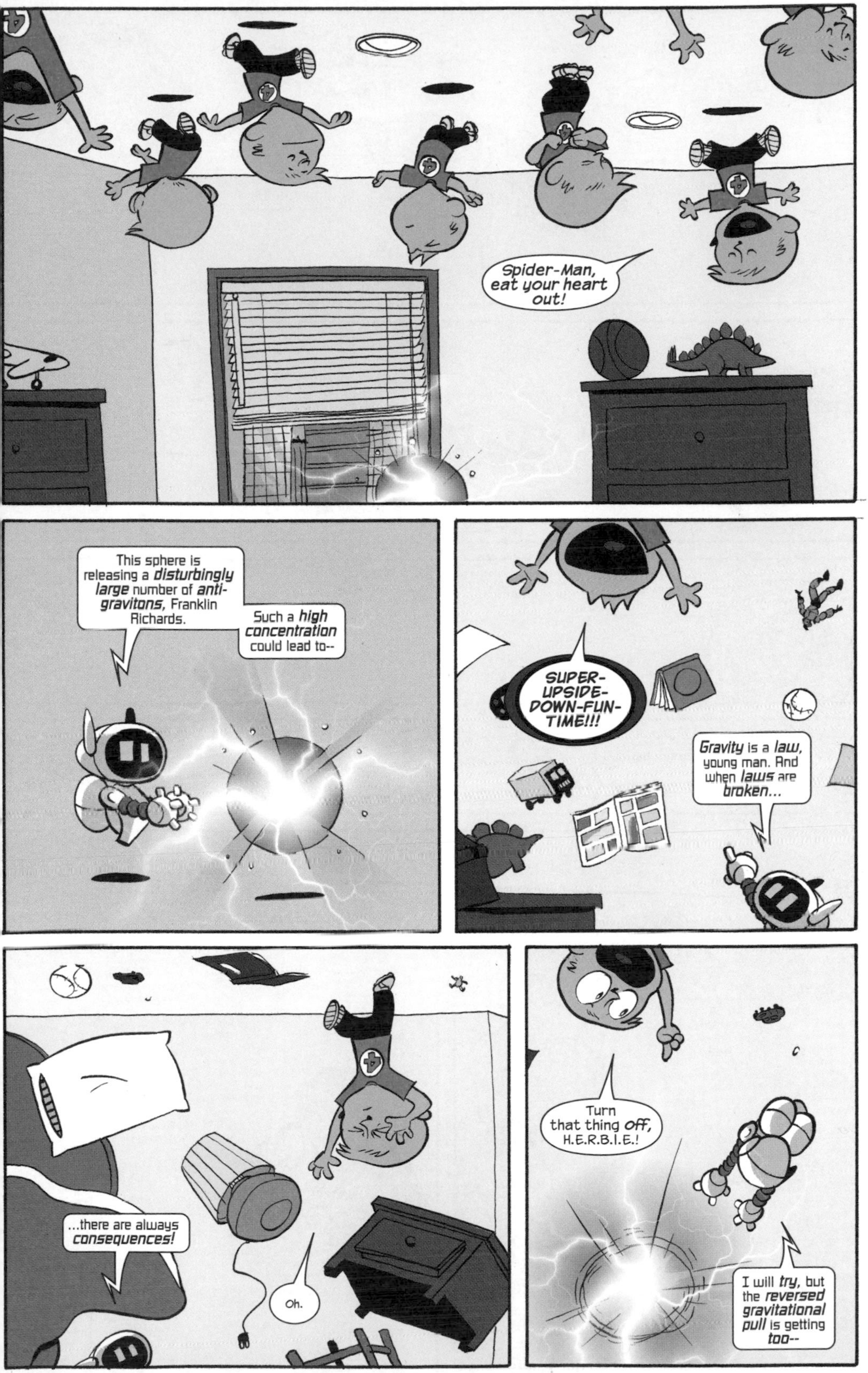
Spider-Man, eat your heart out!
This sphere is releasing a disturbingly large number of anti-gravitons, Franklin Richards.
Such a high concentration could lead to--
SUPER-UPSIDE-DOWN-FUN-TIME!!!
Gravity is a law, young man. And when laws are broken...
...there are always consequences!
Oh.
Turn that thing off, H.E.R.B.I.E.!
I will try, but the reversed gravitational pull is getting too--

THUD!

--100110!

SLAM!

Wait! Maybe I can *reach* it now!

No use...

Arms...too heavy!

But if the *gravity* continues to *increase*, the device could *collapse* in on *itself* and become--

--A BLACK HOLE!

Well, it was *fun* while it *lasted*, buddy...

Heh.

This... is funny, Fran... don't think you understand the gravity of the situation.

Trust me, Mom... if I understand anything right now, it's "gravity"...

END.

You are in big trouble, young man!

You're not leaving this room until every inch is clean and--

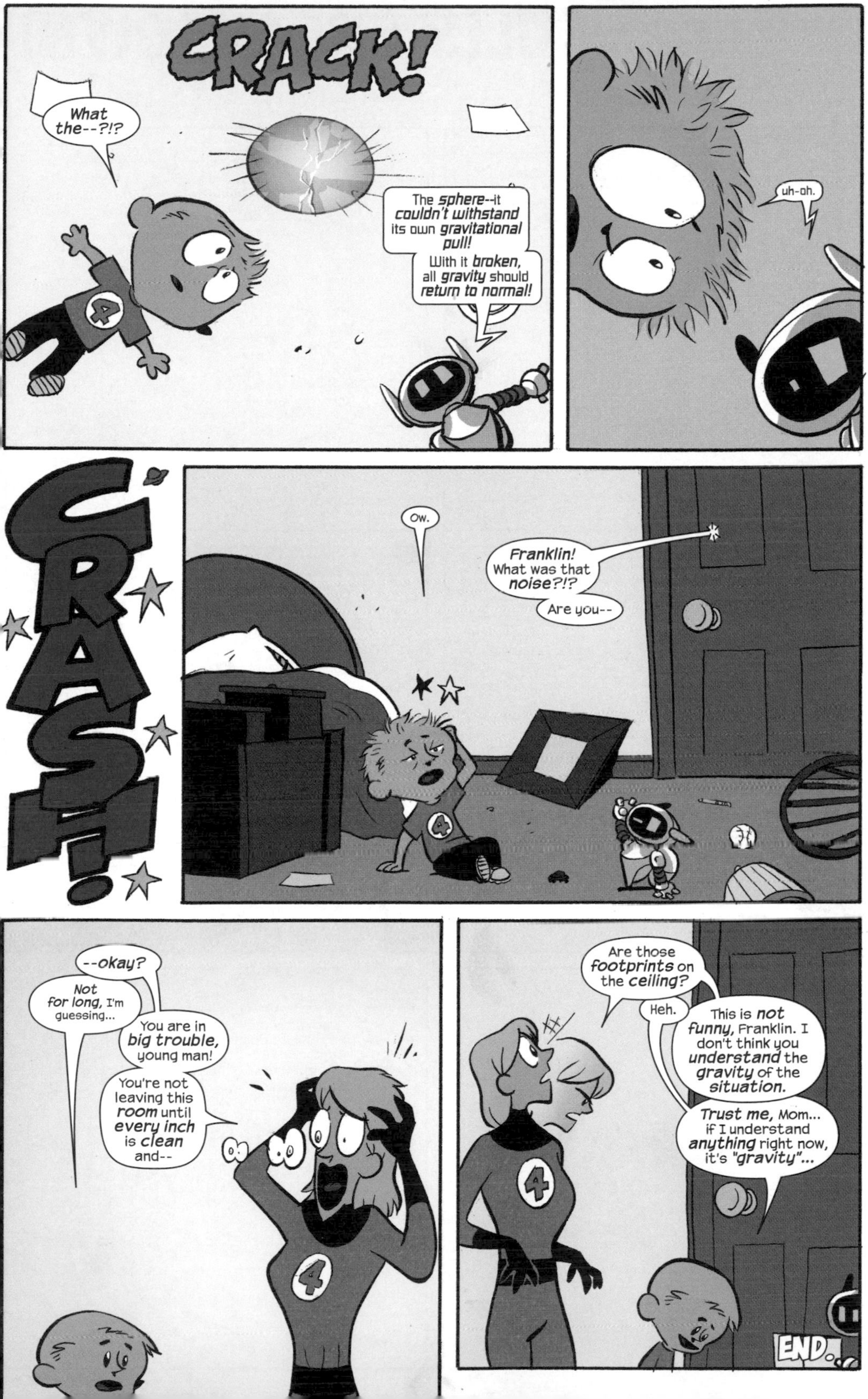
CRACK!
What the--?!?
The sphere--it couldn't withstand its own gravitational pull!
With it broken, all gravity should return to normal!
uh-oh.
CRASH!
Ow.
Franklin! What was that noise?!?
Are you--
--okay?
Not for long, I'm guessing...
You are in big trouble, young man!
You're not leaving this room until every inch is clean and--
Are those footprints on the ceiling?
Heh.
This is not funny, Franklin. I don't think you understand the gravity of the situation.
Trust me, Mom... if I understand anything right now, it's "gravity"...
END.

FRANKLIN RICHARDS: SON OF A GENIUS IN: BULLY BREAKDOWN!

BY CHRIS ELIOPOULOS & MARC SUMERAK
BRAD ANDERSON, COLORS
NATHAN COSBY, ASSISTANT EDITOR
MARK PANICCIA, EDITOR

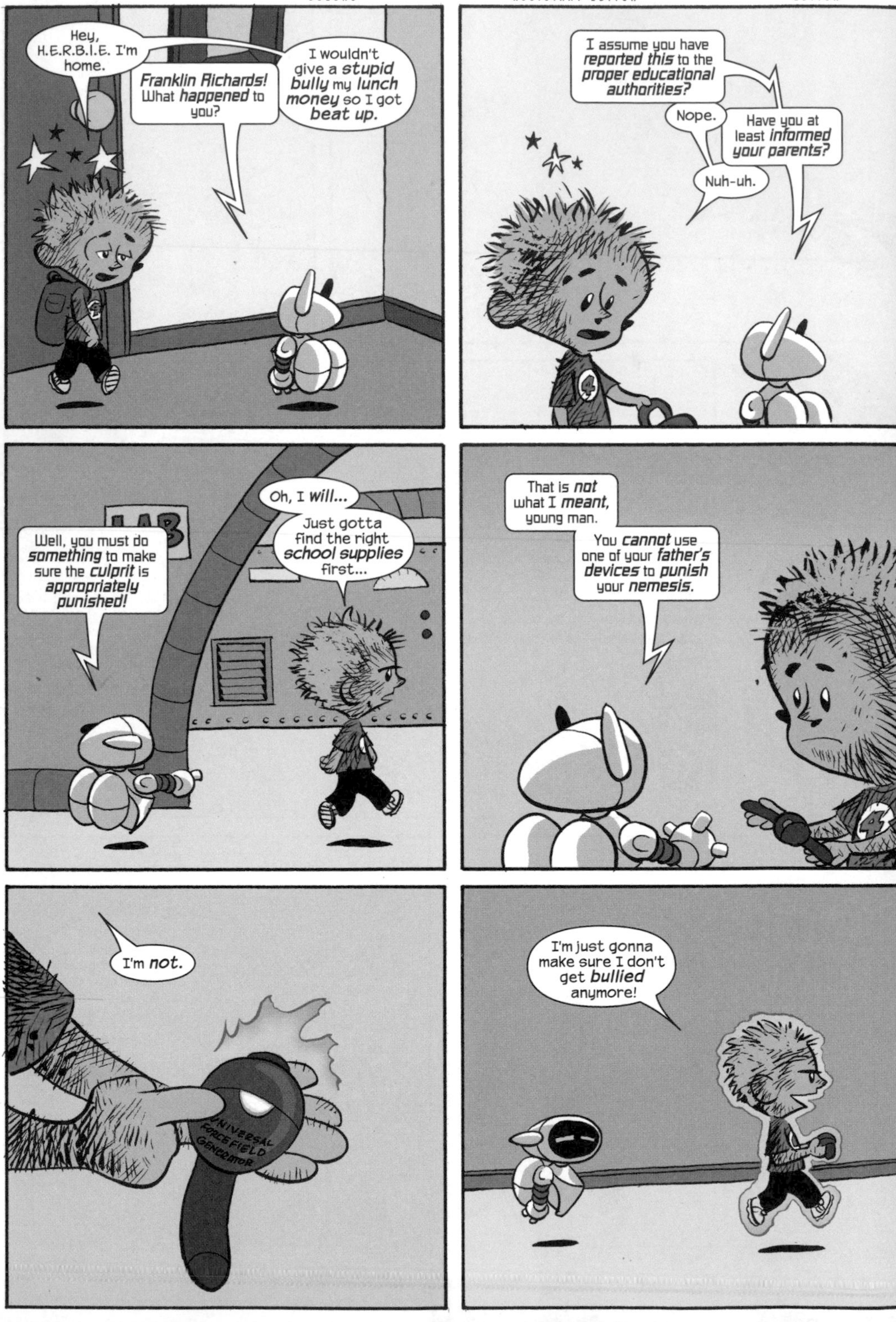
Hey, H.E.R.B.I.E. I'm home.
Franklin Richards! What happened to you?
I wouldn't give a stupid bully my lunch money so I got beat up.
I assume you have reported this to the proper educational authorities?
Nope.
Have you at least informed your parents?
Nuh-uh.
LAB
Well, you must do something to make sure the culprit is appropriately punished!
Oh, I will...
Just gotta find the right school supplies first...
That is not what I meant, young man.
You cannot use one of your father's devices to punish your nemesis.
I'm not.
UNIVERSAL FORCEFIELD GENERATOR
I'm just gonna make sure I don't get bullied anymore!

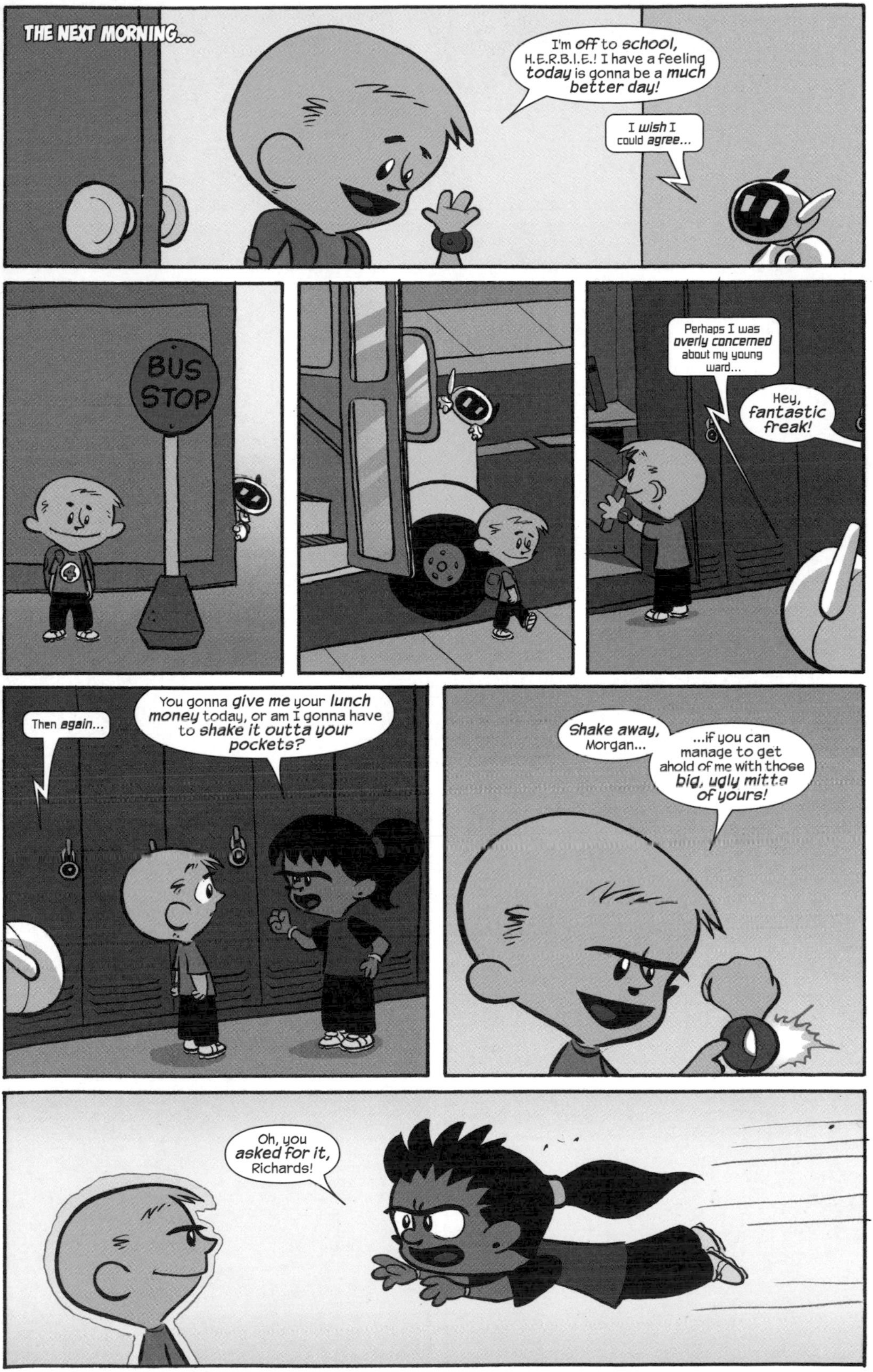
THE NEXT MORNING...
I'm off to school, H.E.R.B.I.E.! I have a feeling today is gonna be a much better day!
I wish I could agree...
BUS STOP
Perhaps I was overly concerned about my young ward...
Hey, fantastic freak!
Then again...
You gonna give me your lunch money today, or am I gonna have to shake it outta your pockets?
Shake away, Morgan...
...if you can manage to get ahold of me with those big, ugly mitts of yours!
Oh, you asked for it, Richards!

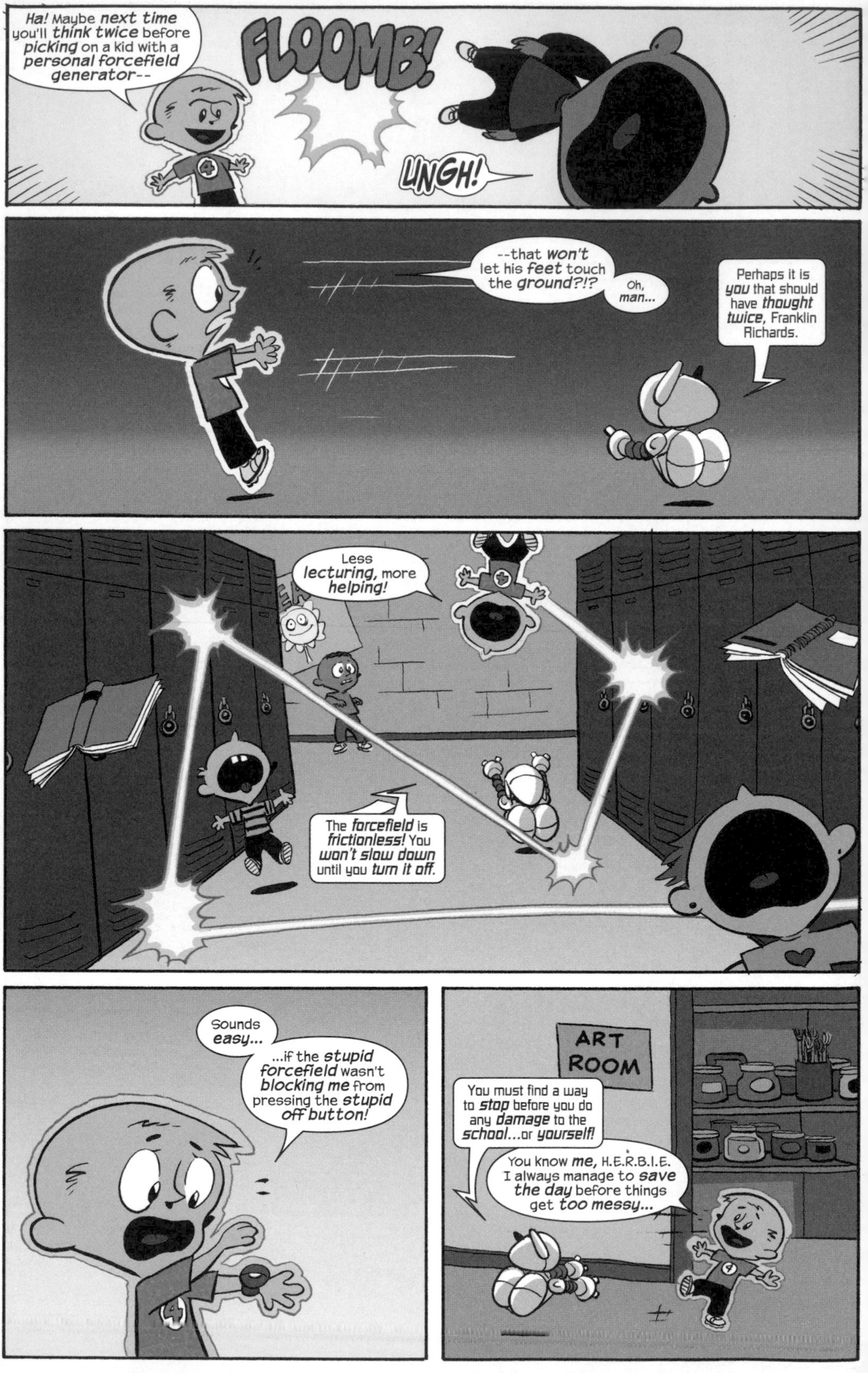

Ha! Maybe next time you'll think twice before picking on a kid with a personal forcefield generator--
FLOOMB!
UNGH!
--that won't let his feet touch the ground?!?
Oh, man...
Perhaps it is you that should have thought twice, Franklin Richards.
Less lecturing, more helping!
The forcefield is frictionless! You won't slow down until you turn it off.
Sounds easy...
...if the stupid forcefield wasn't blocking me from pressing the stupid off button!
ART ROOM
You must find a way to stop before you do any damage to the school...or yourself!
You know me, H.E.R.B.I.E. I always manage to save the day before things get too messy...

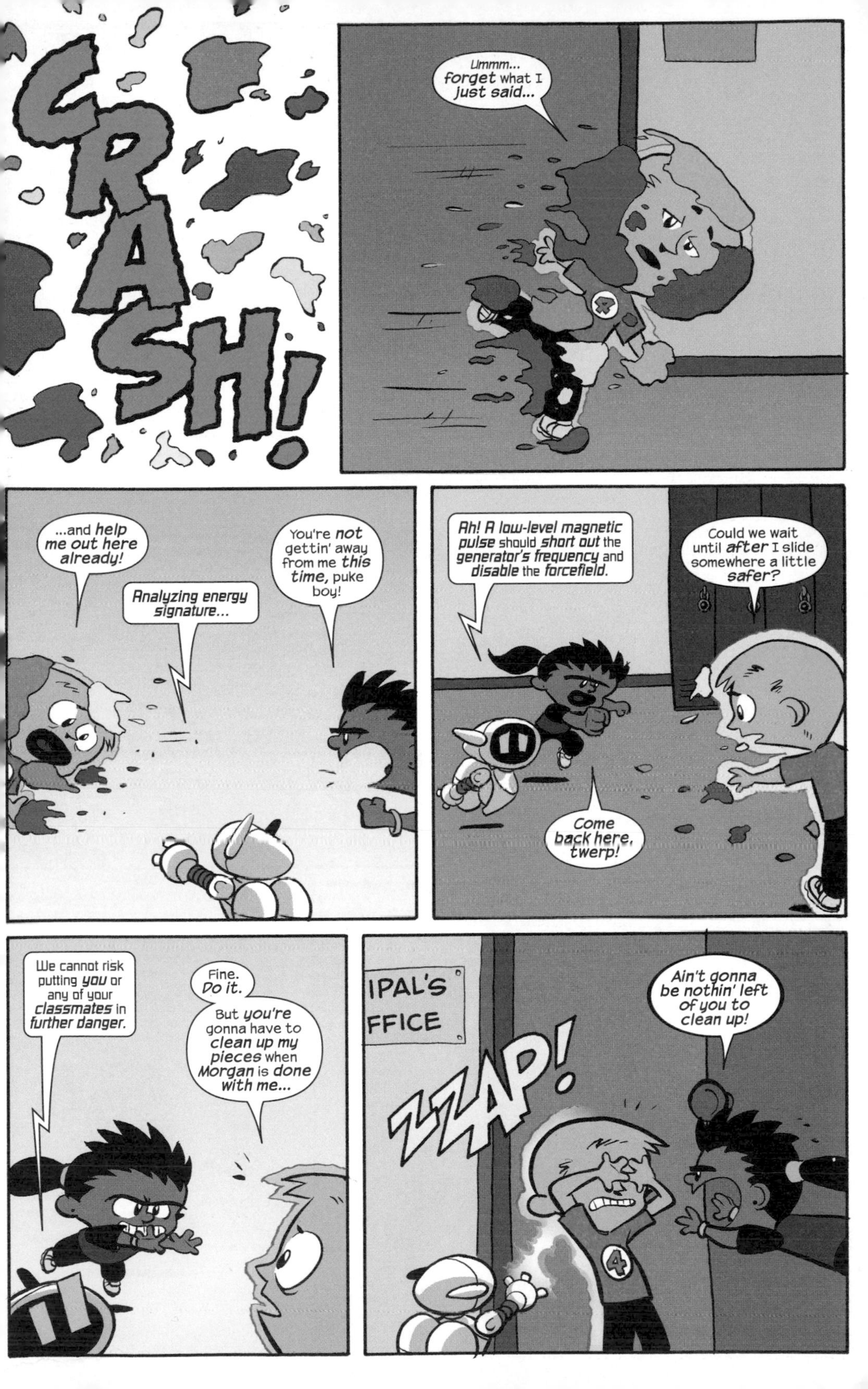
CRASH!
Ummm... forget what I just said...
...and help me out here already!
Analyzing energy signature...
You're not gettin' away from me this time, puke boy!
Ah! A low-level magnetic pulse should short out the generator's frequency and disable the forcefield.
Could we wait until after I slide somewhere a little safer?
Come back here, twerp!
We cannot risk putting you or any of your classmates in further danger.
Fine. Do it.
But you're gonna have to clean up my pieces when Morgan is done with me...
IPAL'S
FFICE
Ain't gonna be nothin' left of you to clean up!
ZZAP!

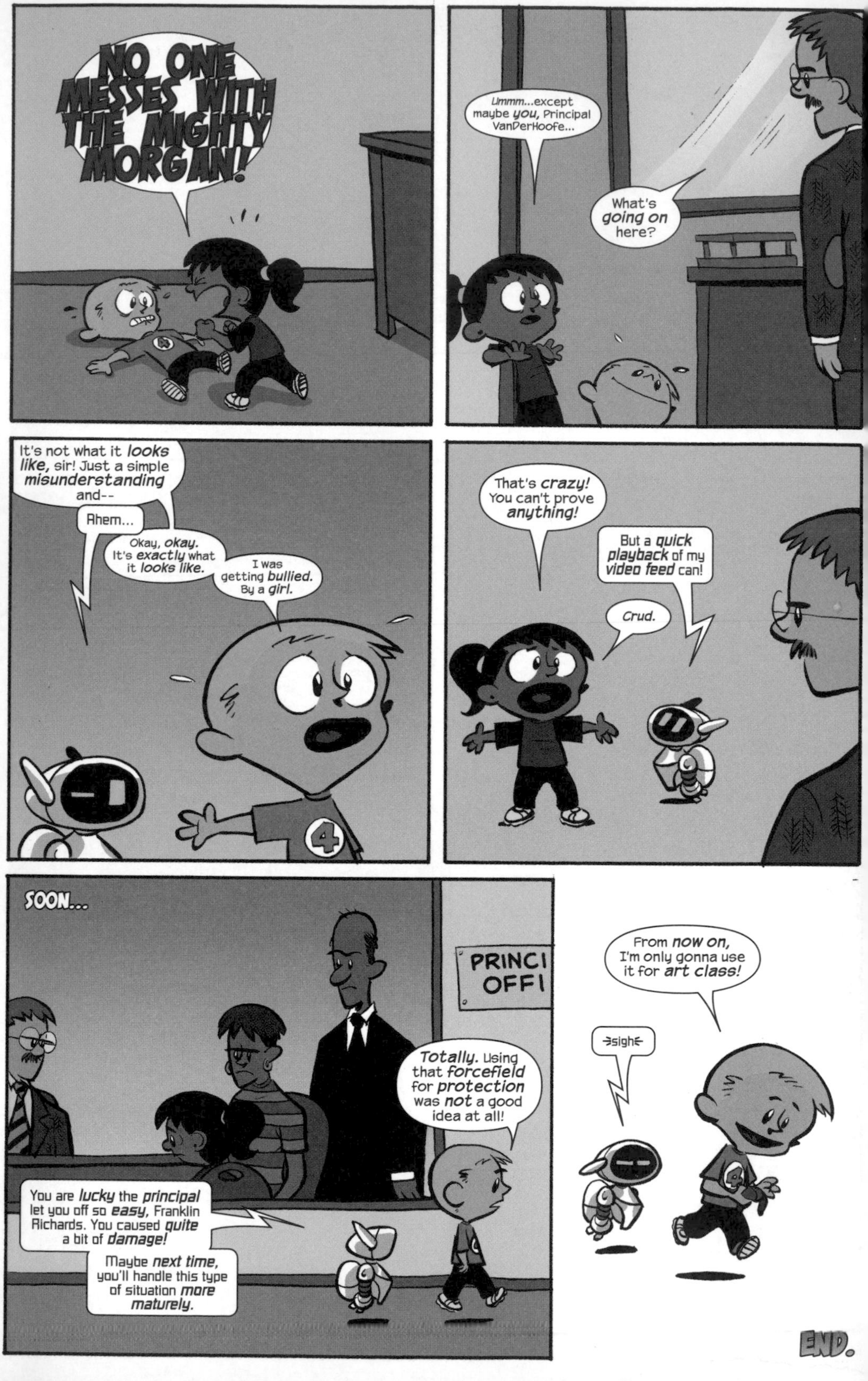
NO ONE MESSES WITH THE MIGHTY MORGAN!
Ummm...except maybe you, Principal VanDerHoofe...
What's going on here?
It's not what it looks like, sir! Just a simple misunderstanding and--
Ahem...
Okay, okay. It's exactly what it looks like.
I was getting bullied. By a girl.
That's crazy! You can't prove anything!
But a quick playback of my video feed can!
Crud.
SOON...
PRINCI
OFFI
Totally. Using that forcefield for protection was not a good idea at all!
You are lucky the principal let you off so easy, Franklin Richards. You caused quite a bit of damage!
Maybe next time, you'll handle this type of situation more maturely.
From now on, I'm only gonna use it for art class!
≽sigh≼
END.

FRANKLIN RICHARDS SON OF A GENIUS IN: MONKEY TALK!

BY CHRIS ELIOPOULOS & MARC SUMERAK

BRAD ANDERSON COLORS
NATHAN COSBY ASSISTANT EDITOR
MARK PANICCIA EDITOR

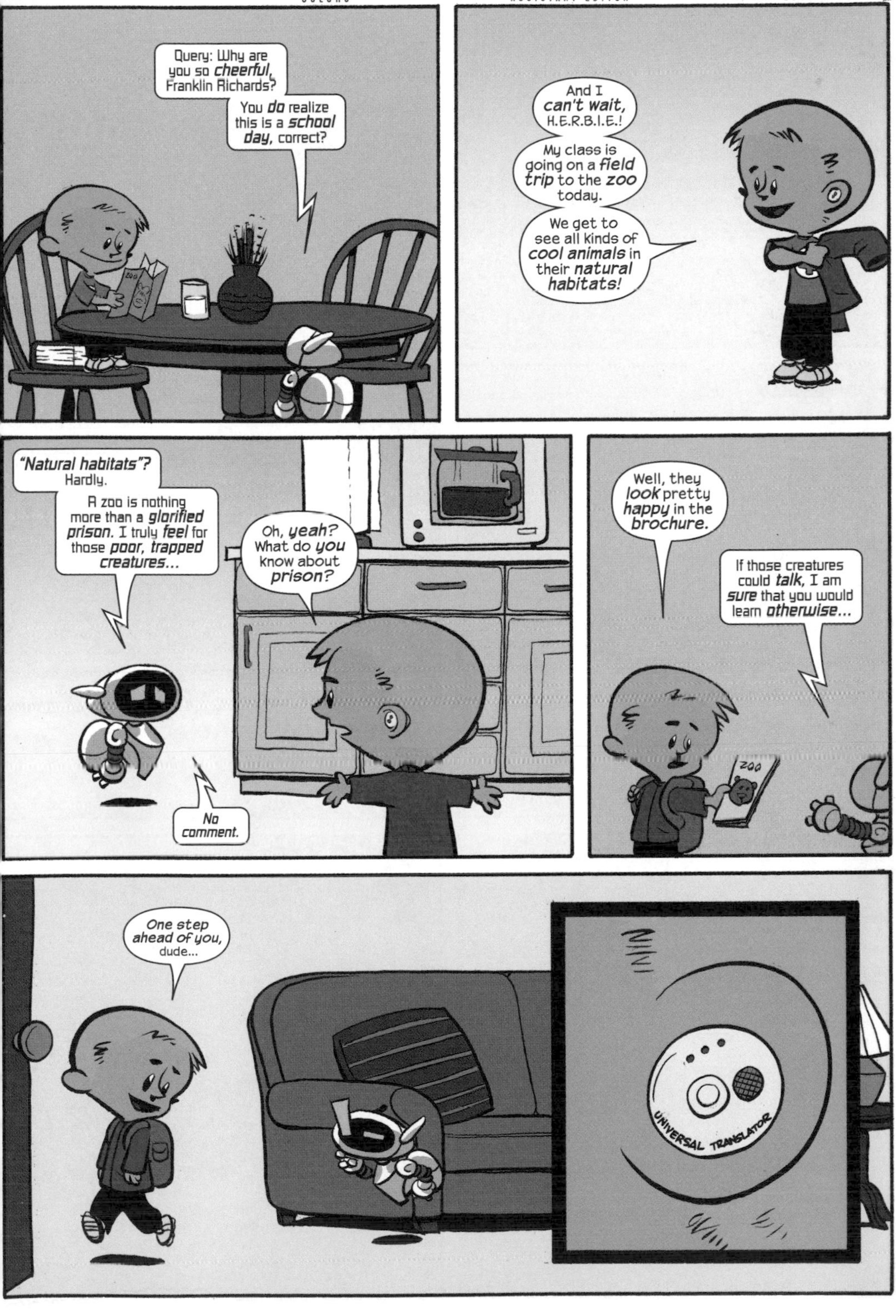

Query: Why are you so *cheerful*, Franklin Richards?
You *do* realize this is a *school day*, correct?
ZOO
And I *can't wait*, H.E.R.B.I.E.!
My class is going on a *field trip* to the *zoo* today.
We get to see all kinds of *cool animals* in their *natural habitats!*
"*Natural habitats*"? Hardly.
A zoo is nothing more than a *glorified prison*. I truly *feel* for those *poor, trapped creatures...*
Oh, *yeah?* What do *you* know about *prison?*
No comment.
Well, they *look* pretty *happy* in the *brochure*.
If those creatures could *talk*, I am *sure* that you would learn *otherwise...*
ZOO
One step ahead of you, dude...
UNIVERSAL TRANSLATOR

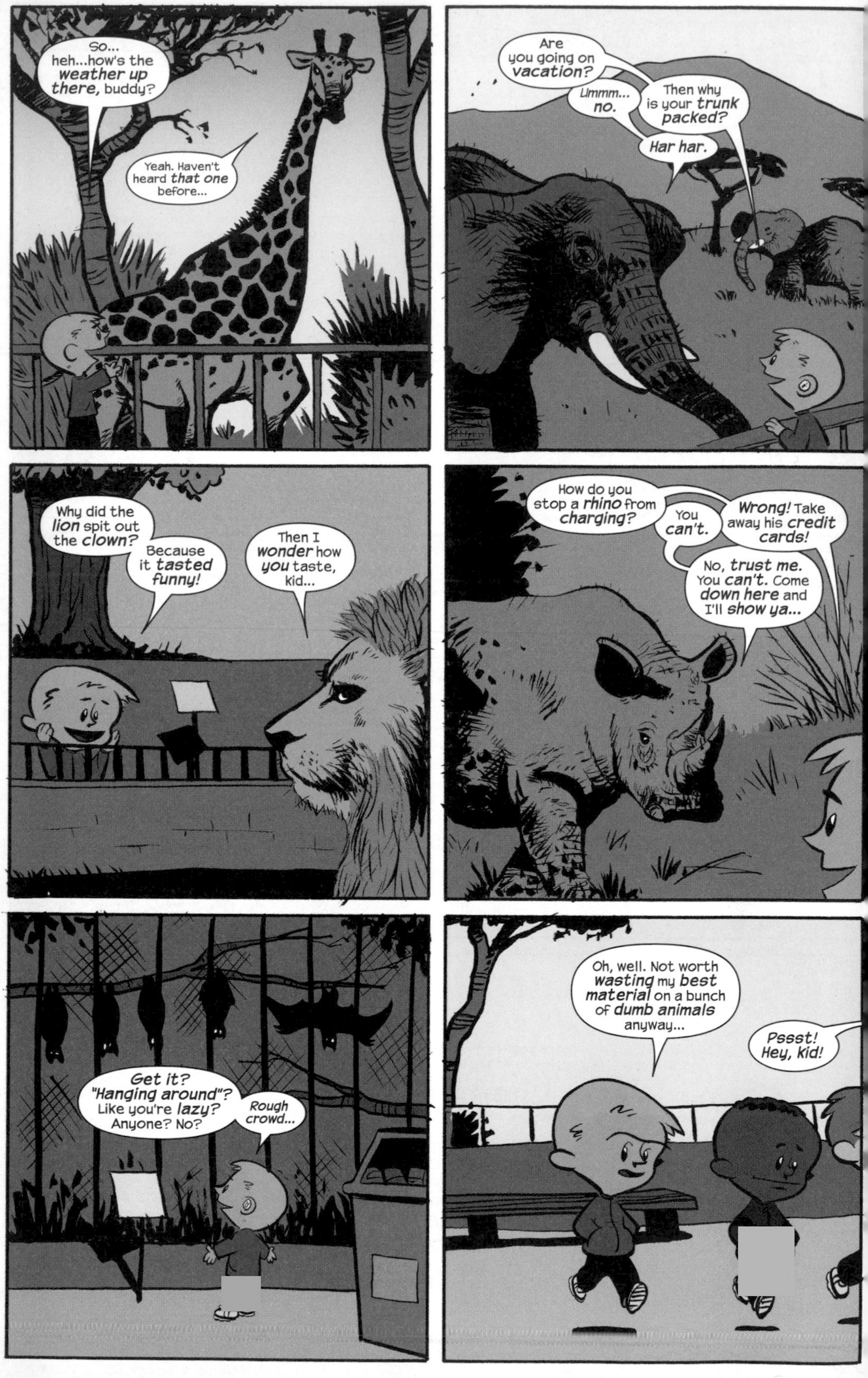
So... heh...how's the weather up there, buddy?
Yeah. Haven't heard that one before...
Are you going on vacation?
Ummm... no.
Then why is your trunk packed?
Har har.
Why did the lion spit out the clown?
Because it tasted funny!
Then I wonder how you taste, kid...
How do you stop a rhino from charging?
You can't.
Wrong! Take away his credit cards!
No, trust me. You can't. Come down here and I'll show ya...
Get it? "Hanging around"? Like you're lazy? Anyone? No?
Rough crowd...
Oh, well. Not worth wasting my best material on a bunch of dumb animals anyway...
Pssst! Hey, kid!

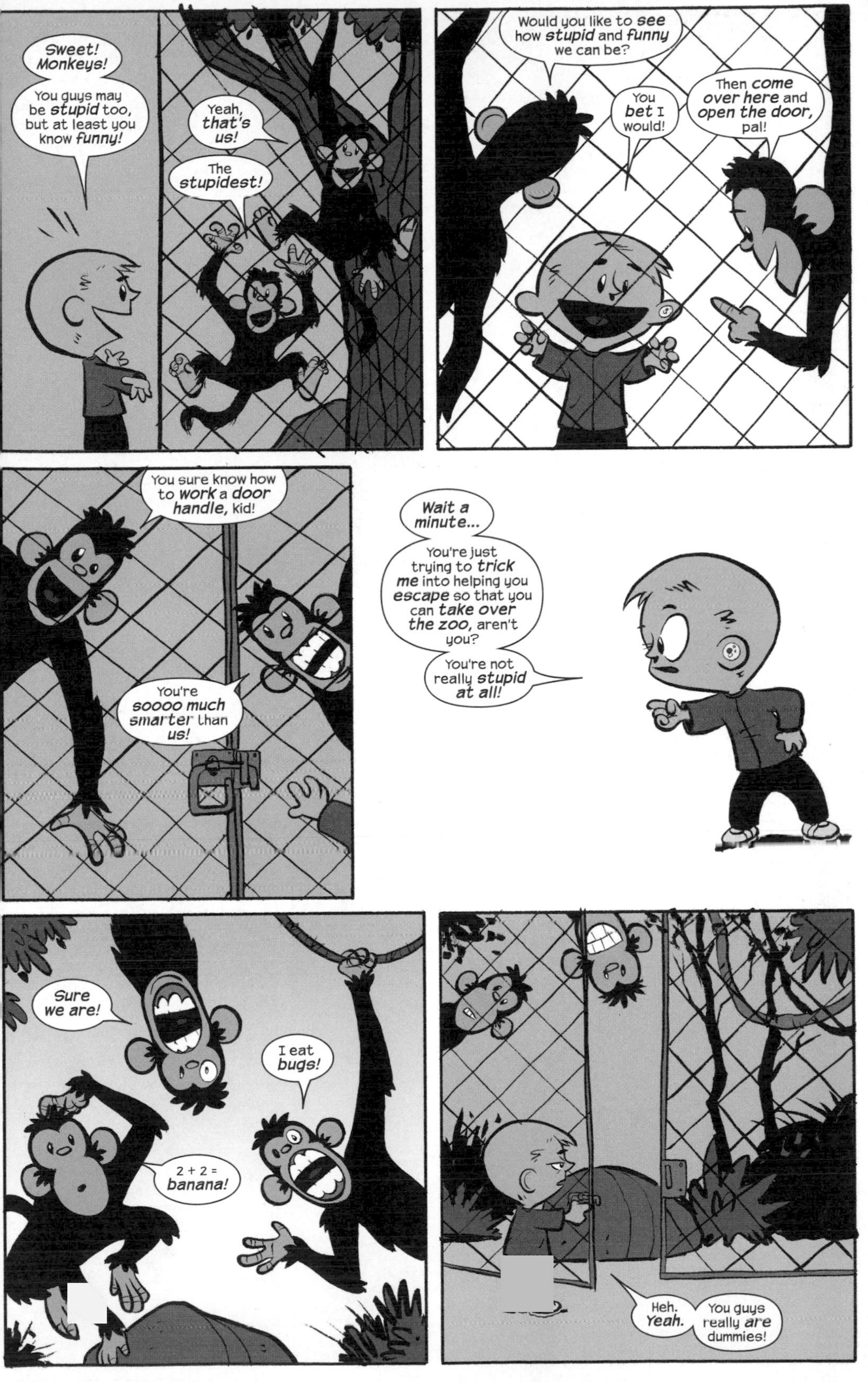

Sweet! Monkeys!
You guys may be stupid too, but at least you know funny!
Yeah, that's us!
The stupidest!
Would you like to see how stupid and funny we can be?
You bet I would!
Then come over here and open the door, pal!
You sure know how to work a door handle, kid!
You're soooo much smarter than us!
Wait a minute...
You're just trying to trick me into helping you escape so that you can take over the zoo, aren't you?
You're not really stupid at all!
Sure we are!
I eat bugs!
2 + 2 = banana!
Heh. Yeah.
You guys really are dummies!

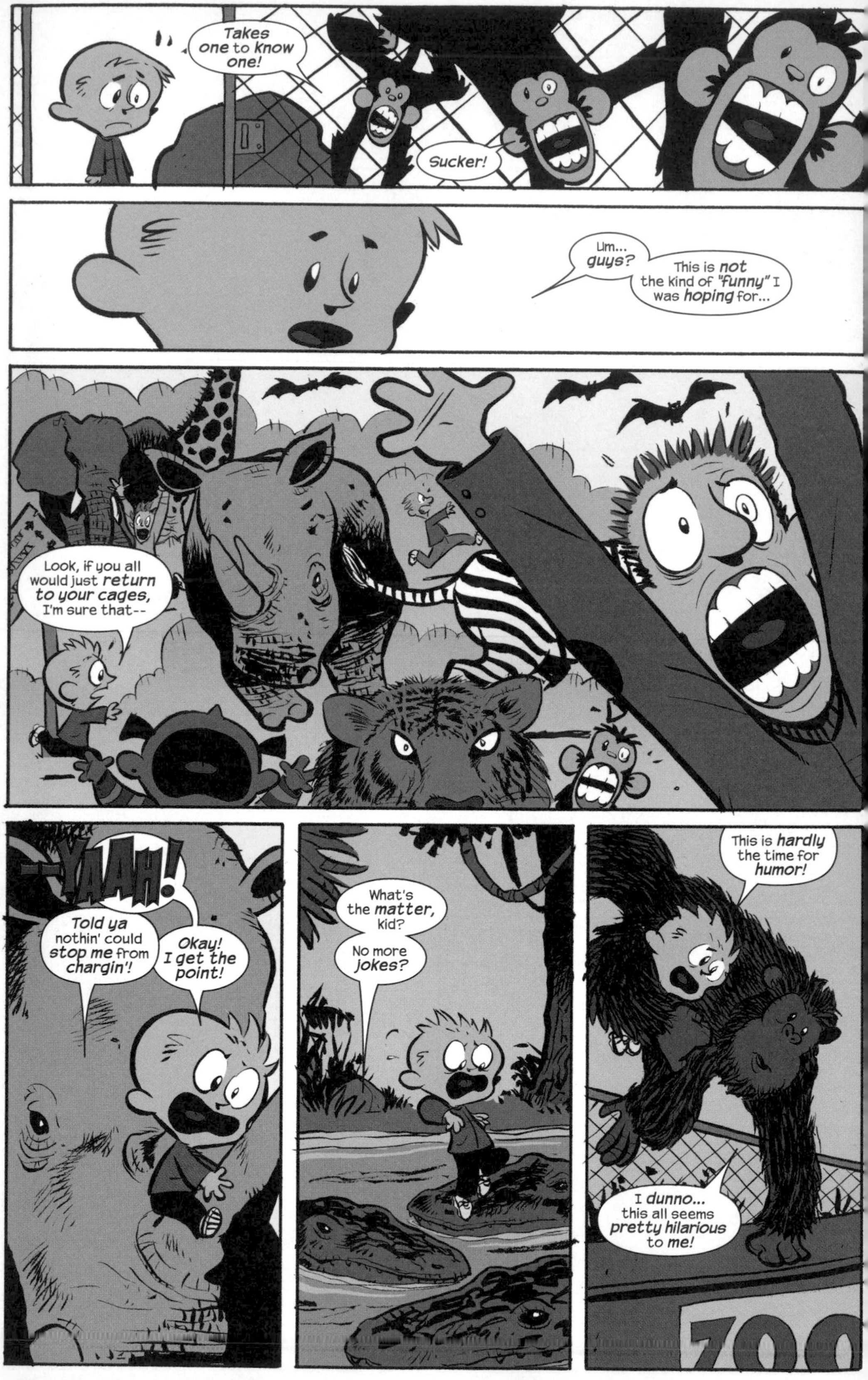
Takes one to know one!
Sucker!
Um... guys?
This is not the kind of "funny" I was hoping for...
Look, if you all would just return to your cages, I'm sure that--
--YAAH!
Told ya nothin' could stop me from chargin'!
Okay! I get the point!
What's the matter, kid?
No more jokes?
This is hardly the time for humor!
I dunno... this all seems pretty hilarious to me!
ZOO

How was your *field trip* to the *zoo*, Franklin Richards?

Completely uneventful. Why? What have you *heard?*

I was doing some *inventory* in the *lab* while you were gone and noticed that your father's *universal translator* was missing.

Do *you* know *where it is?*

I took it to the *zoo* so I could *talk* to the *animals.*

You were *right,* H.E.R.B.I.E. They *hated* being *locked up.*

I knew it! So *what else* did they have to *say?*

Nothing.

Surely they had *something* exciting to share with you. Some *insight* on *inter-species--*

Nope. Nothing at all.

Time to *go* to bed! 'Night, H.E.R.B.I.E.

But it's only 4:00...

Do you mind *watching Franklin* for a while, H.E.R.B.I.E.?

The *city* needs the *Fantastic Four* to *round up* some *dangerous escapees.*

Ah, another *prison break,* sir?

Nope. Just some *zoo* animals.

FRANKLIN!

END.

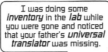

FRANKLIN RICHARDS SON OF A GENIUS IN: BUILD A BETTER 'BOT!

BY CHRIS ELIOPOULOS & MARC SUMERAK

BRAD ANDERSON COLORS | NATHAN COSBY ASSISTANT EDITOR | MARK PANICCIA EDITOR

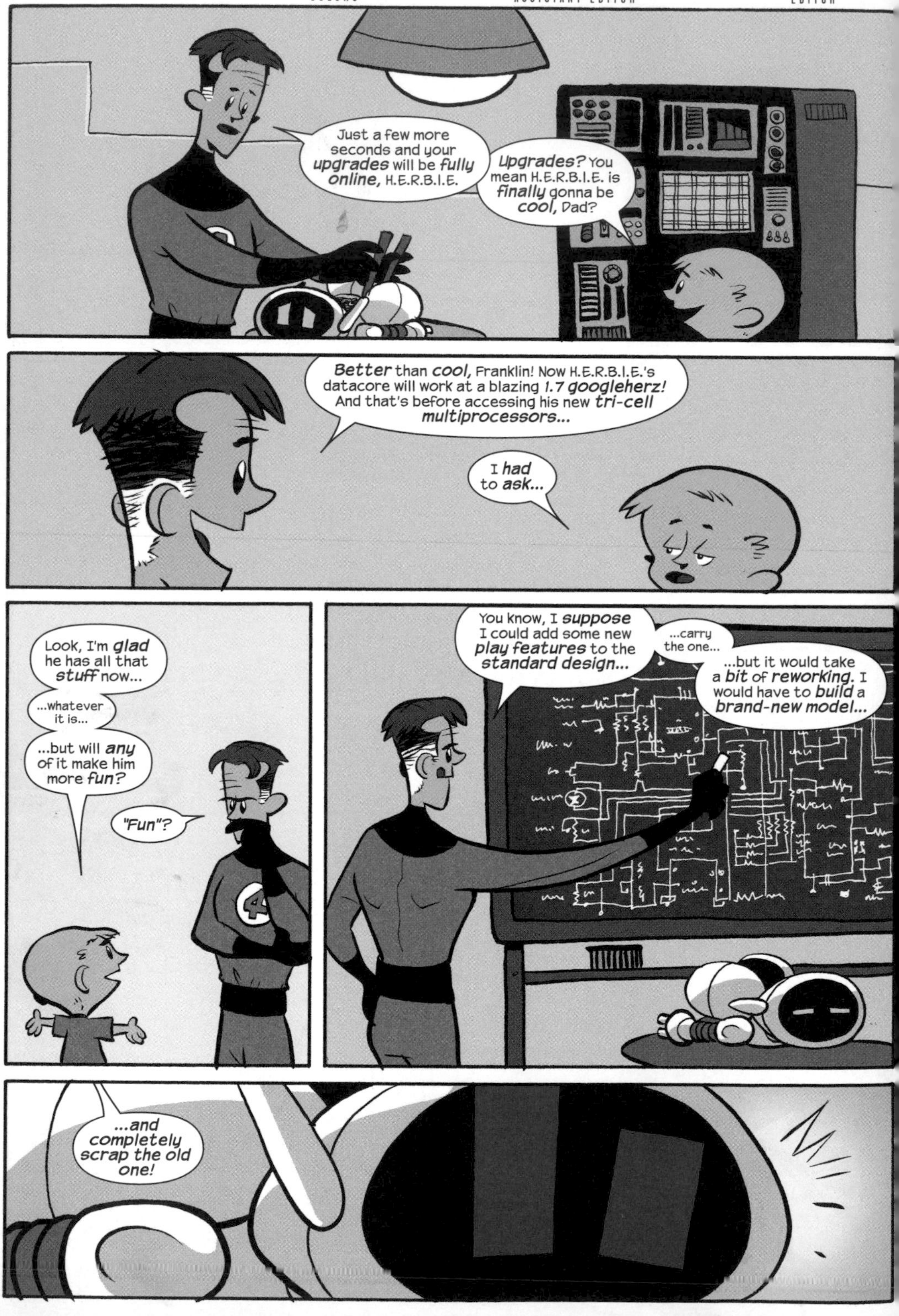

Just a few more seconds and your upgrades will be fully online, H.E.R.B.I.E.
Upgrades? You mean H.E.R.B.I.E. is finally gonna be cool, Dad?
Better than cool, Franklin! Now H.E.R.B.I.E.'s datacore will work at a blazing 1.7 googleherz! And that's before accessing his new tri-cell multiprocessors...
I had to ask...
Look, I'm glad he has all that stuff now...
...whatever it is...
...but will any of it make him more fun?
"Fun"?
You know, I suppose I could add some new play features to the standard design...
...carry the one...
...but it would take a bit of reworking. I would have to build a brand-new model...
...and completely scrap the old one!

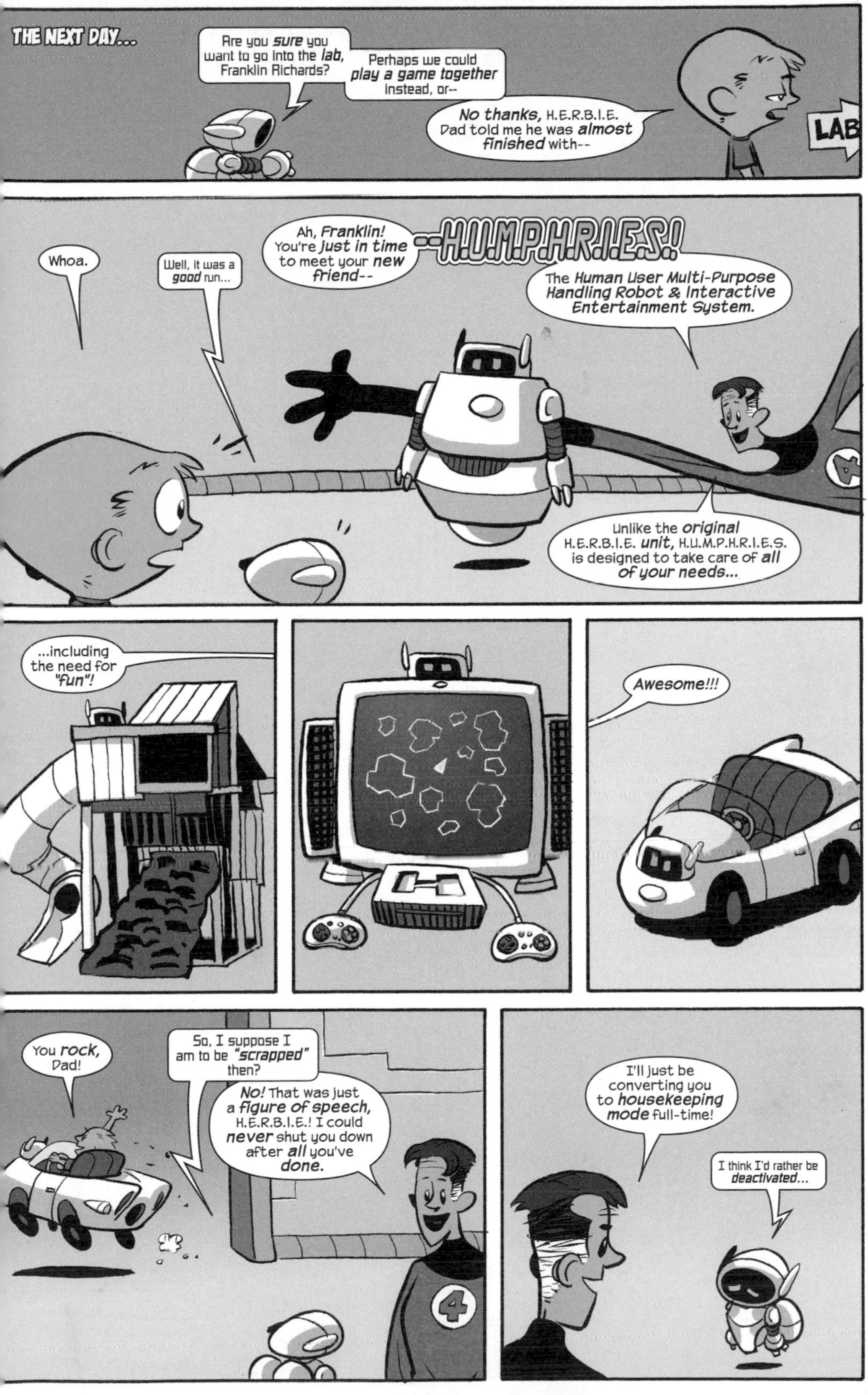
THE NEXT DAY...
Are you sure you want to go into the lab, Franklin Richards?
Perhaps we could play a game together instead, or--
No thanks, H.E.R.B.I.E. Dad told me he was almost finished with--
LAB
Whoa.
Well, it was a good run...
Ah, Franklin! You're just in time to meet your new friend--
--H.U.M.P.H.R.I.E.S.!
The Human User Multi-Purpose Handling Robot & Interactive Entertainment System.
Unlike the original H.E.R.B.I.E. unit, H.U.M.P.H.R.I.E.S. is designed to take care of all of your needs...
...including the need for "fun"!
Awesome!!!
You rock, Dad!
So, I suppose I am to be "scrapped" then?
No! That was just a figure of speech, H.E.R.B.I.E.! I could never shut you down after all you've done.
I'll just be converting you to housekeeping mode full-time!
I think I'd rather be deactivated...

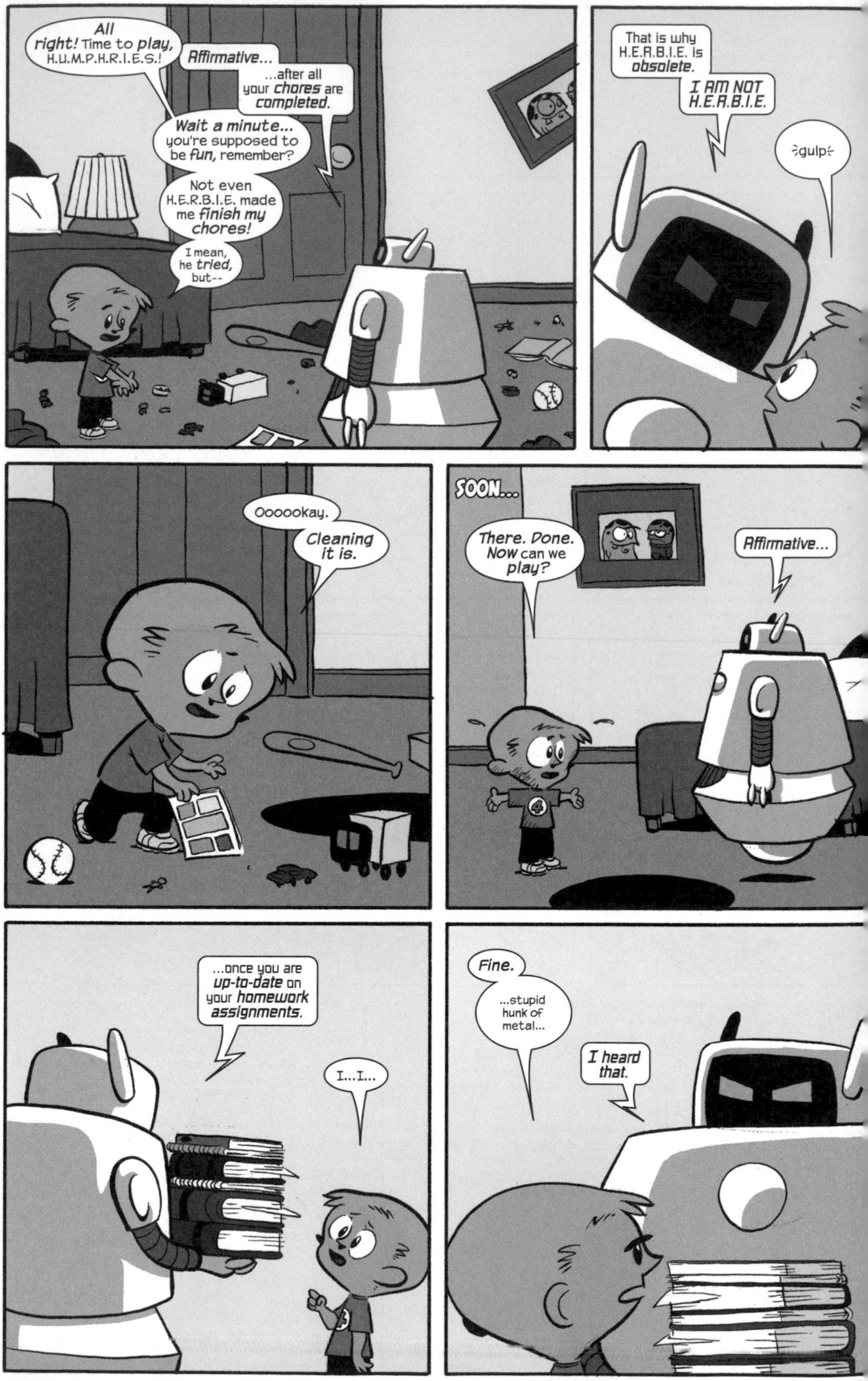
All right! Time to play, H.U.M.P.H.R.I.E.S.!
Affirmative...
...after all your chores are completed.
Wait a minute... you're supposed to be fun, remember?
Not even H.E.R.B.I.E. made me finish my chores!
I mean, he tried, but--
That is why H.E.R.B.I.E. is obsolete.
I AM NOT H.E.R.B.I.E.
gulp
Oooookay.
Cleaning it is.
SOON...
There. Done. NOW can we play?
Affirmative...
...once you are up-to-date on your homework assignments.
I...I...
Fine.
...stupid hunk of metal...
I heard that.

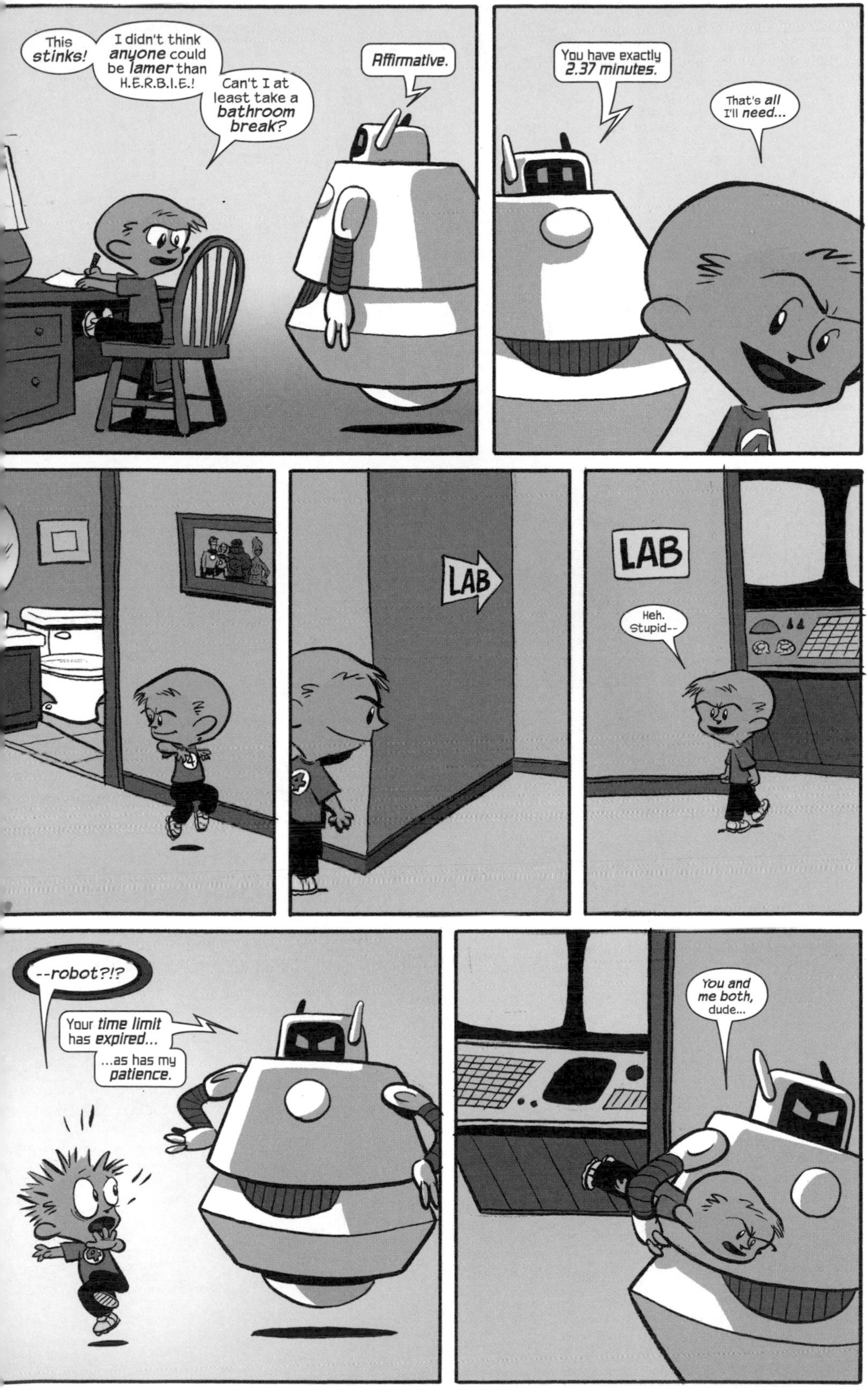
This stinks!
I didn't think anyone could be lamer than H.E.R.B.I.E.!
Can't I at least take a bathroom break?
Affirmative.
You have exactly 2.37 minutes.
That's all I'll need...
LAB
LAB
Heh. Stupid--
--robot?!?
Your time limit has expired...
...as has my patience.
You and me both, dude...

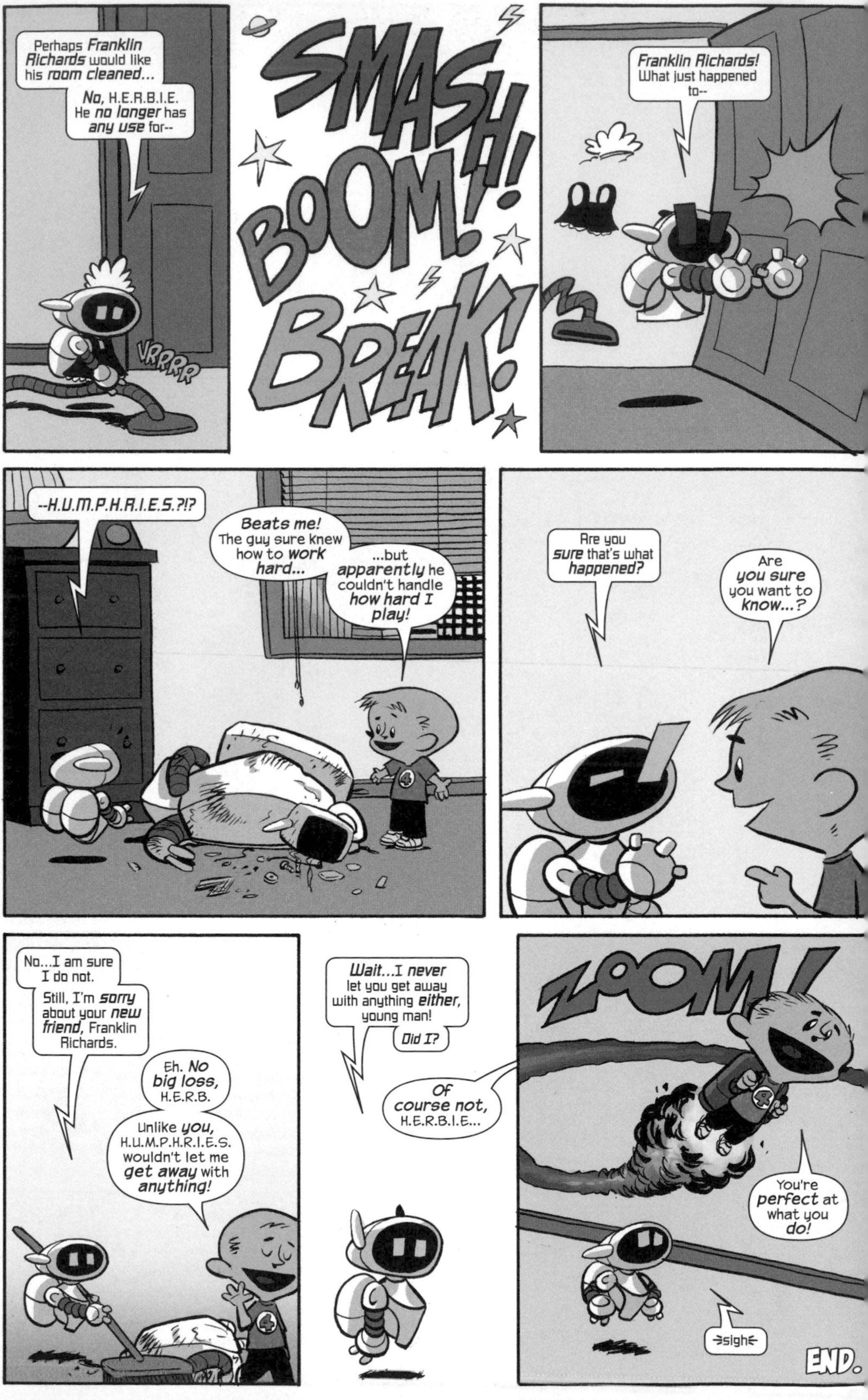
Perhaps Franklin Richards would like his room cleaned...
No, H.E.R.B.I.E. He no longer has any use for--
VRRRR
SMASH! BOOM!! BREAK!
Franklin Richards! What just happened to--
--H.U.M.P.H.R.I.E.S.?!?
Beats me! The guy sure knew how to work hard...
...but apparently he couldn't handle how hard I play!
Are you sure that's what happened?
Are you sure you want to know...?
No...I am sure I do not.
Still, I'm sorry about your new friend, Franklin Richards.
Eh. No big loss, H.E.R.B.
Unlike you, H.U.M.P.H.R.I.E.S. wouldn't let me get away with anything!
Wait...I never let you get away with anything either, young man!
Did I?
Of course not, H.E.R.B.I.E...
ZOOM!
You're perfect at what you do!
≥sigh≤
END.

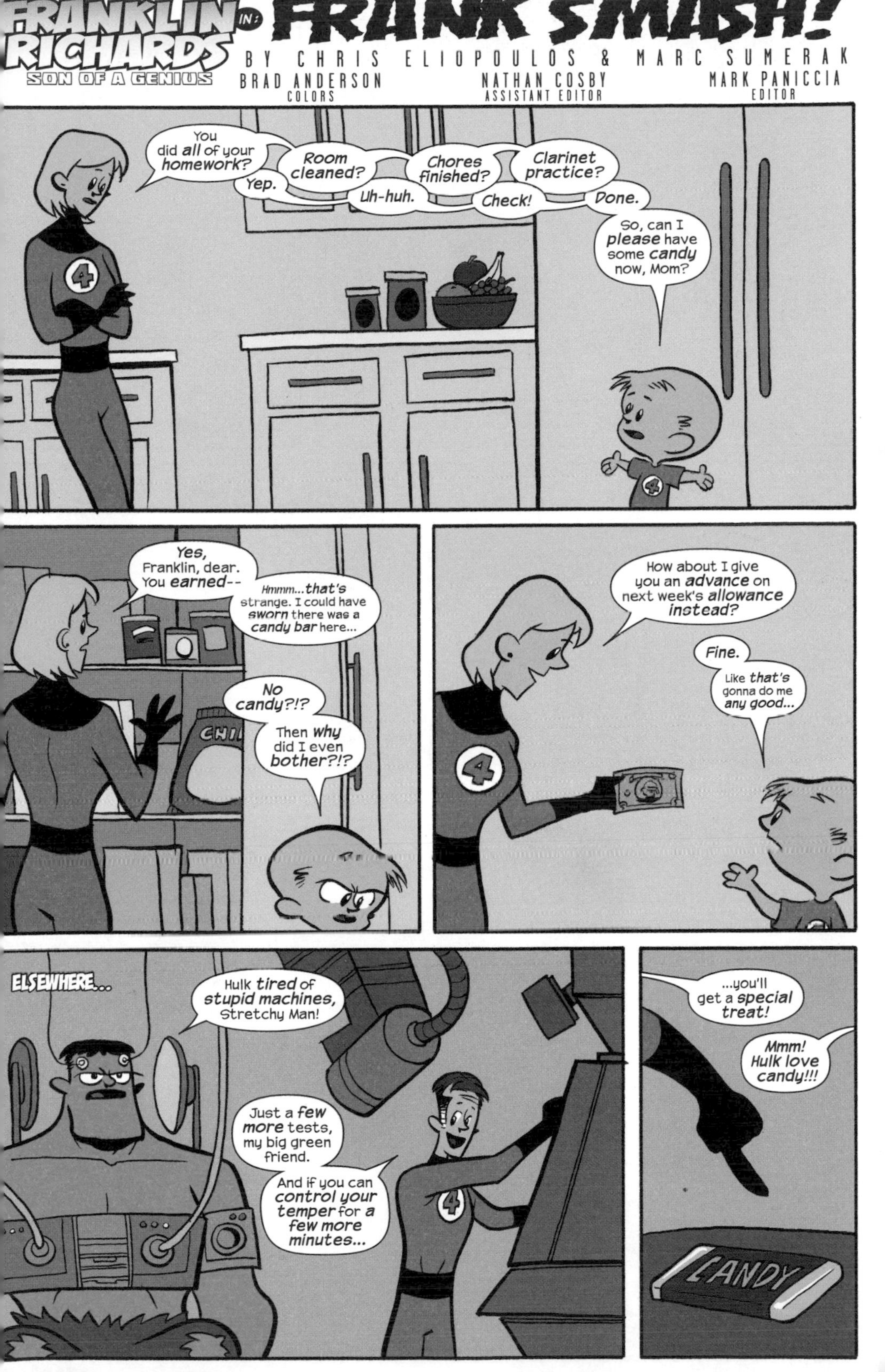
FRANKLIN RICHARDS SON OF A GENIUS IN: FRANK SMASH!
BY CHRIS ELIOPOULOS & MARC SUMERAK
BRAD ANDERSON COLORS
NATHAN COSBY ASSISTANT EDITOR
MARK PANICCIA EDITOR
You did all of your homework?
Yep.
Room cleaned?
Uh-huh.
Chores finished?
Check!
Clarinet practice?
Done.
So, can I please have some candy now, Mom?
Yes, Franklin, dear. You earned--
Hmmm...that's strange. I could have sworn there was a candy bar here...
No candy?!?
Then why did I even bother?!?
How about I give you an advance on next week's allowance instead?
Fine.
Like that's gonna do me any good...
ELSEWHERE...
Hulk tired of stupid machines, Stretchy Man!
Just a few more tests, my big green friend.
And if you can control your temper for a few more minutes...
...you'll get a special treat!
Mmm! Hulk love candy!!!
CANDY

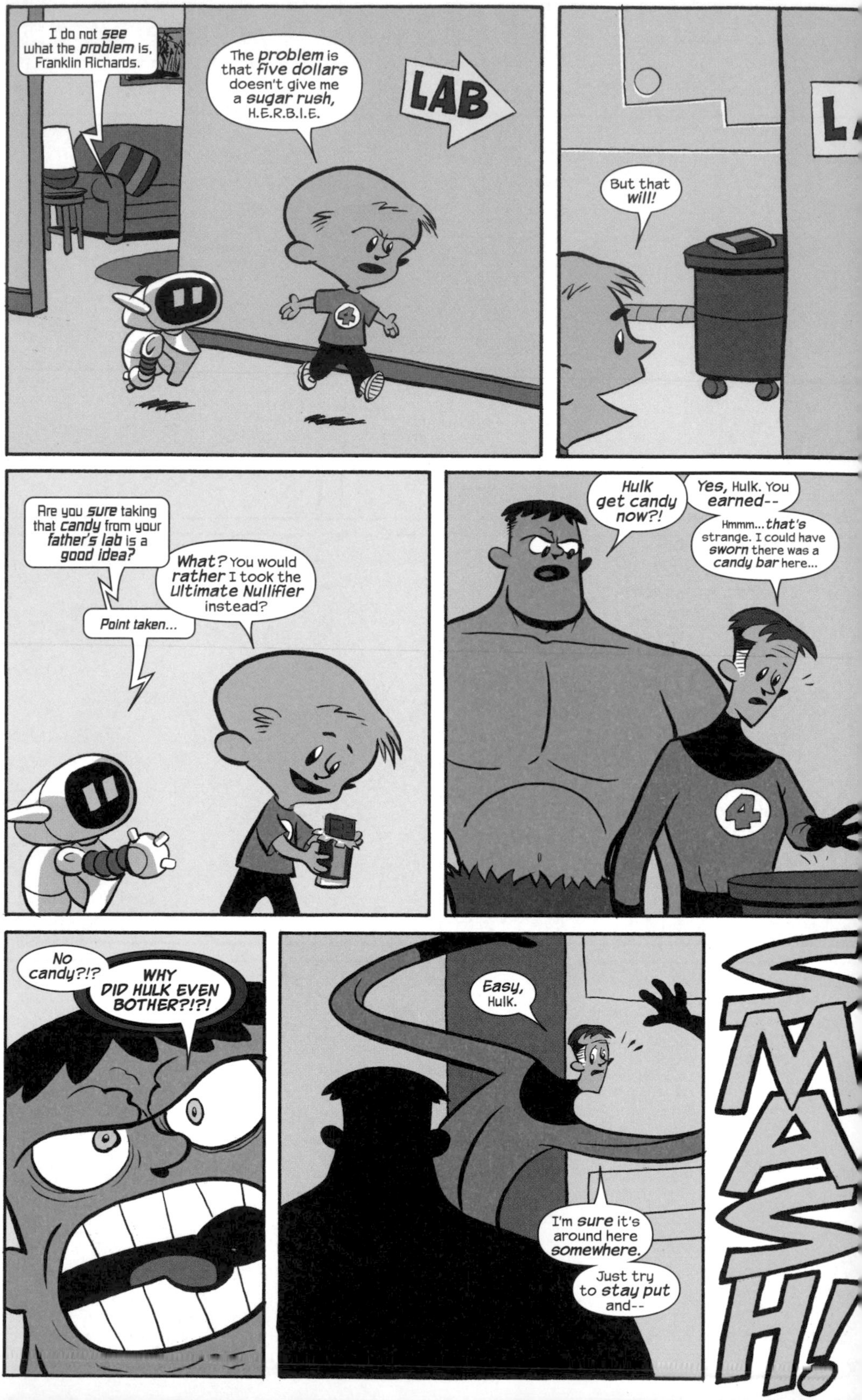
I do not see what the problem is, Franklin Richards.
The problem is that five dollars doesn't give me a sugar rush, H.E.R.B.I.E.
LAB
But that will!
Are you sure taking that candy from your father's lab is a good idea?
What? You would rather I took the Ultimate Nullifier instead?
Point taken...
Hulk get candy now?!
Yes, Hulk. You earned--
Hmmm...that's strange. I could have sworn there was a candy bar here...
No candy?!?
WHY DID HULK EVEN BOTHER?!?!
Easy, Hulk.
I'm sure it's around here somewhere.
Just try to stay put and--
SMASH!

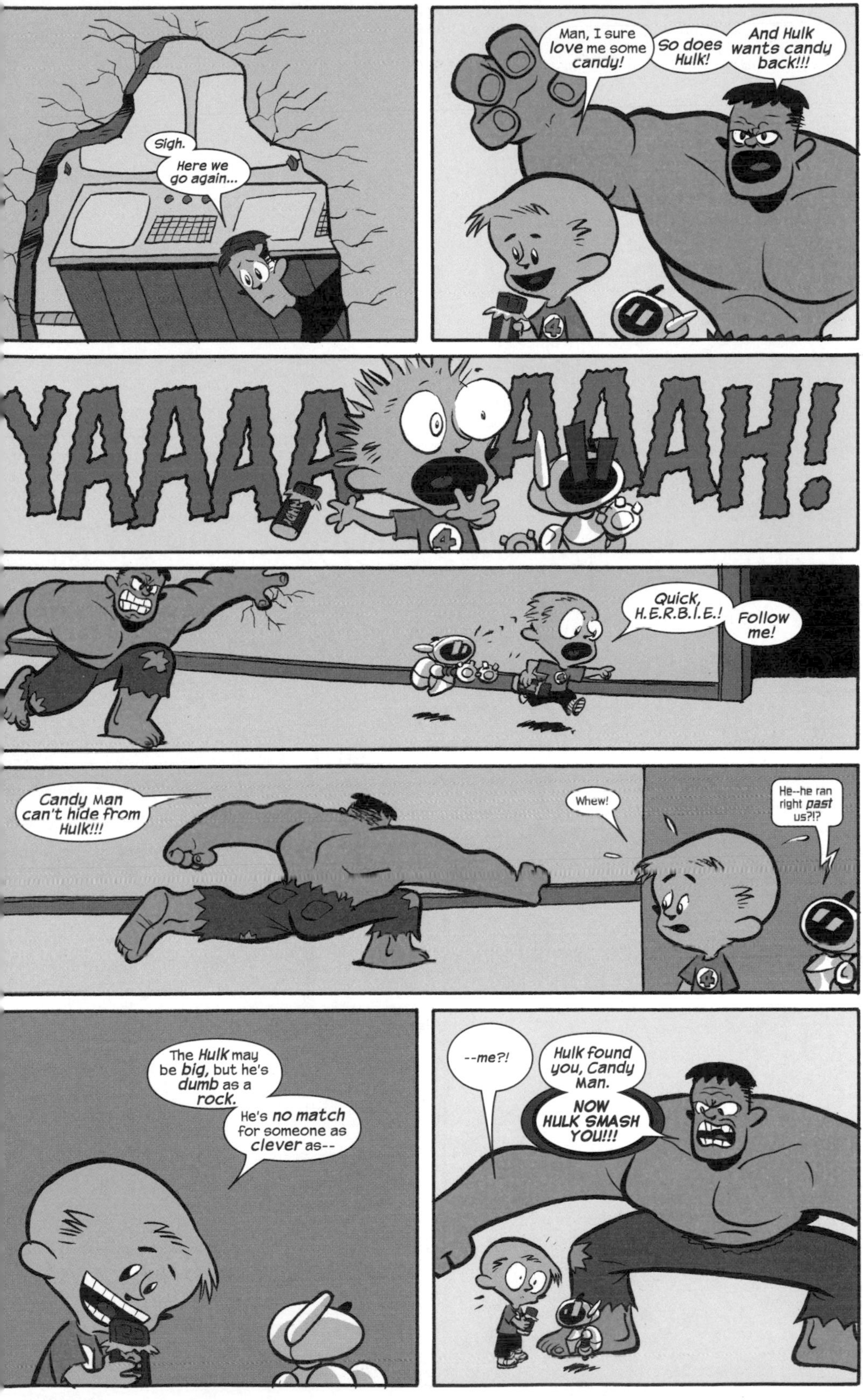
Sigh.
Here we go again...
Man, I sure love me some candy!
So does Hulk!
And Hulk wants candy back!!!
YAAAAAAAAH!
Quick, H.E.R.B.I.E.!
Follow me!
Candy Man can't hide from Hulk!!!
Whew!
He--he ran right past us?!?
The Hulk may be big, but he's dumb as a rock.
He's no match for someone as clever as--
--me?!
Hulk found you, Candy Man.
NOW HULK SMASH YOU!!!

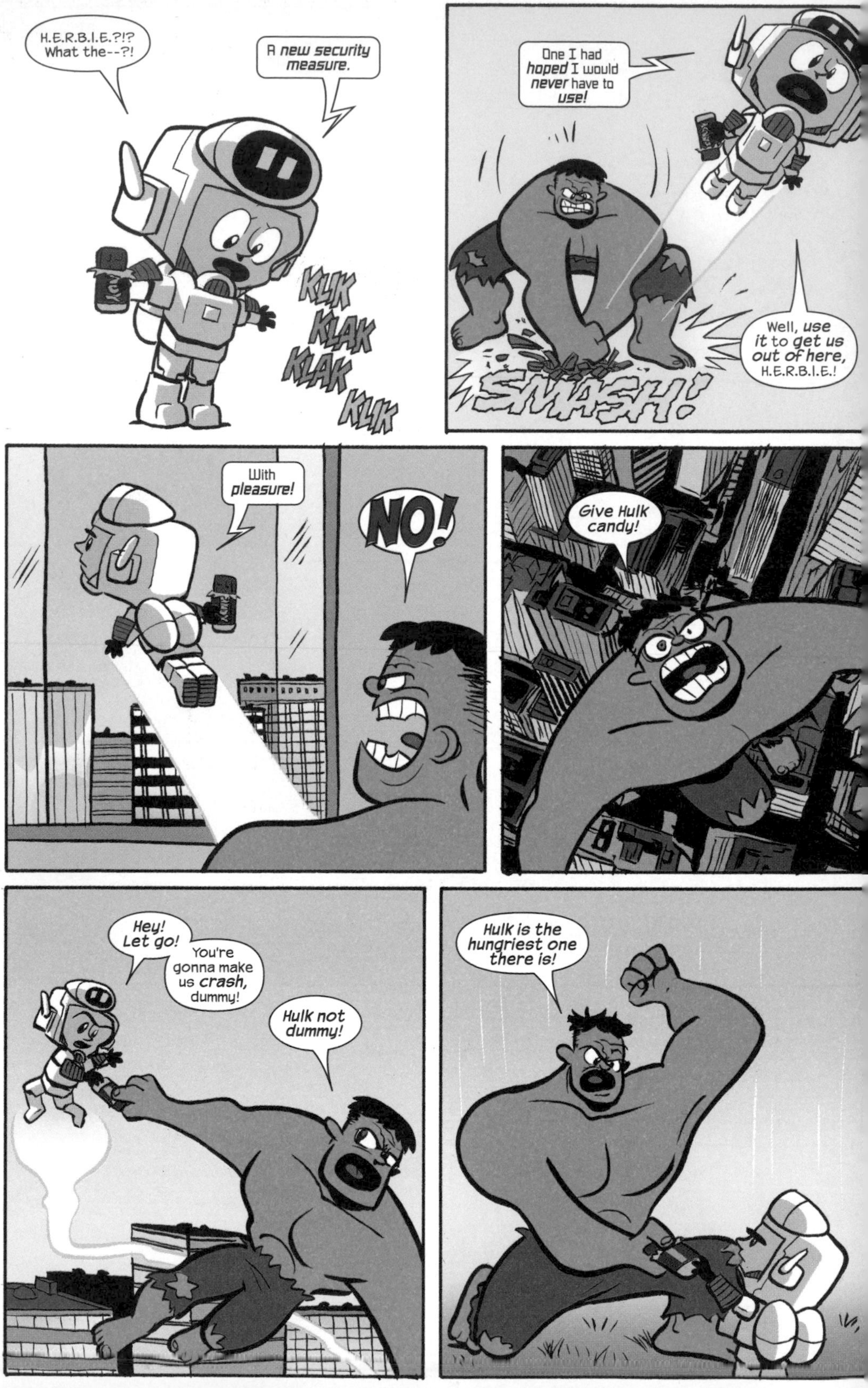

H.E.R.B.I.E.?!? What the--?!
A new security measure.
KLIK KLAK KLAK KLIK
One I had hoped I would never have to use!
SMASH!
Well, use it to get us out of here, H.E.R.B.I.E.!
With pleasure!
NO!
Give Hulk candy!
Hey! Let go!
You're gonna make us crash, dummy!
Hulk not dummy!
Hulk is the hungriest one there is!

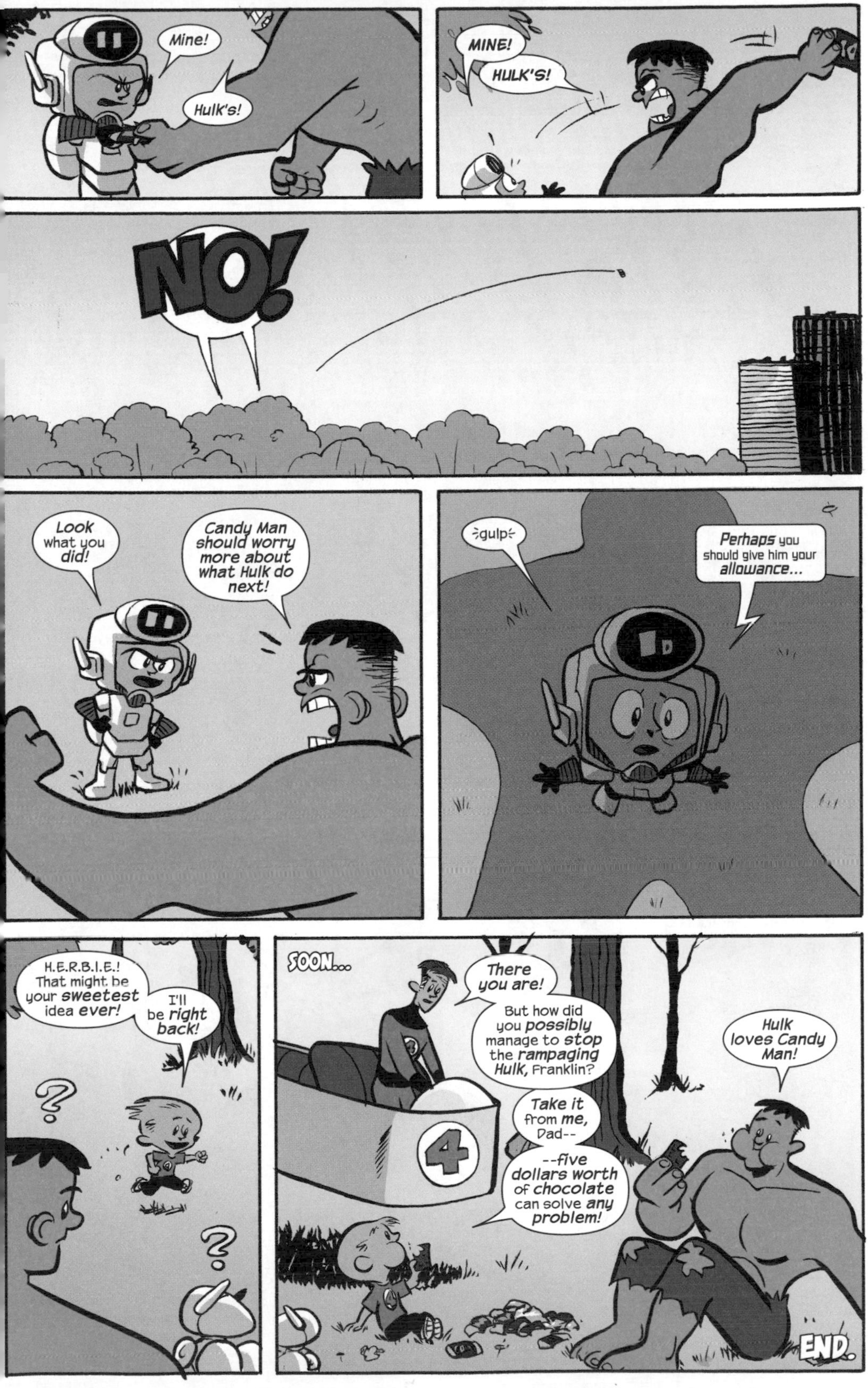

Mine!
Hulk's!
MINE!
HULK'S!
NO!
Look what you did!
Candy Man should worry more about what Hulk do next!
gulp
Perhaps you should give him your allowance...
H.E.R.B.I.E.! That might be your sweetest idea ever!
I'll be right back!
SOON...
There you are!
But how did you possibly manage to stop the rampaging Hulk, Franklin?
Take it from me, Dad--
--five dollars worth of chocolate can solve any problem!
Hulk loves Candy Man!
END.

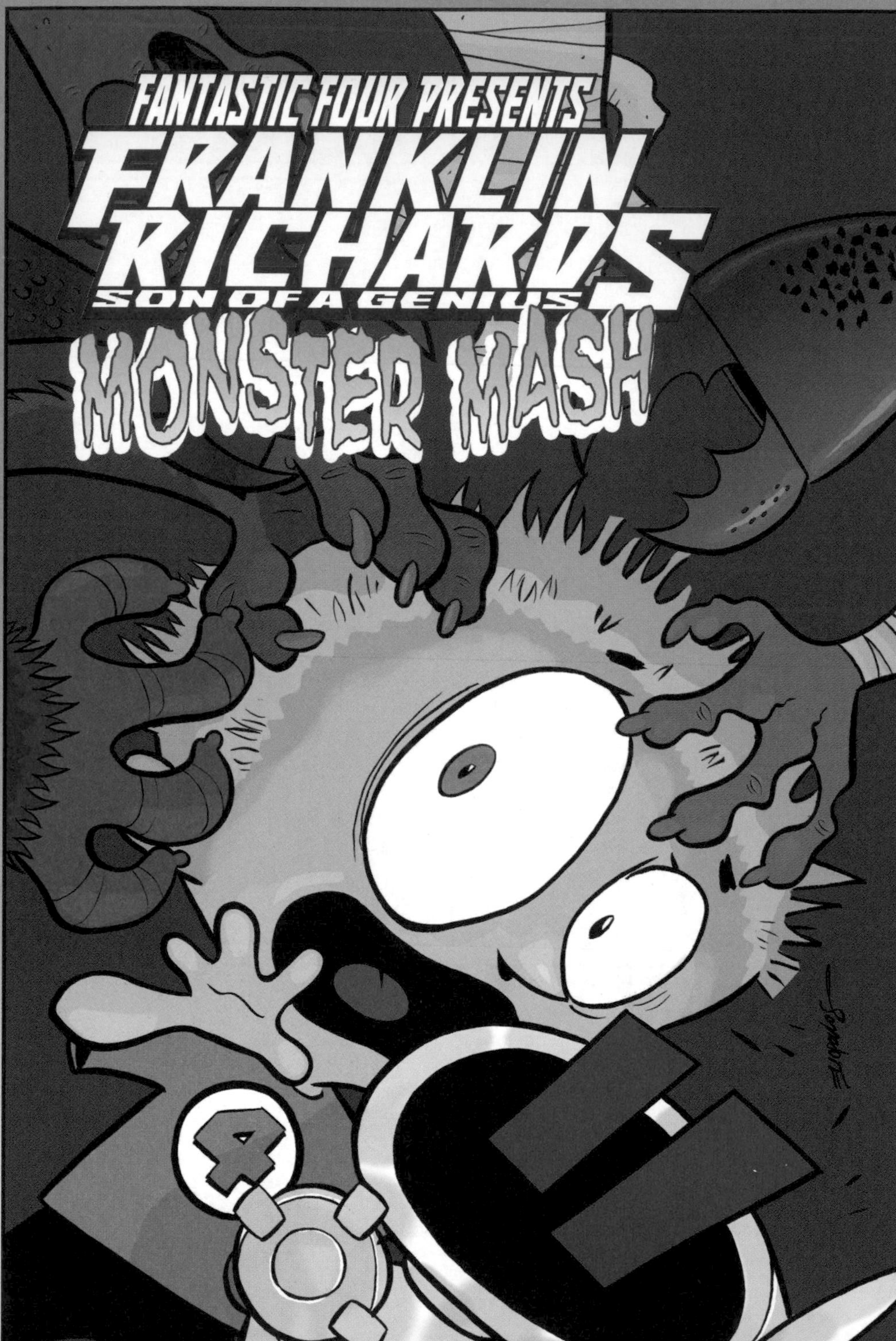
FANTASTIC FOUR PRESENTS
FRANKLIN RICHARDS
SON OF A GENIUS
MONSTER MASH
4

FANTASTIC FOUR PRESENTS FRANKLIN RICHARDS SON OF A GENIUS
MONSTER MASH

CHRIS ELIOPOULOS and MARC SUMERAK
STORY

MARC SUMERAK
SCRIPT

CHRIS ELIOPOULOS
ART & LETTERS

BRAD ANDERSON
COLOR

NATHAN COSBY
ASSISTANT EDITOR

MARK PANICCIA
EDITOR

JOE QUESADA
EDITOR IN CHIEF

DAN BUCKLEY
PUBLISHER

FRANKLIN RICHARDS SON OF A GENIUS IN: READY, STEADY, YETI!

BY CHRIS ELIOPOULOS & MARC SUMERAK

BRAD ANDERSON COLORS

NATHAN COSBY ASSISTANT EDITOR

MARK PANICCIA EDITOR

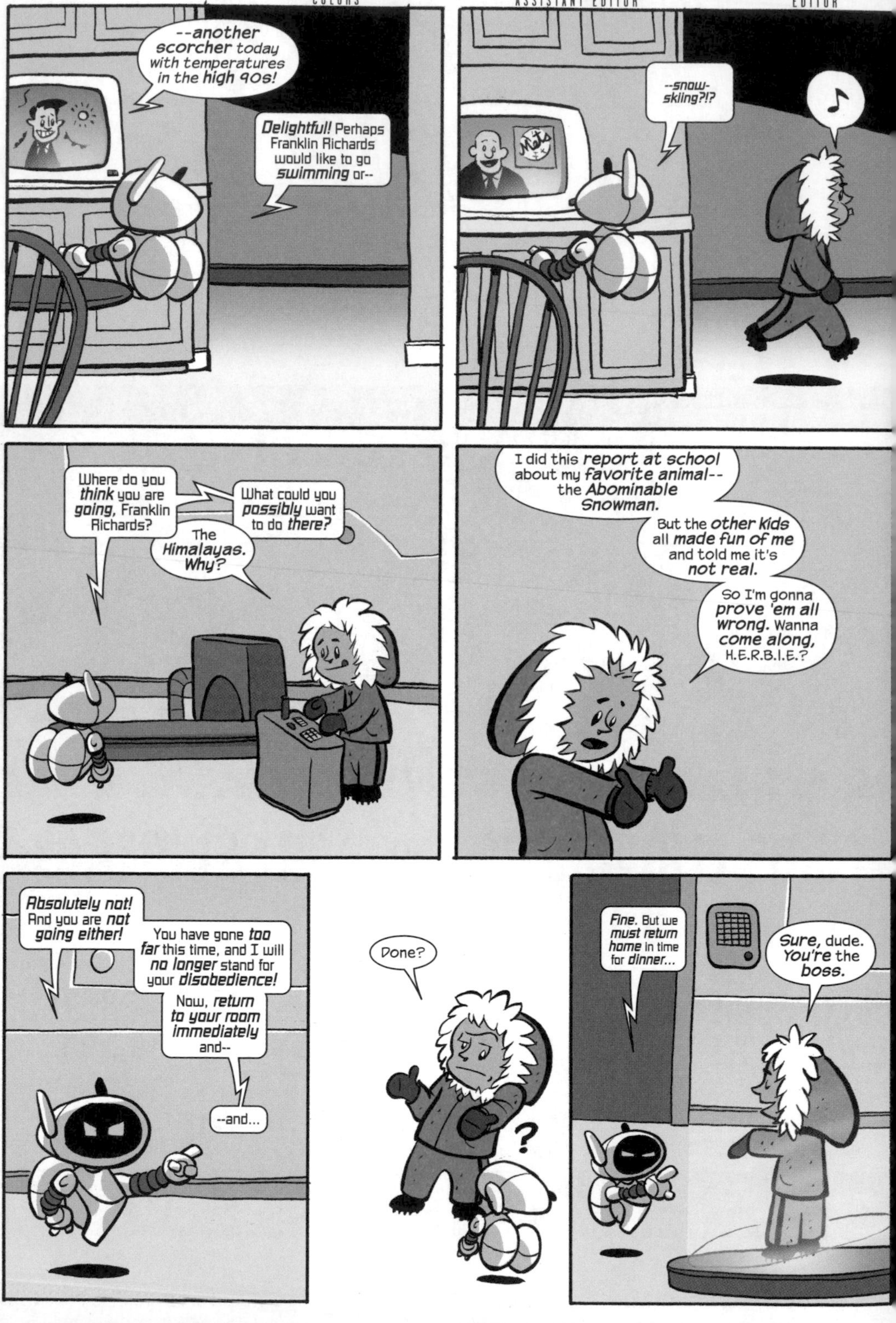

--another scorcher today with temperatures in the high 90s!
Delightful! Perhaps Franklin Richards would like to go swimming or--
--snow-skiing?!?
♪
Where do you think you are going, Franklin Richards?
The Himalayas. Why?
What could you possibly want to do there?
I did this report at school about my favorite animal-- the Abominable Snowman.
But the other kids all made fun of me and told me it's not real.
So I'm gonna prove 'em all wrong. Wanna come along, H.E.R.B.I.E.?
Absolutely not! And you are not going either!
You have gone too far this time, and I will no longer stand for your disobedience!
Now, return to your room immediately and--
--and...
Done?
?
Fine. But we must return home in time for dinner...
Sure, dude. You're the boss.

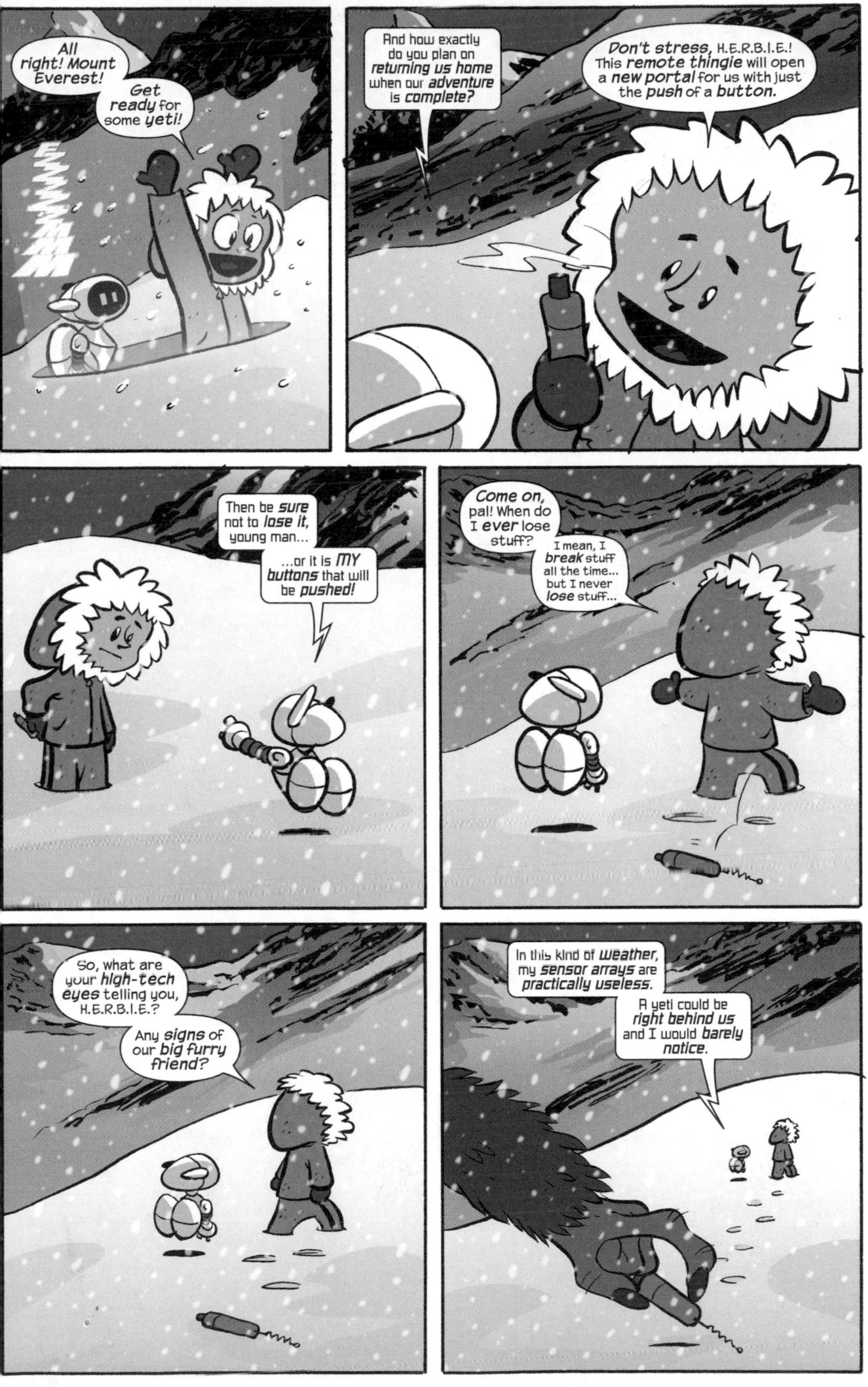
All right! Mount Everest!
Get ready for some yeti!
FZZZZZM
And how exactly do you plan on returning us home when our adventure is complete?
Don't stress, H.E.R.B.I.E.! This remote thingie will open a new portal for us with just the push of a button.
Then be sure not to lose it, young man...
...or it is MY buttons that will be pushed!
Come on, pal! When do I ever lose stuff?
I mean, I break stuff all the time... but I never lose stuff...
So, what are your high-tech eyes telling you, H.E.R.B.I.E.?
Any signs of our big furry friend?
In this kind of weather, my sensor arrays are practically useless.
A yeti could be right behind us and I would barely notice.

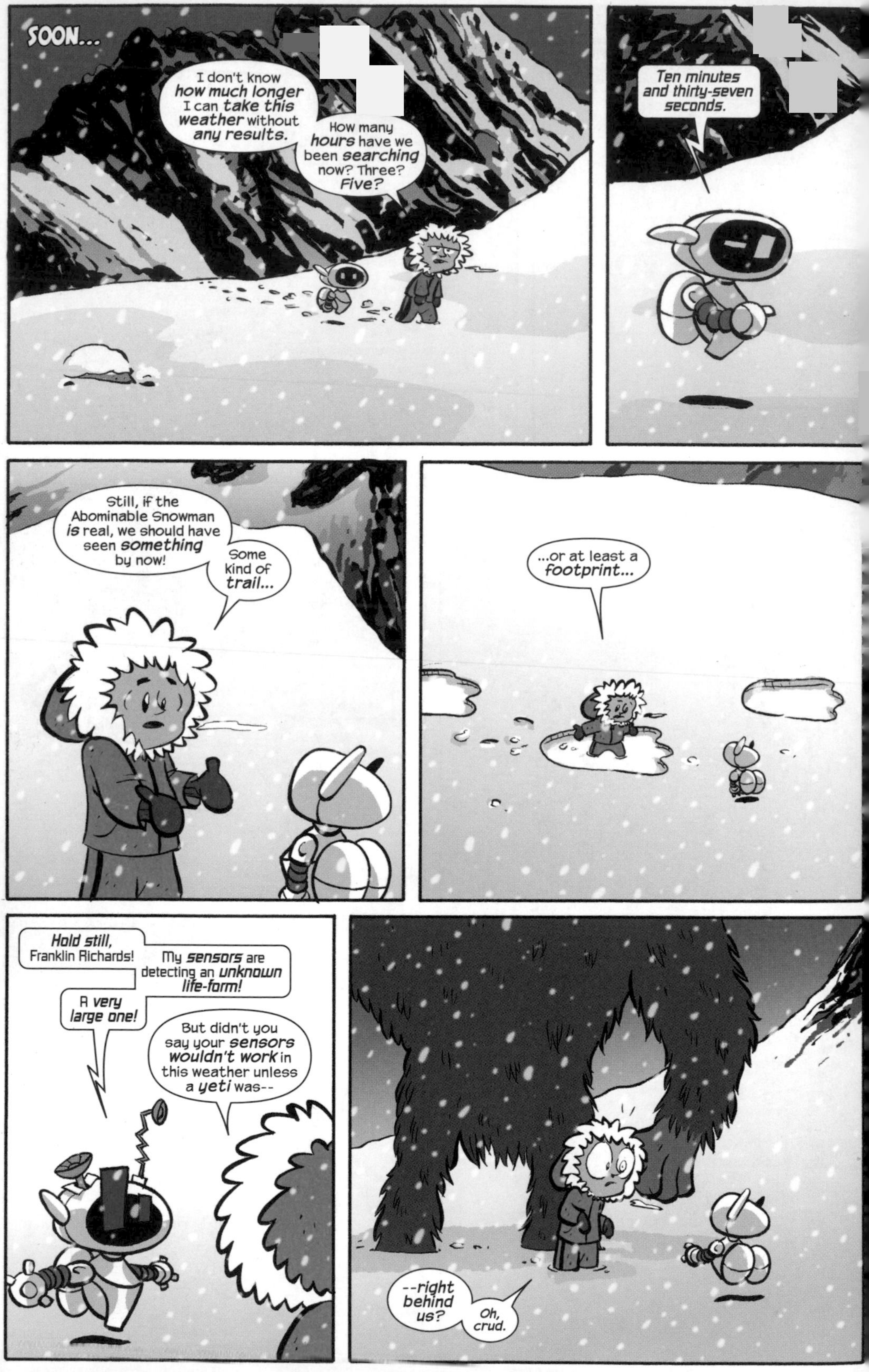
SOON...
I don't know how much longer I can take this weather without any results.
How many hours have we been searching now? Three? Five?
Ten minutes and thirty-seven seconds.
Still, if the Abominable Snowman is real, we should have seen something by now!
Some kind of trail...
...or at least a footprint...
Hold still, Franklin Richards!
My sensors are detecting an unknown life-form!
A very large one!
But didn't you say your sensors wouldn't work in this weather unless a yeti was--
--right behind us?
Oh, crud.

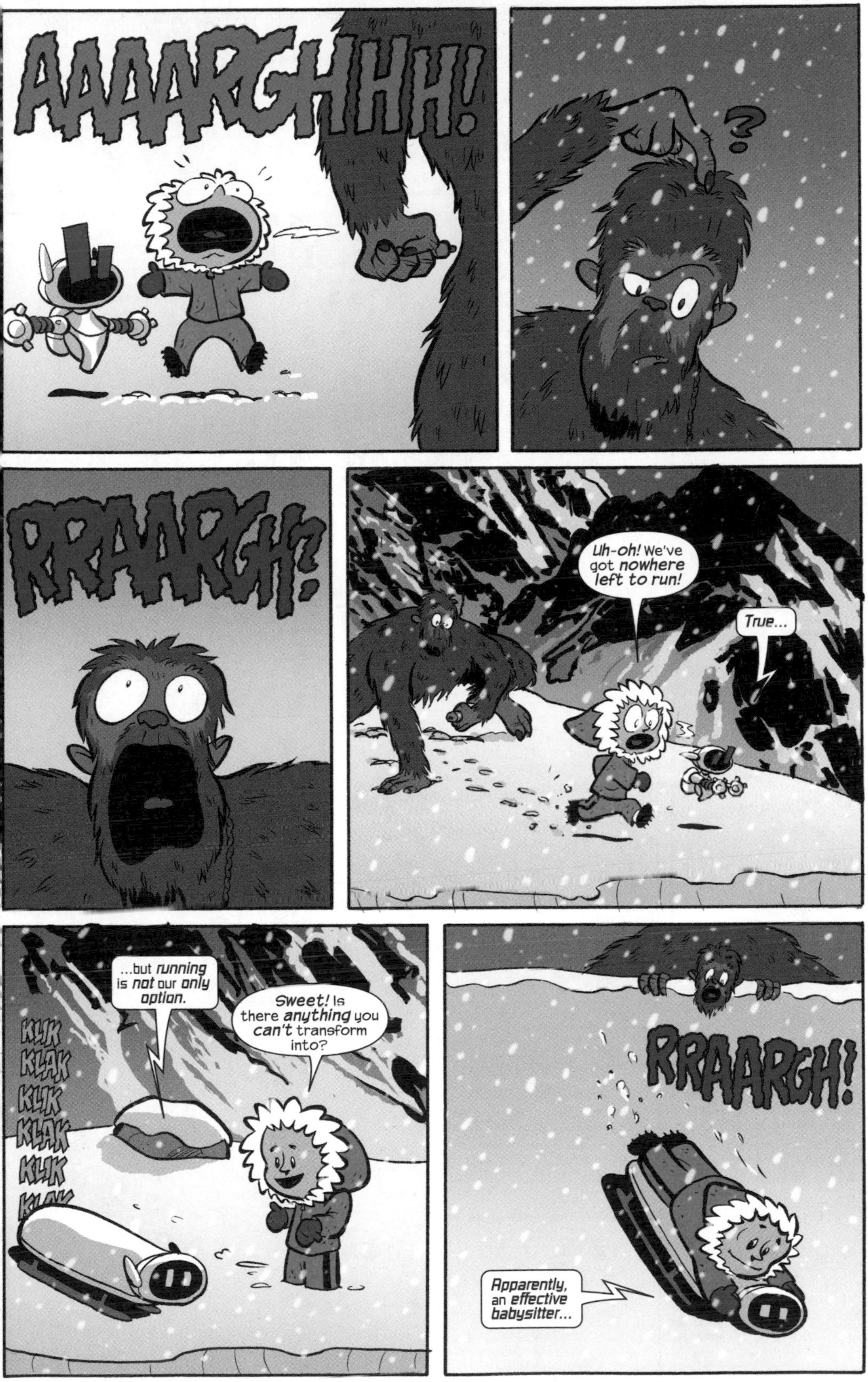
AAAARGHHH!
RRAARGH?!
Uh-oh! We've got nowhere left to run!
True...
...but running is not our only option.
Sweet! Is there anything you can't transform into?
KLIK KLAK KLIK KLAK KLIK
RRAARGH!
Apparently, an effective babysitter...

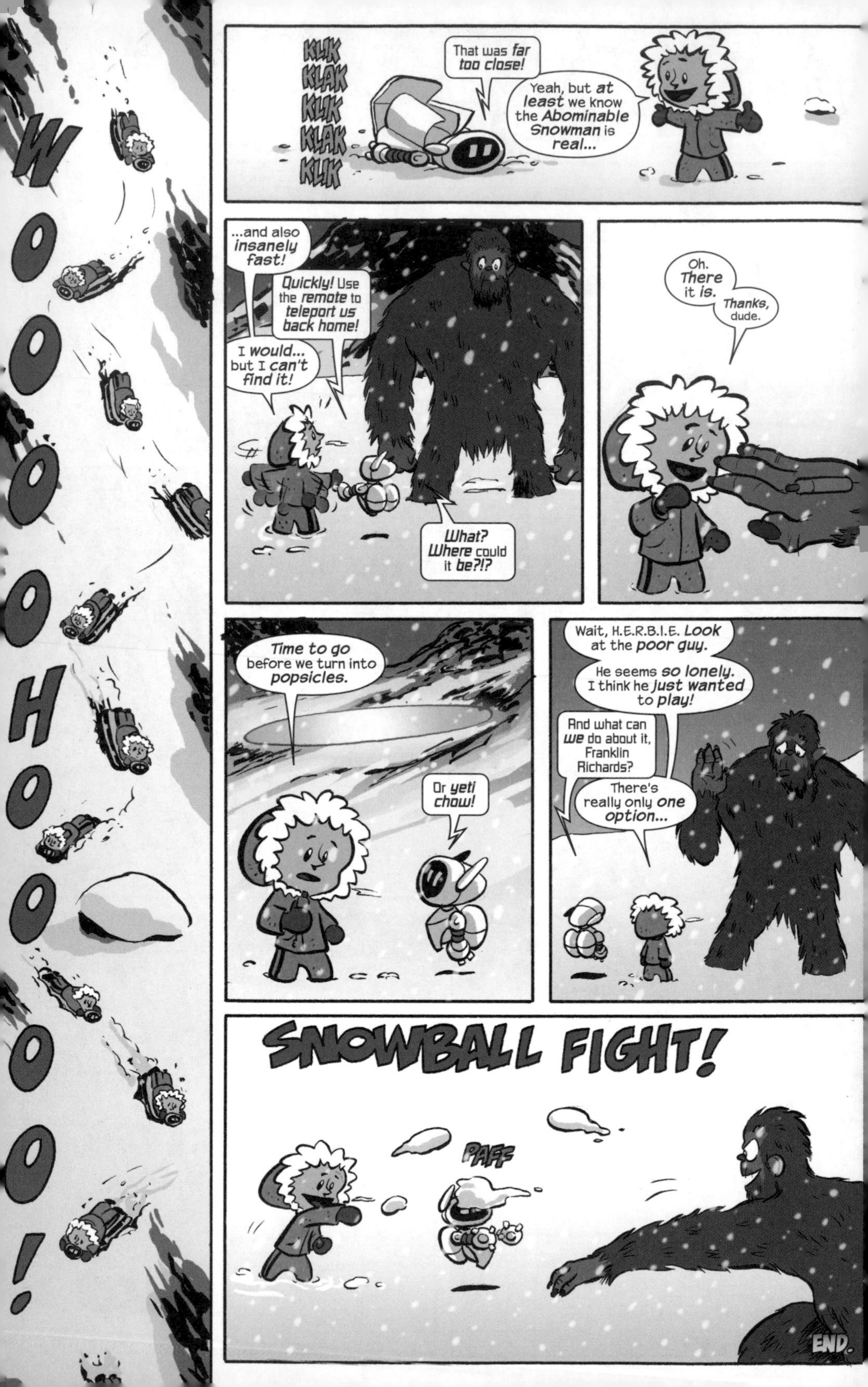
WOOOOOHOOOOOO!
KLIK KLAK KLIK KLAK KLIK
That was far too close!
Yeah, but at least we know the Abominable Snowman is real...
...and also insanely fast!
Quickly! Use the remote to teleport us back home!
I would... but I can't find it!
What? Where could it be?!?
Oh. There it is.
Thanks, dude.
Time to go before we turn into popsicles.
Or yeti chow!
Wait, H.E.R.B.I.E. Look at the poor guy.
He seems so lonely. I think he just wanted to play!
And what can we do about it, Franklin Richards?
There's really only one option...
SNOWBALL FIGHT!
PAFF
END.

FRANKLIN RICHARDS
SON OF A GENIUS
IN: LITTLE MONSTER

BY CHRIS ELIOPOULOS & MARC SUMERAK

BRAD ANDERSON
COLORS

NATHAN COSBY
ASSISTANT EDITOR

MARK PANICCIA
EDITOR

--so then Johnny and Ben *returned* the creature to its *proper dimension* and--

BURP!

'Scuse me.

You are *excused*, young man--*from this table!*

What? I just--

You just *lost your dessert* by being rude.

Seriously, Franklin, *what* has *gotten into you?*

I... I *don't* know...

...but I'm *gonna find out!*

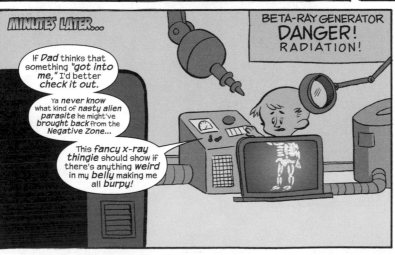

MINUTES LATER...

If *Dad* thinks that something *"got into me,"* I'd better *check it out.*

Ya *never know* what kind of *nasty alien parasite* he might've *brought back* from the *Negative Zone...*

This *fancy x-ray thingie* should show if there's anything *weird* in my *belly* making me all *burpy!*

BETA-RAY GENERATOR
DANGER!
RADIATION!

ZZHOOM!

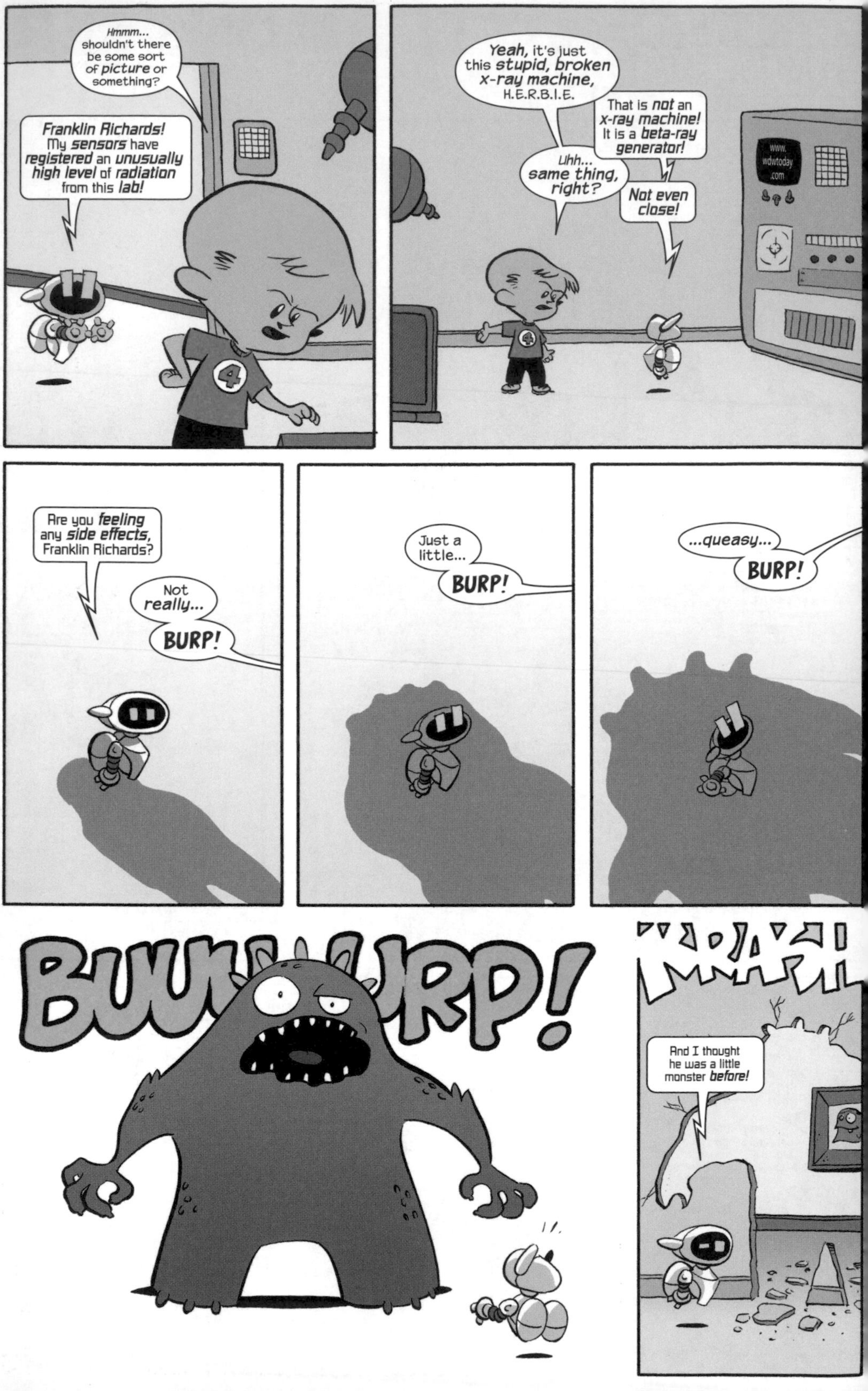
Hmmm... shouldn't there be some sort of picture or something?
Franklin Richards! My sensors have registered an unusually high level of radiation from this lab!
Yeah, it's just this stupid, broken x-ray machine, H.E.R.B.I.E.
That is not an x-ray machine! It is a beta-ray generator!
Uhh... same thing, right?
Not even close!
www. wdwtoday .com
Are you feeling any side effects, Franklin Richards?
Not really...
BURP!
Just a little...
BURP!
...queasy...
BURP!
BUUUURP!
KRASH!
And I thought he was a little monster before!

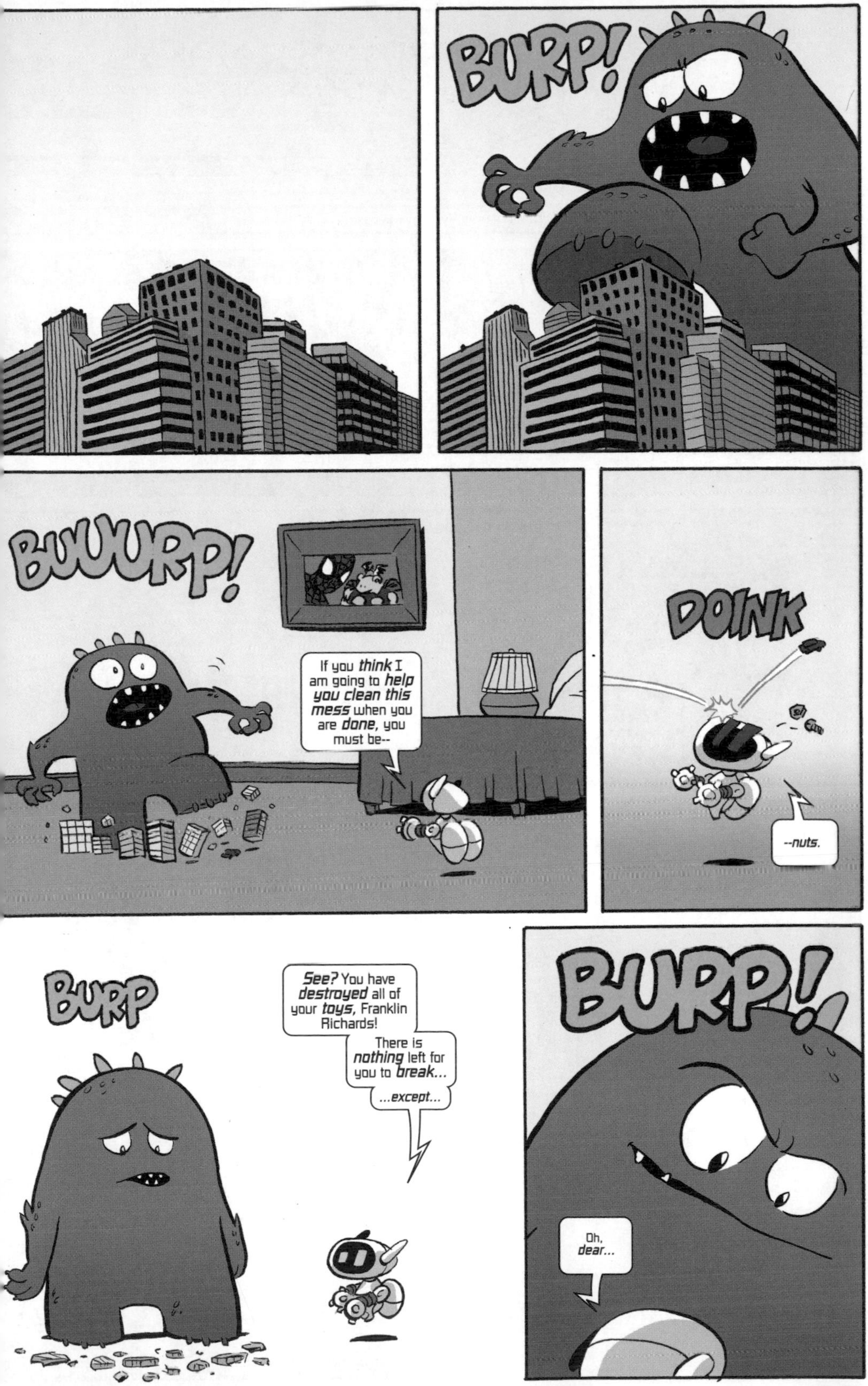
BURP!
BUUURP!
If you *think* I am going to *help you clean this mess* when you are *done*, you must be--
DOINK
--nuts.
BURP
See? You have *destroyed* all of your *toys,* Franklin Richards!
There is *nothing* left for you to *break...*
...except...
BURP!
Oh, *dear...*

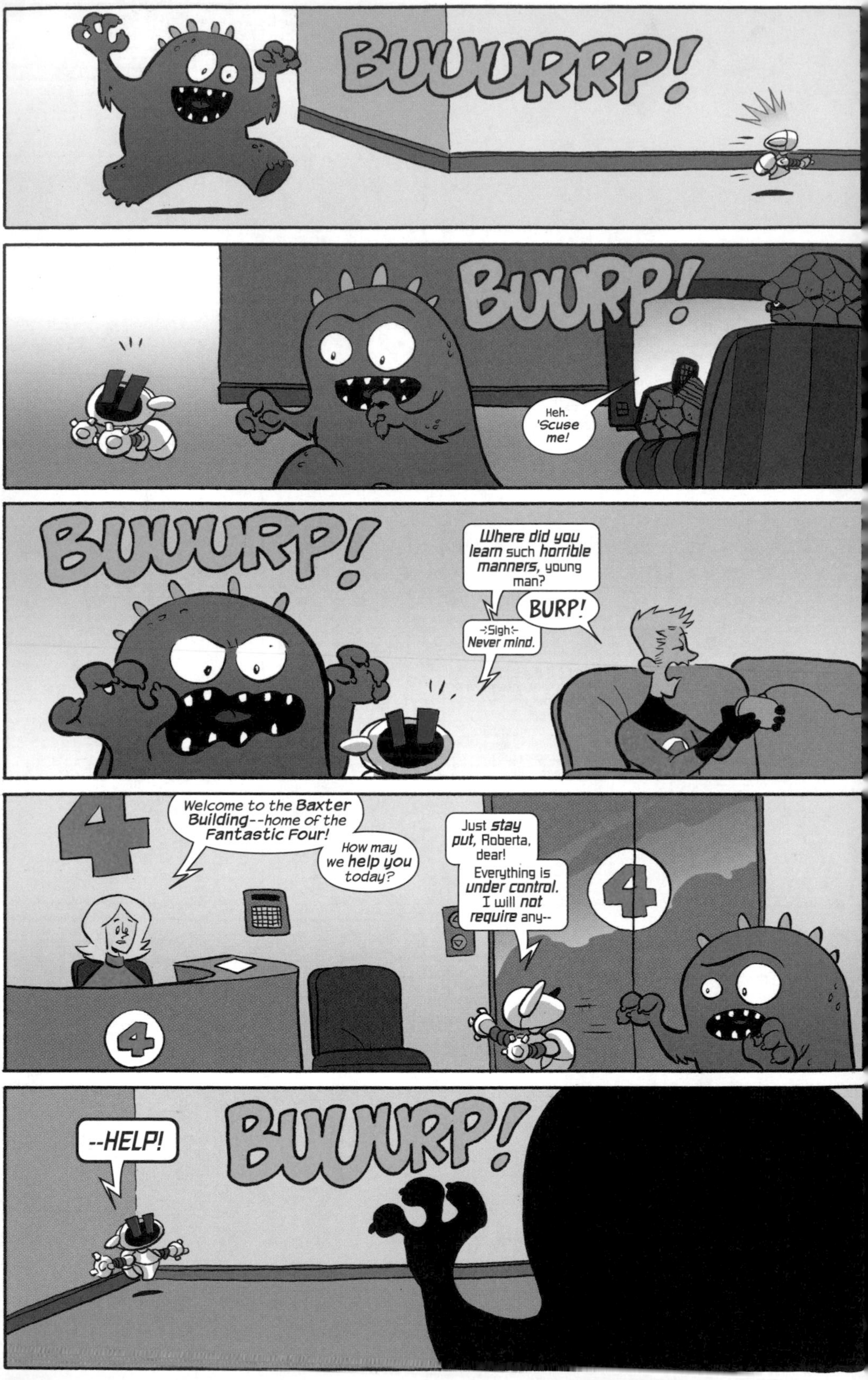
BUUURRP!
BUURP!
Heh. 'Scuse me!
BUUURP!
Where did you learn such horrible manners, young man?
BURP!
-:Sigh:- Never mind.
Welcome to the Baxter Building--home of the Fantastic Four!
How may we help you today?
Just stay put, Roberta, dear!
Everything is under control. I will not require any--
--HELP!
BUUURP!

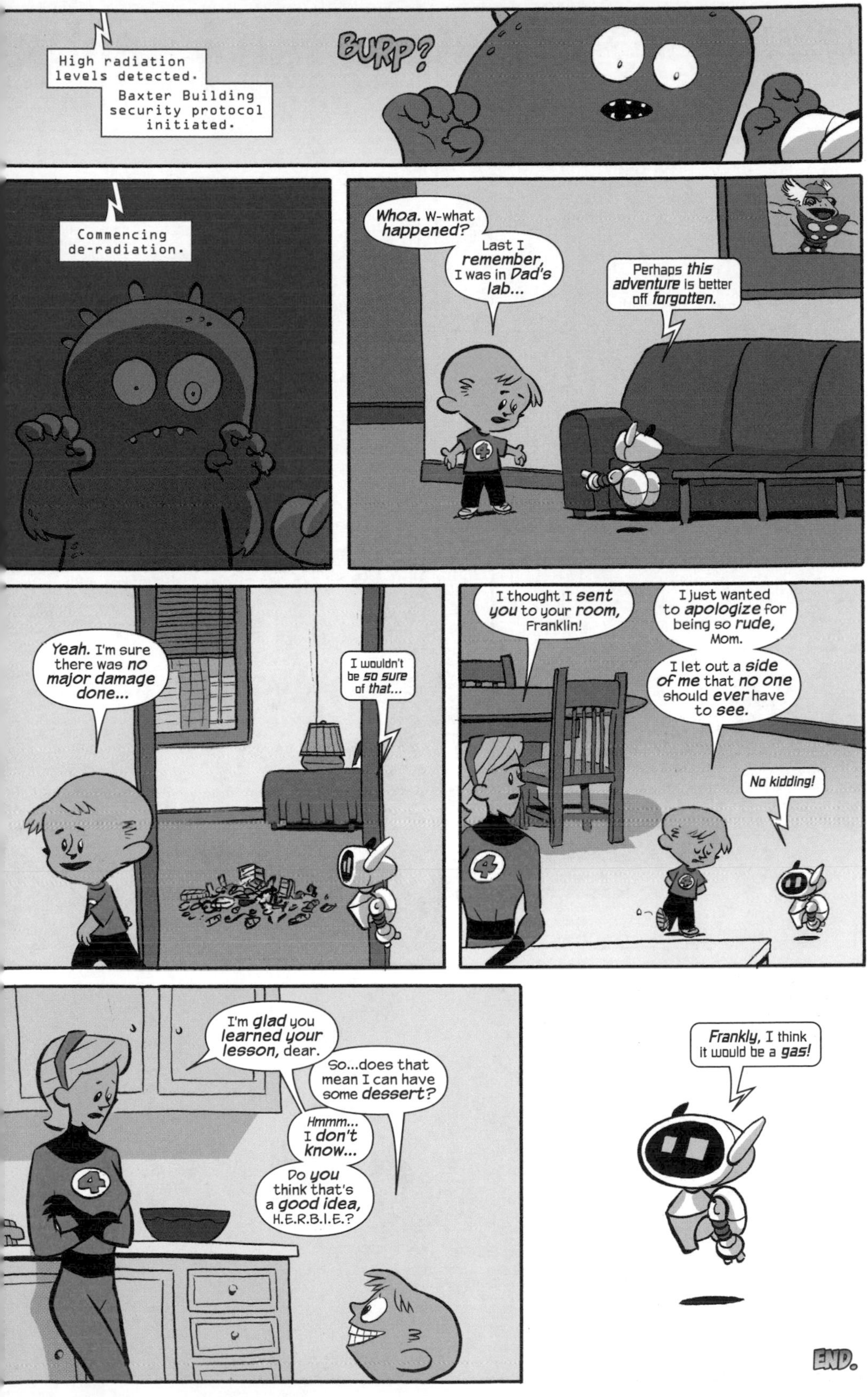
High radiation levels detected.
Baxter Building security protocol initiated.
BURP?
Commencing de-radiation.
Whoa. W-what happened?
Last I remember, I was in Dad's lab...
Perhaps this adventure is better off forgotten.
Yeah. I'm sure there was no major damage done...
I wouldn't be so sure of that...
I thought I sent you to your room, Franklin!
I just wanted to apologize for being so rude, Mom.
I let out a side of me that no one should ever have to see.
No kidding!
I'm glad you learned your lesson, dear.
So...does that mean I can have some dessert?
Hmmm... I don't know...
Do you think that's a good idea, H.E.R.B.I.E.?
Frankly, I think it would be a gas!
END.

FRANKLIN RICHARDS SON OF A GENIUS IN: Ghosts in the Machine

BY CHRIS ELIOPOULOS & MARC SUMERAK
BRAD ANDERSON COLORS
NATHAN COSBY ASSISTANT EDITOR
MARK PANICCIA EDITOR

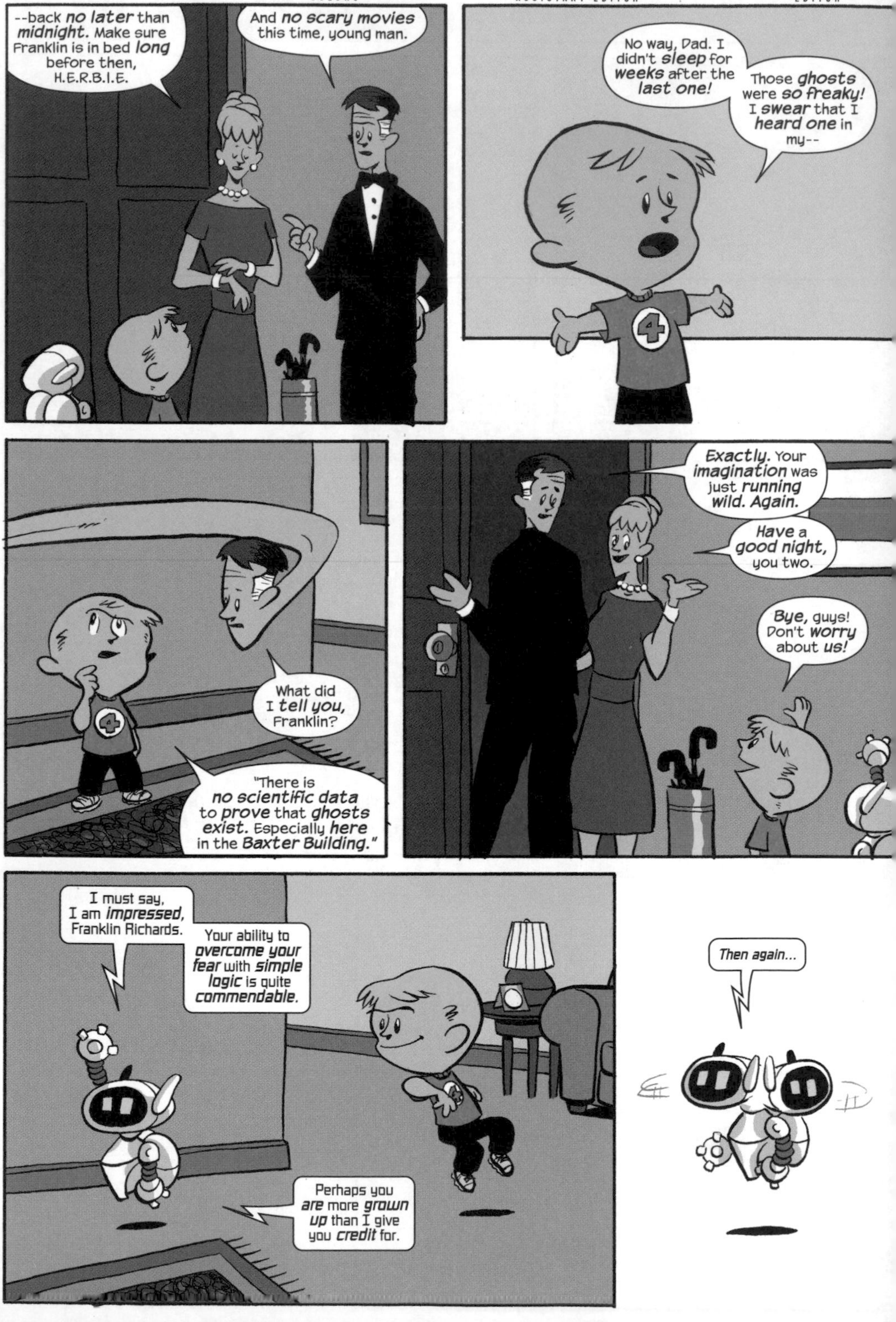

--back no later than midnight. Make sure Franklin is in bed long before then, H.E.R.B.I.E.
And no scary movies this time, young man.
No way, Dad. I didn't sleep for weeks after the last one!
Those ghosts were so freaky! I swear that I heard one in my--
What did I tell you, Franklin?
"There is no scientific data to prove that ghosts exist. Especially here in the Baxter Building."
Exactly. Your imagination was just running wild. Again.
Have a good night, you two.
Bye, guys! Don't worry about us!
I must say, I am impressed, Franklin Richards.
Your ability to overcome your fear with simple logic is quite commendable.
Perhaps you are more grown up than I give you credit for.
Then again...

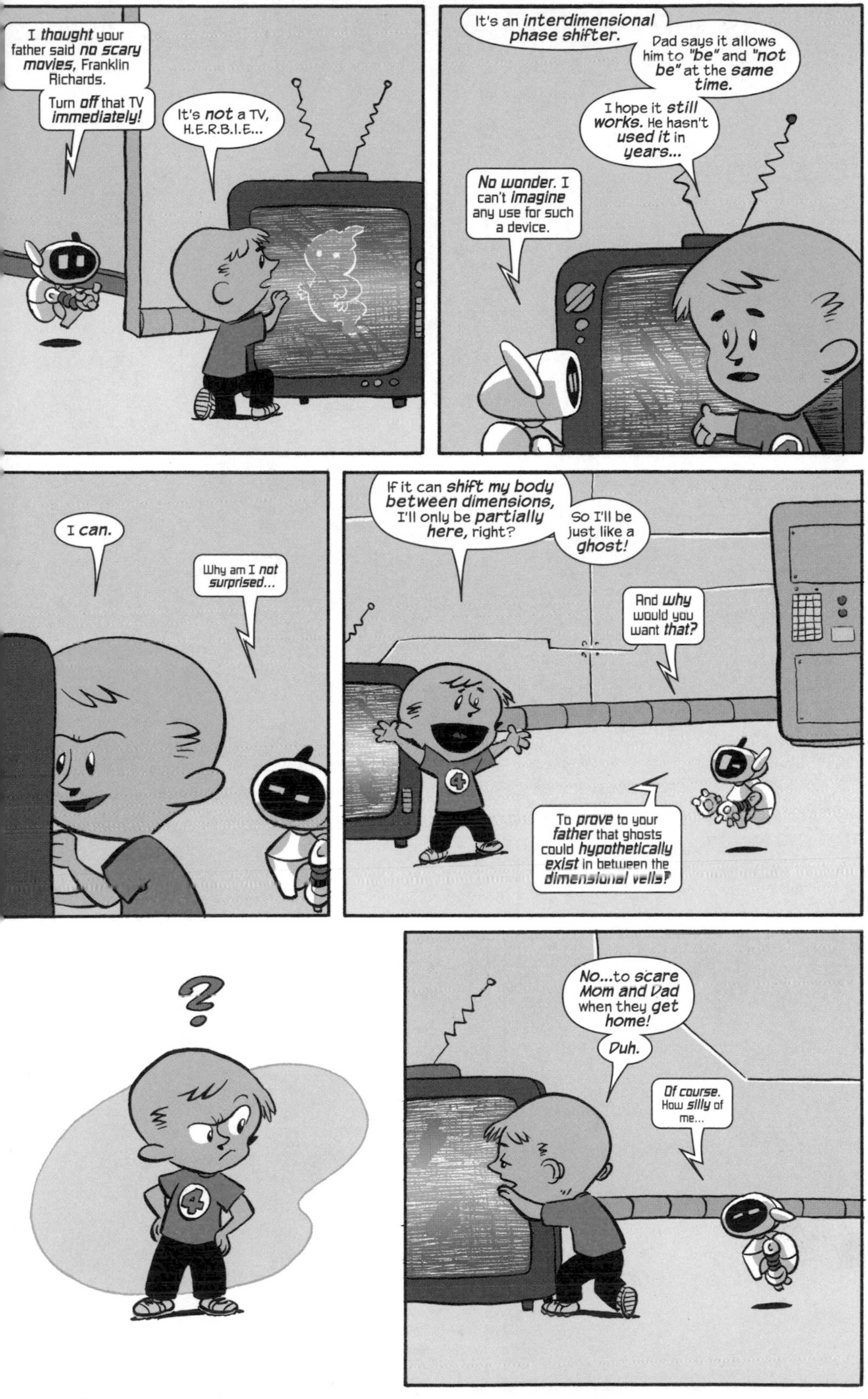
I thought your father said no scary movies, Franklin Richards.
Turn off that TV immediately!
It's not a TV, H.E.R.B.I.E...
It's an interdimensional phase shifter.
Dad says it allows him to "be" and "not be" at the same time.
I hope it still works. He hasn't used it in years...
No wonder. I can't imagine any use for such a device.
I can.
Why am I not surprised...
If it can shift my body between dimensions, I'll only be partially here, right?
So I'll be just like a ghost!
And why would you want that?
To prove to your father that ghosts could hypothetically exist in between the dimensional veils?
No...to scare Mom and Dad when they get home!
Duh.
Of course. How silly of me...

Warning: My *sensors* are *losing track* of you, Franklin Richards!

That must mean it's *working!*

GZZT!

SWEET!

Check it out, H.E.R.B.I.E.! I'm a *real live* ghost!

My *systems* are *unable* to *detect* you...but this *device* seems to allow me to *hear* and *see* you.

Somewhat.

You're ⚡kzzt⚡ *missing out,* dude! I look ⚡kzzt⚡ *awesome!*

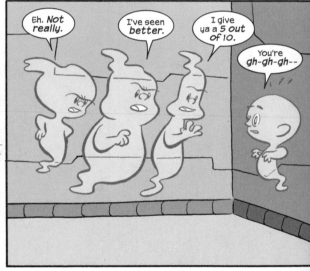

Eh. *Not really.*

I've seen *better.*

I give ya a *5 out of 10.*

You're gh-gh-gh--

GHOSTS!

So are *you* now, buddy.

Welcome to da *club!*

What is *going on,* young man? The *phase shifter* is detecting *other beings* on your *dimensional plane.*

No kidding!

No ⚡kzzt⚡ *kidding!*

Hey! Where ya *goin'*?

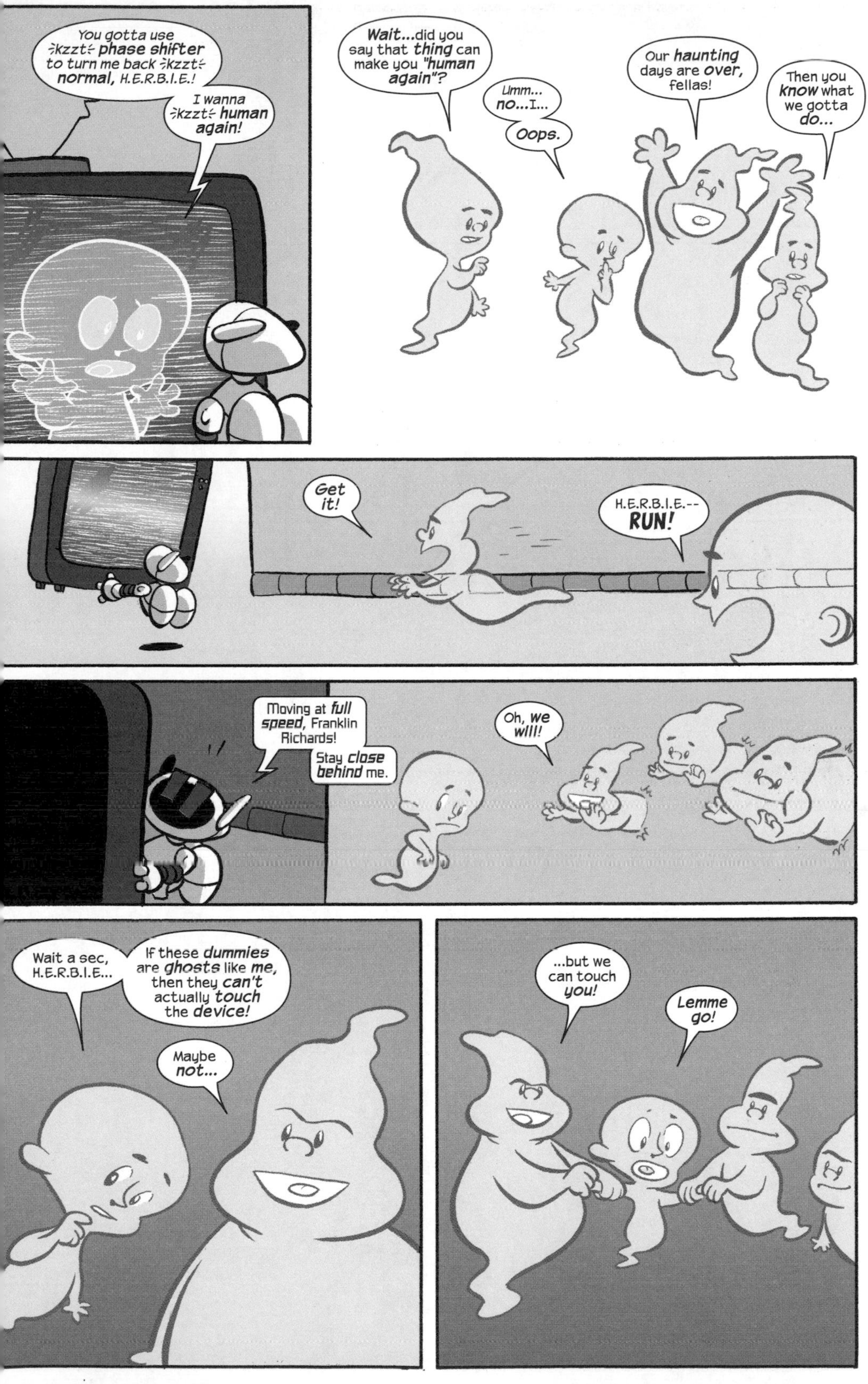
You gotta use ⚡kzzt⚡ phase shifter to turn me back ⚡kzzt⚡ normal, H.E.R.B.I.E.!
I wanna ⚡kzzt⚡ human again!
Wait...did you say that thing can make you "human again"?
Umm... no...I...
Oops.
Our haunting days are over, fellas!
Then you know what we gotta do...
Get it!
H.E.R.B.I.E.-- RUN!
Moving at full speed, Franklin Richards!
Stay close behind me.
Oh, we will!
Wait a sec, H.E.R.B.I.E...
If these dummies are ghosts like me, then they can't actually touch the device!
Maybe not...
...but we can touch you!
Lemme go!

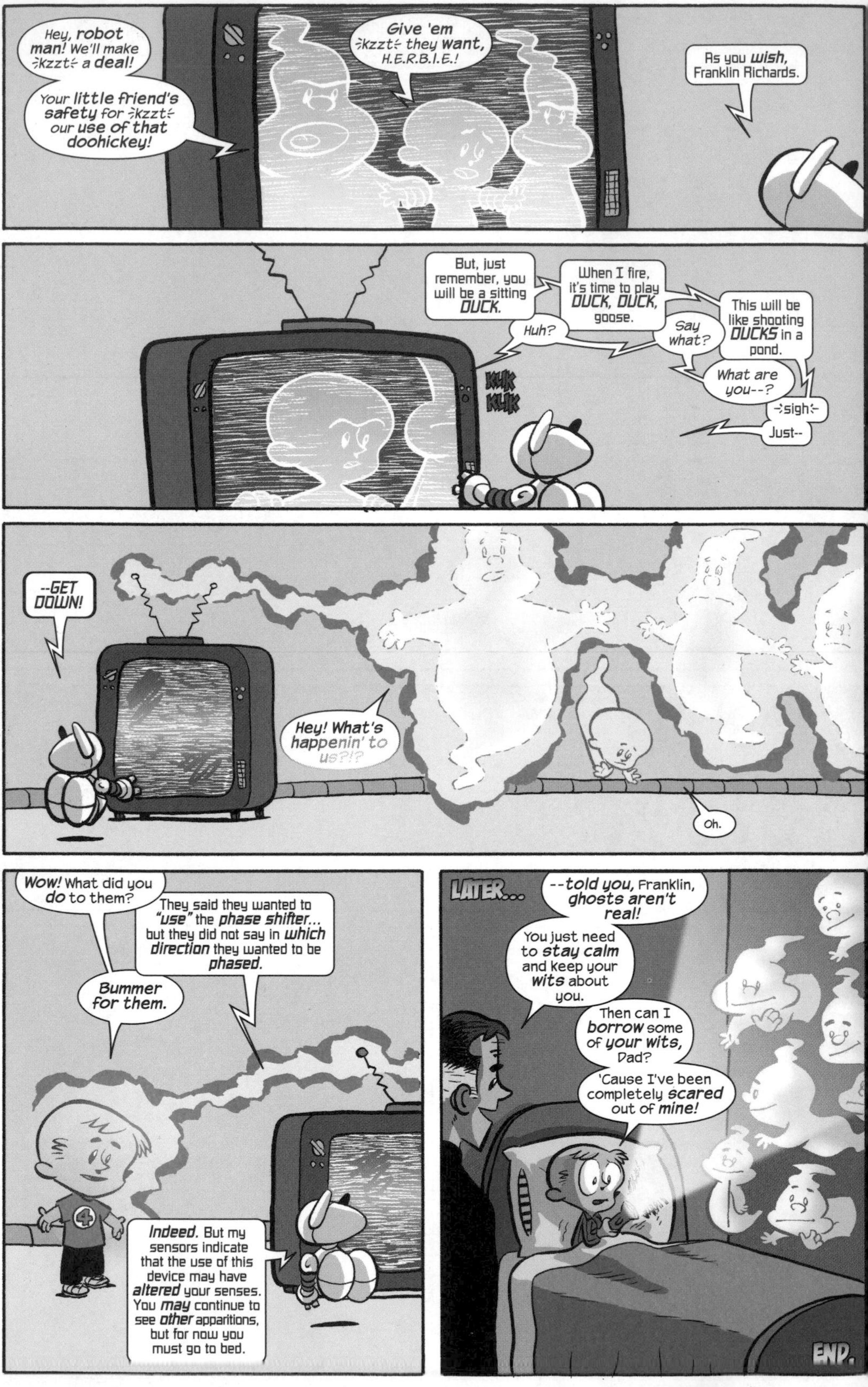

Hey, robot man! We'll make ⊰kzzt⊱ a deal!
Your little friend's safety for ⊰kzzt⊱ our use of that doohickey!
Give 'em ⊰kzzt⊱ they want, H.E.R.B.I.E.!
As you wish, Franklin Richards.
But, just remember, you will be a sitting DUCK.
When I fire, it's time to play DUCK, DUCK, goose.
This will be like shooting DUCKS in a pond.
Huh?
Say what?
What are you--?
KLIK KLIK
⊰sigh⊱
Just--
--GET DOWN!
Hey! What's happenin' to us?!?
Oh.
Wow! What did you do to them?
They said they wanted to "use" the phase shifter... but they did not say in which direction they wanted to be phased.
Bummer for them.
Indeed. But my sensors indicate that the use of this device may have altered your senses. You may continue to see other apparitions, but for now you must go to bed.
LATER...
--told you, Franklin, ghosts aren't real!
You just need to stay calm and keep your wits about you.
Then can I borrow some of your wits, Dad?
'Cause I've been completely scared out of mine!
END.

FRANKLIN RICHARDS IN: UNDER THE BED

SON OF A GENIUS

BY CHRIS ELIOPOULOS & MARC SUMERAK

BRAD ANDERSON
COLORS

NATHAN COSBY
ASSISTANT EDITOR

MARK PANICCIA
EDITOR

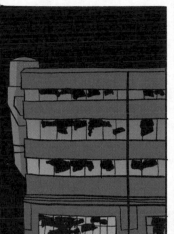

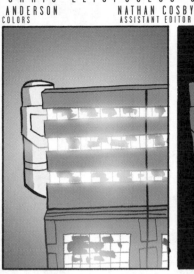

H.E.R.B.I.E.! Mom and Dad are home!

Welcome back, Fantastic Four.

How was your trip?

Just your *normal* extra-dimensional adventure, Frankie.

You callin' those *freaky aliens* that attacked us *"normal,"* Torch?

Uh...yeah. How long have you been on this *team* again?

Heh. I guess that *is* pretty *normal* for us...

What if the aliens *followed* you back?

They *can't*, Franklin. I've *sealed off* the dimensional rift permanently with *this device.*

Do you think I could *use* it to stop the *monster* under my bed?

'Cause I *can't go to sleep* unless--

Nice try, young man.

But you *aren't* going to *fool us* into letting you *stay up any later!*

But, Mom! I'm *not kidding!* There really *is*--

That is *enough,* Franklin Richards.

Now, *off to bed* before you *really* start to *tweak my transistors!*

But-- but--

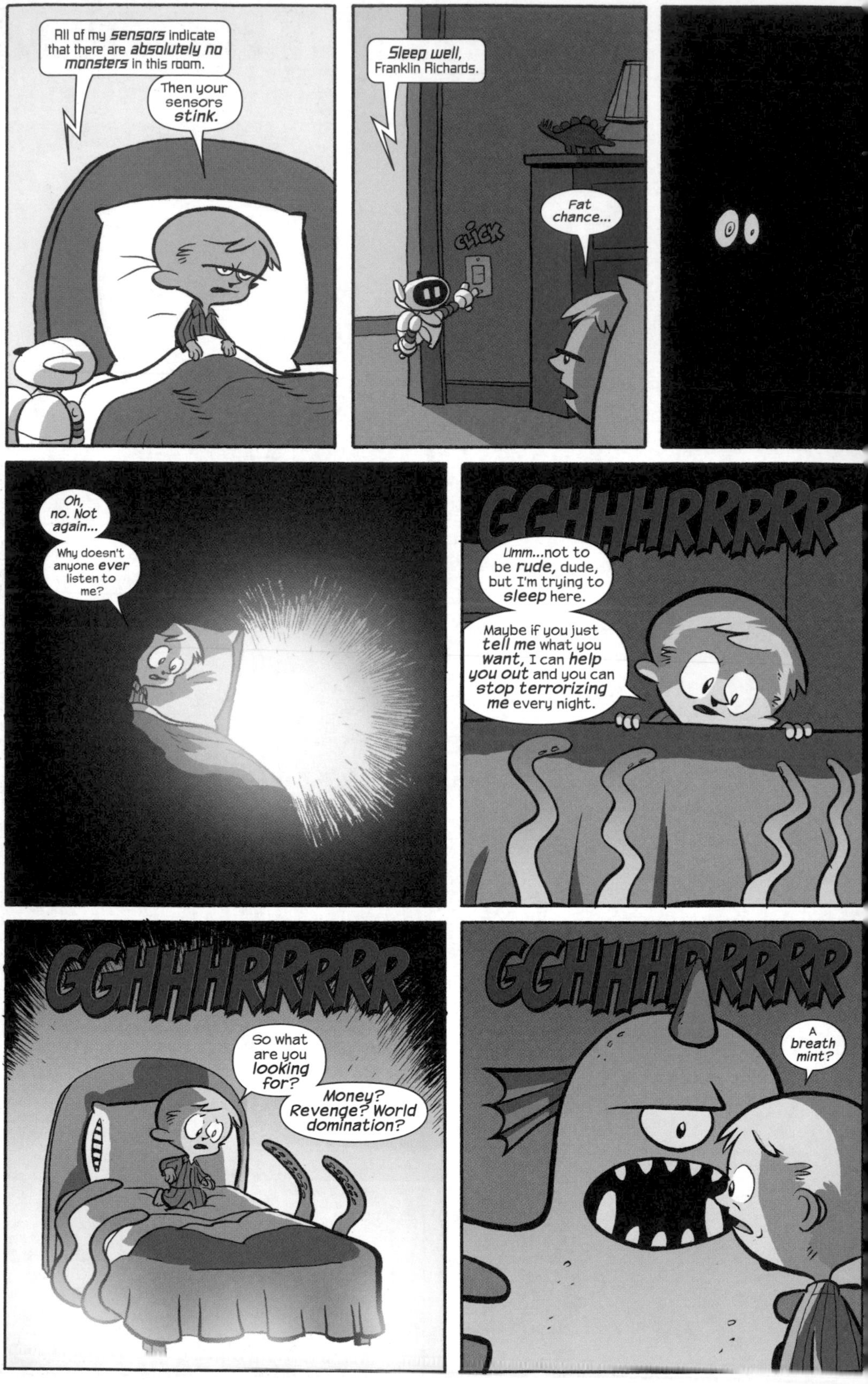
All of my sensors indicate that there are absolutely no monsters in this room.
Then your sensors stink.
Sleep well, Franklin Richards.
CLICK
Fat chance...
Oh, no. Not again...
Why doesn't anyone ever listen to me?
GGHHHRRRRR
Umm...not to be rude, dude, but I'm trying to sleep here.
Maybe if you just tell me what you want, I can help you out and you can stop terrorizing me every night.
GGHHHRRRRR
So what are you looking for?
Money? Revenge? World domination?
GGHHHRRRRR
A breath mint?

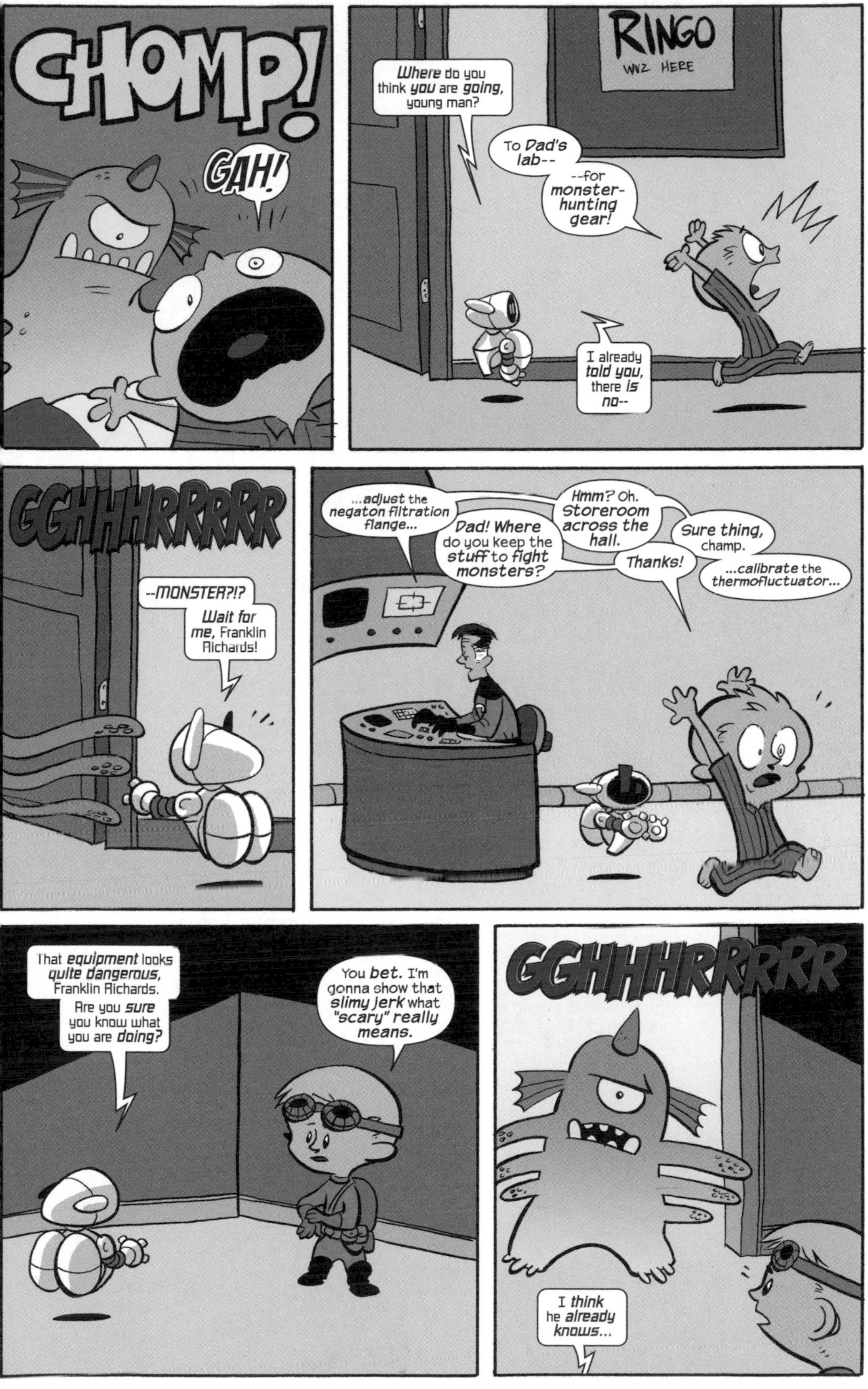
CHOMP!
GAH!
Where do you think you are going, young man?
RINGO WUZ HERE
To Dad's lab--
--for monster-hunting gear!
I already told you, there is no--
GGHHHRRRRR
--MONSTER?!?
Wait for me, Franklin Richards!
...adjust the negaton filtration flange...
Dad! Where do you keep the stuff to fight monsters?
Hmm? Oh. Storeroom across the hall.
Thanks!
Sure thing, champ.
...calibrate the thermofluctuator...
That equipment looks quite dangerous, Franklin Richards.
Are you sure you know what you are doing?
You bet. I'm gonna show that slimy jerk what "scary" really means.
GGHHHRRRRR
I think he already knows...

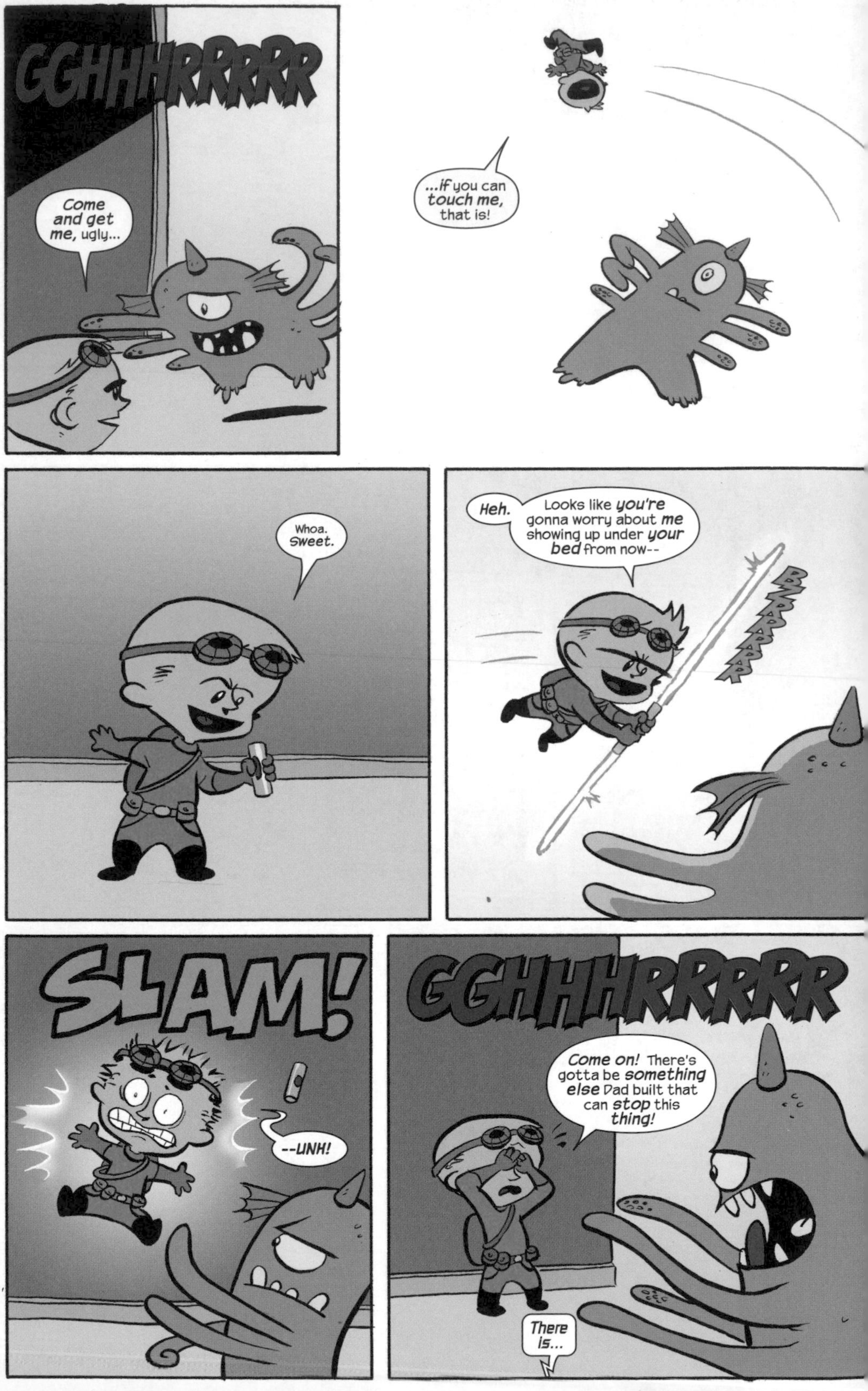

GGHHHRRRRR
Come and get me, ugly...
...if you can touch me, that is!
Whoa. Sweet.
Heh.
Looks like you're gonna worry about me showing up under your bed from now--
BZZAAAP
SLAM!
--UNH!
GGHHHRRRRR
Come on! There's gotta be something else Dad built that can stop this thing!
There is...

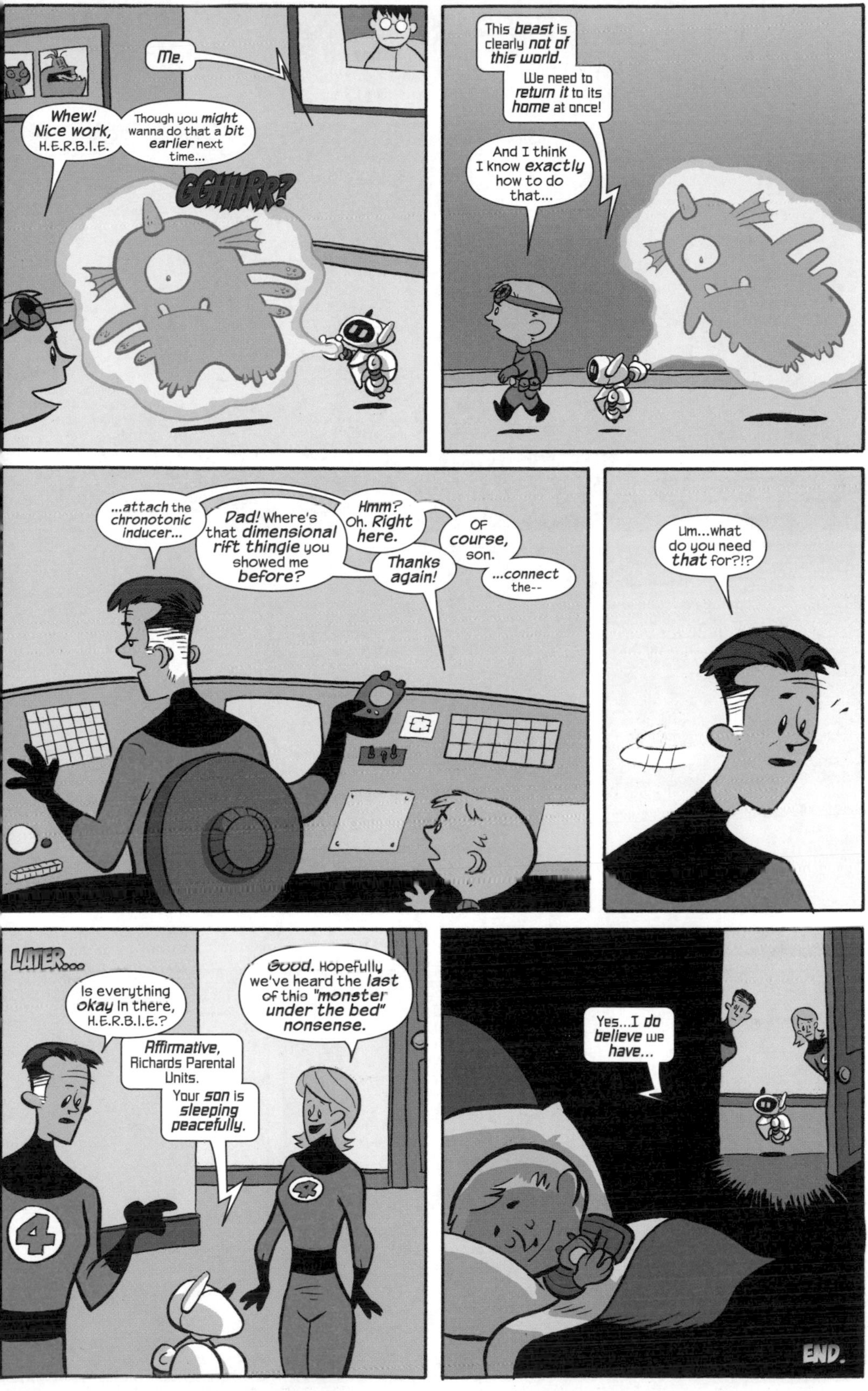
Me.
Whew! Nice work, H.E.R.B.I.E.
Though you might wanna do that a bit earlier next time...
GGHHRR?
This beast is clearly not of this world.
We need to return it to its home at once!
And I think I know exactly how to do that...
...attach the chronotonic inducer...
Dad! Where's that dimensional rift thingie you showed me before?
Hmm? Oh. Right here.
Thanks again!
Of course, son.
...connect the--
Um...what do you need that for?!?
LATER...
Is everything okay in there, H.E.R.B.I.E.?
Affirmative, Richards Parental Units.
Your son is sleeping peacefully.
Good. Hopefully we've heard the last of this "monster under the bed" nonsense.
Yes...I do believe we have...
END.

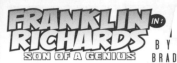

FRANKLIN RICHARDS SON OF A GENIUS IN: POWER TRIP!

BY CHRIS ELIOPOULOS & MARC SUMERAK

BRAD ANDERSON COLORS

NATHAN COSBY ASSISTANT EDITOR

MARK PANICCIA EDITOR

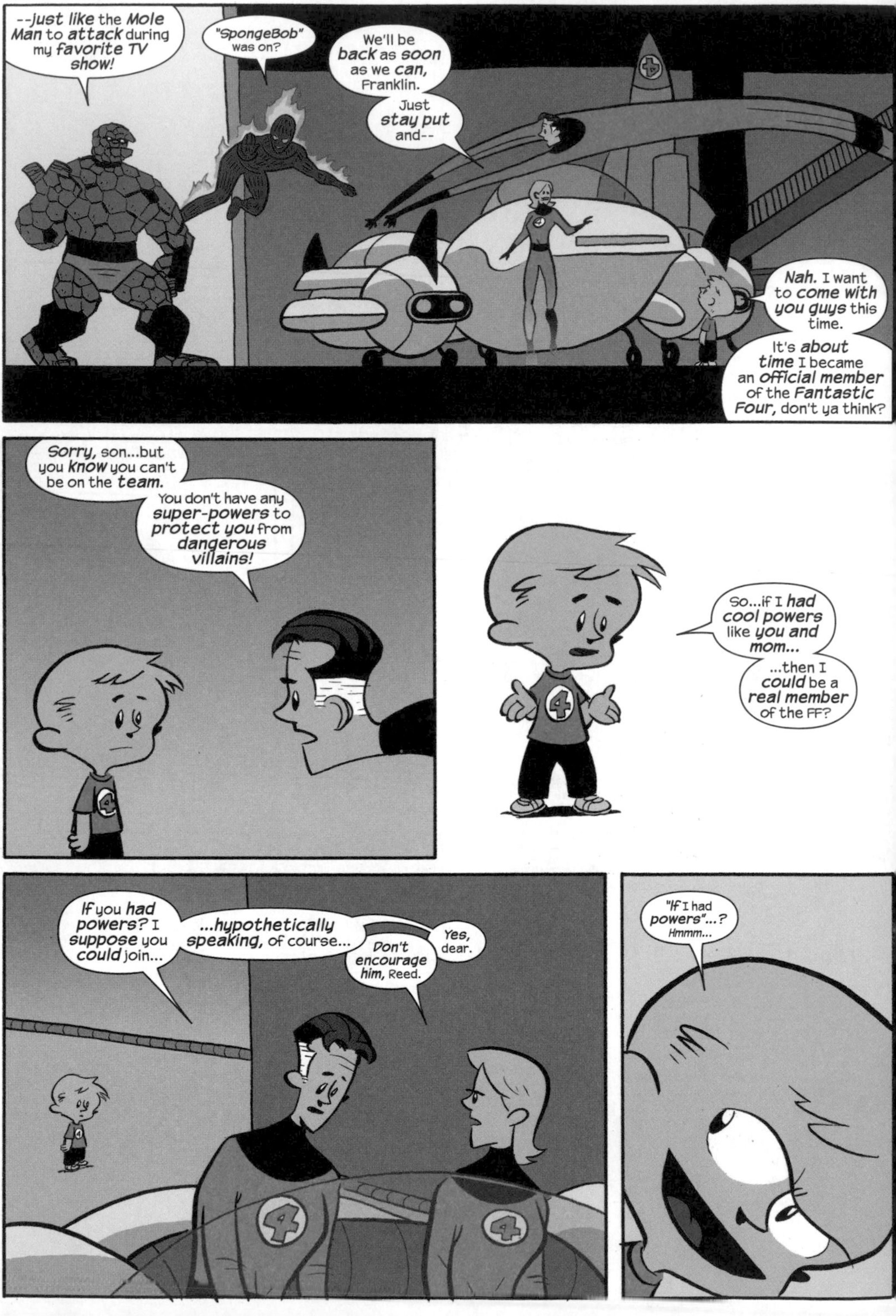

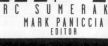

--Just like the Mole Man to attack during my favorite TV show!
"SpongeBob" was on?
We'll be back as soon as we can, Franklin.
Just stay put and--
Nah. I want to come with you guys this time.
It's about time I became an official member of the Fantastic Four, don't ya think?
Sorry, son...but you know you can't be on the team.
You don't have any super-powers to protect you from dangerous villains!
So...if I had cool powers like you and mom...
...then I could be a real member of the FF?
If you had powers? I suppose you could join...
...hypothetically speaking, of course...
Don't encourage him, Reed.
Yes, dear.
"If I had powers"...? Hmmm...

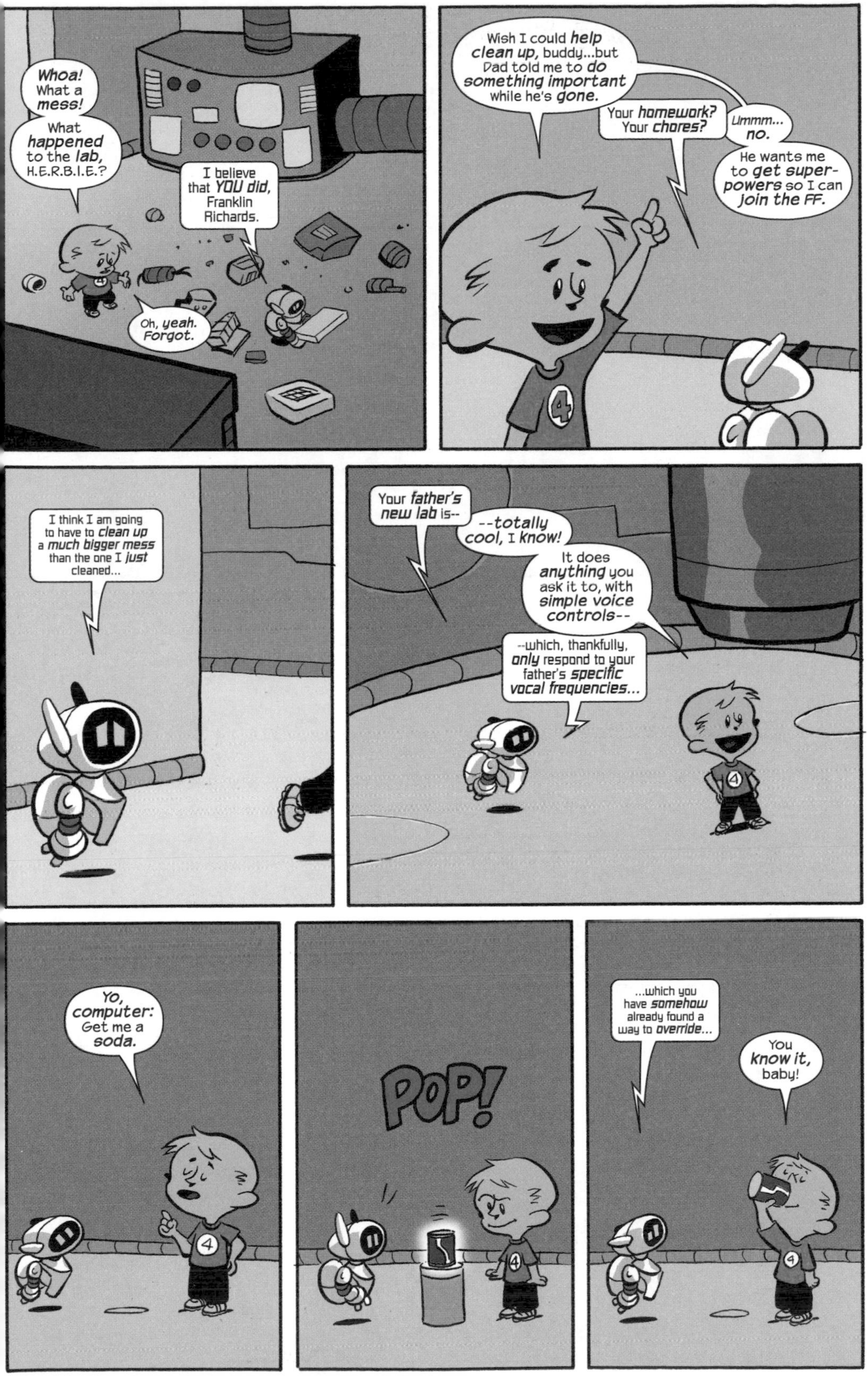
Whoa! What a mess!
What happened to the lab, H.E.R.B.I.E.?
I believe that YOU did, Franklin Richards.
Oh, yeah. Forgot.
Wish I could help clean up, buddy...but Dad told me to do something important while he's gone.
Your homework? Your chores?
Ummm... no.
He wants me to get super-powers so I can join the FF.
I think I am going to have to clean up a much bigger mess than the one I just cleaned...
Your father's new lab is--
--totally cool, I know!
It does anything you ask it to, with simple voice controls--
--which, thankfully, only respond to your father's specific vocal frequencies...
Yo, computer: Get me a soda.
POP!
...which you have somehow already found a way to override...
You know it, baby!

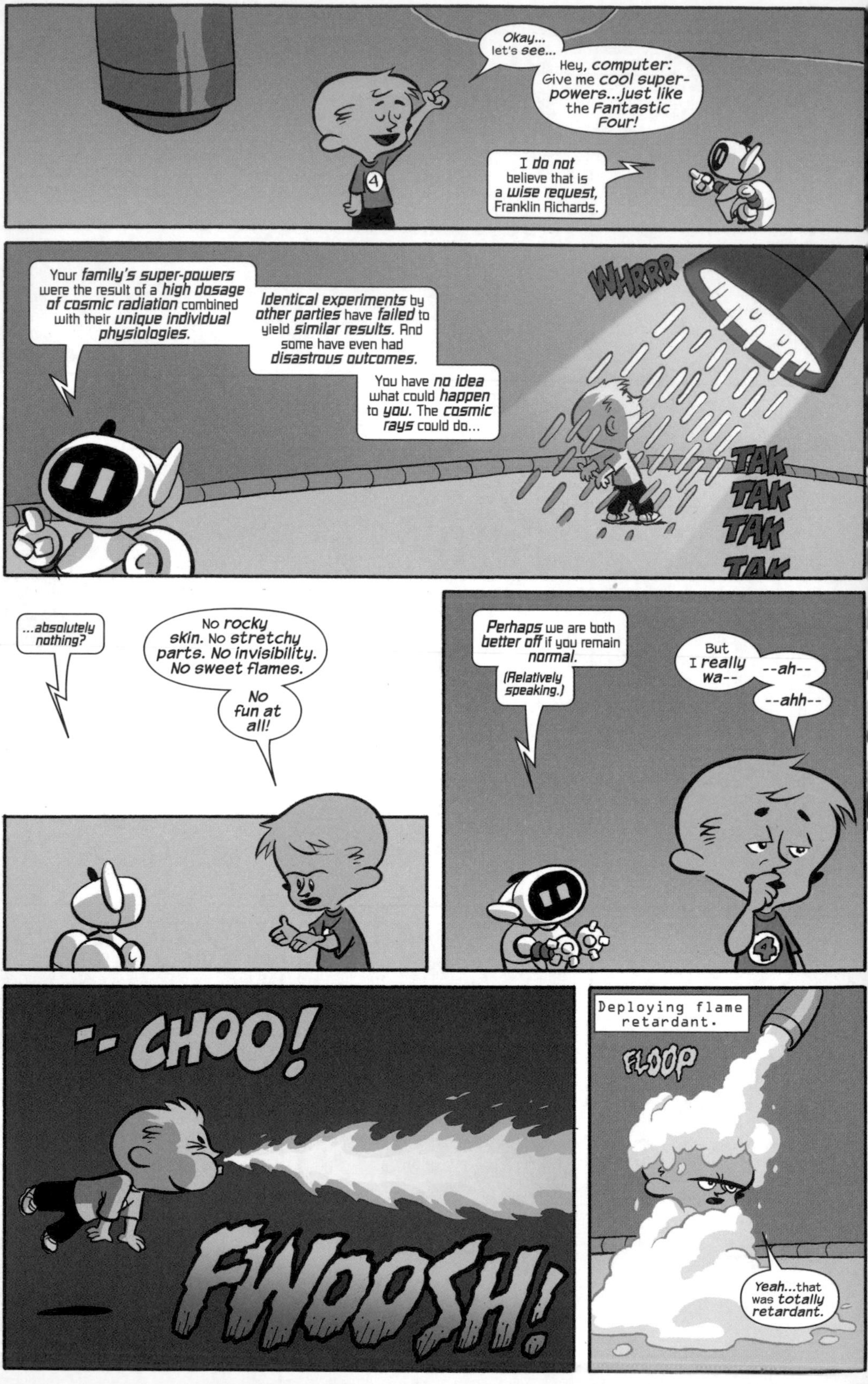

Okay... let's see...
Hey, computer: Give me cool super-powers...just like the Fantastic Four!
I do not believe that is a wise request, Franklin Richards.
Your family's super-powers were the result of a high dosage of cosmic radiation combined with their unique individual physiologies.
Identical experiments by other parties have failed to yield similar results. And some have even had disastrous outcomes.
You have no idea what could happen to you. The cosmic rays could do...
WHRRR
TAK TAK TAK TAK
...absolutely nothing?
No rocky skin. No stretchy parts. No invisibility. No sweet flames.
No fun at all!
Perhaps we are both better off if you remain normal.
(Relatively speaking.)
But I really wa--
--ah--
--ahh--
--CHOO!
FWOOSH!
Deploying flame retardant.
FLOOP
Yeah...that was totally retardant.

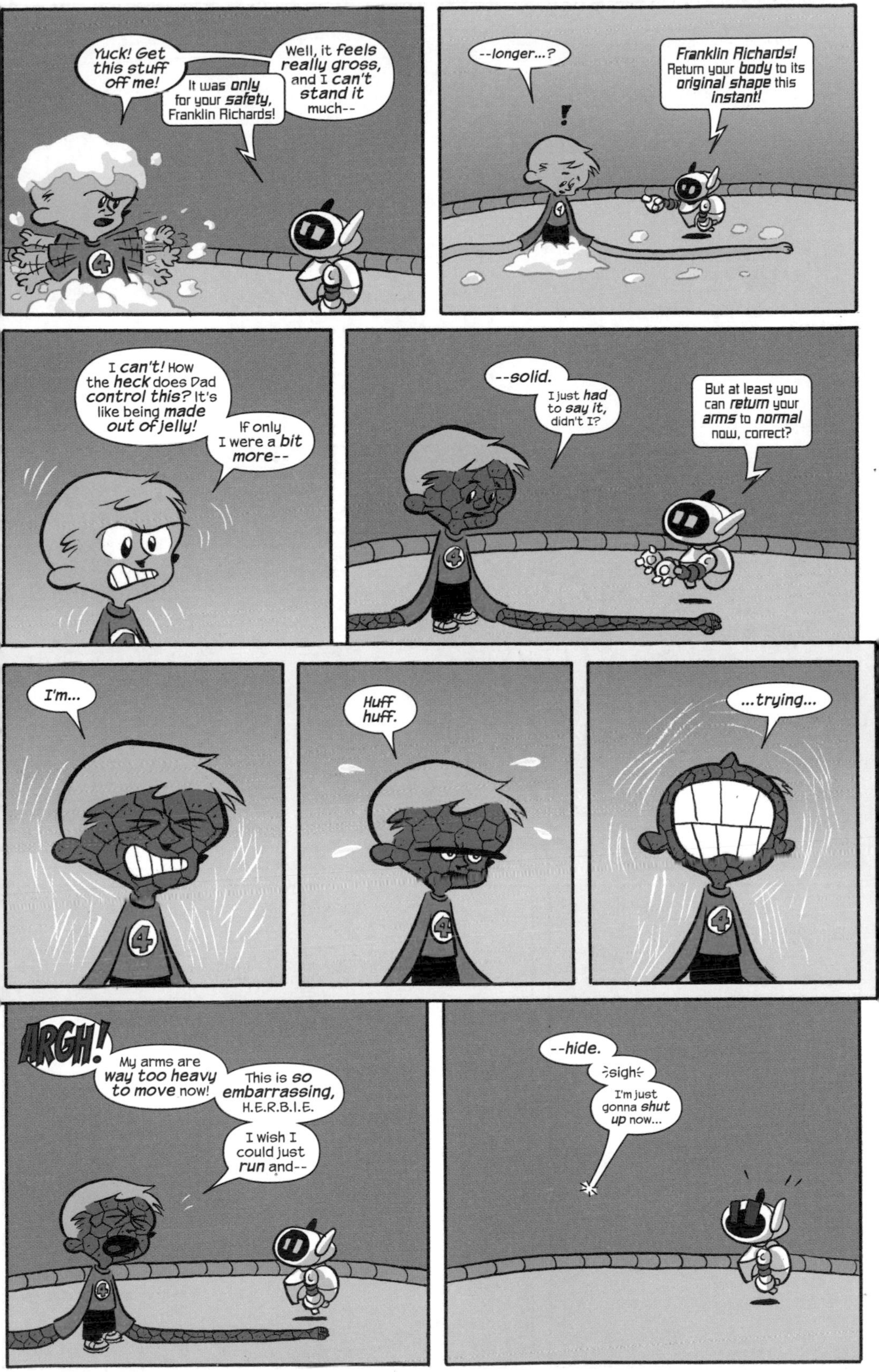
Yuck! Get this stuff off me!
It was only for your safety, Franklin Richards!
Well, it feels really gross, and I can't stand it much--
--longer...?
!
Franklin Richards! Return your body to its original shape this instant!
I can't! How the heck does Dad control this? It's like being made out of jelly!
If only I were a bit more--
--solid.
I just had to say it, didn't I?
But at least you can return your arms to normal now, correct?
I'm...
Huff huff.
...trying...
ARGH!
My arms are way too heavy to move now!
This is so embarrassing, H.E.R.B.I.E.
I wish I could just run and--
--hide.
sigh
I'm just gonna shut up now...

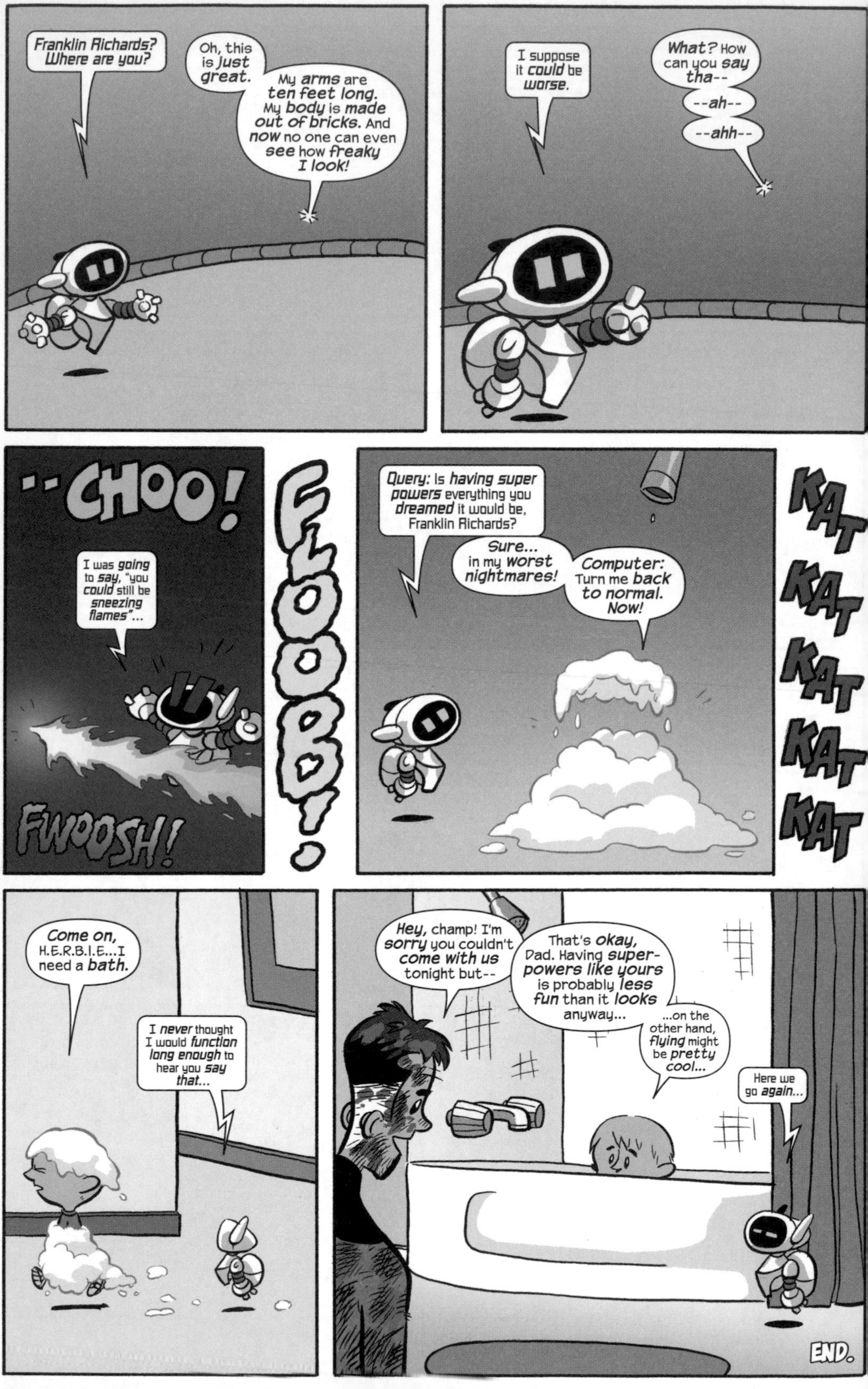

Franklin Richards? Where are you?
Oh, this is just great.
My arms are ten feet long. My body is made out of bricks. And now no one can even see how freaky I look!
I suppose it could be worse.
What? How can you say tha--
--ah--
--ahh--
--CHOO!
I was going to say, "you could still be sneezing flames"...
FWOOSH!
FLOOOB!
Query: Is having super powers everything you dreamed it would be, Franklin Richards?
Sure... in my worst nightmares!
Computer: Turn me back to normal. Now!
KAT KAT KAT KAT KAT
Come on, H.E.R.B.I.E...I need a bath.
I never thought I would function long enough to hear you say that...
Hey, champ! I'm sorry you couldn't come with us tonight but--
That's okay, Dad. Having super-powers like yours is probably less fun than it looks anyway...
...on the other hand, flying might be pretty cool...
Here we go again...
END.

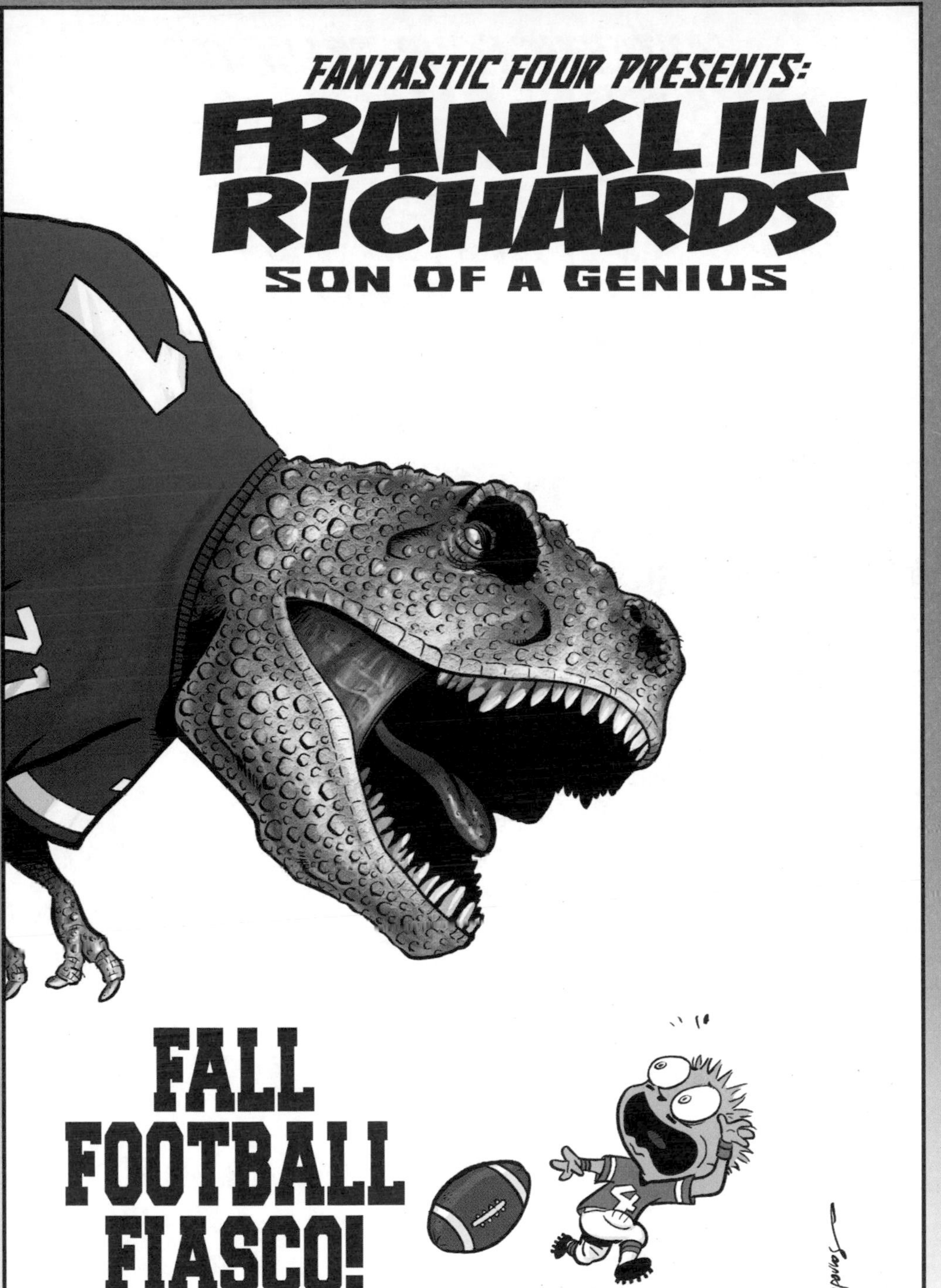

FANTASTIC FOUR PRESENTS:
FRANKLIN RICHARDS
SON OF A GENIUS
FALL FOOTBALL FIASCO!

FANTASTIC FOUR PRESENTS:
FRANKLIN RICHARDS
SON OF A GENIUS
FALL FOOTBALL FIASCO!

CHRIS ELIOPOULOS and MARC SUMERAK
STORY

MARC SUMERAK
SCRIPT

CHRIS ELIOPOULOS
ART & LETTERS

BRAD ANDERSON
COLORS

NATHAN COSBY
ASSISTANT EDITOR

MARK PANICCIA
EDITOR

IRENE LEE
PRODUCTION

JOE QUESADA
EDITOR IN CHIEF

DAN BUCKLEY
PUBLISHER

STORY ONE
FANTASY FOOTBALL!

STORY TWO
LOCKJAW UNLEASHED!

STORY THREE
DOUBLE TROUBLE!

STORY FOUR
TIME AND TIME AGAIN!

STORY FIVE
ALIEN ENCOUNTER!

FRANKLIN RICHARDS SON OF A GENIUS IN:

FANTASY FOOTBALL!

BY CHRIS ELIOPOULOS & MARC SUMERAK

BRAD ANDERSON COLORS — NATHAN COSBY ASSISTANT EDITOR — MARK PANICCIA EDITOR

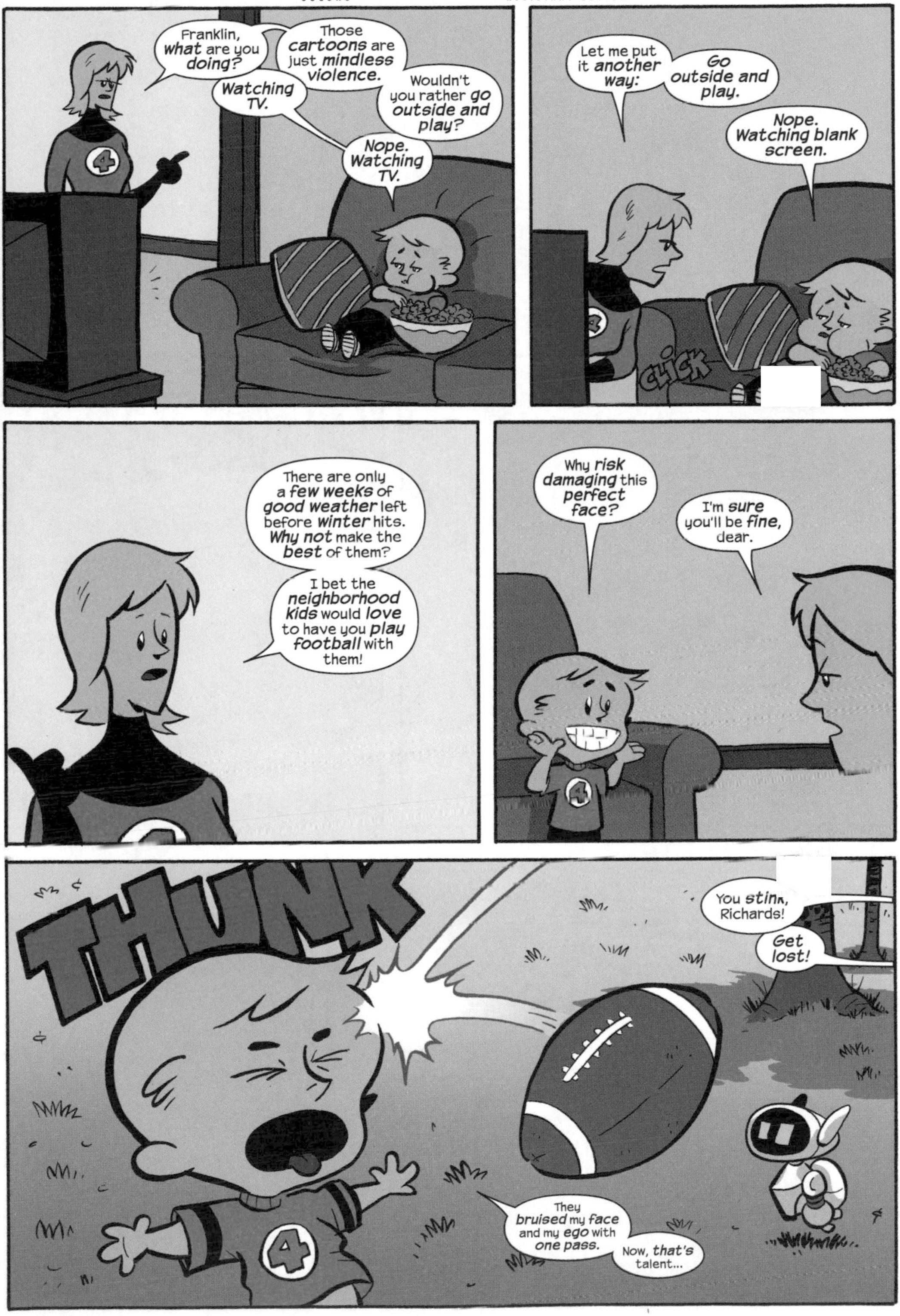

Franklin, what are you doing?
Watching TV.
Those cartoons are just mindless violence.
Wouldn't you rather go outside and play?
Nope. Watching TV.
Let me put it another way:
Go outside and play.
CLICK
Nope. Watching blank screen.
There are only a few weeks of good weather left before winter hits. Why not make the best of them?
I bet the neighborhood kids would love to have you play football with them!
Why risk damaging this perfect face?
I'm sure you'll be fine, dear.
THUNK
You stink, Richards!
Get lost!
They bruised my face and my ego with one pass.
Now, that's talent...

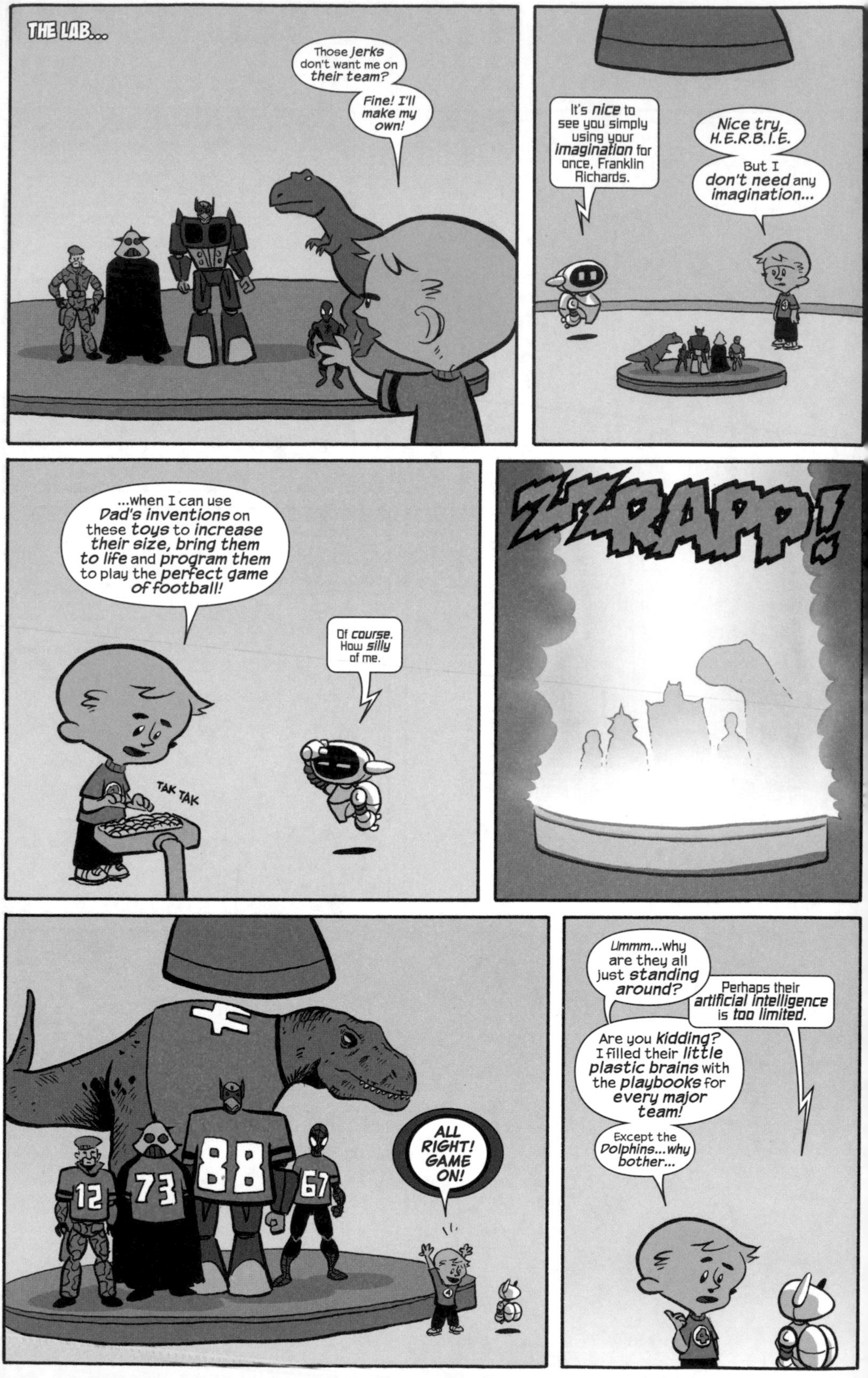
THE LAB...
Those jerks don't want me on their team?
Fine! I'll make my own!
It's nice to see you simply using your imagination for once, Franklin Richards.
Nice try, H.E.R.B.I.E.
But I don't need any imagination...
...when I can use Dad's inventions on these toys to increase their size, bring them to life and program them to play the perfect game of football!
TAK TAK
Of course. How silly of me.
ZZZRAPP!
12
73
88
67
ALL RIGHT! GAME ON!
Ummm...why are they all just standing around?
Perhaps their artificial intelligence is too limited.
Are you kidding? I filled their little plastic brains with the playbooks for every major team!
Except the Dolphins...why bother...

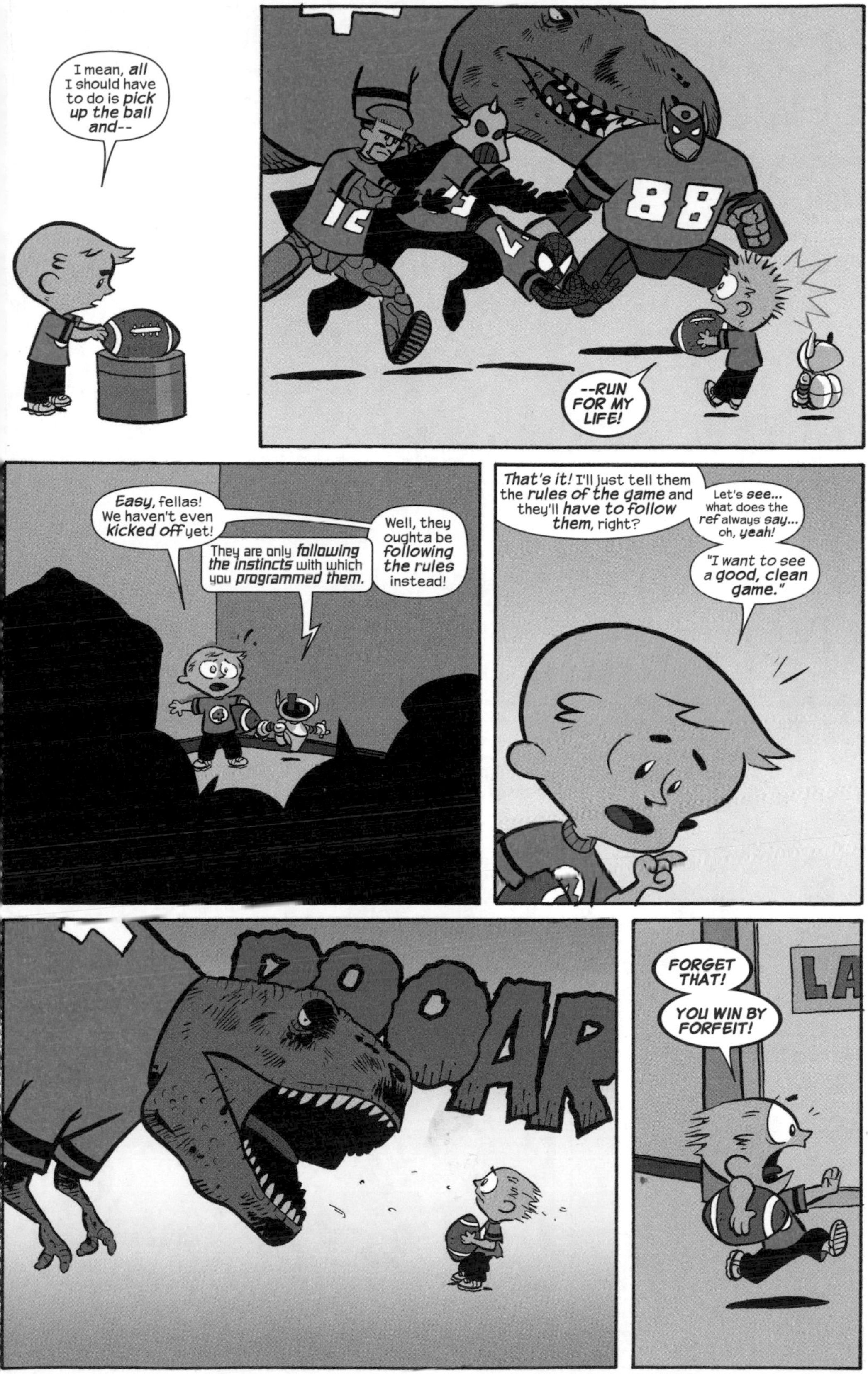
I mean, all I should have to do is pick up the ball and--
88
--RUN FOR MY LIFE!
Easy, fellas! We haven't even kicked off yet!
They are only following the instincts with which you programmed them.
Well, they oughta be following the rules instead!
That's it! I'll just tell them the rules of the game and they'll have to follow them, right?
Let's see... what does the ref always say... oh, yeah!
"I want to see a good, clean game."
ROOOAR
FORGET THAT!
YOU WIN BY FORFEIT!

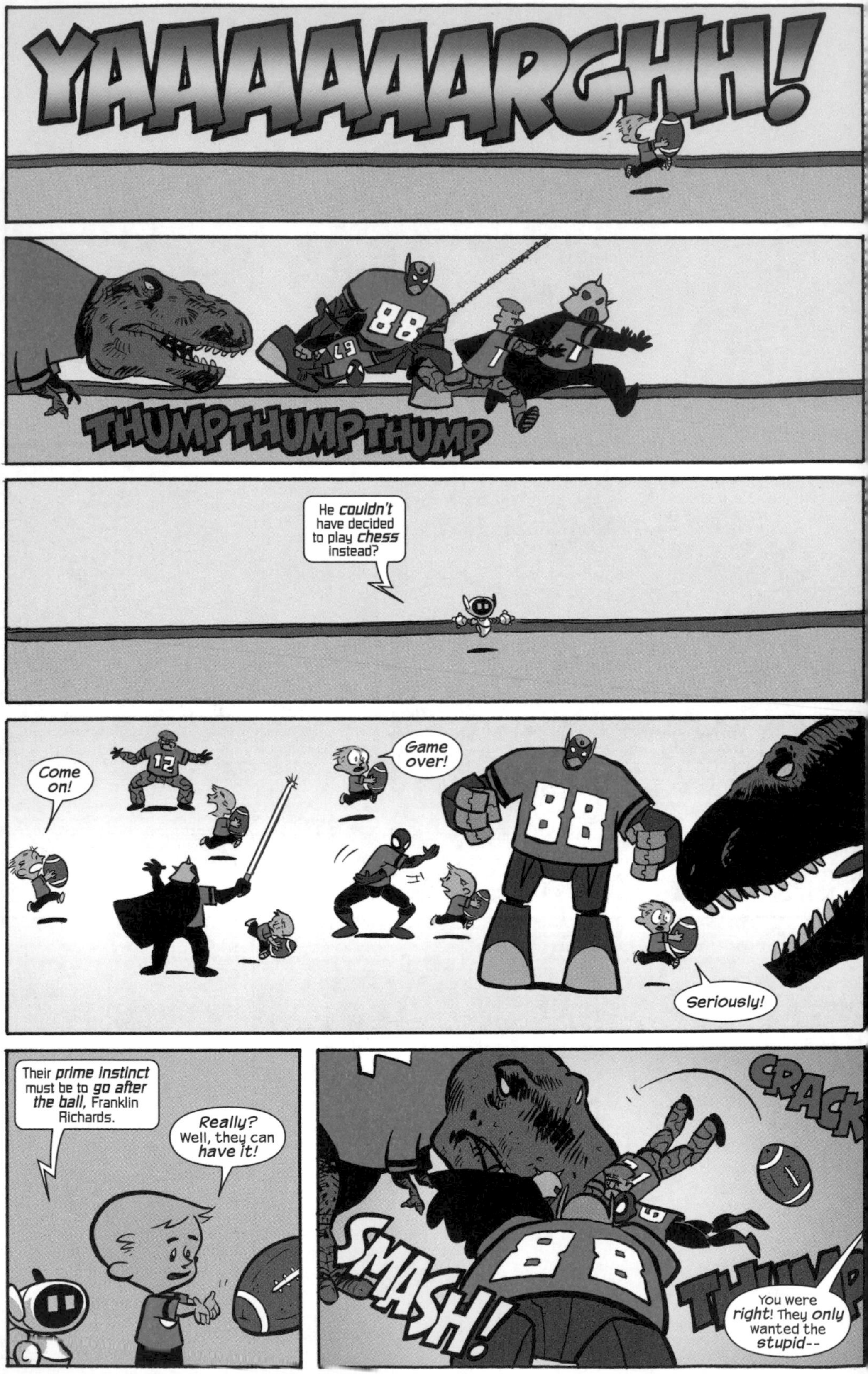
YAAAAAARGHH!
THUMPTHUMPTHUMP
He couldn't have decided to play chess instead?
Come on!
Game over!
Seriously!
Their prime instinct must be to go after the ball, Franklin Richards.
Really? Well, they can have it!
CRACK
SMASH!
You were right! They only wanted the stupid--

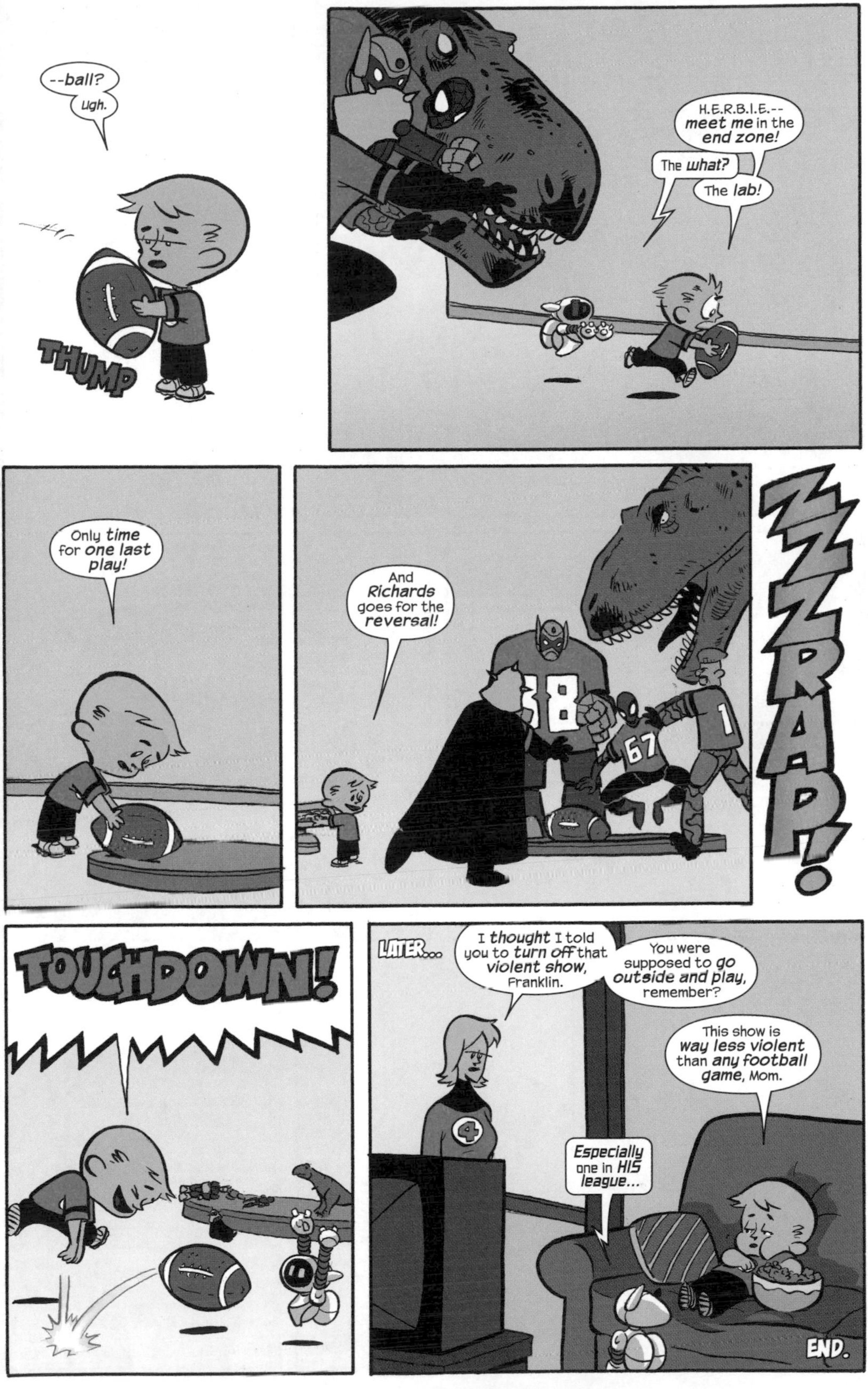
--ball?
Ugh.
THUMP
H.E.R.B.I.E.-- meet me in the end zone!
The what?
The lab!
Only time for one last play!
And Richards goes for the reversal!
ZZZRAP!
TOUCHDOWN!
LATER...
I thought I told you to turn off that violent show, Franklin.
You were supposed to go outside and play, remember?
This show is way less violent than any football game, Mom.
Especially one in HIS league...
END.

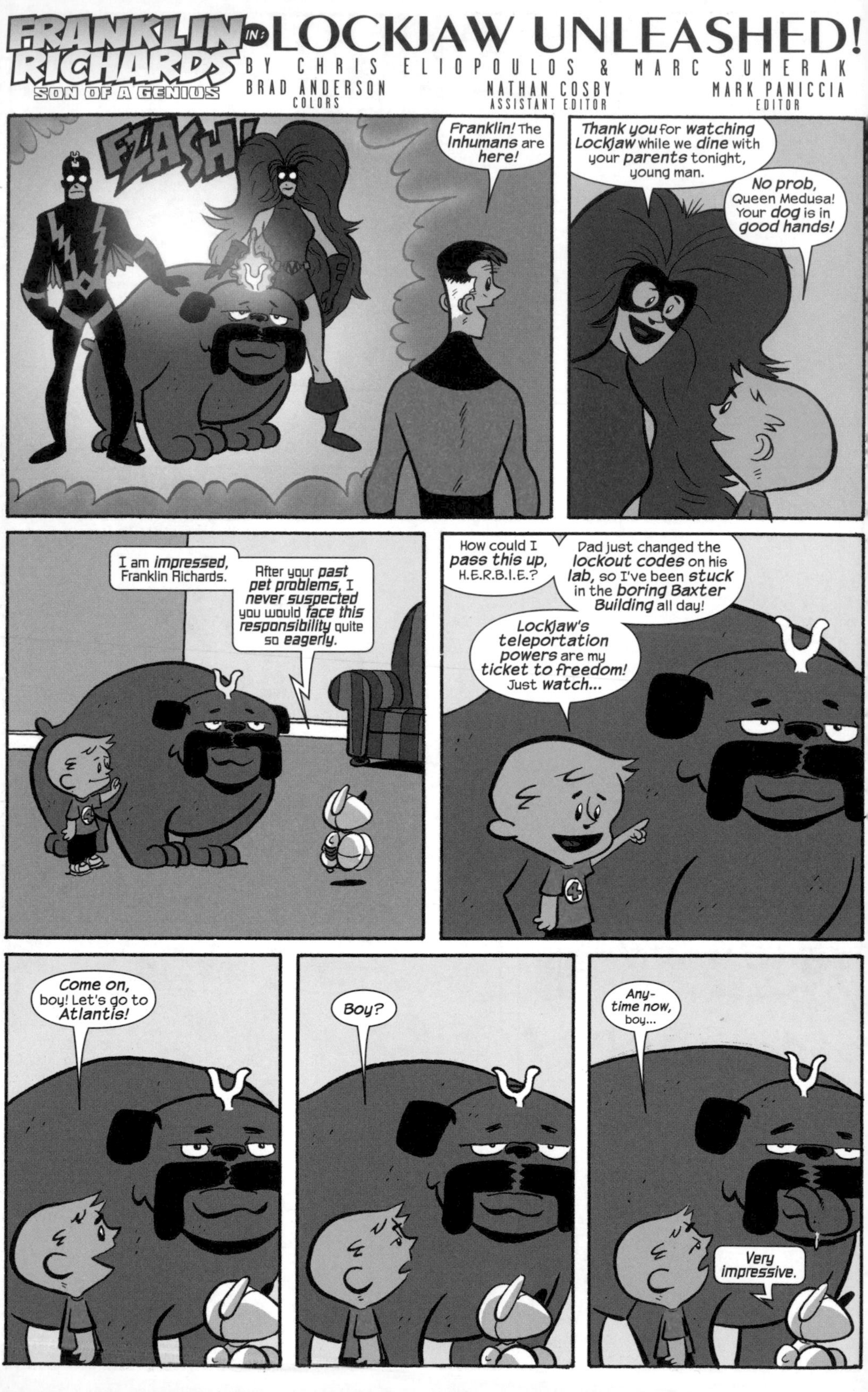
FRANKLIN RICHARDS SON OF A GENIUS
IN: LOCKJAW UNLEASHED!
BY CHRIS ELIOPOULOS & MARC SUMERAK
BRAD ANDERSON COLORS
NATHAN COSBY ASSISTANT EDITOR
MARK PANICCIA EDITOR
FLASH!
Franklin! The Inhumans are here!
Thank you for watching Lockjaw while we dine with your parents tonight, young man.
No prob, Queen Medusa! Your dog is in good hands!
I am impressed, Franklin Richards.
After your past pet problems, I never suspected you would face this responsibility quite so eagerly.
How could I pass this up, H.E.R.B.I.E.?
Dad just changed the lockout codes on his lab, so I've been stuck in the boring Baxter Building all day!
Lockjaw's teleportation powers are my ticket to freedom! Just watch...
Come on, boy! Let's go to Atlantis!
Boy?
Any-time now, boy...
Very impressive.

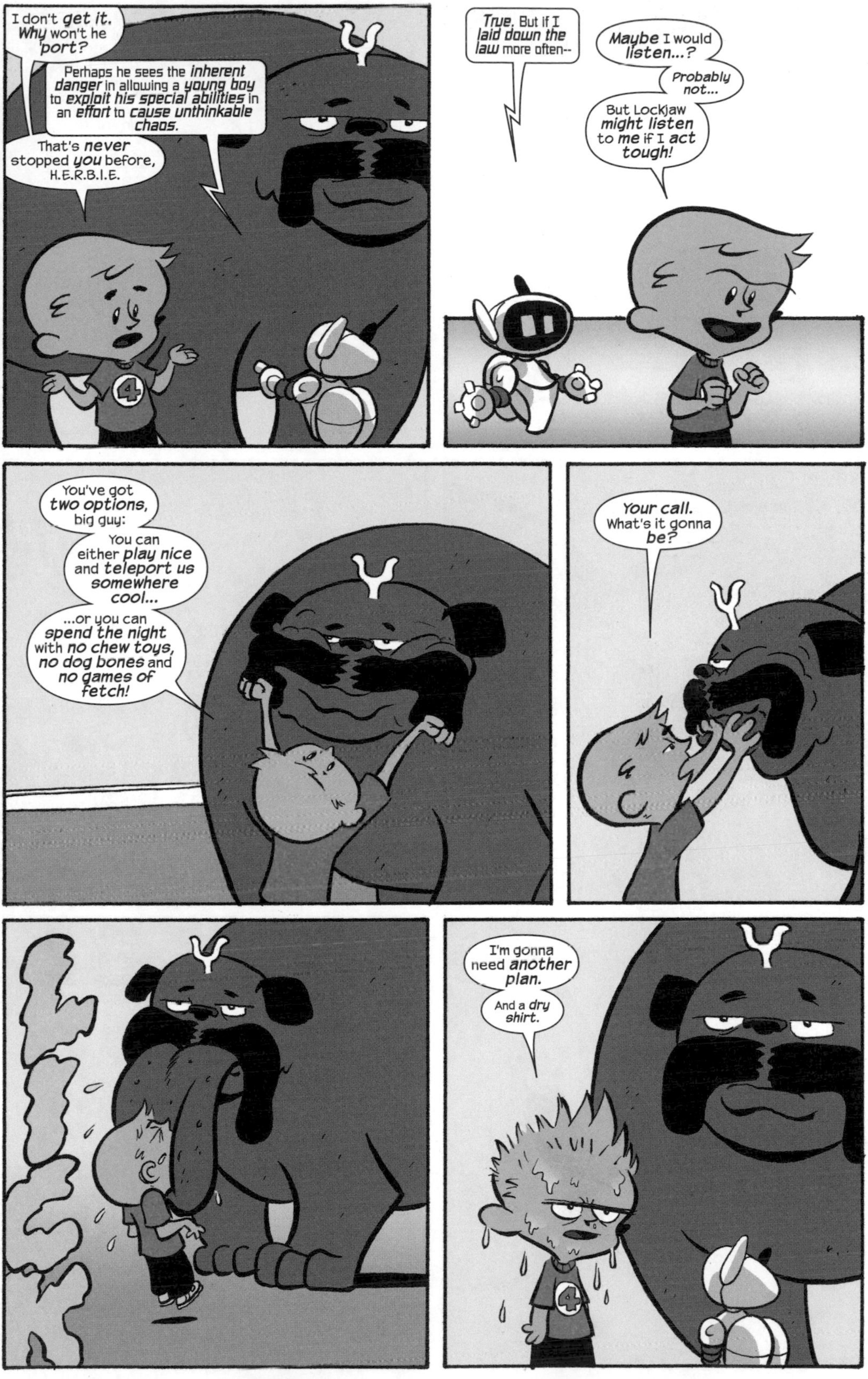
I don't get it. Why won't he 'port?
Perhaps he sees the inherent danger in allowing a young boy to exploit his special abilities in an effort to cause unthinkable chaos.
That's never stopped you before, H.E.R.B.I.E.
True. But if I laid down the law more often--
Maybe I would listen...?
Probably not...
But Lockjaw might listen to me if I act tough!
You've got two options, big guy:
You can either play nice and teleport us somewhere cool...
...or you can spend the night with no chew toys, no dog bones and no games of fetch!
Your call. What's it gonna be?
I'm gonna need another plan.
And a dry shirt.

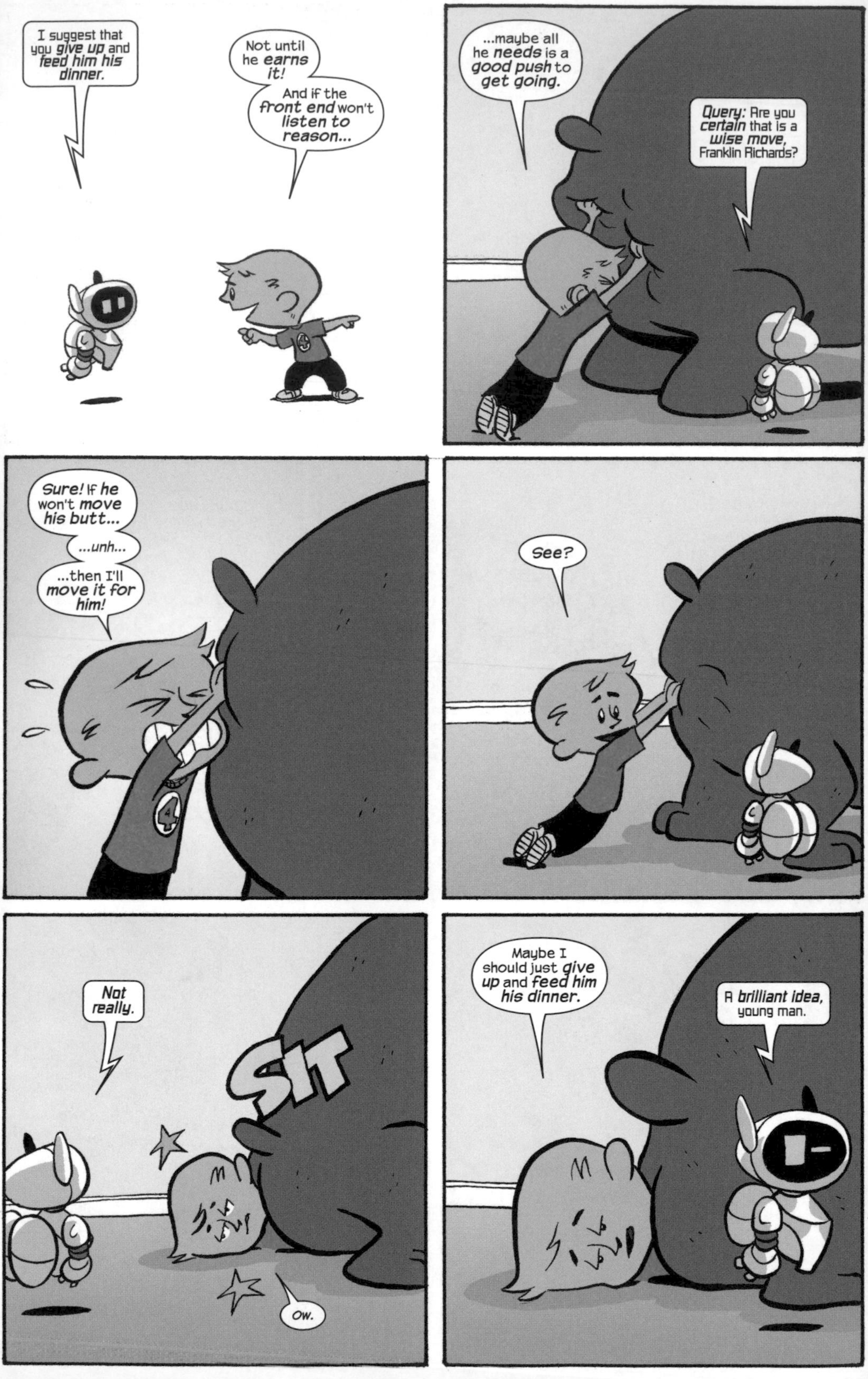
I suggest that you give up and feed him his dinner.
Not until he earns it!
And if the front end won't listen to reason...
...maybe all he needs is a good push to get going.
Query: Are you certain that is a wise move, Franklin Richards?
Sure! If he won't move his butt...
...unh...
...then I'll move it for him!
See?
Not really.
SIT
Ow.
Maybe I should just give up and feed him his dinner.
A brilliant idea, young man.

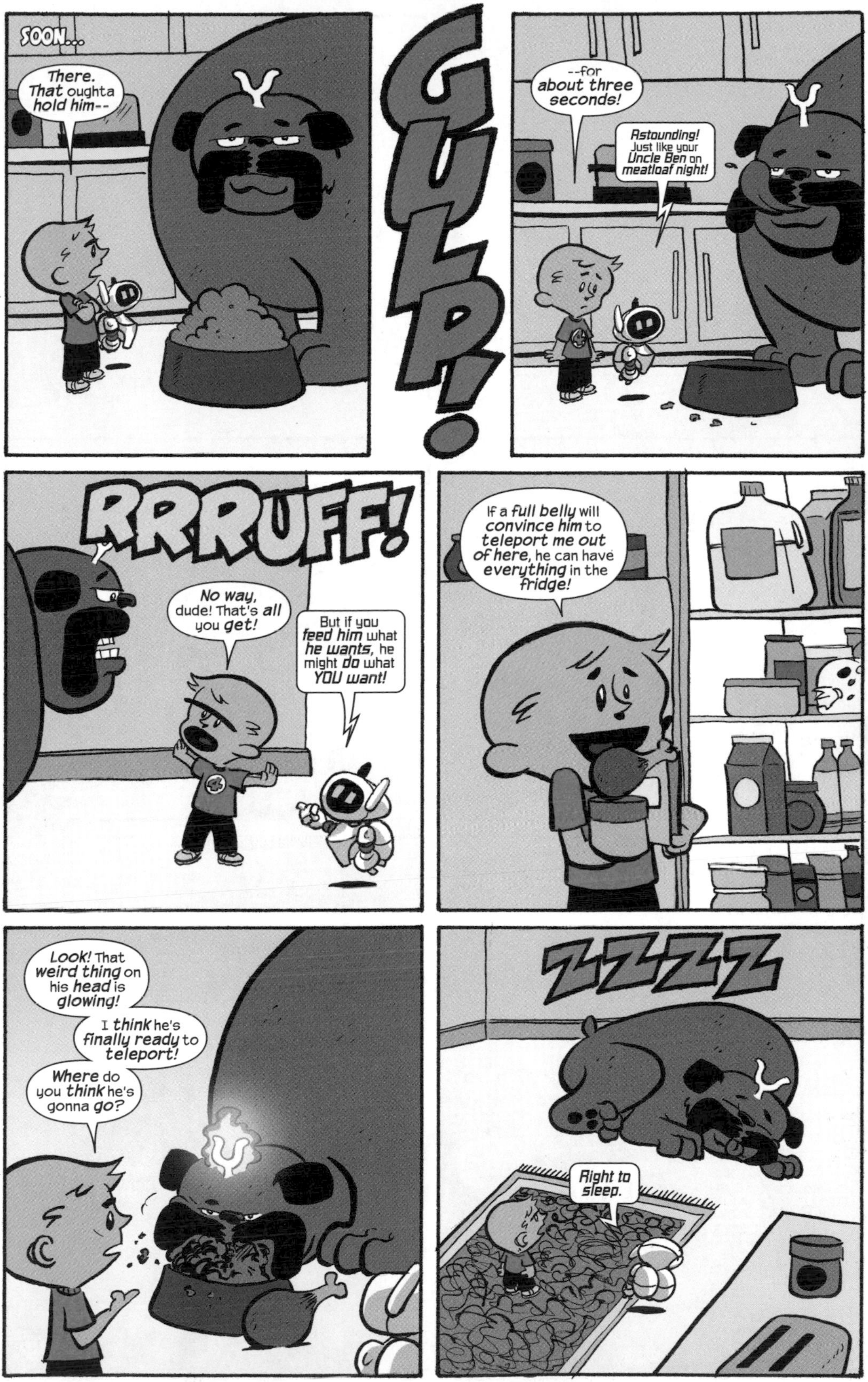
SOON...
There. That oughta hold him--
GULP!
--for about three seconds!
Astounding! Just like your Uncle Ben on meatloaf night!
RRRUFF!
No way, dude! That's all you get!
But if you feed him what he wants, he might do what YOU want!
If a full belly will convince him to teleport me out of here, he can have everything in the fridge!
Look! That weird thing on his head is glowing!
I think he's finally ready to teleport!
Where do you think he's gonna go?
ZZZZ
Right to sleep.

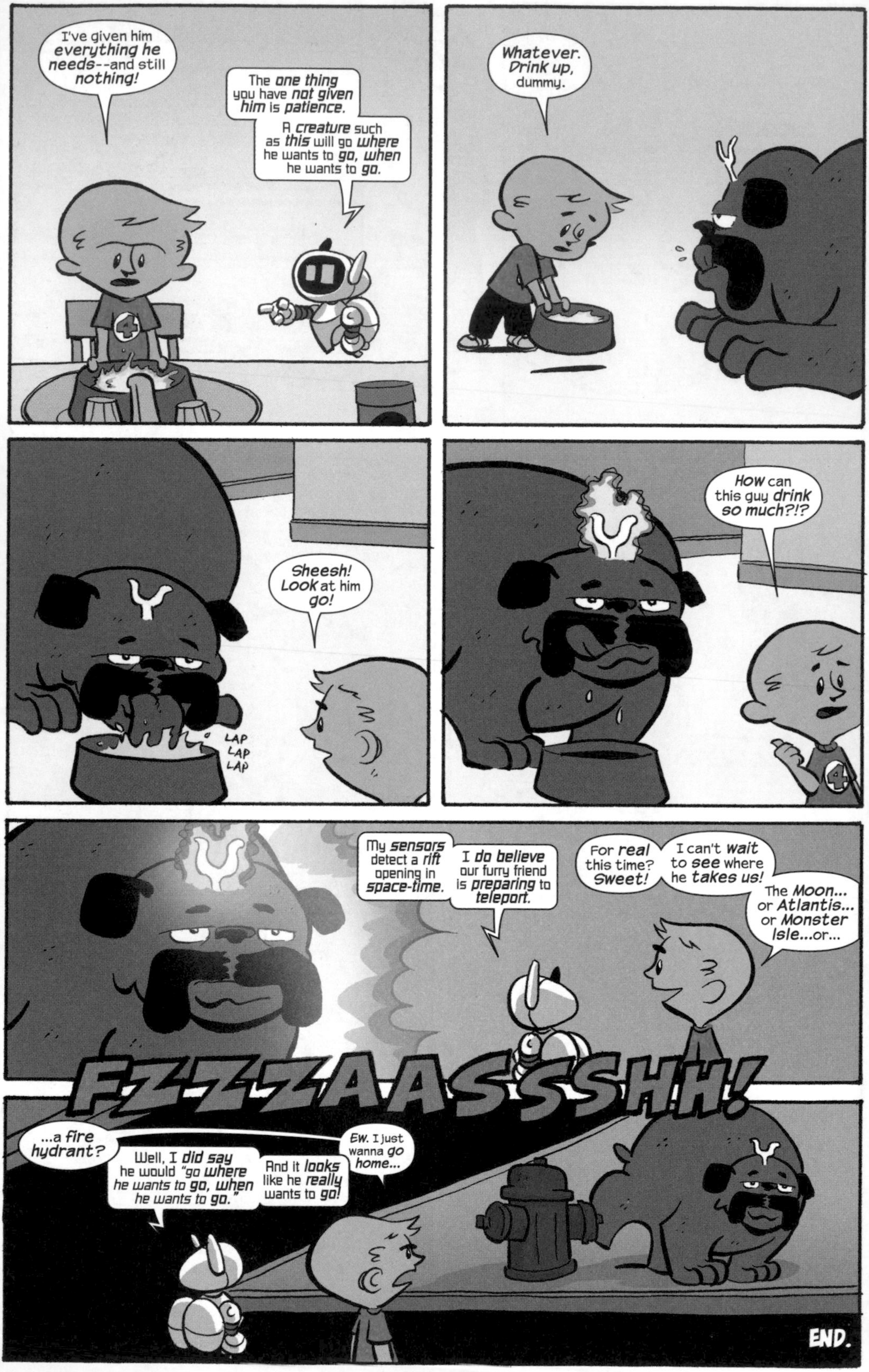
I've given him everything he needs--and still nothing!
The one thing you have not given him is patience.
A creature such as this will go where he wants to go, when he wants to go.
Whatever. Drink up, dummy.
Sheesh! Look at him go!
LAP LAP LAP
HOW can this guy drink so much?!?
My sensors detect a rift opening in space-time.
I do believe our furry friend is preparing to teleport.
For real this time? Sweet!
I can't wait to see where he takes us!
The Moon... or Atlantis... or Monster Isle...or...
FZZZZAASSSHH!
...a fire hydrant?
Well, I did say he would "go where he wants to go, when he wants to go."
And it looks like he really wants to go!
Ew. I just wanna go home...
END.

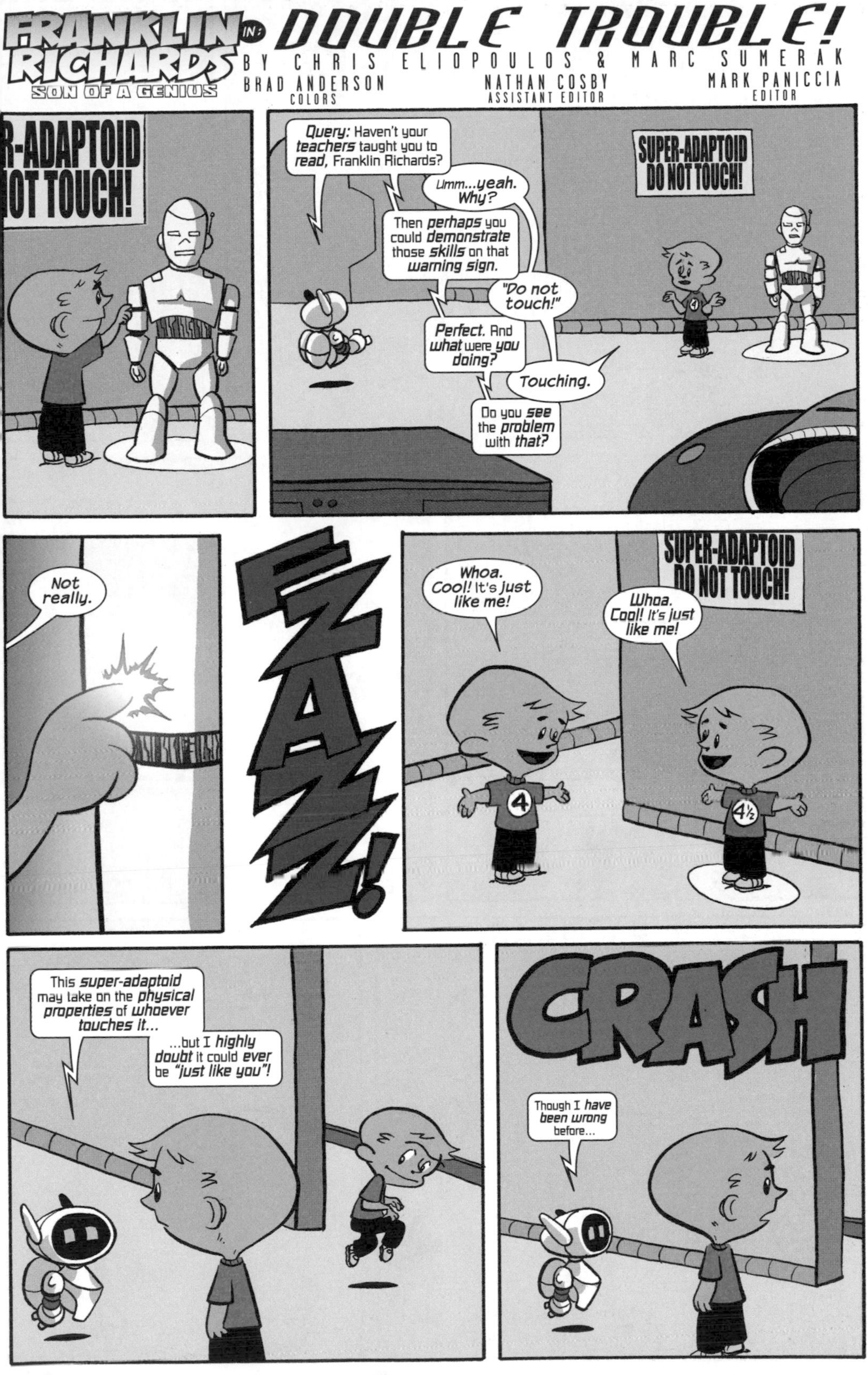
FRANKLIN RICHARDS
SON OF A GENIUS
IN: DOUBLE TROUBLE!
BY CHRIS ELIOPOULOS & MARC SUMERAK
BRAD ANDERSON COLORS
NATHAN COSBY ASSISTANT EDITOR
MARK PANICCIA EDITOR
R-ADAPTOID
IOT TOUCH!
Query: Haven't your teachers taught you to read, Franklin Richards?
Umm...yeah. Why?
Then perhaps you could demonstrate those skills on that warning sign.
"Do not touch!"
Perfect. And what were you doing?
Touching.
Do you see the problem with that?
SUPER-ADAPTOID
DO NOT TOUCH!
Not really.
FZAZZ!
Whoa. Cool! It's just like me!
Whoa. Cool! It's just like me!
SUPER-ADAPTOID
DO NOT TOUCH!
This super-adaptoid may take on the physical properties of whoever touches it...
...but I highly doubt it could ever be "just like you"!
CRASH
Though I have been wrong before...

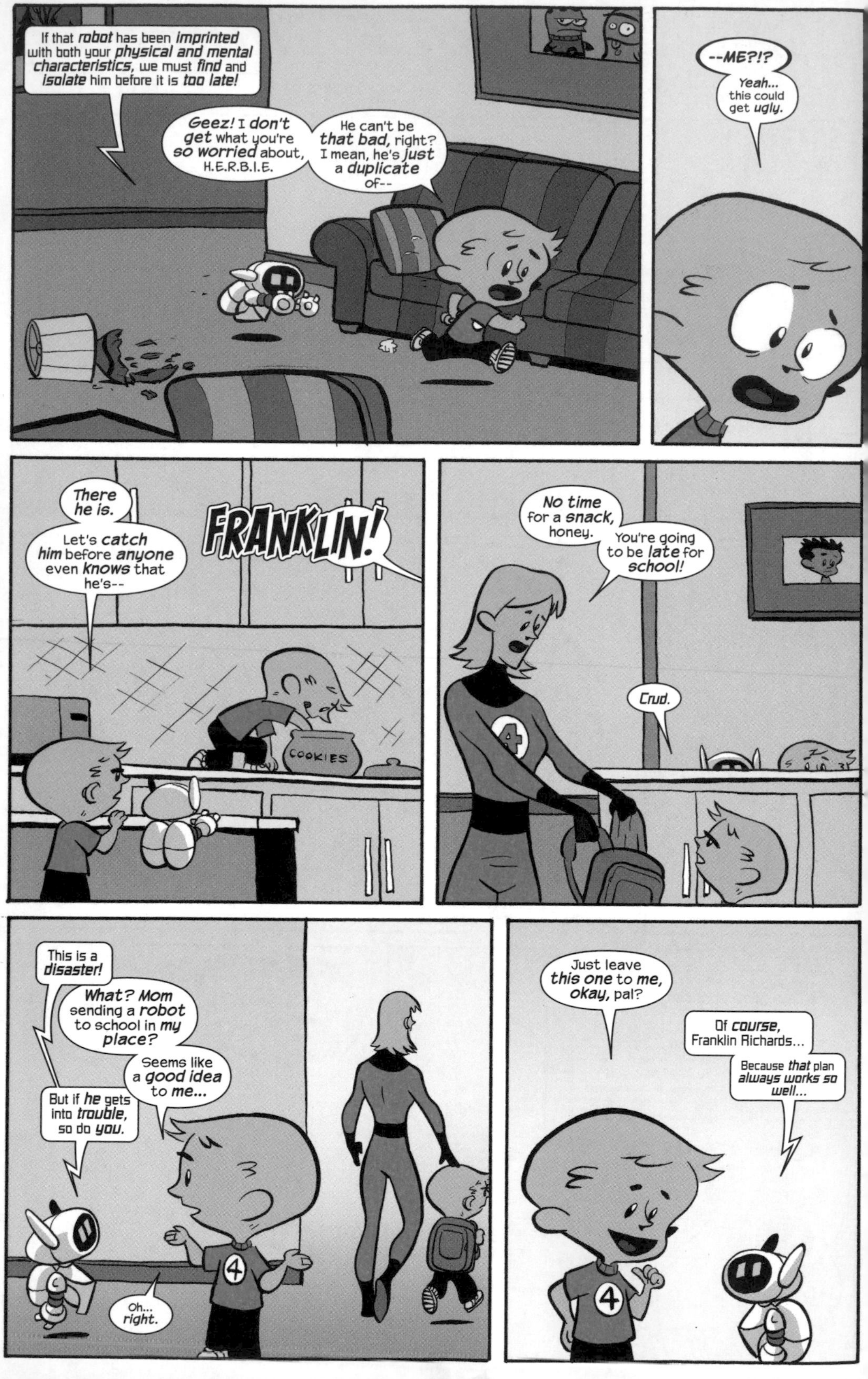
If that robot has been imprinted with both your physical and mental characteristics, we must find and isolate him before it is too late!
Geez! I don't get what you're so worried about, H.E.R.B.I.E.
He can't be that bad, right? I mean, he's just a duplicate of--
--ME?!?
Yeah... this could get ugly.
There he is.
Let's catch him before anyone even knows that he's--
FRANKLIN!
COOKIES
No time for a snack, honey.
You're going to be late for school!
Crud.
This is a disaster!
What? Mom sending a robot to school in my place?
Seems like a good idea to me...
But if he gets into trouble, so do you.
Oh... right.
Just leave this one to me, okay, pal?
Of course, Franklin Richards...
Because that plan always works so well...

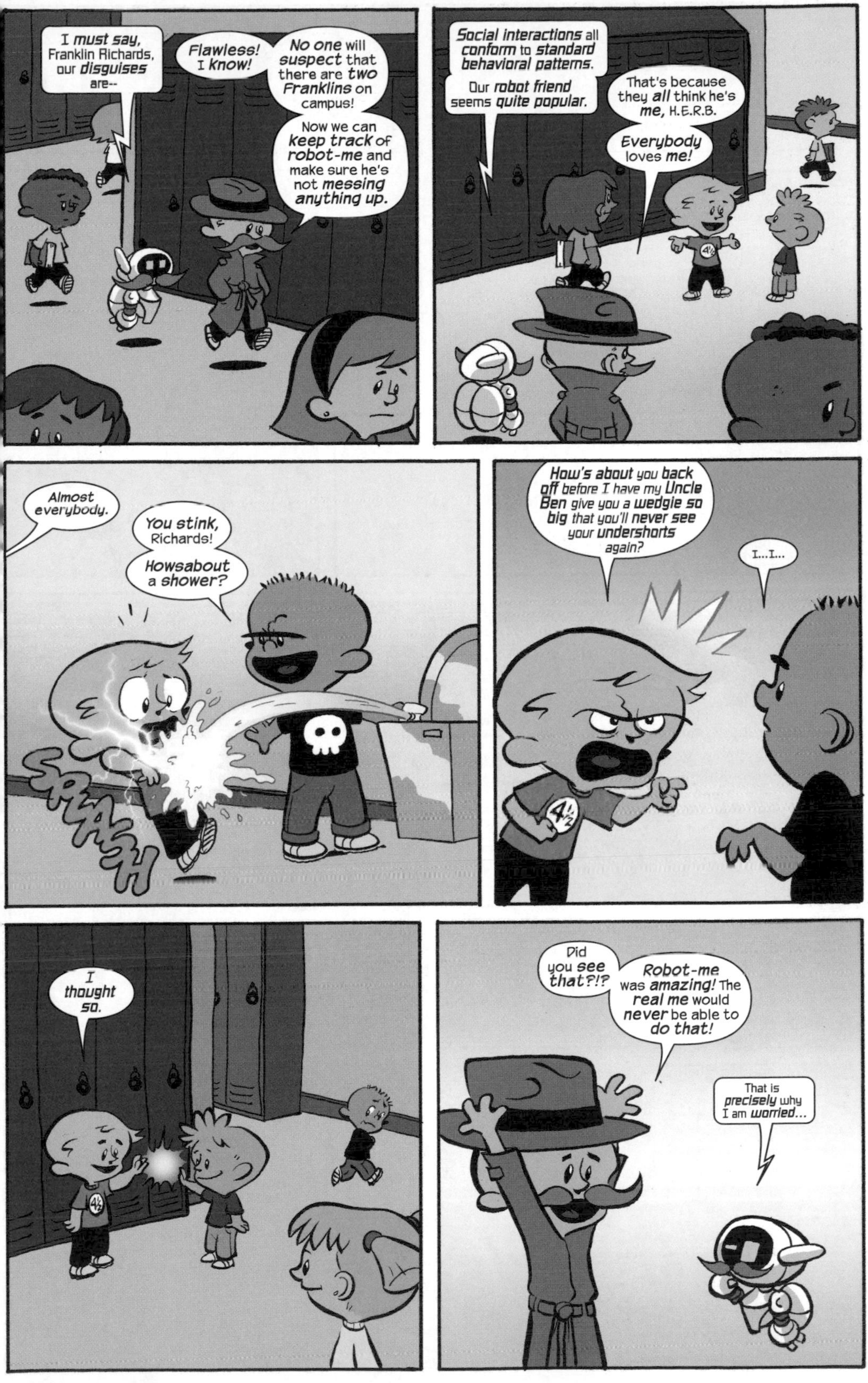
I must say, Franklin Richards, our disguises are--
Flawless! I know!
No one will suspect that there are two Franklins on campus!
Now we can keep track of robot-me and make sure he's not messing anything up.
Social interactions all conform to standard behavioral patterns.
Our robot friend seems quite popular.
That's because they all think he's me, H.E.R.B.
Everybody loves me!
Almost everybody.
You stink, Richards!
Howsabout a shower?
SPLASH
How's about you back off before I have my Uncle Ben give you a wedgie so big that you'll never see your undershorts again?
I...I...
I thought so.
Did you see that?!?
Robot-me was amazing! The real me would never be able to do that!
That is precisely why I am worried...

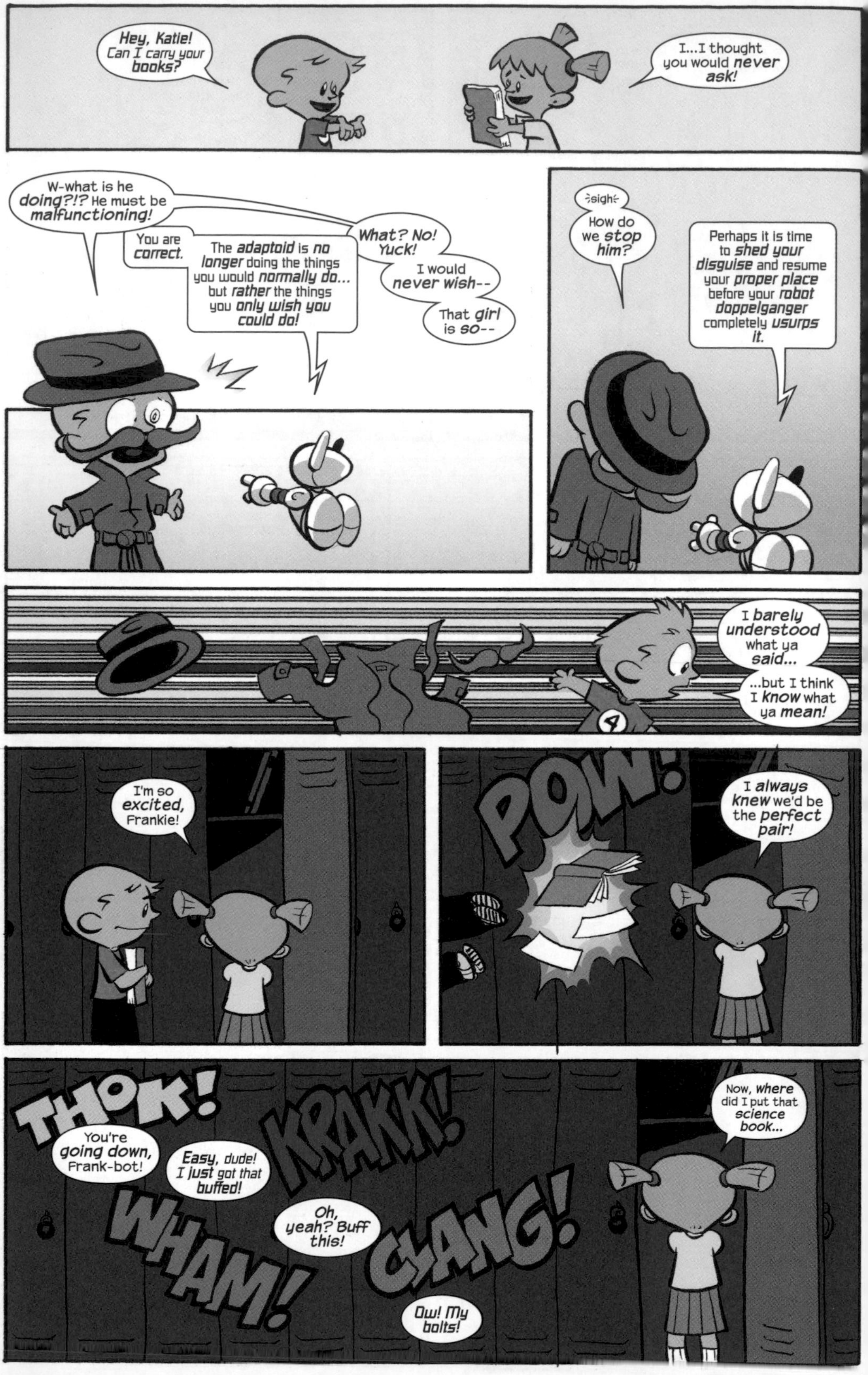
Hey, Katie! Can I carry your books?
I...I thought you would never ask!
W-what is he doing?!? He must be malfunctioning!
What? No! Yuck!
I would never wish--
That girl is so--
You are correct.
The adaptoid is no longer doing the things you would normally do... but rather the things you only wish you could do!
sigh
How do we stop him?
Perhaps it is time to shed your disguise and resume your proper place before your robot doppelganger completely usurps it.
I barely understood what ya said...
...but I think I know what ya mean!
I'm so excited, Frankie!
POW!
I always knew we'd be the perfect pair!
THOK!
You're going down, Frank-bot!
Easy, dude! I just got that buffed!
KRAKK!
Oh, yeah? Buff this!
WHAM!
CLANG!
Ow! My bolts!
Now, where did I put that science book...

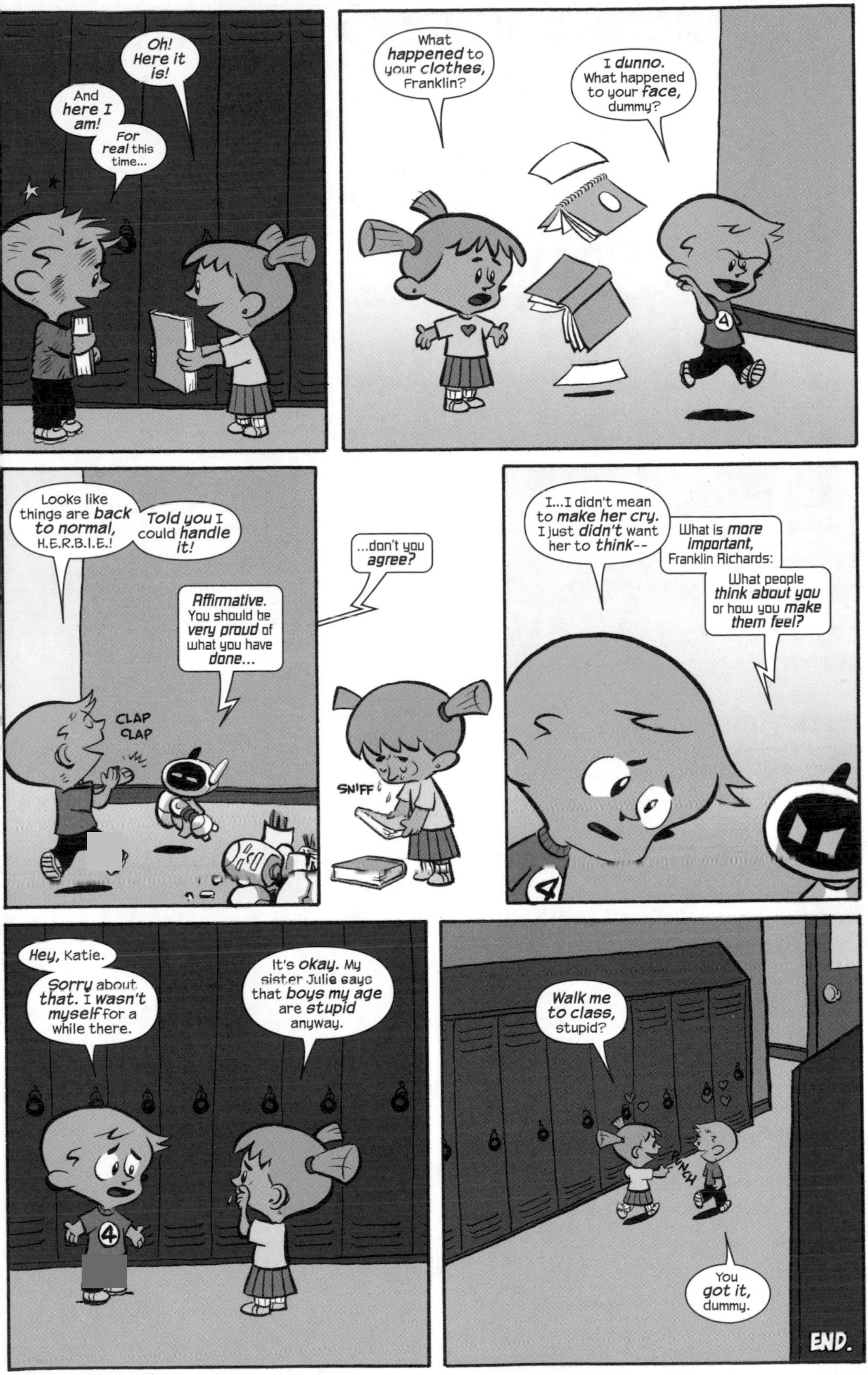

And here I am! For real this time...
Oh! Here it is!
What happened to your clothes, Franklin?
I dunno. What happened to your face, dummy?
Looks like things are back to normal, H.E.R.B.I.E.!
Told you I could handle it!
CLAP CLAP
Affirmative. You should be very proud of what you have done...
...don't you agree?
SNIFF
I...I didn't mean to make her cry. I just didn't want her to think--
What is more important, Franklin Richards:
What people think about you or how you make them feel?
Hey, Katie.
Sorry about that. I wasn't myself for a while there.
It's okay. My sister Julie says that boys my age are stupid anyway.
Walk me to class, stupid?
PUNCH
You got it, dummy.
END.

FRANKLIN RICHARDS SON OF A GENIUS IN: TIME AND TIME AGAIN!

BY CHRIS ELIOPOULOS & MARC SUMERAK

BRAD ANDERSON COLORS | NATHAN COSBY ASSISTANT EDITOR | MARK PANICCIA EDITOR

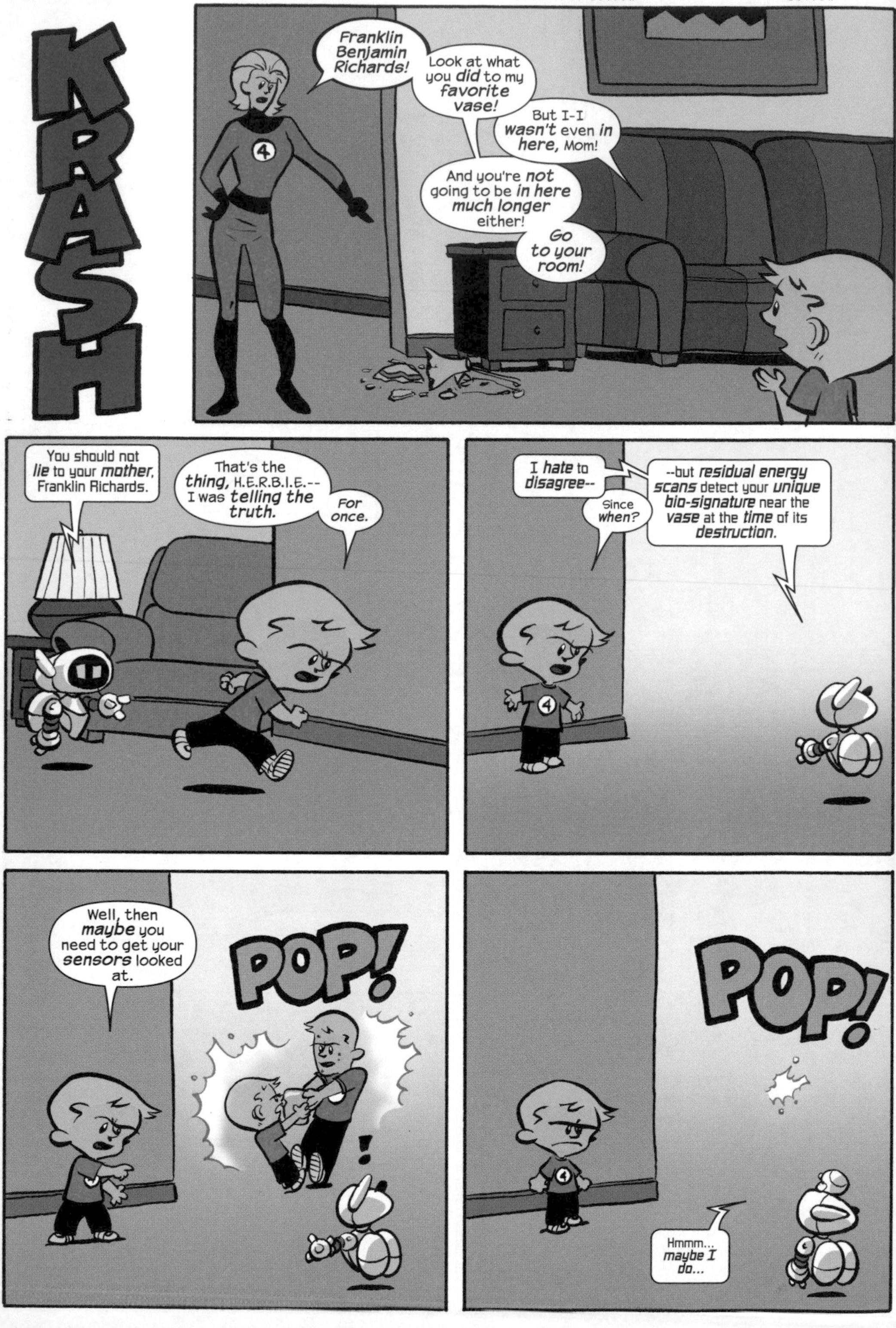

KRASH
Franklin Benjamin Richards!
Look at what you did to my favorite vase!
But I-I wasn't even in here, Mom!
And you're not going to be in here much longer either!
Go to your room!
You should not lie to your mother, Franklin Richards.
That's the thing, H.E.R.B.I.E.-- I was telling the truth.
For once.
I hate to disagree--
--but residual energy scans detect your unique bio-signature near the vase at the time of its destruction.
Since when?
Well, then maybe you need to get your sensors looked at.
POP!
!
POP!
Hmmm... maybe I do...

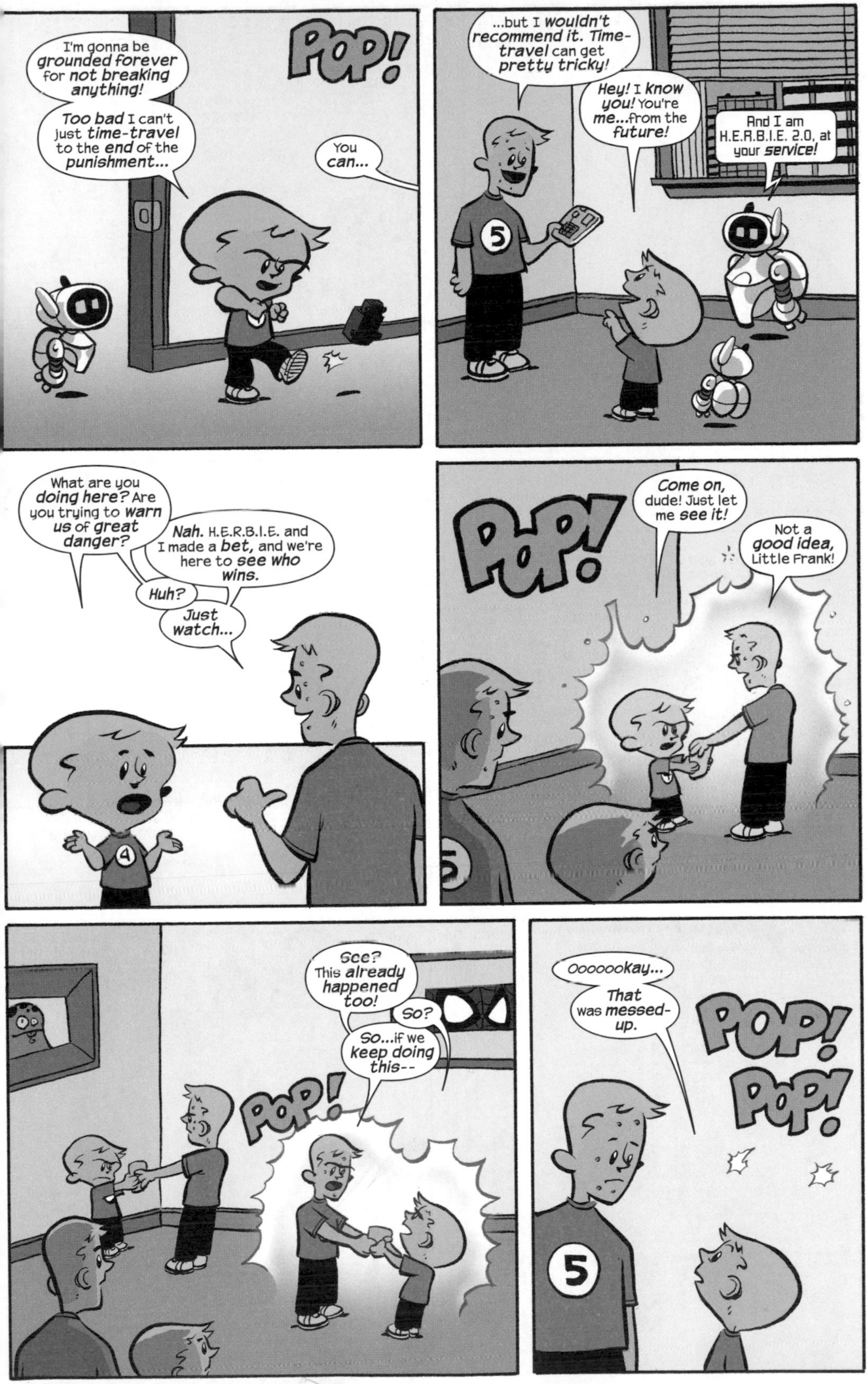
I'm gonna be grounded forever for not breaking anything!
Too bad I can't just time-travel to the end of the punishment...
POP!
You can...
...but I wouldn't recommend it. Time-travel can get pretty tricky!
Hey! I know you! You're me...from the future!
And I am H.E.R.B.I.E. 2.0, at your service!
What are you doing here? Are you trying to warn us of great danger?
Nah. H.E.R.B.I.E. and I made a bet, and we're here to see who wins.
Huh?
Just watch...
POP!
Come on, dude! Just let me see it!
Not a good idea, Little Frank!
See? This already happened too!
So?
So...if we keep doing this--
POP!
Ooooookay...
That was messed-up.
POP!
POP!

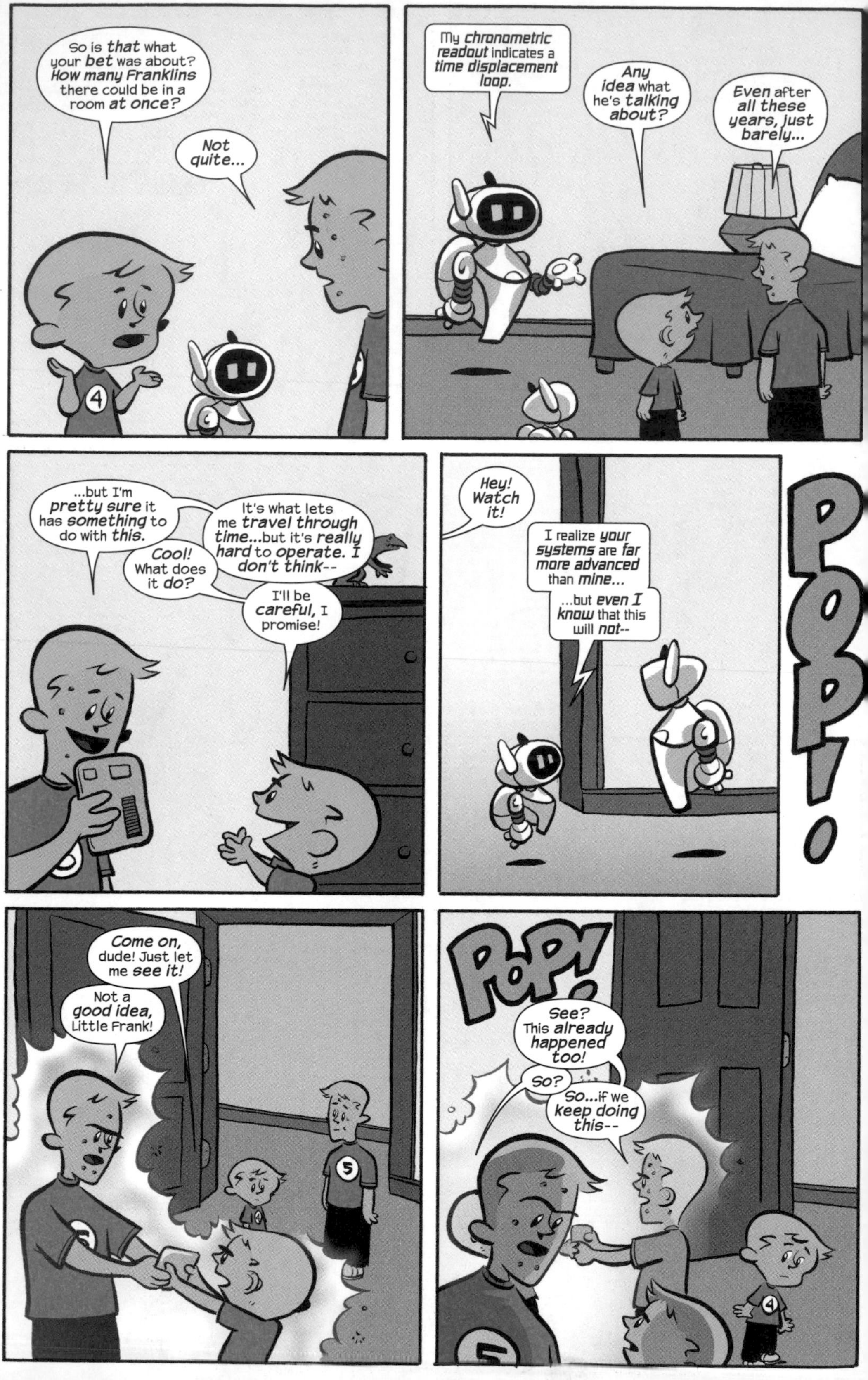
So is that what your bet was about? How many Franklins there could be in a room at once?
Not quite...
My chronometric readout indicates a time displacement loop.
Any idea what he's talking about?
Even after all these years, just barely...
...but I'm pretty sure it has something to do with this.
Cool! What does it do?
It's what lets me travel through time...but it's really hard to operate. I don't think--
I'll be careful, I promise!
Hey! Watch it!
I realize your systems are far more advanced than mine...
...but even I know that this will not--
POP!
Come on, dude! Just let me see it!
Not a good idea, Little Frank!
POP!
See? This already happened too!
So?
So...if we keep doing this--

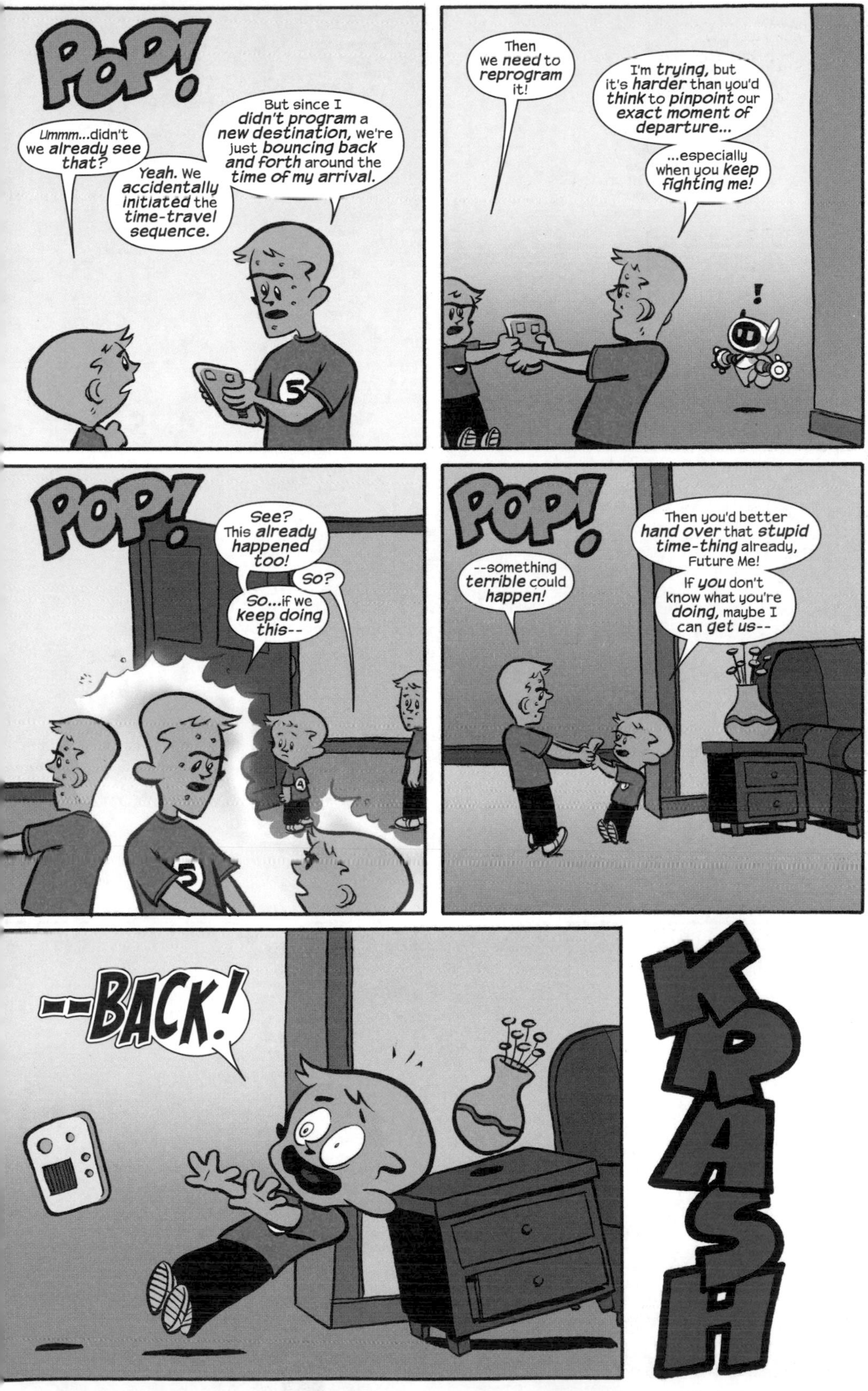
POP!
Ummm...didn't we already see that?
Yeah. We accidentally initiated the time-travel sequence.
But since I didn't program a new destination, we're just bouncing back and forth around the time of my arrival.
Then we need to reprogram it!
I'm trying, but it's harder than you'd think to pinpoint our exact moment of departure...
...especially when you keep fighting me!
!
POP!
See? This already happened too!
So?
So...if we keep doing this--
POP!
--something terrible could happen!
Then you'd better hand over that stupid time-thing already, Future Me!
If you don't know what you're doing, maybe I can get us--
--BACK!
KRASH

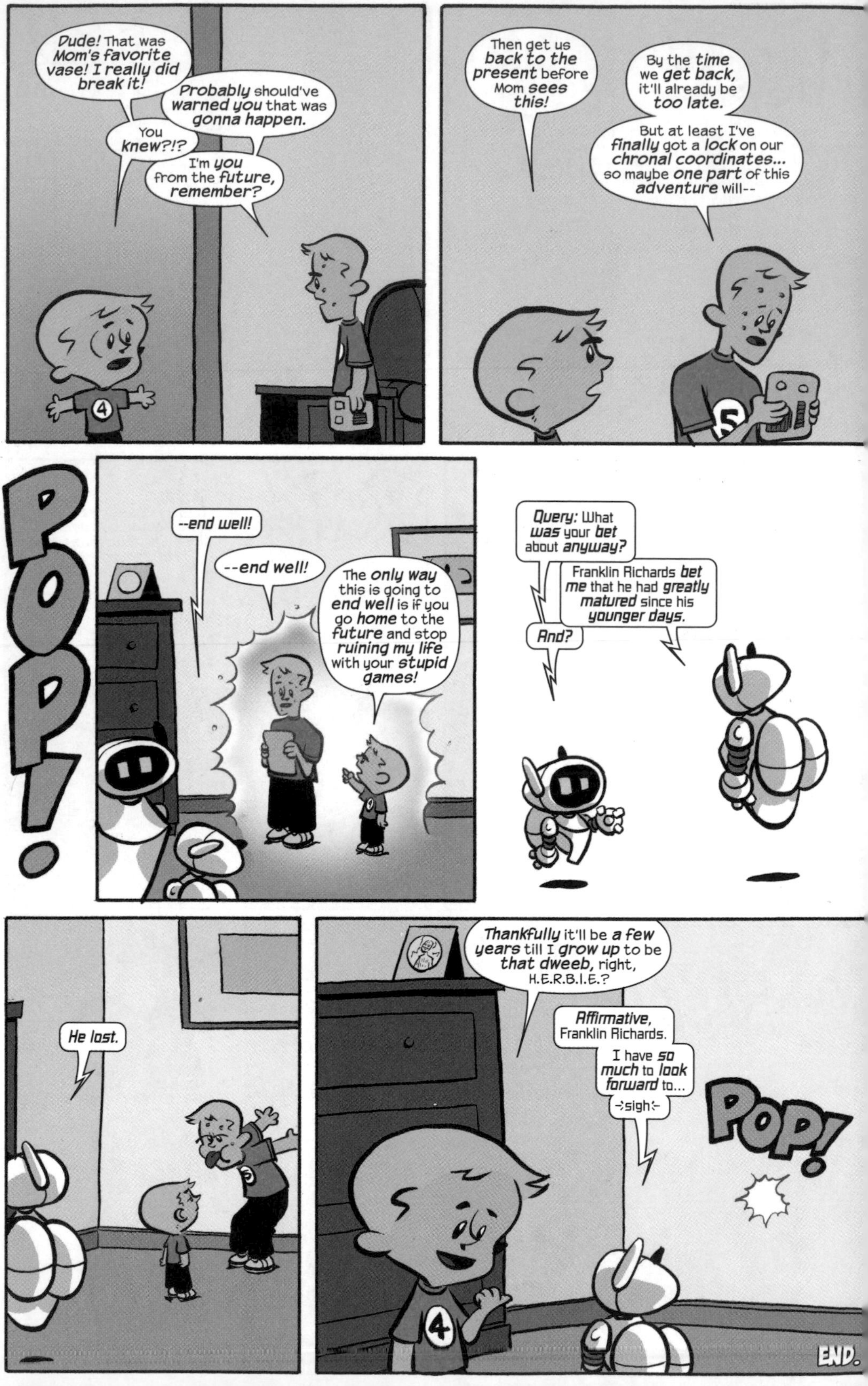
Dude! That was Mom's favorite vase! I really did break it!
Probably should've warned you that was gonna happen.
You knew?!?
I'm you from the future, remember?
Then get us back to the present before Mom sees this!
By the time we get back, it'll already be too late.
But at least I've finally got a lock on our chronal coordinates... so maybe one part of this adventure will--
POP!
--end well!
--end well!
The only way this is going to end well is if you go home to the future and stop ruining my life with your stupid games!
Query: What was your bet about anyway?
Franklin Richards bet me that he had greatly matured since his younger days.
And?
He lost.
Thankfully it'll be a few years till I grow up to be that dweeb, right, H.E.R.B.I.E.?
Affirmative, Franklin Richards.
I have so much to look forward to...
-sigh-
POP!
END.

FRANKLIN RICHARDS SON OF A GENIUS IN: ALIEN ENCOUNTER!

BY CHRIS ELIOPOULOS & MARC SUMERAK

BRAD ANDERSON COLORS · NATHAN COSBY ASSISTANT EDITOR · MARK PANICCIA EDITOR

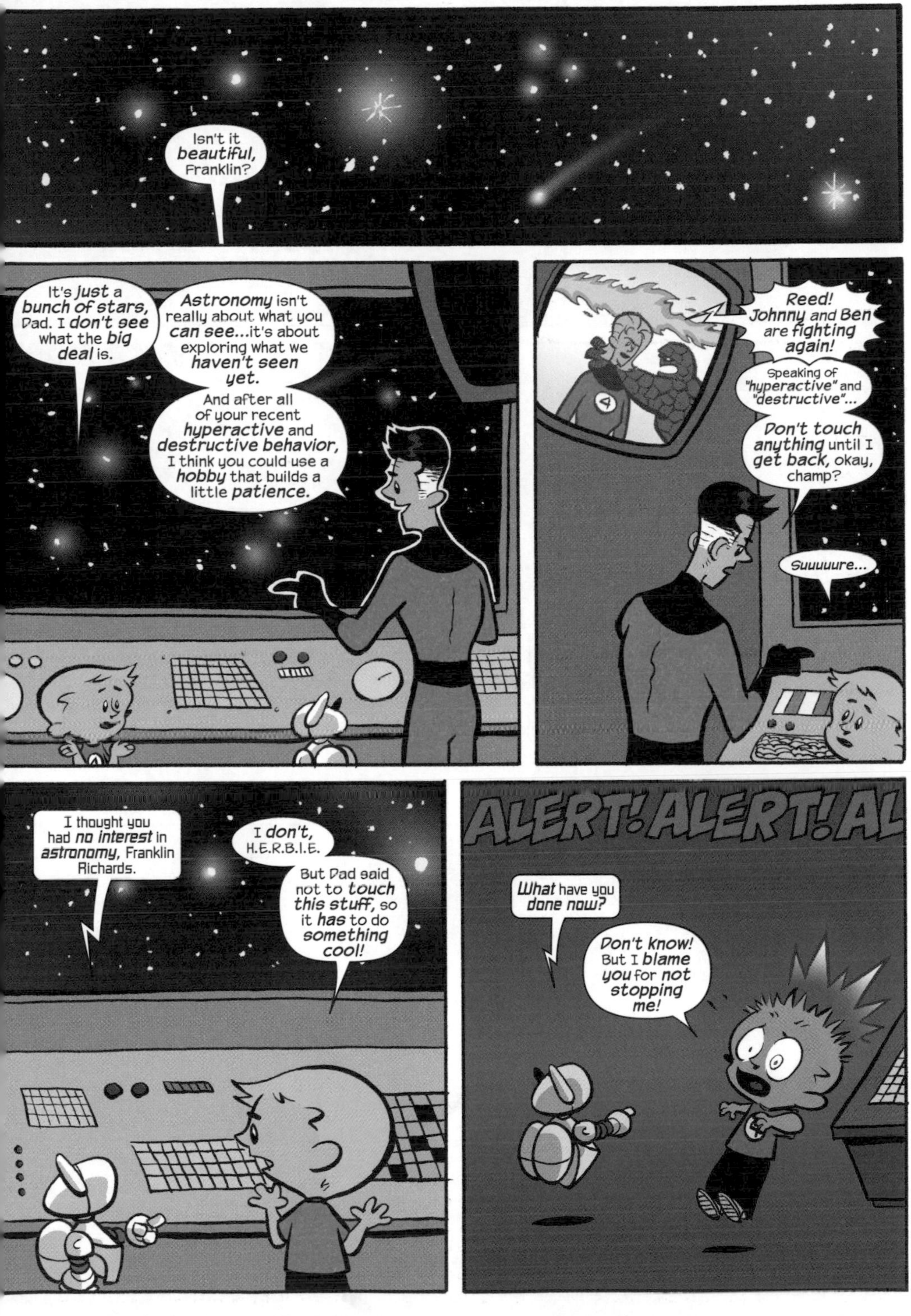

Isn't it beautiful, Franklin?
It's just a bunch of stars, Dad. I don't see what the big deal is.
Astronomy isn't really about what you can see...it's about exploring what we haven't seen yet.
And after all of your recent hyperactive and destructive behavior, I think you could use a hobby that builds a little patience.
Reed! Johnny and Ben are fighting again!
Speaking of "hyperactive" and "destructive"...
Don't touch anything until I get back, okay, champ?
Suuuuure...
I thought you had no interest in astronomy, Franklin Richards.
I don't, H.E.R.B.I.E.
But Dad said not to touch this stuff, so it has to do something cool!
ALERT! ALERT! AL
What have you done now?
Don't know! But I blame you for not stopping me!

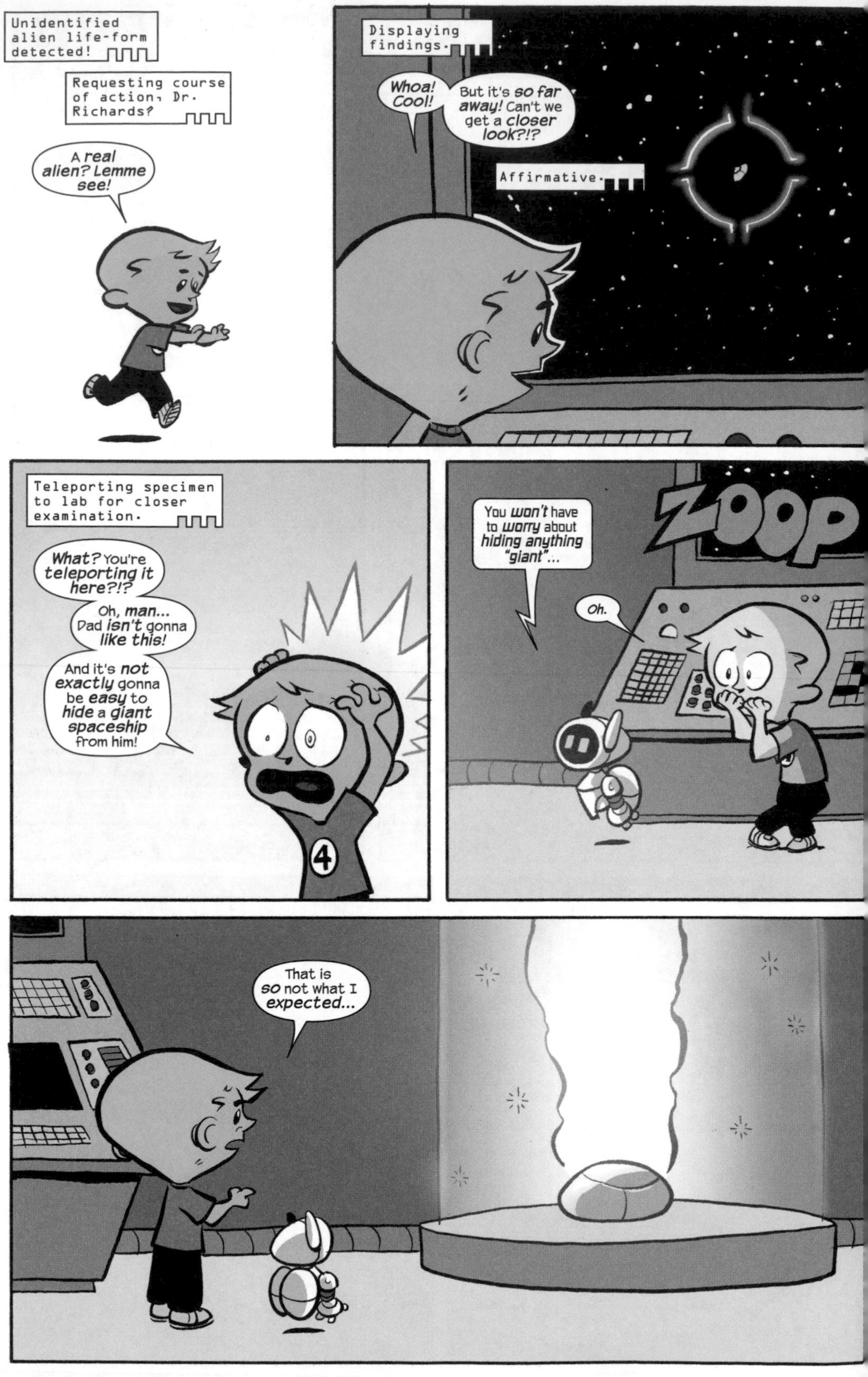
Unidentified alien life-form detected!
Requesting course of action, Dr. Richards?
A real alien? Lemme see!
Displaying findings.
Whoa! Cool!
But it's so far away! Can't we get a closer look?!?
Affirmative.
Teleporting specimen to lab for closer examination.
What? You're teleporting it here?!?
Oh, man... Dad isn't gonna like this!
And it's not exactly gonna be easy to hide a giant spaceship from him!
ZOOP
You won't have to worry about hiding anything "giant"...
Oh.
That is so not what I expected...

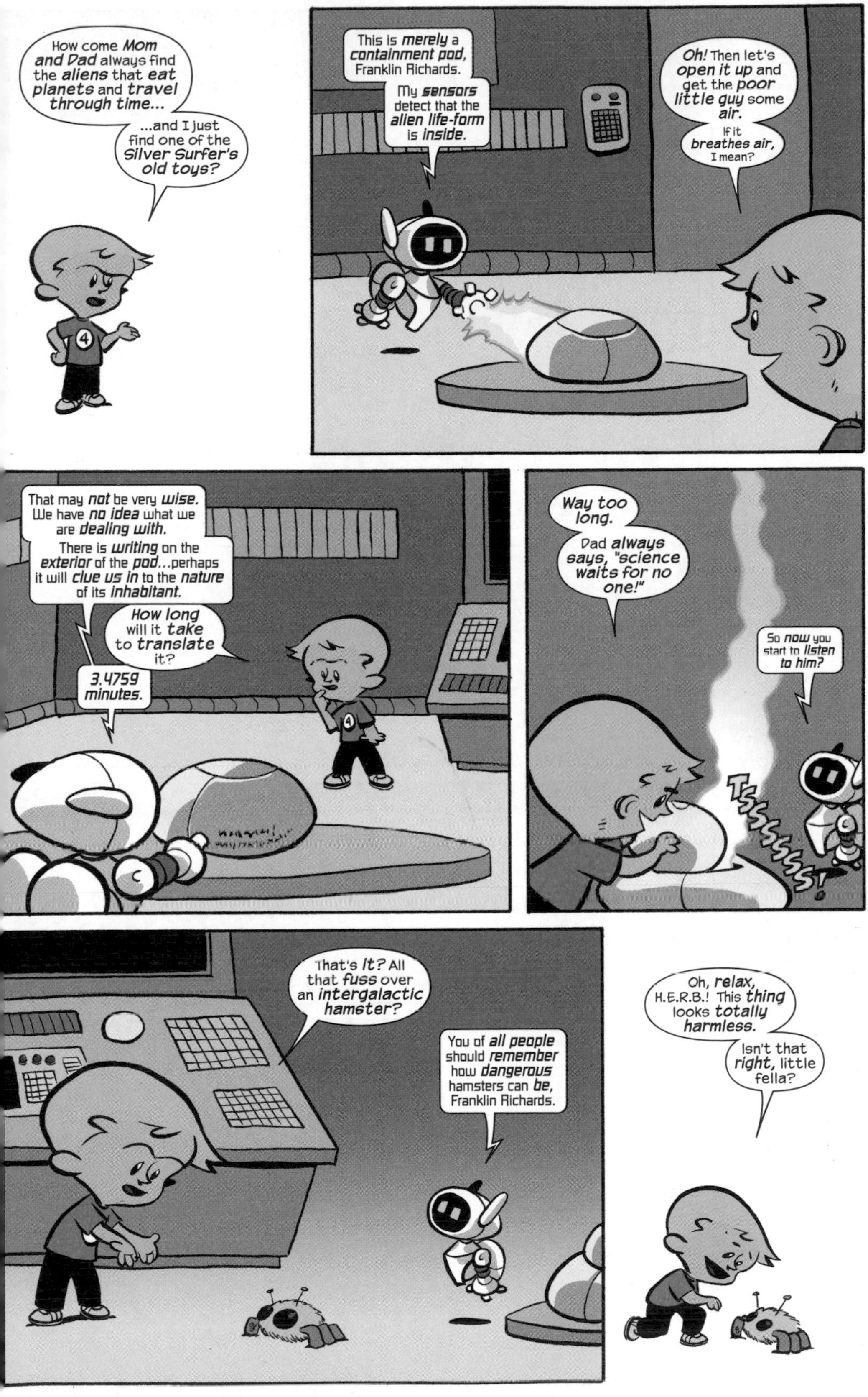

How come Mom and Dad always find the aliens that eat planets and travel through time...
...and I just find one of the Silver Surfer's old toys?
This is merely a containment pod, Franklin Richards.
My sensors detect that the alien life-form is inside.
Oh! Then let's open it up and get the poor little guy some air.
If it breathes air, I mean?
That may not be very wise. We have no idea what we are dealing with.
There is writing on the exterior of the pod...perhaps it will clue us in to the nature of its inhabitant.
How long will it take to translate it?
3.4759 minutes.
Way too long.
Dad always says, "science waits for no one!"
So now you start to listen to him?
TSSSSSSS!
That's it? All that fuss over an intergalactic hamster?
You of all people should remember how dangerous hamsters can be, Franklin Richards.
Oh, relax, H.E.R.B.! This thing looks totally harmless.
Isn't that right, little fella?

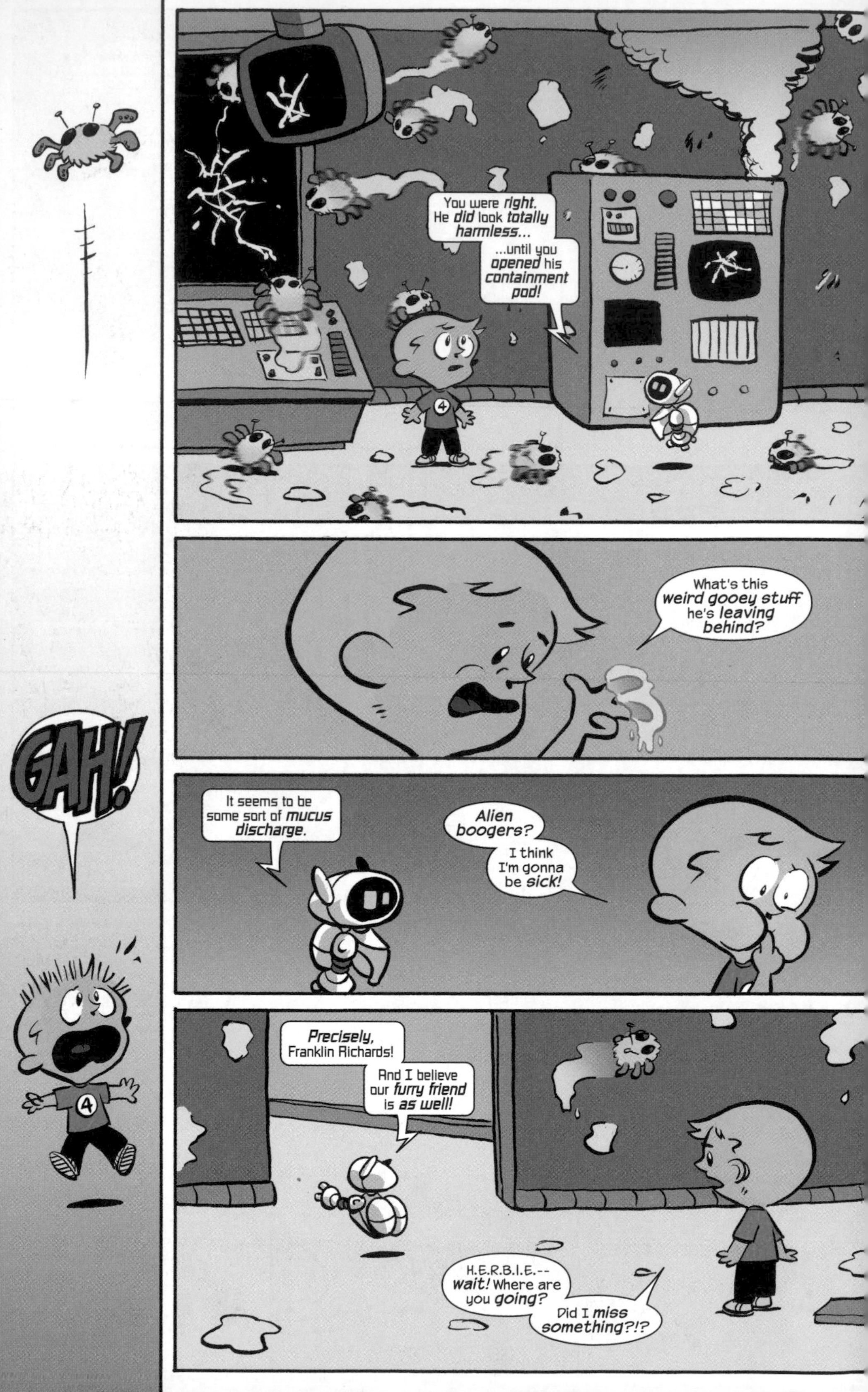
You were right. He did look totally harmless...
...until you opened his containment pod!
What's this weird gooey stuff he's leaving behind?
It seems to be some sort of mucus discharge.
Alien boogers?
I think I'm gonna be sick!
GAH!
Precisely, Franklin Richards!
And I believe our furry friend is as well!
H.E.R.B.I.E.-- wait! Where are you going?
Did I miss something?!?

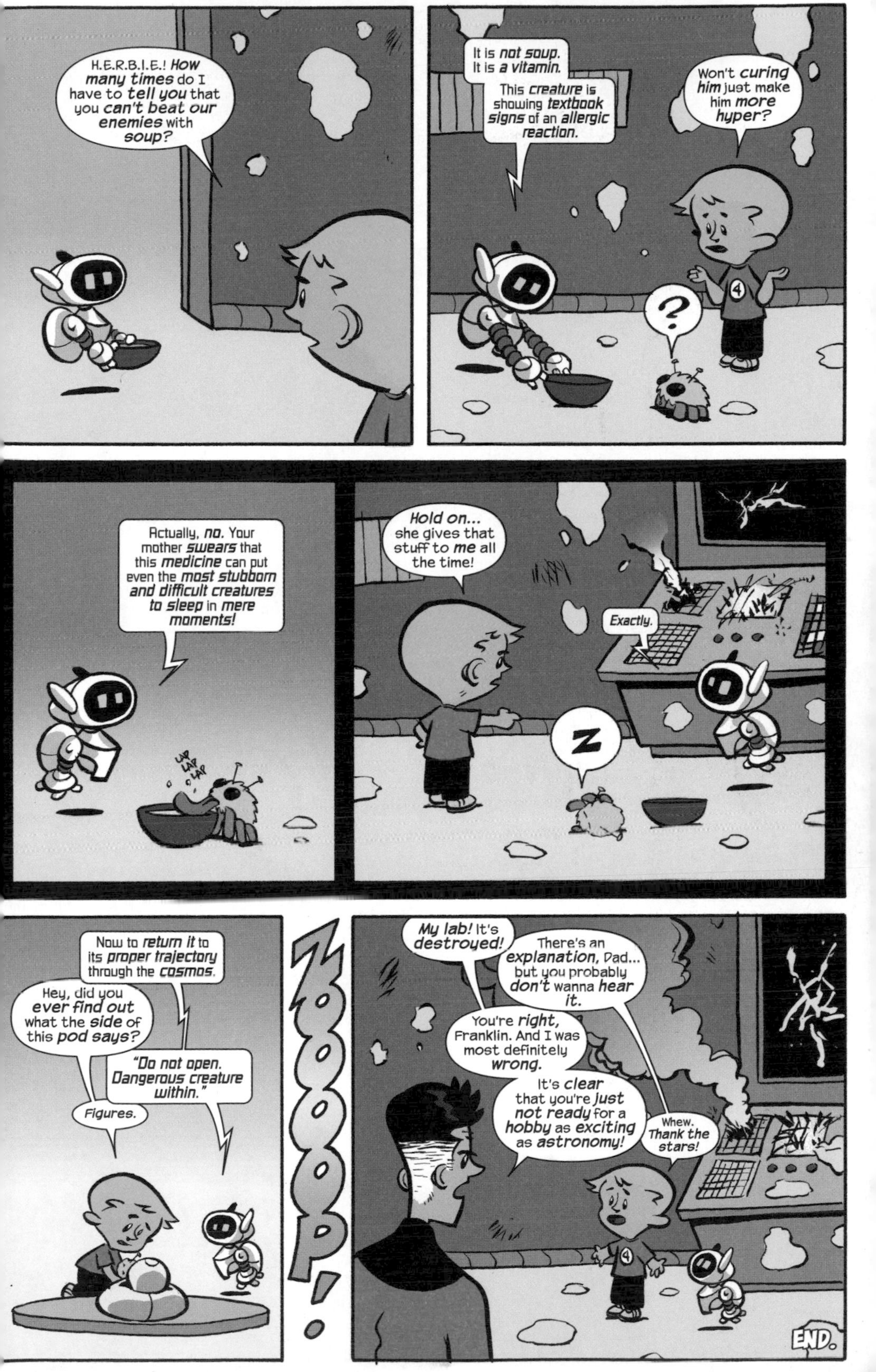
H.E.R.B.I.E.! How many times do I have to tell you that you can't beat our enemies with soup?
It is not soup. It is a vitamin.
This creature is showing textbook signs of an allergic reaction.
Won't curing him just make him more hyper?
?
Actually, no. Your mother swears that this medicine can put even the most stubborn and difficult creatures to sleep in mere moments!
LAP LAP LAP
Hold on... she gives that stuff to me all the time!
Exactly.
Z
Now to return it to its proper trajectory through the cosmos.
Hey, did you ever find out what the side of this pod says?
"Do not open. Dangerous creature within."
Figures.
ZOOOOOOP!
My lab! It's destroyed!
There's an explanation, Dad... but you probably don't wanna hear it.
You're right, Franklin. And I was most definitely wrong.
It's clear that you're just not ready for a hobby as exciting as astronomy!
Whew. Thank the stars!
END.

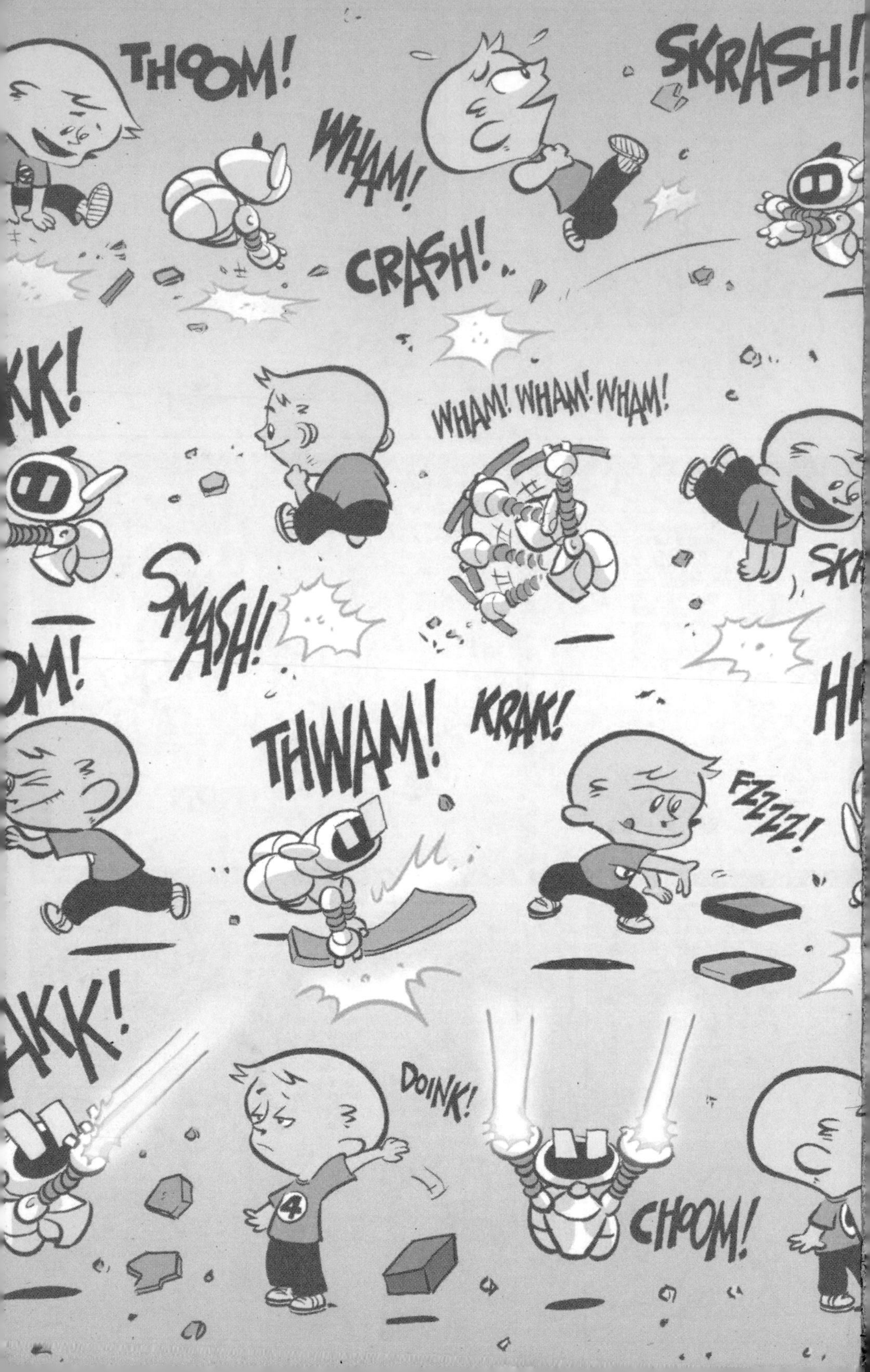
THOOM!
WHAM!
SKRASH!
CRASH!
WHAM! WHAM! WHAM!
SMASH!
THWAM!
KRAK!
FZZZZ!
DOINK!
CHOOM!